C0-DYA-027

Heirs, Kin, and Creditors in Renaissance Florence

Visions of modernity rest in part on a distinction between inherited status (past) and achievement (present). Inheritance is taken as automatic, if not axiomatic; the recipients are passive, if grateful. This study, based on a singular source (Florentine repudiations of inheritance), reveals that inheritance was in fact a process, that heirs had options: at the least, to reject a burdensome patrimony, but also to maneuver property to others and to avoid (at times deceptively, if not fraudulently) the claims of others to portions of the estate. Repudiation was a vestige of Roman law that became once again a viable legal institution with the revival of Roman law in the Middle Ages. Florentines incorporated repudiation into their strategies of adjustment after death, showing that they were not merely passive recipients of what came their way. These strategies fostered family goals, including continuity across the generations.

Thomas Kuehn is a graduate of Carleton College (B.A. 1972) and the University of Chicago (M.A. 1973, Ph.D. 1977). Professor Kuehn taught at Reed College for four years before going to Clemson University, where he has served as the history department chair since 2001. Among his many published works, Kuehn has written *Emancipation in Late Medieval Florence* (1982); *Law, Family, and Women: Toward a Legal Anthropology of Renaissance Italy* (1991); and *Illegitimacy in Renaissance Florence* (2002). His scholarship has been published in journals as diverse as *Renaissance Quarterly, American Journal of Legal History, Continuity and Change*, and the *Journal of Women's History*.

Heirs, Kin, and Creditors in Renaissance Florence

THOMAS KUEHN
Clemson University

CAMBRIDGE UNIVERSITY PRESS

CAMBRIDGE UNIVERSITY PRESS
Cambridge, New York, Melbourne, Madrid, Cape Town, Singapore, São Paulo, Delhi

Cambridge University Press
32 Avenue of the Americas, New York, NY 10013-2473, USA

www.cambridge.org
Information on this title: www.cambridge.org/9780521882347

© Thomas Kuehn 2008

This publication is in copyright. Subject to statutory exception
and to the provisions of relevant collective licensing agreements,
no reproduction of any part may take place without
the written permission of Cambridge University Press.

First published 2008

Printed in the United States of America

A catalog record for this publication is available from the British Library.

Library of Congress Cataloging in Publication Data

Kuehn, Thomas, 1950–
Heirs, kin, and creditors in Renaissance Florence / Thomas Kuehn.
p. cm.
Includes index.
ISBN 978-0-521-88234-7 (hbk.)
1. Inheritance and succession – Italy – Florence – History. 2. Renunciation
of inheritance – Italt – Florence – History. I. Title.
KKH9851.2.K84 2008
346.45′51052–dc22 2007050180

ISBN 978-0-521-88234-7 hardback

Cambridge University Press has no responsibility for
the persistence or accuracy of URLs for external or
third-party Internet Web sites referred to in this publication
and does not guarantee that any content on such
Web sites is, or will remain, accurate or appropriate.

For Teresa

Contents

List of Tables		*page* ix
Preface: The Ambivalence of Inheritance		xi
	Introduction: Of Inheritance and Kinship	1
	A Point of Departure	1
	The Primacy of Testaments	9
	Actions of Heirs	13
	Strategies of Writing	17
1	Family and Inheritance	20
	The Law of Succession and Repudiation	21
	Classical Roman Background	22
	The Nature of Repudiation in Medieval Ius Commune	26
	Capacity to Repudiate	34
	Period for Deliberation	38
	Coheirs and Subsequent Heirs	40
	Partial Repudiation	42
	Problems of Perception and Fraud	45
	Conclusion	49
2	Florentine Laws Regulating Inheritance and Repudiation	51
	Statutory Framework	52
	Lines of Juristic Interpretation	67
	Legislation, Fraud, and the Misuse of Repudiation	71
3	Repudiation and Inheritance	82
	Inheritance in Florentine Family Records	82
	Estate Planning	89
	Obligations of Heirs	95
	Repudiations in Florentine Family Records	100
	Conclusion	107

4	**Profile of Florentine Repudiation and Inheritance**	112
	The Registry and Its Data	112
	Chronology of Repudiations	115
	Repudiating Florentines and Tuscans	120
	Gender Analysis	126
	Geography of Repudiation	130
	Partial Repudiations	131
	Intestate Succession	132
	Conclusions	134
5	**Repudiations and Household Wealth**	136
	1427 Catasto	136
	The Catasto of 1480	142
	Motivations	147
	Repudiation across Generations	151
6	**Repudiation as an Inheritance Practice**	154
	The Data	156
	Strategies	159
	Unclaimed Estates	175
7	**Repudiations in Dispute**	179
	Consilia *and Litigation*	180
	Florentine Repudiation Cases, 1350–1450	182
	Florentine Cases, 1450–1550	192
	Conclusions	207
	Conclusion	209
Appendix 1		215
Appendix 2		216
Appendix 3		217
Appendix 4		218
Appendix 5		219
Appendix 6		221
Sources and Abbreviations		223
Index		227

List of Tables

1	Repudiations, Year by Year	*page* 116
2	Relationship of Deceased to Primary Repudiator	121
3	Relationship to Repudians	124
4	Gender of Repudiantes	127
5	Gender and Relationships to Deceased	129
6	Locations of Repudiations	131
7	Partial Repudiations	132
8	Intestate Successions Repudiated	133
9	Households and Repudiation, 1427	139
10	Households and Repudiation, 1480	143
11	Notarial Repudiations	155
12	Time between Death and Repudiation by Relationship to Deceased	157

Preface
The Ambivalence of Inheritance

I first came across repudiation of inheritance in my initial foray into Florence's rich archives, more than thirty years ago. At that time, I was researching emancipation of children. Repudiation struck me as both similar to emancipation – perhaps too similar, in the concerns it raised about fraud and its consequent parallel registration – and too strange. It was hard to understand why one would turn down an inheritance, even in the face of language that it was *damnosa*. In contrast, it was not so hard for one who grew up in the sixties to understand why a child would want to be free of paternal control or even why a father might want to relinquish such control.

Emancipation turned out to lead to other elements that I had not anticipated, as any fruitful research topic should. It was, as I had hoped, a good point to begin to understand the workings of law within families. Repudiation remained a nagging and puzzling presence on the margins. As part of the large, complex, and foreboding area of inheritance, repudiation seemed beyond reach. Having spent an enjoyable lunch one day in Berkeley dissuading Gene Brucker from tackling inheritance as a research topic because of its vastness and complexity, I only further convinced myself that it was too difficult. Maybe this book will serve to convince readers that my initial premonition was correct.

Inheritance was the vital process – the central moment in the life cycle – by which social reproduction occurred. Passage of titles, especially to land, defined elites and their power over others. Inheritance was too vital to be left to individual whims or to chance. It was hedged about with rigid rules and commanding expectations. In contrast, the great social theorists of the nineteenth century – Henry Sumner Maine, Frédéric Le Play, Émile Durkheim, Max Weber, for example – had all variously posed the passage to modernity in terms of a change from social order based on ascription, largely the result of inheritance, to one based on achievement. Property went from being a collective to an individual attribute.[1]

Against modernistic visions and stories of individual achievement, inheritance, in fact, still matters in the development and consolidation of modern commercial and industrial firms – disguised though it may be by law and accounting mechanisms that separate business from household.[2] Conversely, forms of achievement or the revision or avoidance of inheritance rules operated in the past, as one can see with women's property rights and the social and legal standing of illegitimate children, whose main legal and social disability operated with regard to inheritance. As Beatrice Gottlieb notes, "near unanimity about the rightness of inheritability did nothing to eliminate the ambivalence that surrounded certain aspects of it."[3] The laws of inheritance in the past gave room and means to strategies. Heirs did not have to be heirs; guardians and executors could opt out of the burdens and duties left to them – even if they all faced countervailing moral pressures to undertake the tasks the deceased had, knowingly or unknowingly, imposed.

I took on a partial study of repudiation (published in 1992, which predated that lunch with Brucker by some three years). Work on illegitimacy forced me to confront inheritance in law and practice subsequently. As my study of illegitimacy wound to a conclusion, Jules Kirshner suggested that I needed to return to repudiation. Once again, I took his advice.

There are several points of departure to this study. For one thing, it is a study of inheritance strategies by heirs. These strategies were related to and served the goal of family survival and preservation as Florentines and Tuscans understood it. They were not individualistic in any modern sense, yet they were also not simply the product of a group dynamic. They were worked out by persons, singly or in groups. They were flexible and adaptive – maddeningly so to the governing authorities who sought to extract revenues from households and to protect the integrity of markets. Repudiation was only one device available to heirs, but it was useful. Repudiations of inheritance were a regular feature of the Florentine social landscape and generational progression.

The utility of repudiation rested in good part on the fact that it provided a way to avoid debts and obligations. A second starting point to this book is that the society of Florence operated on a dense but porous web of credit

---

[1] James Casey, *The History of the Family* (Oxford: Blackwell, 1989), esp. 30–37, 138–40. See also Paolo Grossi, *"Un altro modo di possedere": L'emersione di forme alternative di proprietà alla coscienza giuridica postunitaria* (Milan: Giuffrè, 1977); Jane Fishburne Collier, *From Duty to Desire: Remaking Families in a Spanish Village* (Princeton: Princeton University Press, 1997).

[2] See George E. Marcus with Peter Dobkin Hall, *Lives in Trust: The Fortunes of Dynastic Families in Late Twentieth-Century America* (Boulder: Westview Press, 1992).

[3] Beatrice Gottlieb, *The Family in the Western World: From the Black Death to the Industrial Age* (New York and Oxford: Oxford University Press, 1993), 203.

and debt, trust and distrust, honesty and deceit. The economy was volatile, and the best of intentions to meet obligations, to pay off a credit extended to oneself and, to extend credit to others could hit insurmountable obstacles. We can appreciate only with difficulty that planning could meet with apprehension and uncertainty. It is easy to fall into the mindset of Pirandello's narrator, seduced by the fixity and clarity of history in the documents found in a notary's office, compared to the shifting reality of daily life.[4]

Another and related preoccupation in this study has been that a thorough distinction between family and individual – a distinction that also serves as a progression from past to modernity – is not a useful framework for analysis. It could reify the *casa* rather than projecting it as a site of the confluence of interests and sentiments. Fathers could not so control and subordinate their sons that they, in turn, would prove incapable of managing and directing family affairs when their time came. Sons somehow had to be both independent and respectful. As Sylvia Junko Yanagisako nicely expresses it, "patriarchal desires of succession are constituted by a complex array of altruistic and self-serving sentiments of love, attention, respect, and esteem."[5] A device such as repudiation of inheritance could variously suit needs of individuals and family groups, as circumstances seemed to warrant.

There is another point of departure (or is it arrival?) for this book – Florence. The city is a prominent fixture in studies of the Renaissance. It came to dominate most of Tuscany politically and economically. It gave birth to or attracted figures, from Dante to Michelangelo, whose writings and monuments defined the city and an age. And it still possesses the richest and most varied collections of sources, whose preservation makes possible historical research unimaginable for most anywhere else.

It used to be that investigation of some aspect of Florentine history required no justification, or was its own justification. The centrality of events and people in Florence to an understanding of the Renaissance, whose importance in terms of Western history had been undoubted since Burckhardt, meant that any aspect of that city's history was fair game. Things have changed. A recent volume of essays entitled *Beyond Florence* has challenged Florentine exceptionalism, both diminishing the sense that Florence was somehow pivotal to developments in early modern history and asserting that Florence cannot be taken as typical of central and northern Italian cities, as has often been the case. Paula Findlen, one of the editors of *Beyond Florence*, notes that the "decline" of Florence in historiography coincides with the decline of the Renaissance as an organizing principle. Even though Florence had been taken increasingly as a kind of anthropological

---

[4] Luigi Pirandello, *One, No One, and One Hundred Thousand*, trans. William Weaver (New York: Marsilio, 1992).
[5] Sylvia Junko Yanagisako, *Producing Culture and Capital: Family Firms in Italy* (Princeton: Princeton University Press, 2002), 89.

laboratory (by myself, among others) because of its unique records, it has become increasingly evident that even the history of Florence and the history of Tuscany are not the same.[6]

I propose to treat Florence once again as an anthropological lab. I will do so with no illusions about generalizing Florentine experiences, or Florentine laws, to other Italian cities, and I will be at pains where appropriate to draw distinctions between Florence and Tuscany. In fact, Florence shared a legal culture with the rest of Italy, marked by the activities and writings of trained lawyers and notaries,[7] which was the underpinning of inheritance practices. Layered on top of this "common" legal heritage (hence *ius commune*) were cities' own peculiar modifications (termed *ius proprium* in distinction). There was some correspondence in law and legal institutions among them, though we cannot see this correspondence as strict and isomorphic.[8] Florentine legal experiences, therefore, both shared common terms and features with those in many other Italian cities, yet also diverged from them in significant ways.

Florence may have been harsher than most cities in its laws placing legal restrictions on women.[9] And it may be that Florence earlier and more thoroughly saw the adoption of a "male-oriented ideal of lineage" that directed the flow of property to successive generations.[10] But Florence also shared

---

[6] Paula Findlen, "In and Out of Florence," in *Beyond Florence: The Contours of Medieval and Early Modern Italy*, ed. Paula Findlen, Michelle M. Fontaine, and Duane J. Osheim (Stanford: Stanford University Press, 2003), 13–28, esp. 15–19.

[7] Interestingly, Findlen, ibid., 21, poses that historical attention to the notary "surely goes a long way to enriching the comparative history of Italy."

[8] Which can be the result if too hard a distinction is drawn between law (in *ius commune*) and ideology or conscience or sentiment (in *ius proprium*), as per Manlio Bellomo, "La struttura patrimoniale della famiglia italiana nel tardo medioevo," in *Marriage, Property, and Succession*, ed. Lloyd Bonfield (Berlin: Dunckler & Humblot, 1992), 68. In contrast, see Paolo Grossi, *L'ordine giuridico medievale* (Bari: Laterza, 1995).

[9] Cf. Thomas Kuehn, *Law, Family, and Women: Toward a Legal Anthropology of Renaissance Italy* (Chicago: University of Chicago Press, 1991), 212–37; id., "Person and Gender in the Laws," in *Gender and Society in Renaissance Italy*, ed. Judith A. Brown and Robert C. Davis (New York: Longman, 1998), 87–106; id., "Understanding Gender Inequality in Renaissance Florence," *Journal of Women's History* 8 (1996): 58–80; id., "Figlie, madri, mogli e vedove: Donne come persone giuridiche," in *Tempi e spazi di vita femminile nella prima età moderna*, ed. Silvana Seidel Menchi, Anne Jacobson Schutte, and Thomas Kuehn (Bologna: Il Mulino, 1999), 431–60; id., "Household and Family in *Ius Commune* and *Ius Proprium*," in *The Household in Late Medieval Cities: Italy and Northwestern Europe Compared*, ed. Myriam Carlier and Tim Soens (Leuven: Garant, 2001), 37–50; Isabelle Chabot, "'Biens de famille': Contrôle des ressources patrimoniales, gender et cycle domestique (Italie, XIIIième–XVième siècles)," in ibid., 89–104; id., "Seconde nozze e identità materna nella Firenze del tardo medioevo," in *Tempi e spazi*, 493–523; Samuel K. Cohn, Jr., *Women in the Streets: Essays on Sex and Power in Renaissance Italy* (Baltimore: Johns Hopkins University Press, 1996); Stanley Chojnacki, *Women and Men in Renaissance Venice: Twelve Essays on Patrician Society* (Baltimore: Johns Hopkins University Press, 2000).

[10] Samuel K. Cohn, Jr., *The Cult of Remembrance and the Black Death: Six Renaissance Cities in Central Italy* (Baltimore: Johns Hopkins University Press, 1992), 172–80, 196–97.

that tendency with other communities and may even have shown the way, versus previous views that spotted such an "aristocratic" vein only after the definitive triumph of the Medici in the sixteenth century.[11] Access to offices and associated forms of wealth and prestige was not the result of set legal distinctions, as was more so the case for the patriciate of Venice, or would be the case in Florence under the Medici dukes. Manipulation of electoral purses, patronage, and family connections was vital to the identities and practices of those in Florence's elite.[12]

Inheritance was pivotal in Florentine society and politics. Inheritance was also precarious. Florence saw numerous economic swings and was exposed to almost constant disruptions of its markets – beginning most spectacularly with the famines, plagues, and financial failures that were the immediate backdrop to the legislation of 1355 regulating both repudiations of inheritance and emancipations of children. Family fortunes came and went with the winds of economic and political storms. Florentines knew the stories of the formerly great and wealthy and saw some of those stories unfold firsthand. It was in this context that they used repudiations, and perhaps more consistently and ruthlessly than was the case in any other Italian city, although any definitive judgment on this score must await parallel research for other towns.

A final point of departure is the realization that, like the testaments and schemes of intestacy against which it operated, repudiation was a legal institution. As an area of law permitting exceptions to other areas of law, repudiation certainly shows us that "law is only one of the complex and sometimes contradictory forces of kinship that shape the reformulation and renegotiation of the sentiments, interests, and strategies of family members."[13] Law does more than "double kinship" with rules, the normative content of which can in fact be deeply contested. It is a means of expression and enactment of moral commitments and emotional attachments and of

---

[11] Cf. Francis William Kent, *Household and Lineage in Renaissance Florence: The Family Life of the Capponi, Ginori, and Rucellai* (Princeton: Princeton University Press, 1977), 135–44; and Anthony Molho, *Marriage Alliance in Late Medieval Florence* (Cambridge: Harvard University Press, 1994), 333–34.

[12] See the classic examinations of Florentine governance, officeholding, and factionalism: Gene Brucker, *The Civic World of Early Renaissance Florence* (Princeton: Princeton University Press, 1977) and *Florentine Politics and Society, 1343–1378* (Princeton: Princeton University Press, 1962); Lauro Martines, *Lawyers and Statecraft in Renaissance Florence* (Princeton: Princeton University Press, 1968); Nicolai Rubinstein, *The Government of Florence under the Medici (1434–1494)* (Oxford: Oxford University Press, 1965); Dale Kent, *The Rise of the Medici: Faction in Florence, 1426–1434* (Oxford: Oxford University Press, 1978) and "The Florentine 'Reggimento' in the Fifteenth Century," *Renaissance Quarterly* 28 (1975): 575–638; John J. Najemy, *Corporation and Consensus in Florentine Electoral Politics, 1280–1400* (Chapel Hill: University of North Carolina Press, 1982); Marvin Becker, *Florence in Transition*, 2 vols. (Baltimore: Johns Hopkins University Press, 1967–68).

[13] Yanagisako, 83. See also her comments about anthropological theories of kinship, 77–79.

material and nonmaterial interests. My approach to repudiation and inheritance has been guided by a sense of the potential and limits, the rigidity and yet plasticity of the law in relation to daily life.

Acknowledgments

The dynamic between individual and group goes into a book too. The individual author bears the blame for errors, omissions, and patent stupidities. The collective shares the credit for what value there is. Credit then must go first to the National Endowment for the Humanities for a year-long fellowship, coupled with sabbatical leave from Clemson University, that allowed me to do the bulk of the archival research. The Clemson College of Architecture, Arts, and Humanities also provided funding for travel. I am grateful to the professional and efficient staffs of the Archivio di Stato and Biblioteca Nazionale Centrale of Florence for their assistance and kindness. Nor can I forget the gracious assistance of the staff at the Robbins Center at the University of California, Berkeley, Law School, and of its director, Laurent Mayali, and the incredible and invaluable aid of the Clemson University Interlibrary Loan Office. My first exploration of repudiation took the form of a presentation to the Renaissance Society of America meeting in 1990. I thank some of those present then for their comments and encouragement, notably Libby and Tom Cohen, and the late Rona Goffen for tracking me down and asking me to submit the paper to *Renaissance Quarterly*, which subsequently published it. An invitation to an international conference on "Famiglie e poteri in Italia tra Medioevo ed Età Moderna" in Lucca in June 2005 allowed me to present and discuss part of Chapter 2. I thank Anna Bellavitis, Isabelle Chabot, and Silvana Seidel Menchi for the invitation, and Stanley Chojnacki and Caroline Fisher for their comments and questions.

Debts of a personal nature abound. My thanks to Anthony Molho for sharing his digitized version of the 1480 catasto and to Lauro Martines for answering my queries. I am grateful to archival companions Bill Caferro and Lawrin Armstrong for lending an ear and offering suggestions. Daniel Smail endured some painfully obtuse early drafts of various chapters and notably encouraged me to keep the issue of credit and trust at the center of the study. Jules Kirshner has been an invaluable source of insight and an inspiring model of scholarship and intellectual acuity for more than three decades.

Support closer to home sustained my labors. I thank colleagues whose patience I am sure I wore down – Roger Grant and David Nicholas. And I am ever grateful to all my colleagues in the Clemson history department for being day by day a community of engaged scholars and passionate teachers. Amy Matthews provided valuable help in recasting some data so that it could "crunch" through Excel and SPSS, beyond her invaluable work in keeping the department functioning despite me. Trish Nigro found a way to assemble some tables, print copies of this typescript, and observe the Friday color regimen. Ben Stephens slid over to the building from his outpost in the psychology department to show me the ropes with the data software.

My daughter, Allison, endured her father's chatter and grew through the years to show me what a splendid legacy I will leave. The book is dedicated to Teresa Suggs, *amica amatissima*, who still may not like the subject but who helped make it happen and kept me going.

Introduction
Of Inheritance and Kinship

> *Haereditas est successio in universum ius quod defunctus habuit* ('an inheritance is a succession to the entire legal position of the deceased man'). The notion was that, though the physical person of the deceased had perished, his legal personality survived, and descended unimpaired on his Heir or Co-heirs, in whom his identity (so far as the law was concerned) was continued.
>
> It seems, in truth, that the prolongation of a man's legal existence in his heir, or in a group of co-heirs, is neither more nor less than a characteristic of the *family* transferred by a fiction to the *individual*.
>
> – Henry Sumner Maine, *Ancient Law* (London, 1861; reprint ed., London: Oxford University Press, 1931), 151, 154

A Point of Departure

Immediately following his famous and still influential statement that "the movement of the progressive societies has hitherto been a movement *from Status to Contract*," Henry Sumner Maine (1822–88), the English jurist and comparative historian, turned to a discussion of testaments and inheritance. For him, the Romans' development of the testament, a flexible instrument imposing the intentions of testators on their heirs, was the quintessential contract. Its intrusion into succession was the device that melted the rigid quality of ascribed status. It inserted what Maine took as "natural affection" against "the limitations of the family imposed by legal pedantry." The visible Roman horror at intestacy was thus rooted in an early conflict between law and changing sentiment about the family.[1]

Maine's treatment of inheritance remains emblematic. Inheritance is still taken as the process by which the dead live on, or at least influence the

---

[1] Maine, 184–85. Broadly on Maine's views, see Robin Fox, *Reproduction and Succession: Studies in Anthropology, Law, and Society* (New Brunswick: Transaction, 1993), 96–100, 129–33.

living, with their intentions and their possessions. The distinction or even conflict between family and individual is still the pole around which analyses of inheritance rules and strategies gravitate. Legalistic notions of inheritance have even been extended to encompass genetics. A similar fiction of patrimony simplifies social time, inscribing continuity in the heir as custodian of a gene pool, a clear arrangement in which culture domesticates nature and persons own things. "Inheritance made sense," according to anthropologist Alain Pottage, "in societies which imagined it was possible to conserve this form of geometry through time."[2]

One powerful common mode of depiction of the historical progression from the medieval to the fully modern, in fact, is laid out in terms of inheritance. The nineteenth- and early twentieth-century social theoreticians, such as Maine or Alexis de Tocqueville or Émile Durkheim, depicted the historical shift to modernity as a passage from status by ascription (inherited) to status by achievement.[3] Max Weber declared that "with the multiplication of life chances and opportunities [created by bureaucratic government and the capitalist economy], the individual becomes less and less content with being bound to rigid and undifferentiated forms of life prescribed by the group."[4] As an early example of such a "rational," as opposed to "natural" household, Weber invoked the large capitalistic household of Florence, where individuals held separate accounts, in proof, as he saw it, of the solvent forces of a monetary economy.[5] His sense of the Renaissance as a site of rising individualism derived, in turn, from Jakob Burckhardt, who had placed individualism, along with the state, at the center of the Renaissance Italian world.[6]

These theoretical underpinnings continue to inform our historical sense. To quote from one treatment of the history of families,

Inheritance provides one of the contrasts between our time and the centuries before industrialization. What used to be a pervasive principle has become a private one. It is still common for people to inherit property, and there are laws that protect the rights of heirs, but modern Western society does not entirely approve of inherited wealth, and it is not considered necessary to inherit something in order to get on in the world. Inherited wealth is regarded with some suspicion and is heavily taxed. By contrast, in the past *everything* tended to be inherited.[7]

---

[2] Alain Pottage, "Our Original Inheritance," in *Law, Anthropology, and the Constitution of the Social: Making Persons and Things*, ed. Alain Pottage and Martha Mundy (Cambridge: Cambridge University Press, 2004), 249–85, at 251–52, and 278.

[3] James Casey, *The History of the Family* (Oxford: Blackwell, 1989), 18.

[4] Max Weber, *Economy and Society*, 2 vols., ed. Guenther Roth and Claus Wittich (Berkeley: University of California Press, 1978), 1: 375.

[5] Ibid., 376–77.

[6] Jakob Burckhardt, *The Civilization of the Renaissance in Italy*, trans. S. G. C. Middlemore 1860; reprint ed., (New York: Penguin, 1990).

[7] Beatrice Gottlieb, *The Family in the Western World from the Black Death to the Industrial Age* (New York: Oxford University Press, 1993), 201 (emphasis in the original).

A Point of Departure

Inheritance also figures as what one Italian legal historian, Antonio Pertile, came to term the cornerstone of the entire edifice of law.[8] Building on that observation Andrea Romano has stated,

> Defense of patrimonial integrity, the substantial guardian of the family's political-economic interests and social dignity, and attention to the means of transmission of family properties, particularly real estate, constituted in their multiple interconnections, central junctures in the history of law, of political institutions, and of European society in the Middle Ages and early modern era.[9]

So much of law was about inheritance. So many of the suits that came to court were about inheritance. So much of the attention of governments was about securing and taxing inheritance.

Inheritance was not only about the vital reproduction of the social system but, as the comparative anthropologist Jack Goody pointed out, it was and is about "the way in which interpersonal relationships are structured," including household forms.[10] A basic distinction is drawn between rules of impartible inheritance, which seek to keep property together in a bundle across time, often by designating a single heir in each generation, and rules of partible inheritance, which place some assets in the hands of each heir, at the cost of eventual morcelization and division of holdings. Ever since Frédéric Le Play posed a correlation between the multigenerational stem family and impartible inheritance, social historians have investigated the relationship between impartibility or partibility and household forms.[11] For legal historians, the correlation to be drawn is not to household structures so much but to related matters (also of interest to social historians), such as parental power, the timing and arrangement of marriages, the relative freedom of disposition of property by the ascending generation, and the availability of alternatives, such as pre-mortem gifts or dowries.[12] The size and coherence of households varied with these factors as well. The availability of

---

[8] Cited in Andrea Romano, *Famiglia, successioni e patrimonio familiare nell'Italia medievale e moderna* (Turin: Giappichelli, 1994), 2.

[9] Romano, 3.

[10] Jack Goody, Introduction, in *Family and Inheritance: Rural Society in Western Europe, 1200–1800*, ed. Jack Goody, Joan Thirsk, E. P. Thompson (Cambridge: Cambridge University Press, 1976), 1–9, at 1.

[11] For a brief overview, see Michael Anderson, *Approaches to the History of the Western Family, 1500–1914* (London: Macmillan, 1980), 66–69. For examples, in addition to essays in Goody, Thirsk, and Thompson (previous note), see Jean-Louis Flandrin, *Families in Former Times*, trans. Richard Southern (Cambridge: Cambridge University Press, 1979); Peter Laslett, ed., *Household and Family in Past Time* (Cambridge: Cambridge University Press, 1972); Lutz K. Berkner and F. F. Mendels, "Inheritance Systems, Family Structure, and Demographic Patterns in Western Europe, 1700–1900," in *Historical Studies of Changing Fertility*, ed. Charles Tilly (Princeton: Princeton University Press, 1978), 209–223.

[12] Here briefly, Lloyd Bonfield, "Developments in European Family Law," in *Family Life in Early Modern Times, 1500–1789*, ed. David I. Kertzer and Marzio Barbagli (New Haven: Yale University Press, 2001), 87–124, esp. 113–20.

alternative paths to property and/or livelihood, other than by inheritance of land or tools of the trade, was also an important factor.[13] Where inheritance was less singularly important, as was seemingly the case with the advent of industrial capitalism, households too became smaller and weaker.

This book is about inheritance. Indeed, it is about inheritance in that very city that Weber saw as pivotal to historical development of individual economic opportunity, Florence. But it seeks to examine inheritance in a different manner. In particular, this study will examine repudiations of inheritance – heirs' refusals to accept what was left them on the grounds that it was more burdened with debts than blessed with assets. This refusal was a legal act with economic and social consequences.

In light of the acknowledged importance of inheritance in the past, repudiation seems odd, to say the least. When so much rode on inheritance, how could an heir turn it down? Why? The premise behind this study is that examination of repudiation practices can reveal a great deal about how inheritance was supposed to function and what it meant, as well as to place it in contexts that both limited and enabled its operation.

Repudiation of inheritance requires us to consider two matters. First, we are compelled to move beyond the prevailing discourse concerning family and kinship in the past to seeing inheritance in a more financial or economic light. The economic and social life of Florence ran on credit and trust.[14] Consequent problems of indebtedness and mistrust were also pervasive. All sorts of transactions, such as simple sales, in fact involved not just the principals but their heirs, pledged to honor and abide by the terms set forth. The trustworthiness of those with whom one dealt was crucial to the operation of credit. Kin and neighbors were preferred partners in consequence. Market relations were not impersonal; parties knew about each other, their networks and contexts.[15]

---

[13] Cf. Wally Secombe, *A Millennium of Family Change: Feudalism to Capitalism in Northwestern Europe* (London: Verso, 1992); Ulrich Pfister, "Proto-Industrialization," in *Family Life in Early Modern Times*, 63–84.

[14] Cf. James G. Carrier, *Gifts and Commodities: Exchange and Western Capitalism since 1700* (London: Routledge, 1995), 69–74, 91–93. For the immediate area of Florence, see Richard K. Marshall, *The Local Merchants of Prato: Small Entrepreneurs in the Late Medieval Economy* (Baltimore: Johns Hopkins University Press, 1999), 71–100. For a legal perspective, Hélène Angiolini, "I consilia quale fonte per la vita economica: alcuni problemi," in *Legal Consulting in the Civil Law Tradition*, ed. Mario Ascheri, Ingrid Baumgärtner, and Julius Kirshner (Berkeley: Robbins Collection, 1999), 293–315. The classic work is that of Fernand Braudel, *Civilization and Capitalism, 15th-18th Century*, trans. Sian Reynolds, 3 vols. (New York: Harper & Row, 1981–84), esp. vol. 2: *The Wheels of Commerce*, 385–95. Braudel unabashedly proclaimed that "from the artisan to the manufacturer, everyone lived on credit."

[15] Richard Goldthwaite, "The Medici Bank and the World of Florentine Capitalism," *Past and Present* 114 (1987): 3–31; Paul D. McLean and John F. Padgett, "Was Florence a Perfectly Competitive Market? Transactional Evidence from the Renaissance," *Theory and Society*

A Point of Departure

It was not just a matter of credit and debt in the marketplace. There were also numerous instances of what Daniel Smail, for one, has called "circumstantial credit" – obligations rooted in relationships and their material concomitants, such as that to return a dowry on the dissolution of marriage.[16] These credit relationships necessarily rested on affection at some level. They were built on recurring transactions of patronage and clientage; they arose between kin, neighbors, and friends. Recovery of debts rested on personal calculations and not just financial rationales. And recovery was difficult as a result, especially in instances in which fixed terms of repayment did not exist.[17] As dependent as individuals were on others in their constant and shifting credit relations, they were also guarded and fearful of the consequences of failure to fulfill obligations, to falsify, and to deceive.[18] All these debts and obligations facing heirs greatly complicated inheritance.

One does not have to spend much time with the uniquely valuable catasto of Florence to find examples of considerable debt load carried by families against their declared assets. Nor need one look too far in account books to find complaints about the difficulties of tracking down debtors and wringing payment from them. Whiny complaints to tax collectors were legion also.

An outstanding example of the precarious nature of fortunes in Florence is Giovanni Rucellai. Son-in-law to the wealthy Palla Strozzi (himself another example of economic as well as political misfortunes), father-in-law to Lorenzo de' Medici's sister, Rucellai was Florence's third wealthiest head of household according to the catasto of 1458. By 1474, he had suffered grave losses, mainly from mismanagement of his Pisan office by a trusted employee. He was forced to liquidate assets, seek a reassessment and reduction of his fiscal obligations, and by 1479 faced threat of excommunication and exile as a notorious bankrupt. His advice to his sons was to reduce their exposure to others – "bastivi il conservare" (it is enough to hold on to what you have).[19]

---

26 (1997): 209–44; id., "Obligation, Risk, and Opportunity in the Renaissance Economy: Beyond Social Embeddedness to Network Co-constitution," in *The Sociology of the Economy*, ed. Frank Dobbin (New York: Russell Sage, 2004), 193–227.

[16] Cf. Daniel Lord Smail, *The Consumption of Justice: Emotions, Publicity, and Legal Culture in Marseille, 1264–1423* (Ithaca: Cornell University Press, 2003), 144.

[17] In addition to Smail, 137, 145–46, see also William Chester Jordan, *Women and Credit in Pre-Industrial and Developing Societies* (Philadelphia: University of Pennsylvania Press, 1993); Craig Muldrew, *The Economy of Obligation: The Culture of Credit and Social Relations in Early Modern England* (New York: St. Martin's Press, 1998); David Sugarman and Ronnie Warrington, "Land Law, Citizenship, and the Invention of 'Englishness': The Strange World of the Equity of Redemption," in *Early Modern Conceptions of Property*, ed. John Brewer and Susan Staves (London: Routledge, 1996), 111–43.

[18] Ronald F. E. Weissman, *Ritual Brotherhood in Renaissance Florence* (New York: Academic Press, 1982), 35–36.

[19] F. W. Kent, "The Making of a Renaissance Patron of the Arts," and Alessandro Perosa, "Lo Zibaldone di Giovanni Rucellai," in *Giovanni Rucellai e il suo Zibaldone*, vol. 2: A

Repudiation of inheritance secondly impels us to approach inheritance as a process – something that necessarily unfolded over time (though the interval could be brief). It involved much more than the rules of intestacy or the modifications to those rules as worked out in testaments. Inheritance was a process because it involved not just the deceased but his or her heirs, and possibly others (as legatees, guardians, executors, notaries, attorneys, judges, witnesses). Death only opened a new phase in the process. The heirs took steps to enact or thwart the wishes of the deceased or the social and familial desiderata behind the rules of inheritance.

For Maine, there was no process in inheritance, largely because, as he saw ancient societies, there really was no difference between deceased and heir: "The rights and obligations which attached to the deceased head of the house would attach, without breach of continuity, to his successor; for in point of fact, they would be the rights and obligations of the family, and the family had the distinctive characteristic of a corporation – that it never died."[20] Few historians, especially those studying families in Western societies, would accept so simply the reification of families in the past. Yet equally few would disagree with sentiments to the effect that "collectivities took precedence over individuals."[21] The almost singular concern in historical or sociological research has been with the ways in which inheritance mechanisms allowed for the perpetuation of family and property over the generations in the face of undeniable centrifugal forces, or in the face of present needs, versus long-term goals. European aristocracies and patriciates, from the central Middle Ages on, were notably intent on the sorts of material and symbolic solidarities and continuities framed in genealogies and inheritance rules. Italian patrician families especially have been said to exhibit an "extraordinary persistence of the family," rooted at least in part in inheritance practices.[22] Heirs were

---

Florentine Patrician and His Palace (London: Warburg Institute, 1981), 9–95 and 99–152 respectively.

[20] Maine, 153. His view of the indefinite corporate nature of the family and inheritance strategies in the Roman world, it can be safely said, no longer carries weight. See, for example, Richard P. Saller, *Patriarchy, Property and Death in the Roman Family* (Cambridge: Cambridge University Press, 1994), 162–63, who demonstrates that Roman inheritance strategies were household-bound and presentist.

[21] Gottlieb, *The Family in the Western World*, 205. See also Casey, *History of the Family*; Michael Mitterauer and Reinhard Sieder, *The European Family: Patriarchy to Partnership from the Middle Ages to the Present*, trans. Karla Oosterveen and Manfred Hörzinger (Chicago: University of Chicago Press, 1982); Martine Segalen, *Historical Anthropology of the Family*, trans. J. C. Whitehouse and Sarah Matthews (Cambridge: Cambridge University Press, 1986); David Herlihy, *Medieval Households* (Cambridge: Harvard University Press, 1985); and Philippe Ariès and Georges Duby, eds, *A History of Private Life*, 5 vols. (Cambridge: Belknap Press of Harvard University Press, 1987–91).

[22] The phrase is taken from Marino Berengo, *Nobili e mercanti nella Lucca del Cinquecento* (Turin: Einaudi, 1965), 46. See also the influential synthesis of Marzio Barbagli, *Sotto lo stesso tetto: Mutamenti della famiglia in Italia dal xv al xx secolo* (Bologna: Il Mulino,

caught up in these family strategies, even those siblings disadvantaged by practices of single heirship.[23]

Preservation of family property over the generations was rooted in an attitude that Beatrice Gottlieb dubs stewardship.

> In this view of inheritance, the individual counts for little. The heir is a steward rather than an owner. Ideally, the estate passes through his hands untouched. Rather than use it or even add to it, his first duty is to preserve it.[24]

This sort of heirship led, as she notes, to considerable ambivalence on the part of heirs or prospective heirs. The heir was and is not a passive recipient. In each generation, the obligation contained in an inheritance had to be actualized by its executor. The heir had to look in two directions – not only to the demands of the past but to those of the future, whose claims equally had to be allowed for.[25] A bulwark of laws was erected to maintain such stewardship in the face of heirs' ownership of property during their lives. Devices such as the Roman law form of trust, *fideicommissum*, linked with clauses of substitution of heirs into the future – the use of both of which undoubtedly increased over the course of the fifteenth and sixteenth centuries – show how hard some worked to impose stewardship on their heirs.[26]

A device such as repudiation of inheritance or its opposite, acceptance of inheritance (*aditio*), necessarily raises our awareness of the role of the heir. Only a few have investigated this role. Perhaps most systematic in this regard were John Cole and Eric Wolf, who pursued a parallel study of Italian and German Alpine villages with contrasting inheritance rules. They found that impartible (single heir) inheritance customs did not prevent the division of some estates and that partible (multiple heir) customs did not result in total fragmentation of holdings from one generation to the next:[27] "Thus, while the inheritance ideology provides a cognitive framework within which the *de*

1984), but also compare it to Nino Tamassia, *La famiglia italiana nei secoli decimoquinto e decimosesto* (Milan: Sandron, 1910). Note also Cinzio Violante, "Quelques caractéristiques des structures familiales en Lombardie, Émilie, et Toscane aux xie et xiie siècles," in *Famille et parenté dans l'Occident médiéval*, ed. Georges Duby and Jacques Le Goff (Rome: École Franaise de Rome, 1977), 87–148, at 101.

[23] Raffaella Sarti, *Europe at Home: Family and Material Culture, 1500–1800*, trans. Allan Cameron (New Haven and London: Yale University Press, 2002), 59, where she cites Renata Ago, "Giochi di squadra: Uomini e donne nelle famiglie nobili del xvii secolo," in *Signori, patrizi, cavalieri nell'Italia centro-meridionale nell'età moderna*, ed. Maria Antonietta Visceglia (Bari: Laterza, 1992), 256–64.

[24] Gottlieb, 204. Cf. Brian Pullan, "'Three Orders of Inhabitants': Social Hierarchies in the Republic of Venice," in *Orders and Hierarchies in Late Medieval and Renaissance Venice*, ed. Jeffrey Denton (Toronto: University of Toronto Press, 1999), 147–68, esp. 148–49.

[25] Pottage, "Our Original Inheritance," 279.

[26] Gottlieb, 205–7.

[27] John W. Cole and Eric R. Wolf, *The Hidden Frontier: Ecology and Ethnicity in an Alpine Valley* (New York: Academic Press, 1974), 176–95.

facto process must operate, both the mechanics of the process and its results are in the last instance determined by the forces of environment and market, and in spite of ideologies."[28]

What makes each system work, in Cole and Wolf's estimation, is the conduct of persons in each generation. How the heirs interact determines if there are cooperative transitions, smooth distinctions between management and ownership, or conflicts, disruptions, and divisions. Inheritance thus emerges as a process to which heirs vitally contribute their consent or rejection, and the "rules of inheritance are in the nature of ideology and are not guidelines for action."[29]

"Strategies of heirship" is a term one finds with some frequency; but the perspective behind such strategies is always entirely that of the passing generation, of those who were in position and had concern to arrange their affairs, write a will, and so forth.[30] "Yet," cautions Lloyd Bonfield,

the considerable quantity of litigation over dispositions suggests that the designs of property holders were not always respected. Numerous suits were probably initiated and then settled, leaving the historian with some doubt as to the actual distribution of family property. Inheritance in early modern Europe was a complex and oftentimes uncertain process, with customary inheritance law, individual volition, litigation, and compromise all playing a role, and in large measure conspiring to obscure (at least from the historian) 'how much went to whom.'[31]

But it is more than the uncertainty of the records that leaves this dimension of inheritance processes obscure to historians. In many regards, they have not thought to look for such records or even pose the questions that might spur a quest for them.

Emphasis on the use and manipulation of rules by heirs is central to this study. Creative use of legal instruments shaped family relationships, as they continue to do in the present. Although family self-conceptions may celebrate self-reliant founding figures and face-to-face relationships, in contrast to the formal, impersonal, externally grounded legal facade, legal arrangements

---

[28] Ibid., 203.

[29] Ibid., 264. Stephen Wilson, in a study of nineteenth-century Corsica, whose object was not inheritance per se but feud, finds that intrafamilial conflict related mainly to steps to preserve and transmit family property across generations, notably when testators' wishes ran counter to those who stood to inherit. Inheritance was not a "transfer of property from one person to another, but rather a continuous cycle of endlessly matching family to resources," and it was the actions of heirs or prospective heirs that determined real peace and solidarity in the family. Stephen Wilson, *Feuding, Conflict, and Banditry in Nineteenth-Century Corsica* (Cambridge: Cambridge University Press, 1988), 129–57.

[30] Under the heading of "strategies," for example, Saller discusses the flexible use of trusts (*fideicommissa*) by Roman testators to bind their heirs (*Patriarchy, Property and Death*, 168–71). He never raises the legal right of heirs to refuse.

[31] Bonfield, "Developments in European Family Law," 120.

allow families to adjust to political and economic environments.[32] These arrangements vitally involve, but also transcend, testaments.

The Primacy of Testaments

Andrea Romano, in an important legal historical study, traces a shift from a medieval "constant preoccupation to preserve family unity, keeping its components linked together around the patrimony in an extended or even complex structure," to a Renaissance adherence to aristocratic models that identified themselves "more properly in terms of the perpetual survival of the line." The result was that "entire branches and lines of descent were sacrificed economically 'to the honor of the family name,' that was said to be perpetuated in the line of male primogeniture."[33] Romano is not alone and not the first to trace such a shift. He is unique for bringing it to bear within the field of legal history. He places the crisis point in this shift around the end of the Trecento – when it was marked and formed by the continuing impact of plagues and famines that had struck forcefully through the century, by increasing forms of "individualistic" expression, by the growth of communal and signorial powers hostile to competing powerful family associations, and by legal developments that could only poorly mask extended family groups with the terms and rules of civil law. The result was a more dynastic sense of family as a line of descent and a patrimony enduring over generations. It was an image of a family whose prestige rested on its patrimony, preservation of which backed practices such as the testamentary substitutions tying property to a line of descent, even to a single heir.[34]

The testament, imposing the "last wishes" of the deceased on those who follow, takes instrumental pride of place. For obvious reasons, surviving written testaments dominate studies of inheritance. Intestacy, after all, meant a decedent's property passed by general existing rules, which mainly concerned eligibility to inherit, and order of succession (using degrees of relationship, gender, agnation and cognation, and so forth). There is no paper to mark an intestacy usually. There is no way to know the desires and sentiments of the deceased. Only if one had, say, private account books that were unusually complete and forthcoming, could one say how a person positioned himself and his property prior to his intestate death.

---

[32] Cf. George E. Marcus with Peter Dobkin Hall, *Lives in Trust: The Fortunes of Dynastic Families in Late Twentieth-Century America* (Boulder: Westview Press, 1992), esp. 18, 27, 48, 170.

[33] Romano, *Famiglia, successioni e patrimonio familiare*, 18–19. See also J. P. Cooper, "Patterns of Inheritance and Settlement by Great Landowners from the Fifteenth to the Eighteenth Centuries," in *Family and Inheritance*, 192–327.

[34] Romano, 42–46. In addition to works cited below, see Gianna Pomata, "Family and Gender," in *Early Modern Italy, 1550–1796*, ed. John A. Marino (Oxford: Oxford University Press, 2002), 69–86, esp. 75–77.

In contrast, testaments are so compelling. They can be used to examine and extract sentiments and strategies. They are expressive of family ideologies.[35] They have proven useful in tracking attitudes to death and charitable giving. They have provided the basis to some truly impressive and important historical work, most notably in the landmark studies of Michel Vovelle and Jacques Chiffoleau.[36]

For early modern Italian history, the outstanding example of the use of testaments is the work of Samuel Cohn. First in a diachronic study of testaments from Siena, later in a comparative study of six Italian cities, including Florence, Cohn has studied testators' dispositions regarding charity, legacies to kin, and naming of heirs.[37] He has constructed powerful arguments about the impact of the Black Death on testamentary practices and a coherent scheme of variations in practices across different communities. Among other things, he has advanced the finding that the plague, more so after its second occurrence, raised a renewed concern with family name and continuity, traceable in a variety of testamentary clauses.

Testaments have powered other studies as well. Steven Epstein studied Genoese testaments across a century of the Middle Ages. His attention was broadly directed not only to the dispositions and strategies of heirship but to the processes of composition, roles of notaries, assembling of witnesses.[38] One entire line of approach to testaments has been largely concerned with the scribal dimensions of these texts.[39] Simona Ricci has assembled testaments from upper Valdarno, outside Florence, in the fourteenth century to determine what these texts were like, who the testators were, and how they

---

[35] Diane Owen Hughes, "Struttura familiare e sistemi di successione ereditaria nei testamenti dell'Europa medievale," *Quaderni storici* 33 (1976): 929–52.

[36] Michel Vovelle, *La mort et l'Occident: De 1300 à nos jours* (Paris: Gallimard, 1983), and Jacques Chiffoleau, *La comptabilité de l'au-delà: Les hommes, la mort et la religion dans le région d'Avignon à la fin du Moyen ge (vers 1320–vers 1480)* (Rome: École Franaise de Rome, 1980).

[37] Samuel K. Cohn, Jr., *Death and Property in Siena, 1205–1800: Strategies for the Afterlife* (Baltimore: Johns Hopkins University Press, 1988); id., *The Cult of Remembrance and the Black Death: Six Renaissance Cities in Central Italy* (Baltimore: Johns Hopkins University Press, 1992). Also concerned with charitable bequests is Richard Trexler, "Charity and the Defense of Urban Elites in the Italian Communes," in *The Rich, the Well-Born, and the Powerful*, ed. F. Jaher (Urbana: University of Illinois Press, 1973), 64–109.

[38] Steven Epstein, *Wills and Wealth in Medieval Genoa: 1150–1250* (Cambridge: Harvard University Press, 1984).

[39] See the essays in *Nolens intestatus decedere: Il testamento come fonte della storia religiosa e sociale*, ed. Attilio Bartoli Langeli (Perugia: Deputazione per la Storia Patria per l'Umbria, 1985); also Luca Condini, "Un sondaggio fra i testamenti milanesi del secondo Quattrocento," *Archivio storico lombardo* 117 (1991): 367–89. An example of the ways in which careful textual reading of testaments can raise problems is offered by Martin Bertram, "'Renaissance Mentality' in Italian Testaments?" *Journal of Modern History* 67 (1995): 358–69, in conjunction with Cohn's work.

wanted their bodies and goods disposed.[40] Sandra Cavallo has utilized wills, among other things, to illuminate charitable patterns in Turin.[41] Gianna Lumia-Ostinelli has examined Sienese wills, with careful attention to testamentary modifications in contrast to rules of intestacy, in order to "'correct' the rigidly patrilinear image of the inheritance system as delineated by many civic statutes."[42] Her work shares many features with that undertaken for Venice by Stanley Chojnacki and Linda Guzzetti.[43] Maria Luisa Lombardo and Mirella Morelli have done a rigorous examination of late medieval Roman women's testaments.[44] Giovanna Benadusi has added a social class dimension to the gendered study of wills of female servants.[45]

Such studies, valuable as they are, concern themselves only with one part of an inheritance process. They treat inheritance almost exclusively in terms of the bequeathing parties. The only studies that seek out the reactions and strategies of heirs or legatees look at a peculiar subset – hospitals or charitable institutions. One thinks here of Brian Pullan's study of the *scuole* of Venice or Philip Gavitt's of the Florentine foundling hospital, the Innocenti.[46] Gavitt's work is especially revealing of the sorts of lawsuits over testaments that the Innocenti became embroiled in.[47] Studies of widows have looked at

[40] Simona Ricci, *"De hac vita transire": La pratica testamentaria nel Valdarno superiore all'indomani della Peste Nera* (Florence: Comune di Figline Valdarno, Opus Libri, 1998).
[41] Sandra Cavallo, *Charity and Power in Early Modern Italy: Benefactors and Their Motives in Turin, 1541–1789* (Cambridge: Cambridge University Press, 1995).
[42] Gianna Lumia-Ostinelli, "'Ut cippus domus magis conservetur': La successione a Siena tra statuti e testamenti (secoli xii–xvii)," *Archivio storico italiano* 161 (2003): 3–51, quotation at 6. See also her "Morire a Siena: Devoluzione testamentaria, legami parenteli e vincoli affettivi in età moderna," *Bullettino senese di storia patria* 103 (1997): 103–285. Her work supplements earlier explorations by E. D. English, "La prassi testamentaria delle famiglie nobili a Siena e nella Toscana del Tre-Quattrocento," in *I ceti dirigenti nella Toscana del Quattrocento*, ed. Riccardo Fubini (Florence: Papafava, 1987), 463–72, and Salvatore I. Camporeale, "La morte, la proprietà e 'il problema della salvezza': Testamenti e ultime volontà a Siena dal 1200 al 1800 (considerazioni di storia e storiografia)," *Memorie domenicane* 108 (1991): 381–404.
[43] Cf. Stanley Chojnacki, "Dowries and Kinsmen" and "The Power of Love: Wives and Husbands," in his *Women and Men in Renaissance Venice: Twelve Essays on Patrician Society* (Baltimore: Johns Hopkins University Press, 2000), 132–52, 153–68; Linda Guzzetti, "Le donne a Venezia nel xiv secolo: Uno studio sulla presenza nella società e nella famiglia," *Studi veneziani* 25 (1998): 15–88.
[44] Maria Luisa Lombardo and Mirella Morelli, "Donne a Roma tra Medioevo e Età Moderna," *Archivi e cultura*, n.s. 25–26 (1992–93): 25–130.
[45] Giovanna Benadusi, "Investing the Riches of the Poor: Servant Women and Their Last Wills," *American Historical Review* 109 (2004): 805–826.
[46] Brian Pullan, *Rich and Poor in Renaissance Venice* (Cambridge: Harvard University Press, 1971); Philip Gavitt, *Charity and Children in Renaissance Florence: The Ospedale degli Innocenti, 1410–1536* (Ann Arbor: University of Michigan Press, 1990), 107–40.
[47] One of which I examined at some length in "'Nemo mortalis cognitus vivit in evo': Moral and Legal Conflicts in a Florentine Inheritance Case of 1442," in *The Moral World of the Law*, ed. Peter Coss (Cambridge: Cambridge University Press, 2000), 113–33. Unlike other

their strategies and dilemmas in regard to recovery of their dowries or additional testamentary bequests.[48] These studies are at best only partly about inheritance and tend to stress widows' weaknesses in the face of male kin and courts.

Studies based on testaments emphasize the strength of legal rules and moral obligations to bind heirs effectively to the testators' wishes. As Cohn puts it, "in this new litigious culture of the Cinquecento, testators attempted more carefully than before or afterward to foresee and forestall future lawsuits" with the clauses inserted in their wills.[49] Epstein believes that "most of the time the law ensured that the testator's intentions would be carried out, and did not pose any insurmountable barriers to his final wishes."[50] Yet, in the law, heirs and legatees vitally had choices. They by no means always exercised them, but they had options. They could delay, try to ignore, or even on occasion openly contest in court provisions of wills or the very validity of them. If nothing else, they could "walk away." That strategy gained them nothing, but nothing may have been a better deal. And ironically, if there were no contingencies spelled out in the will, their failure to accept an estate might result in an intestacy.

Intestacy, in fact, presents something of a challenge to testament-based studies of inheritance. In part, this challenge has been met by asserting that intestacy was less frequent or even aberrant. Of course, as intestacies left little record, it is impossible to make the case statistically. In lieu of numbers, one powerful argument has rested on the "horror" of intestacy ascribed to the Romans. Historians of Roman law have broadly assumed a preponderance of testamentary transmission in ancient Rome, although one study has raised serious questions about the primacy of testaments among the Romans, largely on the basis of class distinctions.[51] The revival of Roman law in the Middle Ages created a similar renewed loathing of intestacy. Indeed, to the Roman desire not to die intestate was seemingly added a powerful impetus from the Church to use the testament to settle one's moral and charitable

---

Florentine hospitals, such as Santa Maria Nuova, the Innocenti did not appear among the ranks of those repudiating an inheritance.

[48] Cf. Christiane Klapisch-Zuber, "The 'Cruel Mother': Maternity, Widowhood, and Dowry in Florence in the Fourteenth and Fifteenth Centuries," in *Women, Family, and Ritual in Renaissance Italy*, trans. Lydia G. Cochrane (Chicago: University of Chicago Press, 1985), 134–62; Isabelle Chabot, "Widowhood and Poverty in Late Medieval Florence," *Continuity and Change* 3 (1988): 291–311; Giulia Calvi, "'Senza speranza di succedere': Madri, figlie e Stato nella Toscana moderna (xvi-xviii secc.)," in *Madri: Storia di un ruolo sociale*, ed. Giovanna Fiume (Venice: Marsilio, 1995), 157–73.

[49] Cohn, *Death and Property*, 129.

[50] Epstein, 230.

[51] David Cherry, "Intestacy and the Roman Poor," *Revue d'histoire de droit* 64 (1996): 155–72. He finds support in earlier arguments of David Daube and in studies of intestacy in the United States.

accounts, see to burial and memorial masses, and so forth. As Ricci states, "To die *sine condito testamento* is thus a true and proper sin, because the family's reproduction is in risk from this lack of preparation and at the same time the [non]testator compromises his possibilities of entering Paradise."[52]

Increasing use of testaments in the late Middle Ages has certainly been tied to the spread of revived Roman law and, even more so, to religious and charitable impulses. George Dameron has found significant numbers of Florentine wills only from the 1270s, which he links to preoccupations with purgatory and growing attachment to mendicant models of spirituality.[53] One might add that the timing also coincides with the establishment of Guelf and "popular" government in Florence, with its expansion of law, courts, and notarial forms. Cohn has recorded another understandable expansion of testamentary activity in the aftermath of the plagues.[54]

It has also been observed that testaments were not drawn up just by the wealthy. The poor too were familiar with and used testaments. Ricci's work turned up examples from humble *contadini*, and Benadusi's study is based entirely on such lower class wills. Cohn's first study began with the observation that the testaments of peasants offer "a rare moment, if only with short phrases, for listening to those who have had no intellectual history by the traditional standards."[55]

Still, intestacy too happened. No one has been concerned somehow to count intestacies for a medieval or early modern society, or simply to find a way to do so. That some poor made wills does not mean that all did, or that it is not in fact the case that the poor are more likely to die intestate. Even the wealthy do not and did not always exploit wills. One historian, who has limited her gaze to a single, though wealthy and large Florentine clan, has concluded "that, although men and women up and down the social scale wrote wills for familial and religious reasons, more people died without wills than with them."[56] Repudiation of inheritances, testate and intestate, offers a basis for a more systematic, though still very limited, statistical purchase on intestacies.

Actions of Heirs

Even if all inheritances passed through testaments, we still cannot say what happened to the estate after the testator's death, no matter how imposing the

---

[52] The words are Ricci's, *De hac vita transire*, 69, but the idea is taken from Chiffoleau, 68–74.
[53] George Dameron, *Florence and Its Church in the Age of Dante* (Philadelphia: University of Pennsylvania Press, 2005), 133, 168.
[54] In addition to his works cited above, see his *The Black Death Transformed: Disease and Culture in Early Renaissance Europe* (London: Arnold, 2002), 152–53.
[55] Cohn, *Death and Property in Siena*, 2.
[56] Ann Crabb, *The Strozzi of Florence: Widowhood and Family Solidarity in the Renaissance* (Ann Arbor: University of Michigan Press, 2000), 40.

normative force of testaments is taken to be. Only in rare circumstances do documents reveal what became of an estate; "over the rest silence rules."[57] In a real sense, throughout Europe in the past, people (men mainly) anxiously waited for their fathers (or others) to die. Whatever their education, trade, or even marriage had done to situate them in society, it was only at the point of inheritance that they fully entered into political standing and headship in a household. Roman law, with its notion of paternal authority (*patria potestas*) as enduring to the death of the father and with its notion of succession, as Maine captured it, only made this social, economic, and political reality – especially for the wealthiest families – into a glaring legal fact as well. Inheritance was the most important social moment in the lives of generations and generations of Europeans.

As such, it was also a moment of some danger, which has not been generally recognized in historical literature. A consistent feature of historical discussions of inheritance – so consistent that it is absolutely implicit and never expressed – is the assumption that inheritance meant a positive transfer of assets. Testate or intestate, the assumption is that something passed from deceased to heir. But what of debts or any sort of charges against the estate? The very premise behind repudiation of inheritance in law, as we will see, was that an estate could have more liabilities than assets. It was not worth it. An heir could be looking at less than nothing.

Debt and credit were absolutely essential in the economy of Florence and the rest of Italy. Fortunes were made and lost. Good business decisions could become bad ones very rapidly, as weather, wars, and other factors bore on events. And all this was exacerbated by unethical actions on the part of some economic actors. There were obligations that might or might not be triggered by circumstances that were not so overtly matters of business and finance, and that were yet another complication of Florentines' lives. Unwelcome debts and duties could thus arise, likely at very inopportune moments. Against all this, how could any estate look like a sure gain to its heir(s)?

Because an heir came into that sweeping and singular legal personality of the deceased as a *universum ius*, Roman law had to provide an escape. One could refuse to accede to that personality – in its entirety, not to some pick-and-choose portion of it. Maine did not go into that, nor into the overt process of acceptance of inheritance for those for whom succession in Roman law was not so automatic. Repudiation of inheritance does not fit comfortably into his sense of the powerful prerogative of corporate family patrimony. Even for those who study family and succession law, who run across *repudiatio hereditatis* in their source texts, the existence of mechanisms at the service of heirs is minimalized, marginalized, or ignored. Passage of property

---

[57] Ricci, *De hac vita transire*, 70.

to heirs, whether by the rules of intestacy or the dispositions of a testament, has been taken as more or less automatic, immediate, and unavoidable.[58]

Enrico Besta, for instance, in his 1936 study of succession law in Italian history, dismissed acceptance of inheritance (*aditio*) as a mere formality. Repudiation, though it persisted, was not allowed or greatly restricted in some communities, he said, because it did not "conform to the dignity of the families" that inheritance would pass through courts.[59] Only four years later, in the midst of a still valuable study of statutes from Lombard and Tuscan cities, Franco Niccolai repeated Besta's very language.[60]

Still, repudiation was an accepted and operative tool in the legal arsenal available to heirs. Certainly, it was fraught with difficulties and ambiguities. Safeguards around the use of repudiation were erected to protect the interests of creditors of the estate, interests that were perhaps more vulnerable precisely due to statutes' insistence on immediate passage of inheritance to direct heirs. Repudiation could not help but be met with diffidence and caution in some circles. But that is all the more reason to examine, rather than ignore, it.

For example, if it is the case that Florentines (Aretines and Perugians too, according to Cohn) used their testaments to control their heirs and properties from beyond the grave, to block the alienation of property and to preserve earthly fame and memory, and if we are to take this behavior as indicative of the failure of Jakob Burckhardt's image of Renaissance individualism, are we then to take repudiation of inheritance as an assertion of a Burckhardtian individualism on the part of some Florentines?[61] Or was avoiding an inheritance equally a family-identifying strategy, a condition of one's social identity? Was the repudiating heir being a bad kinsman, or was he thereby declaring that the deceased had been a bad kinsman/manager of family assets? Was it even a matter of attributing some moral responsibility for the condition of a family's estate? Was it simply taking advantage of an

---

[58] Cf. Manlio Bellomo, "La struttura patrimoniale della famiglia italiana nel tardo medioevo," in *Marriage, Property, and Succession*, ed. Lloyd Bonfield (Berlin: Duncker & Humblot, 1992), 53–69. See also his *Ricerche sui rapporti patrimoniali tra coniugi: Contributo alla storia della famiglia medievale* (Milan: Giuffrè, 1961); Giulio Vismara, *Famiglia e successioni nella storia del diritto* (Rome: Editrice Studium, 1970); Pier Silverio Leicht, *Storia del diritto italiano: Il diritto privato*, vol. 2: *Diritti reali e di successione* (Milan: Giuffrè, 1960); Manlio Bellomo, "Erede e eredità (diritto intermedio)," *Enciclopedia del diritto*, vol. 15 (Milan: Giuffrè, 1966): 184–95.

[59] Enrico Besta, *Le successioni nella storia del diritto italiano* (Milan: Giuffrè, 1936; reprint ed., 1961), 35–40.

[60] Franco Niccolai, *La formazione del diritto successorio negli statuti comunali del territorio lombardo-tosco* (Milan: Giuffrè, 1940), 145–51.

[61] Cf. Samuel K. Cohn, Jr., "Burckhardt Revisited from Social History," in *Languages and Images of Renaissance Italy*, ed. Alison Brown (Oxford: Oxford University Press, 1995), 217–34; now reprinted in *The Renaissance: Italy and Abroad*, ed. John Jeffries Martin (London: Routledge, 2003), 107–123.

available device to achieve a useful end, as so many clever folks did in the comedic literature of the period?

It is possible to take the approach offered here because a fantastic run of records survives in Florence. In the midst of the immense treasures of that city's archive (here one thinks mainly of the various catasti and the *ricordanze*), there survive twenty-nine volumes under the heading of Ripudie di eredità – the republican government's registry of repudiations.[62] These reveal that over 11,300 times between 1365 and 1534 Florentines and Tuscans repudiated an estate left them. While it is impossible to say what percentage of possible estate acceptances in Florentine Tuscany over 168 years those 11,300 represent, it is equally hard to look at that number and conclude that repudiation was an unimportant, ineffective, little used legal institution. This is not to claim that *repudiatio* was more important than its opposite, *aditio*, which certainly seems to have been numerically predominant.[63] But there was no central registry of *aditiones*, which made heirs liable but also gave them material interests to transact. Acceptance of inheritance did not thwart expectations and thus lead to results that confounded contemporaries and historians.

The monumental study of David Herlihy and Christiane Klapisch-Zuber, based on the Florentine catasto of 1427, shows that a significant proportion of Florentine households fit an extended patriarchal model and that male household heads were generally old (fifty or older).[64] The relative lessening of mortality in the fifteenth century, in comparison to the fourteenth, increased the likelihood of more complex multiple households.[65] Herlihy and Klapisch-Zuber note the prolonged control of family property by the aged patriarch, and the consequent potential for generational conflict, with attempts to defuse such situations through gifts and investments to young adult sons.[66] The practices of repudiation arose in this generational context. Against the idealized image of the patriarchal *capo di famiglia*, we are faced with the failure of fathers and others to be successful managers, with the refusal of sons to accept paternal obligations in repudiation, with their rejection of succession to paternal personhood.

It may be that, as the law assumed, the inheritance was in fact burdensome or useless. But there were also examples of those who used repudiation in more constructive ways – to direct property to certain heirs, or to

---

[62] In fact, two of these are only indexes to other volumes, so there are twenty-seven effective volumes in this registry.
[63] As one example, a single notarial cartulary, Notarile antecosimiano 9038, shows twenty-four *aditiones* against two *repudiationes*, though that ratio should not be taken as paradigmatic.
[64] David Herlihy and Christiane Klapisch-Zuber, *Les toscans et leurs familles* (Paris: Fondation Nationale des Sciences Politiques, 1978), esp. 481–87.
[65] Ibid., 517–20.
[66] Ibid., 606–9.

disguise ownership in largely fraudulent attempts to take advantage of the law.[67] So, while some heirs found their hopes of a lucrative inheritance disappointed, others were implicitly enlisted in, or crafted themselves, strategies to meet, exploit, or redirect social and legal expectations. Their actions serve to remind us that it was not only the kin who waited on death. Government, ecclesiastical bodies, partners, and creditors in general also had a stake in the post-mortem disposition of wealth.

Sources such as the catasto and surviving household accounts foster a tendency to treat family as a social unit. If instead we take family as a set of understandings (in one form, spelled out in law) governing relations between kin, understandings vitally called into play and (con)tested in inheritance, "then property must also not be reified as an object but, rather, as the product of the social relations embedded in its movement over time and space."[68] Repudiation of inheritance allows us one vital window into those movements and understandings, here for one society in the past.

Strategies of Writing

As repudiation existed in and because of law, one has to begin there. On the one hand, law can seem highly autonomous from general cultural, social, and political developments. In the formalized legal systems of the modern West, to be sure, law has its own technical, dense, and arcane language, its own highly trained functionaries versed in that language, and its own sites and rituals. Law thus has a certain inertia and does not simply change because social, economic, or political conditions have. It can be, in consequence, dysfunctional to quite a degree.[69] On the other hand, and it does not take a committed Marxist to see this, law also seems deeply bound up in the play of politics, class interests, and economic change. Legislation and judicial decisions respond to interests and pressures of discrete groups, largely from among social elites. Postmodern variants see law taking identity and meaning from the discourses or narratives in which it is embedded. Instead of standing outside society and history, so as to order or even create society, law appears wholly enwrapped in it.[70]

---

[67] Cf. Thomas Kuehn, "Law, Death, and Heirs in the Renaissance: Repudiation of Inheritance in Florence," *Renaissance Quarterly* 45 (1992): 484–516.
[68] Beshara Doumani, "Endowing Family: Waqf, Property Devolution, and Gender in Greater Syria," *Comparative Studies in Society and History* 40 (1998): 3–41, at 30–31.
[69] Cf. Alan Watson, *The Making of the Civil Law* (Cambridge: Harvard University Press, 1981), 184–87, whose book is a good example of an approach to law as largely autonomous. See also his *The Evolution of Law* (Baltimore: Johns Hopkins University Press, 1985).
[70] For a general presentation of this view, see Alan Hunt, *Explorations in Law and Society: Toward a Constitutive Theory of Law* (New York and London: Routledge, 1993), esp. chaps. 4–5.

In continental and Italian legal history, which is where the present study falls, the autonomy of law has been predominant. Two factors contribute to that. One is that most legal history is written by scholars housed in law faculties. The other is that they concentrate their energies on the doctrinal texts and commentaries of the jurists of the past. For the period under consideration here, that means that legal historical work is almost solely constructed on the academic glosses of civil and canon law and on the commentaries and opinions of authoritative professors of law. Analysis of legislation takes a back seat to jurisprudence.[71] Analysis of use of law within a society, up to and including criminal law enforcement, is left to other historians.[72]

My approach is to split the difference. What the users of law did also (re)shaped the law, even as law set parameters and potentials before them. Law was certainly autonomous in many ways, notably in its language, but only up to a point; and it was dysfunctional at times, on its own terms and not just those of society in general. Law also had to respond to what people did (and we will see some spectacular examples), at least in judicial decisions and legislation, if not in the lecture hall or study. As Peter Fitzpatrick has it, rather than seeking law in one side or the other of the opposition between autonomy and dependence, "we could seek a law which 'is' in-between the opposed dimensions, which 'is' the experienced combination of them, and which has its being because each dimension is inexorable yet unable to be experienced by itself."[73]

It is the conjoined sense of the legal and social-economic nature of repudiation of inheritance that also dictates the approach taken to it in this study. To employ a palaeontological metaphor suggested to me by Daniel Smail, repudiation has left us a host of fossilized traces in a number of different sedimentary (documentary) deposits. These are laws (both "common" and local), case opinions (*consilia*), family records, fiscal accounts (especially the catasto), notarial acts, and most evidently the registers of repudiations. From

---

[71] The parallel in historical studies in the Anglo-American common law tradition is concentration on precedential judicial decisions in the highest courts. As courts are reactive to cases brought to them, they may seem less autonomous than academic jurists, but their decisions are also self-referential with judicial discourse and powerfully resistant to change, if not impervious to it.

[72] Here a respected voice in medieval legal history, Manlio Bellomo, though he engages with communal legislation and other aspects of what is known as *ius proprium*, has been consistent and insistent that the learned and general law, *ius commune*, was the vital ingredient that made law possible and was intrinsic to the works and texts of legislators, notaries, judges, and attorneys. In this regard, he refers to *ius commune*'s "objective and metahistorical consistency." Cf. his *The Common Legal Past of Europe, 1000–1800*, trans. Lydia G. Cochrane (Washington, DC: Catholic University of America Press, 1995), 82–83, 152–55.

[73] Peter Fitzpatrick, *Modernism and the Grounds of Law* (Cambridge: Cambridge University Press, 2001), 72–73.

each, we can reconstruct some piece of the skeleton or even a bit of soft tissue, enough to take an informed leap at the rest. Each source base confirms what others reveal and also adds some new dimension. Each is thus worth examination in its own right and on its own terms.

We begin then with the generic level, the law, in Chapter 1. There we find repudiation elaborated in a context of inheritance rules. We descend from genus to species in Chapter 2, where Florentine legislation shows us both the basic characteristics of the beast and something of its evolution in legislative enactments in the fifteenth century. We gain perhaps some of the soft tissue in the third chapter, when Florentine diaries and account books allow us to see how the institution of repudiation was meaningful to Florentines. Chapter 4 is at the heart of the book, because it uses the source that is dedicated to our subject, the registries of repudiations. From these, we gain a cumulative view of this Florentine species, its growth and decline, its "food source" in the debts and heirship strategies of Florentines. To this, we can add economic and other nuances from the catasto in the next chapter. The sixth then examines the sedimentary layer of notarial texts to gain traces of individuals within the species. We can then try to guess at behaviors and practices. Finally, we turn to *consilia* – perhaps metaphorically analogous to the records of zookeepers with troublesome specimens, but at this point the metaphor, perhaps for the best, begins to dissolve. With these texts, we see problems of control and meaning and tactics adopted to head them off.

The virtue of such an approach is that it respects the integrity and difficulties of the texts, each of which in fact requires a distinctive contextual and linguistic set of tools. The disadvantage is that the connective tissues of the institution of repudiation can fade from view. It is necessary to keep invoking them – the omnipresence of debt, practices of heirship, dowries, kinship, and more – at the risk of repetitiveness. But repetition, happily, is not distortion, and it is the goal of this study to give as accurate, useful, and meaningful a presentation of repudiation of inheritance in Florence as possible. From that, we can begin to understand the true dynamic of family and individual, the process of generational transmission, and the problems a family-rooted sense of property posed for commercial development in the Renaissance.

I

Family and Inheritance

A well-known metaphoric statement of the great Trecento jurist, Bartolo da Sassoferrato (1313–1357), was that "familia accipitur in iure pro substantia" (family is taken in law as its substance).[1] It was in the midst of commenting on the civil law jurisprudence regarding children and their rights to inherit that Bartolo offered his definition of *familia*. His definition was in part intent on setting family into a basis larger than that of natural generation, relationships, and reputation.

It is, in fact, a somewhat enigmatic and ambiguous statement. Substantia is not otherwise much encountered in the writings of medieval glossators and commentators of civil law, nor in their chief source, the *Corpus iuris civilis*. Yet Bartolo chose it in preference to other possibilities – *possessiones*, *res* (*immobiles* or *mobiles*), *bona*, *proprietates*, even *honor*. A nebulous term like substantia, in fact, potentially subsumed all of these.

In the next generation, Angelo degli Ubaldi (1323–1400), working out the legal issues in a Florentine inheritance case, elaborated that

the substance of moveable and immoveable goods [real property] of the world's fabric is visible and corporeal, and consequently palpable. But the substance of rights and actions is incorporeal and invisible.[2]

Interestingly, he went on to observe that the "palpable" substantia of goods could be lost (by legal processes such as *usucapio* or prescription), whereas the invisible substance of rights and actions could not be lost because "they are infixed in our bones" ("infixa sunt ossibus nostris"). If we pose his sense

---

[1] From his commentary to the *lex In suis* to the *Digest De liberis et posthumis* (D. 28.2.11), as cited in Andrea Romano, *Famiglia, successioni e patrimonio familiare nell'Italia medievale e moderna* (Turin: Giappichelli, 1994), 1.

[2] Angelo degli Ubaldi, *cons.* 328, *Consilia* (Frankfurt am Main, 1575), fols. 231rb-32va, at 232ra: "substantia enim mobilium et immobilium unius machinae mundialis est visibilis et corporea: et per consequens, palpabilis. Iurium autem et actionum, incorporea et invisibilis."

of the matter alongside that of Bartolo, we can say that the substance of familia is both the objects that are owned (and may be lost) and the rights of its members to belong, to use, to pass along, and to succeed. Bartolo's contemporary, Alberico da Rosciate (d. 1354), in commenting on widespread municipal rules regarding inheritance, declared that, as a family's material basis was essential for its civic legal standing, statutes had to devise instruments to protect that material basis, the patrimony. A family's *memoria* and *dignitas* were to be perpetuated through a male line of descent (*per prolem masculinam*) and preserved by wealth (*divitias*).[3] *Memoria, dignitas, divitiae* – all were part of familia and its substantia.

One thing that seems clear, especially when we consider the legal context in which Bartolo, Angelo, and Alberico confronted these themes, is that substantia – whatever all it encompassed, both corporeally and incorporeally – was inherited and inheritable. The link between familia and substantia was one that transcended time and person. That transcendence, its meaning and mechanisms, were spelled out for these men, professional jurists, in the terms of the civil law that they had inherited from Rome.

The Law of Succession and Repudiation

In communities such as Renaissance Florence, inheritance operated within the normative structures set by what has come to be known as *ius commune*. This "common" or general (as opposed to local) law was an amalgam based on Roman civil law, as found in the texts of Justinian (the *Corpus iuris civilis*), generously leavened by variant rules and presumptions of canon law (for which a corresponding *Corpus iuris canonici* was assembled in the course of the Middle Ages), as well as norms and practices arising from other bases (Germanic, feudal, mercantile). The ius commune was a learned law – the work largely of university-trained jurists and teachers, who increasingly looked as well to practices and the burgeoning legislation of cities and other bodies to set an agenda of problems and inquiries.[4] And no area of the law raised more problems and questions, practical and hypothetical, than inheritance.

---

[3] Romano, 2; also my "*Memoria* and Family in Law," in *Art, Memory, and Family in Renaissance Florence*, ed. Giovanni Ciappelli and Patricia Lee Rubin (Cambridge: Cambridge University Press, 2000), 262–74.

[4] The literature on the ius commune is far too vast to reproduce here. For more recent interesting, even controversial treatments, see Peter Stein, *Roman Law in European History* (Cambridge: Cambridge University Press, 1999); Manlio Bellomo, *The Common Legal Past of Europe, 1000–1800*, trans. Lydia G. Cochrane (Washington: Catholic University of America Press, 1995); Mario Caravale, *Ordinamenti giuridici dell'Europa medievale* (Bologna: Il Mulino, 1994); A. M. Hespanha, *Introduzione alla storia del diritto europeo* (Bologna: Il Mulino, 2003); Mario Ascheri, *I diritti del medioevo italiano: Secoli xi-xv* (Rome: Carocci, 2000); Paolo Grossi, *L'ordine giuridico medievale* (Bari: Laterza, 1995).

Inherent in the academic nature of ius commune was an abiding discourse that leaves one unable in many instances to state flatly what *the law* was. Much as it might seem appropriate and comfortable to take the stance that law is singular and certain – for that is the position that must be set out in the finding of a court to justify its verdict ("it is the law that....") – such a stance greatly distorts the ius commune. Arguably, it distorts current law too. We cannot seek the legal logic to repudiation without examining areas of discourse among jurists – some areas marked by general consensus, some not; some of practical importance, some of little. By this process, we can tease into the light various dimensions of repudiation and the general realm of heirship in law.

Classical Roman Background

In Roman law, one did not simply inherit property. The heir (*heres*, properly speaking) succeeded to the entire bundle of rights and duties (*universitas iuris*, *hereditas*) of the deceased. The dead person's legal personality lived on by legal fiction in the person of his heir. As Henry Sumner Maine realized in the mid-nineteenth century, "the principle that a man lives on in his Heir" is "the centre round which the whole Law of Testamentary and Intestate succession" circles.[5] This succession from the *de cuius* ("of whose" inheritance) to the heir was to continue to lay at the heart of developments in law through the Middle Ages and up to the modern national codifications, and it was to animate the practices and expectations of those who used that law.

The quality of inheritance as succession in ancient Rome is perhaps best captured in two general maxims that continued to ring through the ages. One was "nemo pro parte testatus pro parte intestatus decedere potest" – one could not die leaving part of the estate by testament and part by rules of intestacy. The succession was singular and universal; it could move only by one of the two means.[6] The other, operating from the other side of the inheritance process, was "semel heres, semper heres" – once an heir, always an heir. Again, the hereditas was a whole, and it could not be shifted onto another once one had undertaken to carry on the personality of the deceased. Any other would have to be one's own heir in turn.[7]

In civil law, a person had to have an heir or heirs. In the normal course of events, heirs were assumed to come from one's children *in potestate*; and in Roman intestate rules, a deceased's children were termed *heredes sui et necessarii* – necessary or obligatory heirs. The key component of the

---

[5] Henry Sumner Maine, *Ancient Law* (London: Oxford University Press, 1861; reprint ed, 1959), 157–58.

[6] P. S. Leicht, *Storia del diritto italiano: Il diritto privato*, vol. 2: *Diritti reali e di successione* (Milan: Giuffrè, 1960), 256–57.

[7] Barry Nicholas, *An Introduction to Roman Law* (Oxford: Clarendon Press, 1962), 241–42.

rules of intestacy was the establishment of lines of succession and degrees of relationship so that in all but a handful of cases some heir could be determined. For their part, testaments served as "in essence a vehicle for moderated deviance from the rules of intestacy."[8] The simple and limited nature of intestacy rules, which at best transmitted property rights without modifying them, did not and could not meet all the needs or concerns of the deceased nor of the heirs. Assignment of differential shares or even the disinheritance of a child, separation of specific legacies to friends or relatives or groups (something more pressing after Christianity's legalization), or other matters had to be handled by a formal testament. As Edward Champlin has stated, the fabled "horror of intestacy" among the Romans arose from a sense of social responsibility to benefit or punish, as appropriate, the wider circle of friends, family, and servants.[9] For his part, Maine attributed the Roman revulsion at intestacy to injustices worked by intestate rules on emancipated sons, who were cut out of paternal inheritance because no longer subject to paternal legal authority.[10] Whatever the reason for a will, the first thing a Roman had to do, the key requirement for the will's validity, was to name an heir or heirs. Whatever modifications were worked in the details, they had to circulate around a clear successory link to the deceased.[11] The distinction between the *heres* and the *legatarius* (beneficiary of a bequest [*legatum*]) lay in the fact that the former took on the deceased's power over the family and patrimonial roles.[12]

The seemingly natural right of *sui heredes* was so strong in Roman classical law that they were also *necessarii*. They had no right or ability to refuse. On the other hand, their succession was so immediate that the classical jurist Paulus was able to opine that with necessary heirs there was not really an inheritance, as they were already owners in a sense (*quodammodo domini*).[13] In contrast, *heredes extranei* (all those not *sui*, which might include a large class of relatives more distant than children or grandchildren in direct line of descent), could refuse to accept an inheritance. There well might be reason to. Such extranei would be both less emotionally and morally attached to the deceased and less knowledgeable about his assets and liabilities.

---

[8] Edward Champlin, *Final Judgments: Duty and Emotion in Roman Wills, 200 B.C.-A.D. 250* (Berkeley: University of California Press, 1991), 8.
[9] Ibid., 21.
[10] Maine, 183–84.
[11] In addition to Champlin, on Roman wills and law of succession, see Nicholas, 235–42; W. W. Buckland, *A Text-Book of Roman Law from Augustus to Justinian*, 3rd ed., ed. Peter Stein (Cambridge: Cambridge University Press, 1966), 305–15; Max Kaser, *Roman Private Law*, 2nd ed., trans. Rolf Dannenbring (Durban: Butterworths, 1968), 278–328; Alan Watson, *Roman Law and Comparative Law* (Athens: University of Georgia Press, 1991), 77–82.
[12] Leicht, 250. He poses a subtle distinction between the Roman heir as successor and the modern situation in which the heir merely succeeds "nell'universalità dei beni."
[13] Champlin, 15.

Whether sui or extranei, successors had to undertake the deceased's duties and obligations. These could be considerable, difficult, and costly. More worrisome, they were unlimited. They could exceed the value of the estate (*ultra vires hereditatis*). If the assets of the hereditas were inadequate to settle outstanding debts or obligations, the heir had to cover them from his own assets. For any heres, there was thus the potential burden of a harmful estate, *damnosa hereditas*, while for extranei there was the added problem of even discovering how *damnosa* the estate was without first entering on it.[14]

Remedies for this problem were first devised, as in so many other areas of Roman law, in the edicts of the praetors (as the judges who would entertain cases and enforce judgments). Heredes extranei had the right to refuse – what was known as *repudiare* (or *omittere*). An extraneus could simply not enter on the estate, or he could make a declaration to that effect. By the same token, an extraneus had to make a special act of entry on an estate (*aditio hereditatis*) to indicate acceptance. In the interval between the de cuius's death and formal acceptance by the heir, the hereditas was said to be vacant, or "lying" (*iacens*).[15] Sui heredes had no such interval to enter the hereditas; their succession in Roman law initially was immediate and not held to any formal act of entry. Judicial modification, in the form of the Praetorian edict, eventually gave the heres suus a remedy in the form of the *beneficium abstinendi*. So long as he had not in fact "intermeddled" (*se inmiscere*) in the estate, his abstention freed him from liability for debts and performances attached to it. He had thus signaled that he would not act as heir or be considered as heir.

Such refusal of inheritance entailed consequences for others. If an heir thus stood aside, who, if anyone, could next be heir? The heir's refusal of an estate was an individualistic act on its face; it touched his or her rights only. An heir could not refuse for others, even those in line of succession, if already born. Generally, it would be the next in line by intestate rules or by the scheme left in a will who would receive the rights the heir had passed up. If there were *coheredes*, they simply took a bigger share. There were complications if the heir himself died before being able to act, but generally the right to consider one's options (*ius deliberandi*) about an estate was transmitted to the heir's heir in turn.[16]

The estate's creditors also had real and legitimate interests, which were greatly complicated by the praetorian rights of heirs to refuse or abstain from an hereditas. Who was going to pay them back? And when? Creditors were allowed to seek a time limit within which the heir had to make up his mind (*tempus deliberandum*). Ultimately, the emperor Justinian (527–565)

---

[14] Nicholas, 239. He adds a third problem, that of "the heavily indebted *heres* of a solvent man," which is not a problem that will occupy us.
[15] Kaser, 305–6.
[16] Kaser, 309; Leicht, 256–57.

set a limit of one year by imperial grant or nine months by judicial decree. If the time expired without the heir acting one way or the other, the creditors could act. The heir's *ius abstinendi* was lost.

By Justinian's decree, lapse of the period for deliberation without action by the heir was construed as acceptance of the inheritance, and the heir was fully liable, without limitation, to the estate's creditors.[17] They could then demand compensation, even involving liquidation of the estate's assets. Obviously, the amount of time lost to such deliberation could be crucial to creditors and debtors alike. The fact that Justinian's layered compilation of jurisprudential texts in the *Digest* and different decrees and judgments in the *Code* preserved several different time frames (100 days, nine months, twelve months) for deliberation about an inheritance would serve to keep things imprecise in this regard.

Both for the sui and the extranei, the key to avoiding liability for debts was thus to stay clear of the inheritance. In reality, that was not so easy and certainly not always desirable. The estate might also contain treasured assets of symbolic, if not economic, value. In embodying the personality of the decedent, the hereditas could give rise to senses of duty to the deceased that lay behind many of the developments in areas of law regarding bequests, trusts (*fideicommissa*), adoption, patronage, and more. A praetorian remedy provided for extranei was the *separatio bonorum*, by which an heir could move judicially to keep assets separately acquired in his own name and capacity from those acquired in succession. In this way, his liability was limited to the substance of the hereditas. In a parallel fashion, creditors of an estate, who feared it being chewed up to cover the debts of an insolvent heir, could move for a *separatio* so as not to lose their opportunity for repayment.[18]

A similar form of relief for the suus heres was definitively provided by Justinian, who introduced the *beneficium inventarii*. An heir could confine his or her liability by making an inventory, before a notary, of all the properties, objects, and credits found in the estate. Consequent liability as heir was limited to those objects or their equivalent value; it did not extend *ultra vires hereditatis*. In that way, one could become heres and the will, if there was one, would not be void for lack of an heir, while legacies and other performances in the will would be kept in order.[19] There was a consequent *inmixtio* of the heir in the estate and clear liability for debts of the hereditas. The *separatio bonorum* and the *beneficium inventarii* simply tried to limit liability to the value (*vires*) that was in the estate.

Despite Justinian's pains to reestablish the classical distinction between sui and extranei, the difference between the *ius abstinendi*, available to the

---

[17] Kaser, 305–6.
[18] Nicholas, 240–41.
[19] Nicholas, 241; Kaser, 314; Enrico Besta, *La successione nella storia del diritto italiano* (Milan: Giuffrè, 1936; reprint ed., Milan: Giuffrè, 1961), 242.

former, and the *repudiatio hereditatis*, available to the latter, became confused.[20] As we will see, by the thirteenth century, if not well before, the two sets of terms had elided into a single institution. Both in texts of doctrine and those of practice, repudiatio and abstentio were used interchangeably, as were aditio and inmixtio to a degree.

The Nature of Repudiation in Medieval Ius Commune

The centuries following Justinian's codification of Roman law and jurisprudence witnessed, in Italy, an abrupt diminution of Roman imperial power. Lombard and later Frankish political and military dominance inserted different populations, with different forms of family and property relations, and different rules for their transformation and transmission. The Church too developed its own concerns, its own sense of families and appropriate rules for marriage, inheritance, guardianship, and more. By the late eleventh and early twelfth centuries, more sophisticated political formations arose, the Norman kingdom in the south and the urban and rural communes in the north of Italy. Within each, whether feudal nobility or urban patriciate, the political class was defined in terms of kinship groups. These became more self-conscious and "dynastic" (that is, driven and defined by agnatic descent) with the aid of the creative and interpretive revival and adaptation of Roman law by learned experts, culminating in the formation of universities, beginning most notably with Bologna.[21]

The revival of Roman law and the parallel academic elaboration of canon law had a profound effect on identities, practices, and possibilities for families. Paternal legal authority (*patria potestas*), testaments, dowries, notions of agnation, guardianship, and so much more came back into social and linguistic usage, but not necessarily with the same range of relevance or meaning that they had at the time of Justinian. And while these terms and rules were part of a "common" language of law and justice, they were also refracted through local customs and laws that were the responsibility of the active courts.

Repudiation of inheritance too was reshaped in the texts of learned law, as well as recontextualized in the statutes and enactments of communes and signories. It became suited to a new sort of normative family model, that was neither the "closed," blood-based communal model of Germanic customs nor the agnatically extended family enabled by Roman patria potestas, with

---

[20] Kaser, 306.
[21] The revival of Roman law in the medieval universities has been the object of countless studies. Among some of the best, with some relevance especially for understanding the social and political dynamic in Italian cities, see Manlio Bellomo, *Società e istituzioni in Italia dal medioevo agli inizi dell'età moderna*, 3rd ed. (Catania: Giannotta, 1982).

its dynamic capacity to freely dispose of property.[22] Blood and legal (artificial) agnation, communal claims, and individual ownership and control – all had a role in shaping the agnatic lineage model, with plenty of variations, that underwrote laws, customs, and practices in Italian communities.

The medieval institution of repudiation rested on the texts gathered in Justinian's *Code* under the titles *De repudianda bonorum possessione* (C. 6.19) and *De repudianda vel abstinenda hereditate* (C. 6.31), and in the *Digest* under *De acquirenda hereditate* (D. 29.2). Scattered texts in other titles of the *Code*, especially *Unde liberi* (C. 6.14) and *De iure deliberandi* (C. 6.30), were also important. Practice was not necessarily required for doctrinal elaboration. The logic of law itself could drive teaching about concepts and institutions of law no longer or little used. Adoption was one prime medieval example in that regard.[23] So when one confronts any legal institution in doctrinal interpretation, one can be yet a long way from practice, let alone from determining how law might regulate everyday behavior.[24]

Historians such as Andrea Romano, Samuel Cohn, and Anthony Molho have argued that by the Renaissance, preservation of family unity, dignity, and memory came to be associated less with drawing various components around a single patrimony than with perpetuating a single line of descent and patrimony over time.[25] Within this complex of concerns and rules, repudiation would seem to have held an anomalous position, at best. Its premise that the hereditas was damnosa seemed to belie the idea that transmission of that patrimony was essential to the preservation of family *memoria* and *dignitas*. Repudiation said the patrimony was worthless, burdened with charges that overwhelmed any assets. It allowed individuals to opt out. It threatened to leave inheritances lying unclaimed, prey only to strangers, as creditors, who could tear into them like so many vultures. Such individualistic legal avenues, among other factors (such as the growth of public power and its hostility to family enclaves of resistance), are cited by Romano as lying behind the "crisis" of family communitary structures that he spots at the end of the Trecento.[26] The legal historian Enrico Besta put it bluntly: repudiation "was not regarded with sympathy anywhere."[27]

---

[22] Romano, *Famiglia, successioni e patrimonio*, 11.
[23] Thomas Kuehn, "Adoption à Florence à la fin du Moyen Age," *Médiévales* 35 (1998): 69–81; Franck Roumy, *L'adoption dans le droit savant du XIIe au XIVe siècle* (Paris: LGDJ, 1998).
[24] See Alan Hunt, *Explorations in Law and Society: Toward a Constitutive Theory of Law* (New York and London: Routledge, 1993), 301–33.
[25] Romano, 18–19, who also reproduces various relevant legal maxims (2), as well as giving a fine general treatment of the subject. In addition to Kuehn, "*Memoria* and Family in Law," Anthony Molho, *Marriage Alliance in Late Medieval Florence* (Cambridge: Harvard University Press, 1994).
[26] Romano, 42–43.
[27] Besta, *Successione*, 40.

Medieval jurists indeed put a negative cast on repudiation at times. Paolo di Castro (c. 1360–1441), who had a hand in the 1415 revision of Florence's statutes, which included provisions controlling and regulating repudiation, noted that formal aditio of an inheritance had features that repudiation did not:

> The reason for the difference is because aditio is favorable, as it acknowledges the one who has died, so it should be expansively treated; but repudiation is odious, because it does the opposite, so it should not receive expansion, and it cannot stand on its own.... Also aditio is a disposition, repudiation is a privation, and a disposition is something, and so it receives expansion; privation is nothing, so it does not receive expansion.[28]

In fact, Paolo di Castro's argument drew on terms devised by Bartolo da Sassoferrato.[29] Both saw repudiation as "hateful" and empty, in comparison to its opposite.

In any case, repudiation remained a viable and actively used portion of the law of succession. For the persons who used it to escape liabilities, it was "favorable" in important ways. Above all, it allowed them to escape liabilities for testamentary bequests, which could go beyond the *vires hereditariae*.[30] Even the negative qualities of repudiation could work in their favor. Aditio could not later be revoked or reversed (why go back on an act that was *favorabilis*?), but repudiation, within time limits, could be.

The jurist who first gave the various texts regarding repudiation a systematic treatment was undoubtedly the Perugian, Angelo degli Ubaldi (1323–1400), active as a teacher and practical legal consultant in Florence in the last decade or so of his life. To be sure, his work built on fertile ground laid out by his illustrious predecessor, Bartolo da Sassoferrato, who, in turn, had built on previous observations by figures such as Cino da Pistoia (d. 1336/37) and Jacopo d'Arena (c. 1253–1296). Jurisprudence was an additive profession, as well as an interpretive and critical one. But Angelo degli Ubaldi was the first to address general themes as well as the particulars of repudiation, and he dedicated an extensive lecture to a text of the *Code* dealing in part with repudiation (a lecture, moreover, that he gave in Florence while teaching there in 1389). In comparison to Angelo, only his brother Baldo (1327–1400) could be said to have conducted as thorough an analysis of repudiation and related

---

[28] Di Castro to D. 29.2.1, *In primam infortiati partem* (Venice, 1593), fol. 108va: "Ratio diversitatis quia aditio est favorabilis, cum faciat quem decederet testatum, ideo ampliatur, repudiatio vero est odiosa, quia operatur contrarium, ideo non recepit augmentum, et per se stare non potest.... Item aditio est habitus, repudiatio est privatio, et habitus est aliquid, et ideo recepit augmentum; privatio est nihil, ideo augmentum non recepit."

[29] Bartolo to D. 29.2.1, *Opera omnia*, 10 vols. (Venice, 1615), vol. 3, *In primam infortiati*, fol. 143ra.

[30] Cf. Angelo degli Ubaldi, *Tractatus de inventario*, in *Tractatus universi iuris*, 29 vols. (Venice, 1584), vol. 8, part 2, fols. 155va–56rb, at 155vb.

issues of acceptance of inheritance, deliberation, and fraud. The more practical emphasis of these two brothers, whose teaching and practice fell in the half century following the first great onslaught of plague in Italy, contrasts with that of their teacher, Bartolo, the bulk of whose teaching and doctrinal elaboration fell before 1348.[31]

Angelo posed a general framework to inheritance in a comment on the rubric of the *Digest* on acceptance of inheritance. There he termed hereditas to be "quoddam intellectuale succedendi" – a phrase that defies simple translation, but that indicates that it involved an understanding or willingness on the part of the heir to succeed. This understanding rested on the legal fact that the inheritance represented the deceased so that the entering heir represented the very person of the deceased ("heres adiens representat personam defuncti"). Angelo noted, however, that according to theologians (as opposed to jurists) hereditas was nothing other than the patrimony of a testator. Thus, for them "in foro conscientiae," an heir was not liable "ultra vires hereditatis," as was formerly the case in civil law, which "now" limited liability in the presence of an estate inventory. The liabilities of heirs were, as he saw it, fundamental:

> From the aforesaid is derived the reason why the heir is held liable to the estate's creditors absolutely and to legatees he is not.... because credits inhere in the person of the deceased to whom he succeeds, but legacies inhere in the heirs.[32]

The distinction that *credita* belonged to the deceased but *legata* established in the deceased's testament belonged to the heir was not directly licensed in civil law, but it was a solution to the difference between obligations existent in the deceased's lifetime and those that arose only after his death. The heir might be overwhelmed by preexisting debts, but bequests could only rise to the level of assets in the estate.

Angelo returned to these broad themes in his commentary on the *lex Gerit pro herede*.[33] There he stated that entering an inheritance was not about being saddled with obligations but about acquiring things and rights.

---

[31] And whose last nine years, to his death in 1357, saw some interesting shifts in his professional activities. For an example, see Osvaldo Cavallar, "River of Law: Bartolus's *Tiberiadis (De alluvione)*, in *A Renaissance of Conflicts: Visions and Revisions of Law and Society in Italy and Spain*, ed. John A. Marino and Thomas Kuehn (Toronto: Centre for Reformation and Renaissance Studies, 2004), 31–129. In this characterization of the difference between the Ubaldi and Bartolo, I follow, among others, Giulio Vismara, *Scritti di storia giuridica*, vol. 6: *Le successioni ereditarie* (Milan: Giuffrè, 1988), 310 and 368; and Julius Kirshner, "Between Nature and Culture: An Opinion of Baldus of Perugia on Venetian Citizenship as Second Nature," *Journal of Medieval and Renaisance Studies* 9 (1979): 179–208, at 203.

[32] Angelo degli Ubaldi to D. 29.2, rubrica, *Super prima infortiati* (Lyon, 1522), fol. 59va: "Ex predictis redditur ratio quare creditoribus hereditariis heres tenebatur in solidum et legatariis non ... quia credita inherent persone defuncto cui succeditur: sed legata inherent heredibus."

[33] For this and all references to the *Code, Digest, Novellae,* and *Institutes*, see *Corpus iuris civilis*, ed. Th. Mommsen, P. Krueger, and R. Schoell, 3 vols. (Berlin: Weidmann, 1928–29).

That was why repudiation and acquisition of inheritance were governed by the same rules and why Angelo took exception to Bartolo's argument that repudiation was about avoiding obligations (rather than acquiring rights). He confronted Bartolo's definitions of aditio and repudiatio as forms of *potentia*[34] and concluded that

> to accept and to repudiate, to intermingle and to abstain is the pure will or unimpeded destination of the soul to be or not to be heir, which happens by the pure and sole aim of the soul.[35]

Volition became the essence of the institution in his eyes. It necessarily preceded and was merely confirmed by and expressed in the formal act of repudiation performed before a judge/notary.

For his part, Baldo degli Ubaldi stated that when deliberation ended limited possibilities came into play for the heir: aditio and repudiatio, inmixtio, and abstentio. Either the heir took the hereditas (positive) or not (privative). But then what exactly did he accept or reject? If, as natural (*ius gentium*) and canon law said, hereditas was defined as succession in the goods that the deceased had, then the heir could not be obligated beyond what was in the inheritance, even without making an inventory. Of course, by that equation, a person who died with nothing could have no heir; but that was certainly not the case in civil law: "The hereditas understood not materially but immaterially and in the manner of civil law has legal meaning even without any substance."[36] Hereditas involved the *universum ius* of the deceased, and in that regard, as Angelo too had noted, hereditas differed from legatum. Thus, that immaterial dimension of hereditas called forth an equally immaterial force behind its acceptance or rejection (*voluntas*).

The act of acquiring an inheritance had two dimensions, verbal and real, or express and tacit; the former was aditio, the latter *gestio pro herede* (using the goods like an heir without formal declaration). In parallel, there were repudiatio in express form and *gestio pro non herede*, as a tacit form of rejection. Either way, as the heir was otherwise liable, the expression of his intent (*animus*) was necessary.

---

[34] Angelo to D. 29.2.88, fol. 70ra-rb: "Sed iste diffinitiones salva sua reverentia non videntur vere prime due dum dicit adire et repudiare esse potentiam adeundi vel repudiandi etc. non videtur vera vel non videntur vere: quia omnia prius sunt in potentia quam in actu secundum Philosophum, et actus executionis est potentie et potentia est causa actus." His response is to Bartolo, to D. 29.2.88, *Opera omnia*, vol. 3, fol. 156vb.

[35] Angelo to D. 29.2.88, fol. 70rb: "adire et repudiare: inmiscere et abstinere est nuda voluntas seu animi destinatio non impedita essendi vel non essendi heres, quod sit nuda et sola animi destinatione"; also to D. 29.2.21,1, fol. 62ra: "Ad adeundum hereditatem sufficit solus animus."

[36] Baldo degli Ubaldi to D. 29.2, rubrica, *Opera omnia*, 9 vols. (Venice, 1577), vol. 3, *In primam et secundam infortiati*, fol. 108rb: "hereditas non materialiter sed immaterialiter et civiliter intellecta iuris intellectum habet sine ullo corpore."

Though not going to the philosophical lengths of his brother, Baldo too made clear that the essence of aditio or repudiatio lay in volition. Differences among jurists such as these lay in concerns regarding the necessity in ius commune (civic statutes, as we will see, were another matter) for overt expression of this volition. Bartolo, for example, posed that volitional statements of the nature of "I do not want to be heir" were not the same as statements such as "I want to repudiate" or "the inheritance does not serve me." The former were merely negative statements. They did not indicate an active will toward something.[37] Angelo degli Ubaldi agreed with Bartolo on this. Statements that one was not heir or did not accept an estate were not equivalent to repudiation, he said, because they indicated only a present intention or state of affairs and not one in respect to all future time ("omne tempus").[38] Subsequent jurists, such as Alessandro Tartagni da Imola (1424–1477), continued to insist that "nolo esse heres" (I do not want to be heir) did not amount to repudiation. Whereas "I am heir" could be taken to mean aditio, "I am not heir" could not be rendered as repudiation.[39] Absent true repudiation, within the deliberative interval, one could still opt to be heir, whereas the rule *semel heres, semper heres* precluded reversal of the first, affirmative statement.

One factor that went along with these conclusions about the *animus* or *voluntas* behind aditio and repudiatio, and that made them possible, was that there was no objective standard or requirement of proof that a given hereditas was in fact, in any way, truly beneficial (lucrosa) or harmful (damnosa). The issue was never raised. Only the perception – perhaps better, the assertion of a perception – on the part of the potential heir was required. As Baldo put it succinctly in a *consilium* on a Pavian case, "in repudiation of inheritance one is not required to show cause" ("in repudiatione hereditatis non requiritur causa").[40]

The practical importance of this nonrequirement cannot be stressed too highly. The legal presumption was that an heir would not allege the sad material and financial conditions of an inheritance if it were not so. The possibility of an estate burdened with obligations and liabilities was easy enough to see. Yet because there was no need to demonstrate the state of

---

[37] Bartolo to D. 28.8.8, *Opera omnia*, vol. 3, fol. 139rb. Before him, Cino da Pistoia had similarly found that stating one was not heir was not the same as saying one repudiated the estate (Cino da Pistoia to C. 6.14.3, *In codicem et aliquot titulos primi pandectarum commentaria*, 2 vols. [Frankfurt, 1575; facsimile ed., Turin: Bottega d'Erasmo, 1964], vol. 2, fol. 354ra).

[38] Angelo to C. 6.14.3, *Super codicem* (Lyon, 1522), fol. 140va.

[39] Alessandro Tartagni to C. 6.14.3, *In primam et secundam codicis* (Venice, 1570), fol. 81va.

[40] Baldo degli Ubaldi, *Consilia*, 6 vols. in 3 (Venice, 1575; reprint ed., Turin: Bottega d'Erasmo, 1970), part 2, *cons.* 144, fol. 35rb, where one also finds the statement "opinio enim (vel metus vel color) eius, qui noluit adire hereditatem, inspicitur, non substantia hereditatis, nec immerito."

the hereditas, repudiation was left entirely at the disposal of the *repudians*. Repudiation was thus available for a number of possible purposes in addition to the presumed (and still massively important) one of avoiding an estate overburdened with debts. What made a hereditas damnosa was entirely at the discretion of the repudians and thus had at least as much to do with his situation, interests, and strategies as it had to do with any "objective" (financial) or subjective (reputation, status) qualities of the estate.

The other side of relying so utterly on the perception and will of the potential heir was that ius commune insisted, as had Roman law, that the repudiating party have certain knowledge of the estate. His perceptions were his own, but the heir's allegation regarding the dismal state of the hereditas rested on the assurance that he or she had at least examined it in some way. Put in its simplest terms, as by Tartagni, the rule was that repudiation could not be made in ignorance.[41] The requirement for certain knowledge went to the point that, if one were in fact a voluntary heir when he thought he was a necessary heir, then aditio or repudiation under that misapprehension was not valid.[42] In sum, "in repudiating an estate or bequest he who repudiates must be certain of his right" ("in repudianda hereditate vel legato certus esse debet de suo iure is qui repudiat" [D. 29.2.23]). The desire for certain knowledge, however, never went to the extent, for example, of demanding a detailed inventory precede a repudiation. Inventories remained the legal device to limit liability for the heir who accepted the estate left him.[43]

By extension of the rule regarding ignorance, an inheritance that had not been actually left (*delata*) to one could not be repudiated. That meant that, among other things, one could not repudiate the estate of someone still alive, no matter how run down that estate was.[44] Nor could one repudiate an estate in which there were doubts that it had been left to him or her. Of course, were it later the case that the hereditas was indeed *delata*, then the repudiation could be repeated, though it was of no validity earlier.[45]

At this point, we can pause to consider a practice closely parallel to repudiation. In practice and in law, despite the juristic declarations prohibiting repudiation of a future inheritance, renunciations of inheritance in advance of death were allowed and occurred. In the interests of steering property to

---

[41] Tartagni to C. 6.19.1, fol. 90va: "quod repudiatio facta per iuris ignorantiam non valeat"; Angelo to D. 29.2.23, fol. 62rb.

[42] Tartagni to D. 29.2.15, *In primam et secundam infortiati* (Venice, 1570), fol. 147rb-va.

[43] On the law of which, in addition to the brief treatise of Angelo degli Ubaldi (note 30), see also in the *Tractatus universi iuris*, vol. 8, part 2, Francesco Porcellini, *Tractatus de confectione inventarii*, fols. 156rb-65ra.

[44] Angelo to D. 29.2.94, fol. 70va: "Hereditas viventis repudiari non potest: et ea repudiata nihil agitur h. d. et est ratio: quia ante mortem hereditas non est delata: ergo repudiari non potest."

[45] Angelo to D. 29.2.13, *Is qui heres* § 1, *si quis dubitet*, fol. 61ra; Tartagni to D. 29.2.13, fols. 146rb-47rb.

male heirs, daughters, who would marry and carry a dowry to another family, and those children, male or female, who were going to enter the religious life, were encouraged or compelled to refuse their portion of the hereditas. As jurists knew well, civil law was hostile to such contracts renouncing future inheritance. Civil law construed such renunciations as, for example, threatening the proper deference and obedience owed to a father on the part of a son who, by renouncing, declined to be his father's heir.[46] Thus, it was *contra bonos mores*. To Bartolo, there was the added factor that refusal of future inheritance diminished the rights of the renouncing party to dispose, in turn, of his own property.[47] Canon law, however, allowed such rejections of future inheritance, notably by a decretal of Boniface VIII (1294–1303), provided that there was a formal oath taken.[48] The powerful and widely known example of St. Francis, who renounced his inheritance and headed off to a religious life rooted in poverty, carried great influence. On this basis, then, even Bartolo could license daughters' singular "voluntary" renunciations of the paternal estate and approve of statutes that deprived all those who would enter monasteries of what they otherwise would inherit, without any expression of consent on their part.[49] Statutes depriving girls of inheritance (beyond their dowry) in favor of their brothers, cousins, paternal uncles, or other agnate males were similarly also licensed on this basis.[50]

Acts of refusal of future inheritance were kept legally and terminologically distinct (in jurisprudence, if not always in civic legislation or notarial texts) from repudiation. They were *renunciationes*. In contrast to repudiation, which was unilateral rejection of an immediate prospect of inheritance, renunciatio was a bilateral contract *de non petendo* to the benefit of a third party. In that regard, renunciatio approached a gift, although it did not see actual transference of ownership. Still, as Paolo di Castro had it, repudiation differed from renunciatio in that "one repudiating an estate, before he accepts it, does not diminish his patrimony but merely does not acquire, nor does he transfer ownership, which he did not have, but he abdicates the power to acquire, which is something different."[51]

The legal concerns with the knowledge of repudiantes could have real consequences. Angelo degli Ubaldi confronted an interesting case that raised the issue. When a man named Giovanni died in Forlì on 5 September 1378, one son, Simone, who was in Forlì, quickly accepted his portion of the estate

---

[46] See Vismara, *Le successioni ereditarie*, 331 (on Baldo) and 420 (Paolo di Castro).
[47] Ibid., 276–84.
[48] Ibid., 285, 291.
[49] Ibid., 253, 284, 329.
[50] Ibid., 413, discussing Paolo di Castro.
[51] "Repudians hereditatem, priusquam ipsam adeat, non diminuit suum patrimonium, sed non acquirit, nec transfert in alium dominium, quod non habebat, sed abdicat a se potentiam acquirendi, quae sunt inter se diversa" (quoted in ibid., 419; but see also 413–14, 418–19).

by terms of the paternal testament. The other son, Pietro, who was away in Fermo, accepted the estate in a notarized instrument on 29 September; however, the very next day, being then in Ascoli, he repudiated the estate. Following Pietro's death, his son Jacopo in turn tried to claim half of his grandfather's estate from his cousin on the grounds of the initial aditio and subsequent acts by Pietro to sell portions of his father's property, as revealed in various notarial instruments. Angelo's finding against Jacopo turned on the issue of what Pietro knew, including that in the aditio he simply described the estate as *delata* to him, while in the repudiation he had specified that it was left "ex testamento." In consequence,

there is enough to conjecture that when he accepted the estate, he believed it was left to him on intestacy, but later when he learned it had been left to him by testament he repudiated it, mainly because of the burdens on the estate established in the will or other matters contained therein.[52]

In other words, the testament might be presumed to have been less advantageous than intestacy for the heir and it seemed that Pietro had learned of the testamentary nature of the estate only after the initial aditio. Thus, the aditio was quashed on the basis of the relative *ignorantia*, and the repudiation stood as based on better knowledge, much to Jacopo's chagrin, no doubt. As there was in this case a coheres, there was no possibility of mistaking or revoking the repudiation, for in law ownership had passed to the other heir immediately following the repudiation. Baldo, confirming Angelo's opinion in the case, agreed that an absent son could not fall under presumption of knowledge as to the testate or intestate nature of the inheritance. It seemed reasonable that new and correct awareness of the testament resulted in reconsideration of the acceptance undertaken the day before. The presence of the coheir with title also removed any effect of subsequent inmixtio on Pietro's part.[53]

Capacity to Repudiate

To provide that the repudians had *certa scientia* and was not ignorant of the estate, the law also had to make accommodations to the types of persons who might repudiate and to the time constraints with which they might find themselves faced. For one thing, to make sure of the repudiator's knowledge and intent, jurists precluded repudiation by means of agents or attorneys

---

[52] In Baldo, *cons.* 403, part 3, fols. 114ra-15ra, at 114rb: "satis est coniecturabile quod postquam adivit, credebat sibi delatam ab intestato, ideo postea quando scivit delatam ex testamento repudiavit forte propter onera in testamento apposita, vel alia ex testamento contenta."

[53] Ibid., *cons.* 404, fols. 115rb-vb, which begins with the possibly tongue-in-cheek bit of humor from Baldo: "Quia dictus consultor, cuius nomen ignoro, profunde materiam tertigit...."

(*procurator* or *advocatus*). One had to be present directly to express one's *voluntas* to be, or refuse to be, heir to another.[54]

Minors presented a particular problem. Their lack of full capacity to have knowledge of an estate and to formulate legally effective voluntas had to be compensated for by some means in order for a repudiation to their benefit to occur. As the interests of creditors or legatees were also involved, it would not do simply to wait until the minors reached maturity. How that wait could be abbreviated would vary by whether they were still in patria potestate and their fathers were still alive (thus looking at inheriting from someone other than the father) or if their fathers were deceased and they were subject to guardianship (*tutela* or *cura*) of an adult (and probably contemplating inheritance of the paternal patrimony).

If the father were still alive and the child still in potestate, there was a simple option. The father could accept or reject an estate left to his minor child. However, there was the complication that the father acquired what came to a child under his potestas and so was a far-from-disinterested party when it came to accepting or refusing an inheritance.[55] Jacopo Bottrigari (d. 1348) concluded that a father could not repudiate an estate left to his son to the son's detriment. Such property might include the estate of the child's mother, for which ownership (*proprietas*) passed to the child, while usufruct went to the father.[56] Repudiation of such *bona adventitia* (coming from the mother or her side of the family) might only land it all, ownership and use, in the father's hands. Bartolo, commenting on a different text, from the *Digest*, similarly denied that a father could repudiate *bona profectitia* (coming from his side of the family) left to his child, for title in that case came to him, without the child's consent. Instead, Bartolo said, stressing the other side of the equation, a father could not accept an inheritance without the corroborating consent of the child to whom it had been left. In essence, neither father nor child could repudiate to the other's loss.[57] Baldo went so far as to state that a father could not refuse any rights that came to his son.[58] Angelo stated that father and child both had to repudiate an estate

---

[54] Baldo to D. 29.2.6, *Opera omnia*, vol. 3, fols. 109rb-10ra.

[55] On the potestas and proprietary capacities, see the classic legal analysis of Manlio Bellomo, *Problemi di diritto familiare nell'età dei comuni: Beni paterni e 'pars filii'* (Milan: Giuffrè, 1968), and Thomas Kuehn, *Emancipation in Late Medieval Florence* (New Brunswick: Rutgers University Press, 1982), 18–25.

[56] Jacopo Bottrigari to C. 6.19.2, *Lectura super codice* (1516; reprint ed., Bologna: Forni, 1973), fol. 9vb. Also Baldo to C. 6.19.2, vol. 7, fol. 46vb.

[57] Bartolo to D. 29.2.13,3, vol. 4, fol. 145va: "Quero an hec lex habeat locum in hereditate adventitia. Gl. dicit quod sic, specialiter hodie, ubi apud filium debet remanere proprietas verum est quod olim et hodie non poterat filius repudiando nocere patri, nec pater filio, ut hic, et sic repudiatio non valebat." On the different types, based on provenance, of property that might come to children, see Kuehn, *Emancipation*, 19–20.

[58] Baldo to C. 6.30.11, vol. 7, fol. 101rb.

left the child, adding that such was what he had observed in practice in Florence.[59]

By the same token, a child whose father had died, and thus was under guardianship, required the guardian's consent to repudiate.[60] Here the problems were (1) the age and understanding of the child and (2) the possible self-interest of the *tutor*, who was likely to be of the paternal line and in the order of succession (possibly even next in line) to the estate. One protection against possible exploitative self-interest by the tutor was offered by Cino da Pistoia. A minor, without a tutor, could still repudiate with the authority of a judge.[61] Bartolo followed this solution, which he attributed to the earlier glossator Azo (d. c. 1230).[62] The rationale was that a tutor could not alienate his ward's property without judicial authority, and repudiation was tantamount to alienation.[63] Baldo expanded this procedurally to specify that the judge had to inquire into the state of affairs, calling into court the friends and relatives of the ward to gauge from their testimony the true quality of the estate. Here then, mere allegation as to the worth or state of the inheritance was not to be taken at face value.

There also was jurisprudential support for the position that a guardian could in no case repudiate the inheritance fallen to an *infans* (a child younger than seven).[64] A *pupillus maior infante* (between seven and fourteen years of age) could repudiate with a tutor; an *impubes* (between fourteen and twenty-five) could with a *curator*.[65] But an *infans* was just too young. Instead, the jurists entertained the option of the ward, later grown up, to reverse an early tutelary act, such as an aditio. The *lex Sicut maior* (C. 6.31.4) said that someone over twenty-five could not later seek a repudiated inheritance nor repudiate one previously taken, but it raised the possibility of an heir later repudiating if taken to court by creditors. C. 6.31.6, on the other hand, allowed anyone who had refused an estate, to which no one else had emerged as heir, and from which no property had been alienated, three years to reverse his decision and accept the estate. A minor was accorded four years, upon reaching majority. Minors also had their right to seek cancellation of legal

---

[59] Angelo to D. 29.2.13,3, fol. 61rb: "Et no. hoc quia de facto vidi practicari Florentie." Baldo to D. 29.2.13,3, vol. 3, fol. 110va.

[60] Also Bottrigari to C. 6.31.5, fol. 24ra: "Pupillus hereditatem sibi delatam sine tutore non repudiat." Bartolo to C. 6.31.5, vol. 6, fol. 33ra; Angelo to C. 6.31.5, fol. 168vb.

[61] Cino to C. 6.31.5, vol. 2, fol. 391va.

[62] Bartolo to D. 37.1.8, vol. 4, fol. 152rb, where the text made clear a *tutor* had power to seek elements of the ward's property but not to repudiate. In general on the law of guardianship, see Gigliola Villata di Renzo *La tutela: Indagini sulla scuola dei glossatori* (Milan: Giuffrè, 1975), esp. 255–303.

[63] Indicative, perhaps, of a disfavor for repudiation by guardians was Paolo di Castro's decision in one case where the mother was deemed not to be the legitimate guardian, because she had remarried. Paolo di Castro, *Consilia*, 3 vols. (Venice, 1571), vol. 2, *cons.* 324, fols. 157rb-va.

[64] Angelo to D. 29.2.18, fol. 61va.

[65] Angelo to D. 29.2.57, fol. 65va.

actions during guardianship (*in integrum restitutio*) to get back anything alienated from the estate. There was implicitly a clash between the interests of the creditors in a quick disposition and settlement and the need of the heirs for time to grow up and learn of their rights and duties.

Women were equated with minors in many ways through the ideologically driven notion of *fragilitas sexus*.[66] Bartolo stated that when by law an administration was set up over persons "because of their mental deficiency, as in Italy statutes are commonly enacted that say that women cannot obligate themselves without the consent of blood relatives," they could not accept an inheritance without a guardian's authority. They also gained the minor's privilege to reverse a repudiation. He agreed with Jacopo d'Arena's distinction between simple acquisition and acquisition in which expenses might be attached, as certainly was the case in acquiring an inheritance. For that, a guardian was necessary.[67]

Angelo degli Ubaldi, who had extensive legal experience of life in Florence, referenced the "Tuscan" statutes requiring a special guardian (*mundualdus*) for women. As they could not obligate themselves without a guardian, they could not accept an inheritance or even take part in a simple contract. But he also agreed with his brother Baldo that such a statute was repugnant to common law ("repugnat iurei communi"). As aditio was not a contract, he argued that acceptance of an estate unencumbered with debt, which meant the woman was not liable for anything, was possible without a *mundualdus*. He even essentially broadened that ability by placing the onus of proof on whomever would oppose her doing so. He further distinguished that, though a woman could not obligate herself for or through another, she could undertake acts tending to acquisition, even if later some obligation arose.[68] This

---

[66] On this, see Thomas Kuehn, *Law, Family, and Women: Toward a Legal Anthropology of Renaissance Italy* (Chicago: University of Chicago Press, 1991), 212–20; id., "Daughters, Mothers, Wives, and Widows: Women as Legal Persons," in *Time, Space, and Women's Lives in Early Modern Europe*, ed. Anne Jacobson Schutte, Thomas Kuehn, and Silvana Seidel Menchi (Kirksville: Truman State University Press, 2001), 97–115, at 97–101; id., "Person and Gender in the Laws," in *Gender and Society in Renaissance Italy*, ed. Judith Brown and Robert C. Davis (London: Longman, 1998), 87–106, at 87–88; Manlio Bellomo, *La condizione giuridica della donna in Italia: Vicende antiche e moderne* (Turin: Edizione RAI, 1970); Suzanne Dixon, "Infirmitas Sexus: Womanly Weakness in Roman Law," *Tijdschrift voor Rechtsgeschiedenis* 52 (1984): 343–71, at 344; and generally Yan Thomas, "The Division of the Sexes in Roman Law," in *A History of Women in the West*, ed. Georges Duby and Michelle Perrot, 5 vols., vol. 1: *From Ancient Goddesses to Christian Saints*, ed. Pauline Schmitt Pantel (Cambridge: Harvard University Press, 1992), 83–137.

[67] Bartolo to D. 29.2.5,1, vol. 3, fol. 143rb: "propter imbecillitatem consilii, ut sunt statuta communiter per Italiam que dicunt quod mulieres non possunt obligari sine consensu consanguineorum."

[68] Angelo to D. 29.2.5,1, fol. 60va: "municipali propter imbecillitatem forte consilii ut mulieribus in Tuscia que se obligare non possunt sine consensu mundualdi: nam nec poterit hereditatem adire sine eius consensu:... Adverte tamen tu advocate quod semel obtinui in quadam aditione facta per mulierem faciendo poni quod in hereditate nullum erat debitum vel legatum naturaliter vel civiliter vel utroque modo debitum: unde per hanc aditionem mulier

was a fairly liberal position. By implication, the preventive function of such guardianship was fully called for in the opposite case of repudiation. A further protection for a woman was the assurance that, should she repudiate her rights in her father's estate, she did not thereby lose her right to a dowry.[69] The law was not always and everywhere reluctant to see property go to women or dyspeptic about their ability to manage it in their interests or those of their children. Indulgence could be shown them with regard to aditio, while maintaining protection of their ideologically presumed *imbecillitas* regarding repudiation.[70]

However, one must keep in mind that in most Italian communities, women's inheritance rights were limited by statute.[71] Their brothers, fathers, sons, uncles, and paternal cousins excluded them in many instances. So the reality was that women generally inherited only when there were no close male agnates. As we will see, in Florence repudiations by women or from women were only a small fraction of all repudiations. Their repudiations, moreover, could work to the advantage of more distant agnatic kin.[72]

Period for Deliberation

Whoever inherited faced a time limit to make a decision, repudiatio or aditio, even if he or she also might later reverse that decision. The general rule was that for repudiation heirs had one year from the time they learned of the

se non reperit obligata: unde tenuit aditio nullo debito probato: et adversario incumbit onus probandi.... Attende tamen quia mulier licet non possit se obligare: tamen gerere potest bene actum qui ad acquirendum principaliter ordinatur: licet in quandam consequentiam postea obligetur."

[69] Cf. Baldo, *cons.* 59, vol. 2, part 3, fol. 15va-b, at 15vb: "huic questioni alia incidit, utrum si filia repudiat hereditatem patris, nihilominus sit dotanda de bonis paternis. Et videtur quod sic, hoc ius ad eam pertinet, non tanquam ad heredem sed tanquam ad filiam. In contrarium videtur: quia ista dos succedit loco legitime portionis, que non debetur repudianti. De istis duobus punctis forte non habemus aliquam legem expressam pro filia. Tamen facit, quia si pater tenebatur dare in vita sua, ergo ista dos non mortis causa capitur, sed seorsum: ut quemadmodum si fuisset dotata a patre in vita, haberet dotem hereditate repudiata... ita si non est tradita, sed debita."

[70] In addition to the works cited above, see Thomas Kuehn, "Understanding Gender Inequality in Renaissance Florence: Personhood and Gifts of Maternal Inheritance by Women," *Journal of Women's History* 8 (1996): 58–80, 64–65.

[71] Cf. Kuehn, *Law, Family, and Women*, 238–57; id., "Person and Gender in the Laws"; Franco Niccolai, *La formazione del diritto successorio negli statuti comunali del territorio lombardo-tosco* (Milan: Giuffrè, 1940), 65–108.

[72] Roselli, *Tractatus de successionibus ab intestato*, in *Tractatus universi iuris*, vol. 8, part 2, fols. 357vb-71va, at fol. 365rb, argued that a daughter's repudiation did not prejudice her grandson, by her daughter, because entering an inheritance in place of one's mother was a legal privilege not lost by the mother's renunciation. Paolo di Castro authored a case opinion in line with his position on this issue: Paolo di Castro, *cons.* 54, vol. 3, fols. 57ra-vb.

de cuius's death and possible inheritance.[73] In contrast, as Tartagni in one instance noted, the right to enter an inheritance was perpetual; it was not lost if unexercised over a long period, at least for as much as thirty years.[74] So if one did not learn of an inheritance right for years, it was still actionable.

Time frames, however, might also vary by the form in which one chose to express intentions regarding the inheritance. Consider the following from Bartolo:

> I pose a question: what if someone said "I want to repudiate" or instead he said that the estate does not serve him. You say either he said this after the time given him for deliberating, and then these words produce repudiation.... Or he said this before deliberation [ended], and then these words produce repudiation after three months.... But what if he said "I do not want to accept"? I say that in that case where he says he does not want to accept, repudiation is produced after a year.... And the reason for the difference between this and what I said in the preceding question is that these words are expressive of consent.[75]

Similarly, a declaration of desire to accept ("volo adire vel puto mihi hereditatem expedire"), even if made after the deliberation period, led to aditio only after three months. However, if a judge set a time limit, at the end of which one had neither repudiated nor accepted, he could not take the property.[76]

Provision of such time limits, along with the de facto abstention from the inheritance, meant that jurists had to allow for two types of repudiation – express and tacit – as well as exercise their ingenuity on possible variant consequences of them. Bartolo noted that, whereas in express repudiation father and son had to concur, if they both gained inheritance rights, in tacit repudiation the son's (in)action could hurt the father without his consent; and at the same time Bartolo said that tacit repudiation occurred when time limits were set by ius commune, by civic statute, or by a judge.[77] Both Bartolo and Paolo di Castro noted that there was some latitude for reversing a tacit repudiation resulting from a judicially imposed time limit, but they conceded no such reversal against legislated limits.[78] For our purposes, as we will see

---

[73] Angelo to C. 6.30.19, fol. 164vb.
[74] Tartagni to C. 6.30.8, fol. 149rb.
[75] Bartolo to D. 28.8.8, vol. 4, fols. 139rb-va: "Quaero quid si aliquis dixit volo repudiare vel dixit hereditatem sibi non expedire. Dic aut hoc ipse dixit post tempus datum sibi ad deliberandum, et tunc ista verba inducunt repudiationem.... Aut hoc dixit ante petitam deliberationem et tunc ista verba cum cursu trium mensium inducunt repudiationem.... Sed quid si dixit nolo adire? Dico quod in illo qui dicit nolle se adire cum cursu anni, inducitur repudiatio.... Et est ratio differentiae inter hec et ea que dixi in precedenti questione, quia hec verba sunt abnegativa voluntatis deficientis."
[76] Ibid., fol. 139va.
[77] Bartolo to D. 29.2.13,3, vol. 3, fol. 145va: "in repudiatione tacita que fit per cursum temporis statuti a lege communi, vel municipali vel forte a iudice preiudicaret patri."
[78] Paolo di Castro to C. 6.31.6, *In secundam codicis* (Lyon, 1548), fol. 89va.

in the next chapter, it was the civic statutes that effectively set time limits to the deliberation period, at least regarding inheritance from fathers.

Coheirs and Subsequent Heirs

One could repudiate a bequest (as opposed to the hereditas itself). The *legatarius* was not heres, and one's sense is that most bequests were of specific objects or values that were no doubt lucrosa and thus easily accepted. But conditions and obligations could be attached as well. A repudiated legatum, said Baldo degli Ubaldi, was treated as if it had never been left in the first place ("fingitur non relictum").[79] As such, the rejected legatum was absorbed back into the hereditas and enriched the heir(s).

Repudiation of hereditas was different, if only because the hereditas was not so bound to a specific recipient. Therefore, it did not dissolve upon rejection. If there were two or more heirs, repudiation by one meant his share accreted to the coheir(s), what was known as the *ius accrescendi*.[80] In other words, if one heir repudiated and another accepted, the one accepting took on all burdens and benefits of the hereditas.[81] Another way of putting the matter was that an heir who accepted an estate conditionally was not considered to have "intermingled" in it if there were a coheir.[82] In practical terms, this meant, for example, that a man with children of his own, who inherited an estate along with his brothers, would repudiate to the benefit of his siblings, not his offspring. Only his acceptance would put his children in line for his share, unless his brothers all either died or also repudiated, in which case his children would be next in line (along with any cousins, with proportions by lines, not by individuals).

When a coheir accepted what another had repudiated, the estate had an heir. The repudiating heir might still enjoy some benefit of the estate through the coheir, but it was gratuitous. A repudiating heir who had an accepting coheir could still claim a testamentary substitution to a minor (thus to be heir by virtue of someone other than the testator directly).[83] Baldo, in expanding on this point, drew out the case of a man who abstained but had been substituted to his brother in a will. There were differences between being substituted heir to the brother by paternal testament and being heir to him on intestacy.[84] The key was that repudiation by a coheres ceded his claims to the other coheres.

---

[79] Baldo to D. 30.[1].86, 2, vol. 3, fol. 138vb-39ra. He went on to state that *dominium* transferred to the accepting *legatarius* at acceptance. Tartagni to D. 29.2.13,3, fol. 150ra, noted further that "Per aditionem hereditatis acquirit heres dominium rerum hereditariarum etiam si possessionem non apprehendat, et eas vendicare potest adversus possidentes."
[80] See Leicht, *Diritti di successione*, 256–57.
[81] Angelo to D. 29.2.99, fol. 70vb.
[82] Angelo to D. 29.2.20,4, fol. 61vb.
[83] Baldo to D. 29.2.40, vol. 3, fol. 114ra.
[84] Baldo to D. 29.2.42, vol. 3, fol. 114ra-rb.

In a treatise that was among the first systematic treatments of law regarding testamentary substitutions, Raniero Arsendi (d. 1358) posed the problem of several sons, instituted heirs and substituted to each other in their father's testament, one of whom repudiated. Did the others acquire by right of accretion or by right of substitution? Could they repudiate one right and accept the other (in effect becoming heir not to their father but to their brother)? The glosses did not seem to help, as one said they could and another they could not (D. 29.2.17, 1 and D. 29.2.35 respectively). Arsendi resolved the problem by arguing that the coheirs could not repudiate the substitution but accept the accretion, because then they could casually empty or avoid ("evacuare vel evitare") a burden imposed by the testator. However, they could repudiate the accretive right and yet accept by right of substitution, because then they could not avoid the obligations on the estate.[85]

The period of deliberation (one year) began immediately on the de cuius's death for a suus heres, because there was assumed to be no intervening period between the death and knowledge of it. But were the heir to pass away within that year, having not yet accepted or rejected the estate definitively, he or she did not transmit an unacknowledged hereditas to ascendants, extranei, or even descendants.[86] In the words of Baldo, the "common opinion" was that a suus who had neither accepted nor rejected an estate transmitted not the hereditas but an *ius deliberandi*.[87] Where several jurists enjoyed pouring their energies and ingenuity was the instance of a son who chose to repudiate his father's estate but accept his paternal grandfather's, which came to him through his father. The locus for this discussion was the *lex Qui se patris* of the title *Unde liberi* (C. 6.14.3). The text itself indicated that one who denied being heir (*negat se heredem*) to his father could not take the grandfather's property except by *bonorum possessio*. He could be *bonorum possessor* but not heres.

The first to turn thorough attention to this law seems to have been Cino da Pistoia, who stated that it "has the reputation of being difficult and subtle and useless among some ignorant attorneys, who never study it. But in truth it is useful and necessary, as will appear, and so it is well to direct attention to it."[88] It was certainly *utilis* for the prolonged treatment Cino gave it, in the course of which he noted that whatever the grandson did (deny or repudiate) was of no effect, as either the father had accepted his father's estate, in which case the grandson could not have the *hereditas avi* apart from the *hereditas paterna*, or he had repudiated it, and it remained separate from the paternal

---

[85] Andrea Romano, ed., *Le sostituzioni ereditarie nell'inedita "Repetitio de substitutionibus" de Raniero Arsendi* (Catania: Giannotta, 1977), cxxvi-cxxvii.
[86] Angelo to C. 6.30.19, fols. 164vb-65ra.
[87] Baldo to C. 6.30.3, vol. 7, fol. 98vb-99ra.
[88] Cino to C. 6.14.3, vol. 2, fols. 353vb-55vb, at 354ra: "Lex ista reputatur difficilis et subtilis et inutilis per quosdam advocatos ignorantes, qui nunquam studuerunt in ea. Sed in veritate utilis est et necessaria, ut infra patebit, et ideo bene advertenda."

42   *Family and Inheritance*

hereditas, such that two separate acts of repudiation and/or acceptance were required.[89]

It was Angelo who dedicated the most attention to *Qui se patris*, offering a long commentary and a *repetitio* delivered in Florence in 1389 (included in printed editions of his commentaries).[90] He used the law to investigate the difference between merely denying heirship and actually repudiating. He arrived at some interesting findings. For one, a child who repudiated a maternal estate could reverse himself within a year if no one else had accepted it.[91] He also found that a child, as suus heres, who died during the period of deliberation, transmitted only his *ius deliberandi*; but if he died afterward, he transmitted *hereditas non agnita*.[92] Other types of heirs transmitted the *ius deliberandi*.[93] Another jurist active in Florence, Antonio Roselli (1381–1466), in a treatise systematically exploring intestate succession, reported

> if the father should repudiate the estate of his father, the grandsons from him would not succeed their grandfather, and thus it was determined in Florence. But if their father should die, then these grandsons succeed their grandfather by right of transmission.[94]

They had no such right if they were conceived after their grandfather's death.

Partial Repudiation

Jurists generally denied that one could accept part of a hereditas and repudiate or simply ignore other parts. On the one hand, such parcelling of the hereditas ran against the sense that succession was to the entirety of the deceased's legal existence (*universum ius*). On the other, such a parcelling of the estate would effectively allow heirs to extract all positive value from it while leaving creditors empty handed.

---

[89] Ibid., fol. 355rb.
[90] A manuscript copy of the *repetitio* is in Biblioteca Nazionale, Florence, Magliabechiano xxix, 174, fols. 19r-22r, which appears in *Super codice* of 1522 on fols. 141ra-42va. For Bartolo's treatment, see Bartolo to C. 6.14.3, vol. 6, fols. 9va-10ra.
[91] Magliabechiano 174, fol. 19r-v, 22r.
[92] Ibid., fol. 20r: "Et ex hoc magni effectus sequuntur, primo quod si filius infra tempora deliberationis decedit, transmictit solum ius deliberandi et non hereditatem.... Transmictit ergo solum hereditatem non agnitam si decedit post tempora deliberationis, quia post illa tempora suitas et necessitudo suas vires que cessaverunt pendente deliberationis tempore reassumunt, et eas resummere potest, quia nunquam fuerunt extincte sed cessaverunt durante deliberationis tempore."
[93] Ibid., fols. 20r-v, 22r.
[94] Antonio Roselli, *Tractatus de successionibus ab intestato*, fols. 367vb-68ra: "et ideo si pater nepotis repudiasset hereditatem patris sui, nepotes ex sua persona non succederent avo, et ita obtinuit Florentie. Sed si pater eorum fuisset mortuus, hereditate non agnita, non tamen repudiata, tunc isti nepotes succedunt avo ex iure transmissionis."

The central text here was the very first under the title *De acquirenda hereditate*. In his commentary to that text, Bartolo sided with the *glossa ordinaria*, that overt acceptance of a portion meant acquisition of all of a hereditas, at least when the heir knew there was more than he or she was accepting. As the heir could not accept part and repudiate part, the result had to be acceptance of all. Aditio overrode repudiation.[95] Angelo's treatment was similar to Bartolo's in all regards.[96] It was not permitted to reject part and accept another part, although cities such as Florence could force something like an unwilling acceptance on the sons of delinquent taxpayers or criminals in order to make them shoulder paternal liabilities.[97] Repudiation of part with aditio of the rest ended up as aditio of all, whereas repudiation of part without mention of the rest ended up as repudiation of all.

What if an heir repudiated the hereditas but claimed his *legitima* (the obligatory minimum provision for a direct heir) at the same time? Baldo and Paolo di Castro, as Tartagni reported, had declared that such a repudiation was nullified because legitima was owed only to an heir. One could not claim the legitima without claiming the hereditas. The general rule would hold – repudiating part and accepting part was, in effect, accepting all.[98] Paolo di Castro had considered that rule in a variety of lights, always concluding that any partial aditio resulted in total aditio. If the heir repudiated at one moment and only later tried to gain the legitima, he could not. One could only have legitima "tanquam heres."[99]

Many of these themes came together in a case that involved Tartagni. The object of the dispute was a piece of land, but the legal issue was whether it had been repudiated. The plaintiff acted on the basis of the claims of four sisters, who, in accordance with the usual statutory provisions, had been excluded from paternal inheritance by their brother, who, however, had repudiated it, so that on his death it had passed to his daughter, the defendant in the suit. Plaintiffs' claim was that repudiation meant that they were next in line to their father's estate, not their niece. On the other side, there was the fact that the girl's father, despite his repudiation, had indeed seemed then to intermingle himself in the estate, probably managing it for her.

---

[95] Bartolo to D. 29.2.1, vol. 3, fols. 142va-43ra.
[96] He found one instance in which that was not the case, namely when one accepted on condition that other part had not been left to him, which meant the aditio was rendered null and void. Angelo to D. 29.2.1, fol. 59va-b.
[97] Ibid., fol. 59vb: "non tamen est licitum pro parte acceptare et pro parte renunciare: et ideo si ex forma statuti bona immobilia patris condemnati filiis conservantur ne mendicare cogantur non possunt acceptare partem eorum et partem repudiare. Quinimmo si civitas statuens habet privilegia fiscalia: ut Florentia, talia bona tales filii coguntur agnoscere si obnoxia sunt debitis fiscalibus: et nisi illa agnoscant privantur aliis bonis iam quesitis ut a paterna substantia ex alio capite."
[98] Tartagni to D. 29.2.1, fol. 140ra-va.
[99] Paolo di Castro to D. 29.2.1, fols. 108rb-vb.

Tartagni rehearsed a variety of legal arguments in favor of taking such inmixtio as being "tanquam heres." Were the father still alive he could reveal the *animus* by which he had acted, but in his absence his actions had to stand for his intentions. In this case, the daughter's testimony as to her father's intent had force of law. This daughter insisted on oath, in line with legal presumptions, that her father intended to act as heir and thus revoke the repudiation done earlier. In the sisters' favor, there was the fact that the father, who had repudiated as a minor by notarial act in 1424, had lived for more than forty years after the repudiation, and he had never used his capacity, once an adult, to reverse his repudiation.[100] Tartagni, however, argued for a tacit revocation of the repudiation due to his subsequent acts of "intermingling," which was probably a legally weak position.[101] He tried to bolster it with the argument that the repudiation was also invalid from scribal error, because the notarial instrument of repudiation used the term "repudiavit" but not "abstinuit." As the son was suus, and technically abstentio was the pretorian remedy for sui, he had evidently not had correct knowledge of his status as suus.[102] As a minor at the time, ignorance could be presumed, and there was no countervailing demonstration of knowledge on his part.

This argument was a stretch. The fact that the verb *abstinuit*, a regular part of notarial formulas in repudiations (as we will see) was probably simply covered under an "etc." in the copy available in court was left out of account. Nor was the legal fact of being suus heres so obscure that ignorance need be assumed. Tartagni was probably acting as advocate for the daughter, rather than as adviser to the judge, so he had no interest in making potential points for the other side.[103] He was posing that the language of the notarial text indeed was controlling:

[F]or there it is said that he has knowledge of his father's death and that the estate was ruinous, yet he does not express any other knowledge, and ambiguous words in

---

[100] Alessandro Tartagni, *Consilia*, 7 vols. in 4 (Venice?, 1536), vol. 7, *cons.* 126, fols. 73ra-vb, at 73rb. By some calculus, Tartagni claimed a minor had until age thirty-two, rather than twenty-nine, to revoke a repudiation of the paternal estate.

[101] Ibid., fol. 73rb.

[102] Ibid., fols. 73rb-va.

[103] On the roles of *consultores*, see Julius Kirshner, "*Consilia* as Authority in Late Medieval Italy: The Case of Florence," in *Legal Consulting in the Civil Law Tradition*, ed. Mario Ascheri, Ingrid Baumgärtner, and Julius Kirshner (Berkeley: The Robbins Collection, 1999), 107–40; Guido Rossi, *Consilium sapientis iudiciale: Studi e ricerche per la storia del processo romano-canonico* (Milan: Giuffrè, 1958); Osvaldo Cavallar, *Francesco Guicciardini giurista: I Ricordi degli onorari* (Milan: Giuffrè, 1991); id., "Lo 'stare fermo a bottega' del Guicciardini: giuristi consulenti, procuratori e notai nel Rinascimento," in *Consilia im späten Mittelalter: Zum historischen Aussagewert einer Quellengattung*, ed. Ingrid Baumgärtner (Sigmaringen: Jan Thorbecke, 1995), 113–44.

the instrument must be interpreted against the one who produces them, because one must reach some conclusion.[104]

Whether or not his was the opinion with which the court aligned itself, his *consilium* shows that issues of knowledge, age, revocation, intermingling, and notarial language were all pertinent in practice.

Problems of Perception and Fraud

Every jurist addressed with careful attention the first two *leges* of the *Code* dealing with repudiation. Confusingly, in the medieval scholastic reference system, using the first words of the text as a title, both *leges* began *Si paterna*. These laws, both rather brief, struck at the difference between legal reality and social appearance. The first stated that an heir who abstained, but in fact occupied the paternal house as a tenant or custodian or by some right other than as heir, could not be sued "ex persona patris." The second held that an heir who abstained but also in good faith bought lands from creditors of his father, or was a creditor of his father, would not be liable to similar paternal creditors who emerged later. Thus, both texts allowed for repudiating heirs to hold property from the estate by some other title. The key was whether the abstention from the paternal hereditas was in good faith. The burden of proof lay with the repudians.[105]

The heart of the problem was that the law was quite capable of fragmenting the living human being into an amalgam of rights-bearing personae (in keeping with the original meaning of the word persona, mask). A single individual could be heir to his father, heir to his mother, heir to yet others conceivably, as well as owner of things in his own right. He could have rights over a single object by more than one claim. So a son could repudiate his father's estate – thus not be his heir and not be liable – yet be his mother's heir. And her property would have been in fact intermingled in her husband's, while remaining distinct in law. Quite commonly, the husbands pledged their property for the value of their wives' dowries. Thus, as heir to his mother, against this pledge, a repudiating heir could in fact remain in his father's house or otherwise use his property. How were others (that is, paternal creditors) to know by what right he remained there?

That an heir could legally repudiate and yet be in possession of and use paternal property by some other right opened up all sorts of potential confusions, for creditors and for jurists. We have to recall also that one could renege on a repudiation, and "intermingling" oneself in the estate could be

---

[104] Tartagni, *cons.* 126, vol. 7, fol. 73va-b: "nam ibi exprimitur quod habuit scientiam, scilicet mortis et quod hereditas erat damnosa, non autem exprimit aliam scientiam, et verba ambigua instrumenti debent interpretari contra producentem: quia debet de necessitate concludere."

[105] As per Angelo to D. 29.2.12, fol. 61ra.

the sort of *gestio* that could be taken to that effect – adding another layer of complication. Jacopo Bottrigari conceded that the suus, as opposed to the *emancipatus*, had the possibility of reversing himself by actions. The burden of proof thus fell on him to show that he had repudiated and continued to live in the paternal house in a manner other than as heir ("non animo adeundi").[106] Cino da Pistoia concluded "that today there is no difference insofar as the right and the effect of acceptance of inheritance, for today acceptance consists of intent...and is not the result of fact; therefore, the same right is to be presumed from intent."[107] Bartolo similarly decided that in living in his father's house a son conducted himself as heir unless it could be proved otherwise.[108] Angelo degli Ubaldi agreed.[109]

Baldo characteristically sought underlying rationales. The repudiating son living in the paternal home faced a presumption of inmixtio because there did not seem to be change but rather continuity after death. He went on to pose a larger picture:

And so if a son remains in his father's house by right of his mother's dowry, for return of which the house had been specifically or generally pledged, intermingling is not presumed, according to Odofredus [d. 1265]. And what I say about the dwelling holds if he possesses a field or vineyard that belonged to his father and receives the fruits thereof, for there is the same rationale as with the house. For in the house the fruit is not separate from possession, for its fruit is precisely in living there, and intermingling is more effectively presumed as it is connected to receiving fruits; so unless he prove the contrary, the law holds the suus heres as heir by intermingling himself in the estate, which is reasonable.[110]

Possession of the paternal house as heir to the maternal estate (dowry) was a complication that would elicit increasing concern. Tartagni's treatment of C. 6.31.1 was almost entirely devoted to the issue, drawing on Paolo di Castro (who, as we will see in the next chapter, was heavily influenced by his practical experiences in Florence).[111]

---

[106] Bottrigari to C. 6.31.1, fols. 23va-24ra.
[107] Cino to C. 6.31.1, vol. 2, fol. 390vb: "Credo quod hodie quantum ad ius et effectum aditionis non sit differentia, cum aditio consistat hodie in animo, etiam in persona emancipati, nec sit opus facto: ergo idem ius, quantum ad animum praesumendum."
[108] Bartolo to C. 6.31.1, vol. 6, fol. 32va: "filius habitando in domo patris videtur se gerere pro herede nisi probetur quod ex alia causa fecerit."
[109] Angelo to C. 6.31.1, fol. 168va.
[110] Baldo to C. 6.31.1, vol. 7, fol. 111rb: "Et ideo si filius remansit in domo patris occasione dotis materne, pro qua dote domus erat specialiter vel generaliter obligata, non presumitur immixtio secundum Od<ofredum>. Et quod dico in habitatione domus, idem dico si possedit agrum, vel vineam patris, et fructus percepit: nam tunc est eadem ratio que in domo. Nam in domo non est separatus fructus ab ipsa possessione, quia fructus eius est ipsa habitatio: unde efficacius presumitur immixtio, cui est connexa fructuum perceptio, nisi ergo probet contrarium, lex habet suum heredem pro immixto hereditati quod est rationabile."
[111] Tartagni to C. 6.31.1, fol. 157vb.

Of course, when there was no title, one could presume that possession was an act of bad faith (*mala fides*). Mala fides and fraudulent intent were apparent by certain circumstances: if, following a declared abstentio, the heir was found to have paternal goods and not to have bought them in his own name; if the property were stealthily bought through another; or if the heir had paternal property right away, even on the very day he declared his abstentio.[112] Jacopo Bottrigari noted that if the heir had the goods as purchases he could not be held as heir; but presumptions of mala fides arose if he were discovered to possess all his father's property (as opposed to discrete purchases), if he had it immediately, or if he had it secretly.[113] In any case, such mala fides nullified repudiation.

Cino da Pistoia examined the good faith/bad faith issue at some length. The problem was not that acting in mala fides gained the heir something, for the rule was that it surely did not. The tough case was when there was doubt. Cino found three presumptions of mala fides: possession of all the paternal property, secret possession through another, immediate possession. Purchase from the estate during the period of deliberation, if followed by inmixtio, had to be nullified and the property made subject to creditors' demands.[114] In the end, having become heir to the estate from which the purchase had been made, one had effectively bought it from oneself; hence, there was no sale, as Bartolo succinctly pointed out.[115]

Angelo turned the three presumptions into four (purchase of all the property, purchase through another, possession immediately, clandestine possession).[116] Baldo got more inventive. He raised numerous other situations of mala fides: when the price was too low, when part was purchased and part was a gift, when there was no price. Immediate possession also figured as mala fides for him, as it had for others, because immediate actions were likely premeditated ("incontinenti fit premachinatum").[117]

Suspicion of fraud became jurisprudentially more widespread and differentiated in the course of the fifteenth century, perhaps for good practical reasons. The presence of the heir, especially the son, in the home of the deceased, created presumptions that were not so easily rebuttable:

[I]ndeed many sons are found who hesitate to acknowledge the paternal estate, while the moneys and much else that remain in the estate, and other things that can easily be hidden, furnishings and similar things, they grab up, and yet they deny that these can be found. An attorney for legatees and creditors may try to prove this with

---

[112] Jacopo d'Arena to C. 6.31, *Super iure civili* (1541), fol. 246vb-47ra.
[113] Bottrigari to C. 6.31.2, fol. 23vb.
[114] Cino to C. 6.31.2, vol. 2, fols. 390vb-91rb.
[115] Bartolo to C. 6.31.2, vol. 6, fol. 32vb, and to D. 29.2.91, vol. 4, fol. 158va-b.
[116] Angelo to C. 6.31.2, fol. 168va.
[117] Baldo to C. 6.31.2, vol. 7, fol. 111rb-va, where he also gave more extended consideration to the purchaser later become heir.

production of such items, by proof of which their removal may come to light, and the son can be sued as heir with loss of benefit of abstaining from the estate that is granted him by ius pretorium. And note well that he is understood to have hidden and removed things even if he drank a bit of wine with a servant and denies that he drank it, or if he ate grain and similarly denies it.... So a son has only one remedy, that before he touches anything from the estate, he declare by public instrument and before witnesses that he renounces the estate.[118]

This was eloquent testimony to the difficulties of making the case for abstentio based on behavior alone. The centrality of notarial acts and legal witness – the very essence of legality in so many institutions regarding family (dowry and marriage, emancipation, legitimation) – was evident.

The noted late Trecento jurist, Pietro d'Ancarano (c. 1330–1416), handled a case, dated 20 June 1397, part of whose legal complications involved repudiation with subsequent possession. It is a fitting point on which to draw this inquiry into repudiation law to a close. A set of testamentary substitutions had served to move property through several sets of hands. The problem was whether heirs to the last substituted heir to die could extract two quarters of the estate. What was in question was the force of a repudiation by two brothers and a subsequent renunciation in their favor by the deceased's daughters, their sisters. They pretended that their title to the property was not by virtue of being heirs but as beneficiaries of their sisters' largesse. Both by statute and ius commune repudiation followed by possession was presumed to be simulated and fraudulent. But d'Ancarano asserted that possession might also be had by *ius* other than *hereditarium*, so mere possession was not enough to overturn the repudiation, which otherwise had been properly drawn up by a notary. The powerful statutory presumption against such possession was overridden. The testator had obviously shown by his substitutions a concern for the lineage (*domus* and *progenies*) rather than particular individuals. Repudiation by any heir meant that the estate went to the next in order, and sons were not disadvantaged by paternal repudiation because they were next in line by providence of the testator.

---

[118] Angelo to D. 29.2.71,3, fol. 67rb: "multi enim inveniuntur filii qui titubantes agnoscere hereditatem paternam pecunias et multa alia que in hereditate relinquuntur et alia que de facili possunt occultari: ut localia et similia ad eorum manus reducunt et negant se invenisse. Studeat enim advocatus legatariorum et creditorum probare hanc proventionem, qua probata apparebit amotio et conveniri poterit filius tanquam heres sublato sibi beneficio abstinendi quod tribuitur de iure pretorio. Et no. bene quia intelligitur occultasse et amovisse etiam si vegetem vini bibit cum familia et se bibisse negat: aut comedit frumentum, et similiater negat ut patet infra ver. amovisse ibi consumpsit etc. tene menti. Solum ergo unum remedium haberet filius ut antequam aliquid hereditatis contingat declaret per publicum instrumentum et coram testibus quod hereditati renunciat."

By this it is manifest that the concession and transfer of rights belonging to the heirs, namely to monna Giovanna and her sister Marta, made by them to Niccolò and Francesco, does not prejudice those following in degree.[119]

Thus, they could retain the two quarters come by way of their sisters, while the two quarters they had repudiated passed to the next in line by the terms of the substitution. *Onera hereditaria* (the estate's outstanding obligations) were to be equally divided, so if the sons had hoped to avoid them by their maneuver with their sisters, they had failed. On paper, they were not their father's heirs, but they still had to meet, among other things, the terms of a perpetual *legatum* to give money annually to the poor for the soul of the testator. In the end, d'Ancarano had managed to retain intact all the legal acts – the testament and substitution, the repudiation, the renunciation by the sisters. Other repudiations would not be so easily maintained, in part because of statutory hostility.

Conclusion

Just as heirs might accept or reject the estates left to them, the late medieval jurists could change the inheritance they received from Roman law. To be sure, they largely accepted that inheritance, including all the texts of the *Corpus iuris civilis*. It was an inheritance that served them well (deeply and unendingly *lucrosa*). They maneuvered among those texts, and those from canon law and other sources, with an eye to legislation and practices in the Italian cities from which they hailed and in which they worked and taught. Though they may not have always found them a nice fit with the ideologies that drove inheritance and law in their day, they accommodated those texts and recognized their potential utilities and disutilities. They kept the terms of civil law, whose complex layers of meaning they plumbed with professional relish, but they also assisted in a broad elaboration of *repudiatio* and *abstentio* (and *aditio* and *pro herede gestio*) into a single institutional nexus. And though they did not necessarily arrive at consensus on a number of matters, such as repudiation by and for minors or the time limits that applied to them, their treatment of repudiation and their general endorsement of the validity of local customs and legislation meant that repudiation could serve a function in each jurisdiction that contemplated it.

The jurists broadly agreed on the deeply voluntary nature of repudiation, and of *aditio* for that matter, which included knowledge of the estate in

---

[119] Pietro d'Ancarano, *Consilia* (Pavia, 1496), cons. 27, fols. 12vb-13va, quotation fol. 13va: "Per ista manifeste patet quod concessio et translatio iurium competentium heredibus, scilicet domine Iohanne et sorori Marthe per eas facti in Ni<ccolaum> et Fran<ciscum> non tenuit in preiudicium sequentium in gradu."

question and its mode of transmission. No more so than their Roman predecessors did they attempt to elaborate any tests for the harmful quality of a hereditas. Based on those Roman legacies, they conceded that the repudians might still hold estate properties by some other valid title, and here they did embroider a number of examples and tests, surpassing anything left to them by the Romans. Still, they may have been more than a step behind what was being placed before them daily by their contemporaries.

2

Florentine Laws Regulating Inheritance and Repudiation

Ius commune defined and governed inheritance in Italian communities at one remove. Local statutory regulation of inheritance took precedence, aiming to produce desired modifications to the rules of ius commune. Every Italian community seems to have crafted at least a set of rules laying out lines of intestate succession. Perhaps the overriding purpose of such laws was to disadvantage women in the inheritance of important family property, while protecting and defining their dowry rights. These statutes thus "corrected" (to use the language of jurisprudence) the ius commune which, by the legislation of Justinian, treated men and women, male and female lines of descent, equally.[1] Florence's statute governing women's inheritance claims was perhaps more extensive in its exclusion of them in favor of male agnates, but it was generally unexceptional in this regard.[2] Communities regularly sought to preserve family property in the hands of agnatic kin (*favor agnationis*), one consequence of which was a general assumption that one's sons took immediate possession on death, without requiring a formal act of acceptance, aditio. Only in the course of the late fifteenth and sixteenth centuries, would more communities demand aditio. But it never became a general rule.[3]

Another vital area of civic legislative concern was the trustworthiness and transparency of markets. Forgery, counterfeiting, falsifying records,

---

[1] In general, see Franco Niccolai, *La formazione del diritto successorio negli statuti comunali del territorio lombardo-tosco* (Milan: Giuffrè, 1940); Thomas Kuehn, "Memoria and Family in Law," in *Art, Memory, and Family in Renaissance Florence*, ed. Giovanni Ciappelli and Patricia Lee Rubin (Cambridge: Cambridge University Press, 2000), 262–74; id., *Law, Family, and Women Toward a Legal Anthropology of Renaissance Italy* (Chicago: University of Chicago Press, 1991), 238–57.

[2] Thomas Kuehn, "Person and Gender in the Laws," in *Gender and Society in Renaissance Italy*, ed. Judith A. Brown and Robert C. Davis (New York: Longman, 1998), 87–106; and Gianna Lumia-Ostinelli, "'Ut cippus domus magis conservetur': La successione a Siena tra statuti e testamenti (secoli xii-xvii)," *Archivio storico italiano* 161 (2003): 3–51.

[3] Niccolai, 45–50, surveys the statutes of numerous cities with an eye toward "un certo formalismo risorgente" in the period.

defaulting on credit obligations, bankruptcy, and fraud were countered by an ever-growing body of enactments. Healthy markets and communal collection of taxes and duties rested on countering such nefarious practices.[4] While on face of it, this area of legislative concern may seem quite distinct from inheritance, in fact domestic and commercial possession and ownership were interwoven, and thus too were legal and moral concerns. As Evelyn Welch has demonstrated, commercial transactions in Italian communities were complex matters, "dependent as much on time, trust, social relations and networks as on the seemingly impersonal issues of price, production and demand."[5] Debt and credit were pervasive in the flow of goods and regulation was needed.

Repudiation cut across both areas of concern: inheritance and fraud. It cried out for regulation. Creditors could be harmed when heirs refused to shoulder obligations on an estate. They could easily be deceived when their assumptions about heirs were quietly undermined by a legal repudiation, even more so when, as ius commune clearly allowed, repudiating heirs could continue to reside on and use patrimonial property by some right other than as heir to the deceased. It may not be correct to go as far as Enrico Besta and say that civic statutes were consistently hostile to repudiation, but it certainly is the case that town after town sought to control its use.[6] Franco Niccolai posed that repudiation of inheritance was so much the opposite of the automatic family succession assumed by statutes, that it was in fact an "offense to the deceased and the other kin" and "not only unseemly but also damaging" to the community.[7] This negative characterization of repudiation was the reason for the registration procedures established in Florence and elsewhere. Still, as Niccolai himself notes, it was equally the case that proper use of repudiation was protected.[8]

Statutory Framework

The Obligations of Heirs

What the legislative record in Florence shows is how this community tried to cope with the paradox that repudiation created. What was a useful device

---

[4] Cf. Thomas Kuehn, "Multorum Fraudibus Occurrere: Legislation and Jurisprudential Interpretation Concerning Fraud and Liability in Quattrocento Florence," *Studi senesi* 93 (1981): 309–50; Ronald F. E. Weissman, "The Importance of Being Ambiguous: Social Relations, Individualism, and Identity in Renaissance Florence," in *Urban Life in the Renaissance*, ed. Susan Zimmerman and Ronald F. E. Weissman (Newark: University of Delaware Press, 1989), 269–80.

[5] Evelyn Welch, *Shopping in the Renaissance: Consumer Cultures in Italy, 1400–1600* (New Haven and London: Yale University Press, 2005), 303.

[6] Enrico Besta, *La successione nella storia del diritto italiano* (Milan: Giuffrè, 1936; reprint ed., 1961), 243.

[7] Niccolai, 51. He relies on the statutes of the small town of Cannobbio, which were indeed hostile to repudiation of paternal inheritance.

[8] Ibid., 53–54.

for an heir had evident disutilities for those outside the household or lineage (even for some within). In a society such as Florence, where "indebtedness was a way of life," death marked the time at which final repayment was expected.[9] Repudiation presented an obstacle to smooth settlement. It ran up against the presumptions based on appearances relating to personal and household possessions that signaled social standing and credit-worthiness. In a society such as that of Florence, where the demand for it was all-pervading but "trust was a commodity in short supply," as Gene Brucker notes, legal regulation took on enormous importance.[10] At one and the same time, local legislation provided and permitted legal innovations and flexibility, yet it also attempted strict regulation and control.[11] Preambles and justifications to statutes echoed the sentiment that careful regulation was necessary to safeguard trust in the marketplace, which included making relevant information certain and available. Florence's markets were active through the fourteenth, fifteenth, and sixteenth centuries, with notable periods of boom and bust, giving rise to both great fortunes and spectacular bankruptcies.

Florence's statutes were redacted at three points in the city's republican era: 1322–25, 1355, and 1415.[12] These were points at which both the confused state of accumulating legislation and pressing political needs combined to hasten the enterprise. The statutes of 1355 were certainly a response to the recent devastating epidemic of 1348 and to record keeping problems that had arisen since the turbulent rule of the Duke of Athens in 1343.[13] Only the 1322–25 redaction has received anything like a modern edition, which with all its inadequacies, has recently been reissued.[14] The second survives only in manuscript; the third was printed in the 1780s, at a time when political and cultural imperatives drove a rush to press without scholarly pretensions. The first two versions of Florence's statutes were gathered under two headings – statues of the Capitano del Popolo and those of the Podestà, each consisting of five books. Rules regarding inheritance fell generally in the second book of the Podestà, which contained the essence of civil procedure and private law, to use anachronistic labels. Even in 1415, when the division of Capitano and

---

[9] Welch, *Shopping*, 92.
[10] Gene Brucker, "Fede and Fiducia: The Problem of Trust in Italian History, 1300–1500," in his *Living on the Edge in Leonardo's Florence* (Berkeley: University of California Press, 2005), 83–103, at 84.
[11] As Philip Jones has noted, *The Italian City-State, 500–1300: From Commune to Signoria* (Oxford: Oxford University Press, 1997), 33.
[12] A recent exhaustive account of the processes of statutory construction and legislation in Florence is Lorenzo Tanzini, *Il governo delle leggi: Norme e pratiche delle istituzioni a Firenze dalla fine del Duecento all'inizio del Quattrocento* (Florence: Edifir, 2007).
[13] Cf. Andrea Zorzi, "Le fonti normative a Firenze nel tardo medioevo: Un bilancio delle edizioni e degli studi," in *Statuti della repubblica fiorentina*, new ed., 2 vols. (Florence: Olschki, 1999), 1: liii-ci.
[14] Romolo Caggese, ed., *Statuti della repubblica fiorentina*, 2 vols., vol. 1: *Statuto del capitano del popolo degli anni 1322–25* (Florence: Galileana, 1910), vol. 2: *Statuto del podestà dell'anno 1325* (Florence: Ariani, 1921).

Podestà was abandoned, the materials in what had been the second book of the Podestà were again placed in the second book.

It is hard to say when repudiation entered into consistent use in Florence. It is worth noting that notarial formulary books of the thirteenth century, which contained examples of so many other legal acts, did not present examples of repudiatio.[15] Still, as Manlio Bellomo has said, such books also "show a noteworthy incomprehension of the reality and needs of practitioners."[16]

Florence was not the only community that tried to regulate use of repudiation, but it certainly had plenty of economic incentive to do so aggressively. The bedrock on which repudiation of inheritance in Florence rested was that city's acceptance of the civil law's principle that all contracts, liabilities, and obligations of the deceased were transmitted to each and all of his successors. This principle was tacit in the redactions of 1325 and 1355. In 1415, it gained explicit form in a brief rubric of its own.[17] This premise caused the need for a long and difficult statute, surviving with minor variations in all three redactions, defining just where and how heirs were liable. It was in this context that repudiation figured.

Basically, an adult heir (eighteen being age of majority in Florence) to whom an inheritance had been left, and who was found after fifteen days of the previous owner's death to be in possession of *immobilia*, even though he had otherwise abandoned the estate ("licet bona ipsius hereditatis exiverit seu deseruerit"), was considered to have accepted the estate, "ut verus successor." He would be liable to all outstanding claims, including *legata, fideicommissa*, and *credita*, "nor by pretext of maternal or grandmaternal dowry or repudiation or abstention from said succession, nor by any other right may he claim such property for himself, not even as a debt against the estate, nor under any pretext of inventory."[18] In effect, the one-year period of deliberation allowed in ius commune was drastically reduced to fifteen days

---

[15] Cf. *Formularium florentinum artis notariae (1220–1242)*, ed. Gino Masi (Milan: Giuffrè, 1943); and Bolognese examples of Salatiele, *Ars notariae*, ed. Gianfranco Orlandelli, 2 vols. (Milan: Giuffrè, 1961) and Rolandino de' Passaggieri, *Apparatus super summa notariae* (Bologna, 1478).

[16] Manlio Bellomo, *Società e istituzioni in Italia dal medioevo agli inizi dell'età moderna*, 3rd ed. (Catania: Giannotta, 1982), 447.

[17] *Statuta populi et communis Florentiae, anno salutis mccccxv*, 3 vols. (Freiburg [Florence], 1778–83), vol. 1, liber 2, rubrica 35, 137.

[18] "Nec praetextu dotis maternae, vel avitae, aut repudiationis, seu abstinentiae dictae successionis, aut aliquo alio iure, talia bona, vel se defendere possit, nec etiam quantum ad debita hereditaria, sub praetextu inventarii." The first version of the statute (1325) was labeled De heredibus conveniendis pro debito defuncti (Statuto 1325, liber 2, rubrica 65, 123–24). In 1355, the rubric became De modo et forma conveniendi heredes pro debito defuncti (ASF, Statuti 16, liber 2, rubrica 67, fols. 94v–95v). In the more sophisticated statute redaction of 1415, in which Paolo di Castro and Bartolomeo Vulpi (1359–1435) had a hand, the rubric became De heredibus et hereditate debitoris conveniendis (Statuta, liber 2, rubrica 29, 131–34). On the role of these two jurists in the compilation and editing of these statutes, see now

for all heirs, sui or extranei, and possession after fifteen days resulted in tacit aditio, even if there were legal grounds for the opposite conclusion, notably maternal dowry right and even repudiation itself. The statute demanded that abstention from the estate be real and total, even to the extent of implicitly voiding legally valid repudiations.

These features – fifteen-day limit, no exemption to hold property as compensation for or equivalent to maternal dowry, nor even for repudiation or an inventory – were consistent across the three statute redactions.[19] The assumed unity and solidarity between de cuius and heir (probably of the same family and even the same household) made for harsh and rapid enforcement of liabilities, at least on paper. This law sought to grind out any ambiguities regarding inmixtio (mingling oneself in the assets of an estate). In doing so, however, it also contravened ius commune expressly by abrogating heirs' rights to maternal dowries, to enjoy up to a year to decide to accept or reject, and to take advantage of benefit of inventory to limit their liabilities. Florentine lawyers, as we will see, were well aware of the conflicts between this statute and the learned law to which they were ideologically wedded.

Comparative Perspective

The Florentine statute set a tighter control on repudiation than did contemporary statutes in other Italian communities. Nearby Arezzo in its statutes of 1327 (prior to absorption into the Florentine domain) voided repudiations when heirs were subsequently found in possession, but made exception for maternal dowry and *donatio propter nuptias*.[20] A second statute permitted Aretines to claim benefit of inventory. If summoned to court to answer charges against an estate, an Aretine had five days to produce a copy of the inventory, or, if it had not yet been drawn up, ten days to complete one.[21]

In nearby Montepulciano, like Arezzo subordinated decades later to Florence, there were similar provisions. Anyone seeking compensation from an estate could petition to have the heir judicially summoned to court. If the heir did not appear after ten days, the creditor was to be awarded possession of estate property sufficient to meet his claim. If the heir alleged that he or she was still deliberating about acceptance or repudiation, the creditor could request an end be put to the term for deliberation. If after three more days the heir had not responded either way, the Montepulciano statute ordered that the heir be considered heir and creditors could proceed against him or

---

Lorenzo Tanzini, *Statuti e legislazione a Firenze dal 1355 al 1415: Lo statuto cittadino del 1409* (Florence: Olschki, 2004).
[19] Statuto 1325, liber 2, rubrica 65, 123–24.
[20] *Statuto di Arezzo (1327)*, ed. Giulia Marri Camerani (Florence: Deputazione per la Storia Patria per la Toscana, 1946), liber 3, rubrica 59: De abstinentibus ab hereditate paterna, 171.
[21] Ibid., rubrica 60: De respondentibus se esse heredes cum benefitio inventarii, 171–72.

her. If the heir sought benefit of inventory to limit his exposure, a period of ten days was set and failure to complete the inventory in that time would not protect against claims.[22] As Florence clearly respected (within limits) local laws and customs of her subject towns, such provisions as these in Arezzo and Montepulciano remained in effect there.[23]

Florence's great rival, Siena, in a late redaction (1545) under the influence of legal teaching and case-generated problems, took a weaker stance on inventory and repudiation. Time for deliberation was limited to thirty days, when and if a creditor came forth. Anyone, even someone not in fact the heir, who inserted himself into the estate and conducted himself as heir, was to be held liable for obligations on the estate.[24] Repudiation was permitted otherwise with a deliberation period of one year (heirs under age fourteen had one year after reaching that age). Tacit acceptance was the result of failure to act explicitly. But by the sixteenth century Siena had enacted its own involved procedure for repudiation, which had to be done before the General Executors of the *gabelle*, who had to satisfy themselves from testimony of neighbors and friends of the deceased, through a subcommission of citizens, that there was no malicious or fraudulent purpose behind the proposed repudiation. It was then passed to the Consiglio del Popolo for approval, and creditors on the estate were to be summoned and expressly informed. Creditors could cash out a maternal right by paying the equivalent sum, then take possession of all the estate, if they wished.[25] So elaborate a procedure may only have made repudiation unattractive, while permitting it in practice.

Farther north, Bergamo in 1331 effectively prohibited all use of *beneficium inventarii*. The statute also voided as fraudulent repudiations in which the supposed repudiator was later found to be in possession of goods of the deceased worth at least a quarter of what he or she stood to gain as heir.[26] In contrast to Florence and Arezzo, Bergamo notably was willing to tolerate possession of some portion of the property before denouncing the holder for fraud and voiding his repudiation. Treviso by statute of 1385 was much more

---

[22] *Statuto del comune di Montepulciano (1337)*, ed. Ubaldo Morandi (Florence: Le Monnier, 1966), rubric 1: De in ius vocando et libelli oblatione et primo decreto, 95–98, at 97–98.

[23] This is not to deny that Florence oversaw revisions of local statutes and demanded conformity on jurisdictional and fiscal matters; but areas like inheritance and family law remained at local discretion. See Mario Caravale, *Ordinamenti giuridici dell'Europa medievale* (Bologna: Il Mulino, 1994), 693.

[24] *L'ultimo statuto della Repubblica di Siena (1545)* (1545), ed. Mario Ascheri (Siena: Accademia Senese degli Intronati, 1993), distinctio II, rubric 159: De tempore ad deliberandum, et quod creditoribus satisfiat in totum, etiam confecto inventario, 254–55.

[25] Ibid., distinctio , rubric 174: De repudiatione haereditatis paternae vel avitae, and 175: De repudiante et retinente, seu retinere volente, bona haereditatis repudiatae pro iure matris vel alterius, 263–65.

[26] *Lo statuto di Bergamo di 1331*, ed. Claudia Storti Storchi (Milan: Giuffrè, 1986), collatio 5, rubrica 16: De non adheundo hereditatem cum benefitio inventarii et fraudulose repudiantibus hereditatem, 109.

liberal, not even mentioning repudiation and allowing benefit of inventory with generous terms (one month to begin and two more months to complete it, following judicial demand by creditors).[27]

In fact, some communities found it unnecessary to extend any special statutory attention to inventories and repudiations. In places such as Volterra and Savona, the ius commune was seemingly left to govern such matters without statutory adjustment.[28] Other communities provided statutory remedies for very specific matters without any general statutory structure regarding heirs' assumption of liabilities. Verona, for example, posited in statutes of the early Trecento that possession of a deceased's goods fell to his heirs, testamentary or intestate, immediately "even if the possession does not occur in fact" ("eciam si de facto non fuerit apprehensa").[29] This statute seemed to embody a horror at doubtful possession for any length of time. A statute of Perugia forbade anyone merely to take possession on his own authority of what had been left him. However, the statute's clarification that it did not apply to the universal heir named in a testament would indicate that it was mainly, if not solely, concerned with legatees.[30] Closer to Florence than that Umbrian city and ultimately subject to Florence, the community of Colle Val d'Elsa, in its statutes of 1341, while not directly addressing repudiation or aditio or heirs' obligations, set a penalty on anyone who denied being someone's heir, unless he or she could demonstrate some other title to possession.[31] At least the legislators of Colle betrayed some awareness of the complications of inheritance that limited the common sense desire to equate the visible holder and occupier of property with its legal owner. A statute of Pavia had to point out that at least for one week, in a period of mourning and funeral preparation, living in or entering the home of the deceased was not to be construed as tantamount to aditio.[32]

Legislative pursuit of certainty of ownership and obligations following on inheritance was thus not something peculiar to Florence. What seems exceptional about Florence in this legal area is the thoroughness with which the entire matter of heirs' obligations was laid out. In a city of such size

---

[27] *Gli statuti del comune di Treviso (sec. xiii-xiv)*, ed. Bianca Betto, 2 vols. (Rome: Istituto Storico Italiano per il Medio Evo, 1986), vol. 2, Appendix 4: Lo statuto carrarese del 1385, liber 2, tractatus 3, rubrica 5: Ut heres inventarium conficere teneatur, 376.

[28] *Statuti di Volterra (1210–1224)*, ed. Enrico Fiumi (Florence: Deputazione di Storia Patria per la Toscana, 1951), esp. 9–10, 52; *Statuta antiquissima Saone (1345)*, ed. Laura Balletto, 2 vols. (Genoa: Istituto Internazionale di Studi Liguri, 1971), esp. 2: 181–88.

[29] *Statuti di Verona del 1327*, ed. Silvana Anna Bianchi and Rosalba Granuzzo, 2 vols. (Rome: Jouvence, 1992), 1: 356.

[30] *Statuto del comune e del popolo di Perugia del 1342, in volgare*, ed. Mahmoud Salem Elsheikh, 3 vols. (Perugia: Deputazione di Storia Patria per l'Umbria, 2000), 2: 166–67.

[31] *Statuta antiqua communis Collis Vallis Else (1307–1407)*, ed. Renzo Ninci, 2 vols. (Rome: Istituto Storico Italiano per il Medio Evo, 1999), 1: 307.

[32] Niccolai, *Diritto successorio*, 53–54.

and so much relatively mobile, if not downright volatile, wealth, where even land titles changed hands with some rapidity and credit and debt were so ubiquitous, it was prudent to be thorough.

What Florence shared with other communities was a revealing scepticism regarding the probative value of notarial instruments. Use of notaries to record transactions and events, typical or unusual, was pervasive in Italy and many other areas of Europe, and formative of social practices, especially from the thirteenth century on. The notary's document bestowed on an event *publica fides*; from a merely private undertaking it became public and proven.[33] Notaries reduced the messy and specific features of social life to legal forms and formulas. The truth they provided lay in good part in this very regularity of events, such as repudiation of an inheritance.[34]

Yet what notaries recorded was in fact the result of a collaborative process. Their clients had interests to shape and protect. The very regularity of notarial documents also fiercely conceals a great deal. The notarial text was formed in negotiation and had strategic uses. Neither the notaries' contemporaries nor historians can afford to take these texts at face value without question.[35] Clients were not interested in a full record of actions and interests. They sought a paper trail to use if needed to assert a right.[36] So it was that not only were notaries stock figures of corruption and greed in cultural reflections, they were actively prosecuted for crimes and their documents were disputed in courts.[37] Certainly, regarding repudiation of inheritance in Florence, statutes made clear that a notarial instrument was not adequate proof of the matter. A paper trail may have been necessary, but it was not sufficient. An heir's repudiation had to be actual, not merely legal.

Minors and Mothers

Those communities, like Florence, that eliminated the *beneficium inventarii* (a general tendency according to Niccolai) still preserved it for minors.[38]

---

[33] A succinct presentation of the status of notarial records and the role of the notary is Attilio Bartoli Langeli, "'Scripsi et publicavi': Il notaio come figura pubblica, l'instrumentum come documento pubblico," in *Notai, miracoli e culto dei santi: Pubblicità e autenticazione del sacro tra xii e xv secolo* (Milan: Giuffrè, 2004), 55–71.

[34] Kathryn Burns, "Notaries, Truth, and Consequences," *American Historical Review* 110 (2005): 350–79, at 352.

[35] That being the essential point of Burns's essay, esp. 355–57.

[36] Ibid., 372: "Notarial records are in this sense always in implicit dialogue with an imagined litigious future."

[37] Cf. Laurie Nussdorfer, "Lost Faith: A Roman Prosecutor Reflects on Notaries' Crimes," in *Beyond Florence: The Contours of Medieval and Early Modern Italy*, ed. Paula Findlen, Michelle M. Fontaine, and Duane J. Osheim (Stanford: Standord University Press, 2003), 101–114.

[38] Niccolai, *Diritto successorio*, 59–62.

Young children who had lost their father and inherited from him could have their liability limited to the inventoried assets of the estate, presuming that their guardian was responsible and had one made. Inventories could be quite tricky, especially in the appraisal of household items.[39] As we will see later, Florentines were aware of this added protection for minors and deliberately used it. Minors were also exempt from the fifteen-day limit facing those over eighteen. For minors between the ages of sixteen and eighteen, liability commenced not on the sixteenth day but when a creditor came forth. In the 1355 version of the statute concerning heirs' liabilities, that of adult women was more narrowly drawn; it had to rest on a prior aditio or some indication (such as paying a credit or meeting an obligation) of intent to be heres, beyond mere continued residence or incidental use. No such precondition to liability, other than possession, remained after 1415.[40] That change, whatever overt reason lay behind it, put adult female heirs on the same footing as men. Creditors' summons of such minors or women to court had to be answered within only five days.

Maternal Dowry

The 1415 statute produced another important variation, as it allowed some exemption for heirs to be in possession of all or part of a hereditas for a dowry right. In law, a husband's ownership and administration of his wife's dowry (property brought by her to the marriage) was restricted and rather ambiguous, as ownership lodged with the wife. He could use and even alienate the goods his wife brought, but she retained a tacit security (*hypoteca*) of first priority against other creditors over all her husband's property for return of the value of her dowry. The tacit security of the dowry over his property remained in place, in other words, until the maternal estate was formally settled on her heirs.[41] In Florence, if there were children from the marriage, they were her heirs, in which case a surviving husband retained a right of use while ownership devolved on the children. The rule in Florence, however, in distinction to many other cities, was that sons or their sons inherited from mothers to the exclusion of daughters. A woman's property thus fell even

---

[39] Welch, *Shopping*, 86.
[40] ASF, Statuti 16, fol. 94v.
[41] Among the now vast literature on dowry, the reader is referred to Julius Kirshner, "Wives' Claims against Insolvent Husbands in Late Medieval Italy," in *Women of the Medieval World*, ed. Julius Kirshner and Suzanne F. Wemple (Oxford: Blackwell, 1985), 256–303; id., "'Maritus Lucretur Dotem Uxoris Sue Premortue' in Fourteenth- and Fifteenth-Century Florence," *Zeitschrift der Savigny Stiftung für Rechtsgeschichte* (Kan. Abt.) 77 (1991): 111–55; Isabelle Chabot, "Seconde nozze e identità materna nella Firenze del tardo medioevo," in *Tempi e spazi di vita femminile tra medioevo ed età moderna*, ed. Silvana Seidel Menchi, Anne Jacobson Schutte, and Thomas Kuehn (Bologna: Il Mulino, 1999), 493–523; id., "La loi du lignage: Notes sur le système successoral florentin (xive-xve, xviie siècles)," *Clio: Histoire, femmes et sociétés* 7 (1998): 51–72.

more fully to her husband's line of descent than would have been the case if sons and daughters shared it, as they frequently did elsewhere.[42]

By the 1415 statute, children or grandchildren resident with a mother or grandmother having a dowry right on paternal property were expressly exempted from the need to vacate the property as well as formally repudiate. Following a valid repudiation of their inheritance right to their father, these sons and grandsons could not be sued for paternal or grandpaternal debts and were not to be considered to have intermingled in the estate, as long as they lived with their mother or grandmother, whose dowry was secured against the property. Presumably, after her death, they might remain as her heirs; but it was not clear if the statute's opening statement exposing them to liability might not then come into play, barring repudiation. Their claims on the estate, while privileged as maternal dowry, were limited to its value. Creditors had full rights to pursue their claims, with the sole requirements that a copy of their petition be lodged with the court of the Podestà, the usual tribunal with jurisdiction in these matters, and that a herald announce the suit in the deceased's neighborhood.

This statutory emendation protected dowry rights only in the presence of a prior repudiation of the husband's estate. The jurist Paolo di Castro, who had a large role in shaping Florence's 1415 statutes, recognized this when he reflected on Florentine law and practice in the midst of an academic lecture. Law, he said, could deprive someone of a benefit he might obtain, but it could not take away one already obtained:

[A]nd here is an example from what is practiced in Florence, where there is a statute to the effect that if someone to whom an estate is left should have any hereditary property or have entered it, even if not as heir but by some other right, cause, or pretext–for example, if he should claim that it is obligated to him for his mother's dowry–he is nonetheless considered to be heir and held fully liable to all creditors. And drawing up an inventory will not help him, though a [minor] son will have that remedy. If one does not want the estate of his father and yet wants his mother's dowry, for which the father's estate is obligated and his property is pledged, certainly the remedy is that first and before all he openly repudiate the paternal estate, and there [Florence] there is a statute that repudiation must be done in the public council of the commune, so as to avoid frauds. Once this is done, he may petition a judge and occupy hereditary property on his authority, and the statute will not hurt him. Thus the statute must be understood to have effect even when he occupies the property by judicial authority before he expressly repudiates, otherwise if afterward.[43]

---

[42] Isabelle Chabot and Anna Bellavitis, "A proposito di Men and Women in Renaissance Venice di Stanley Chojnacki," *Quaderni storici* 118 (April 2005): 203–238, at 222.

[43] Paolo di Castro to D. 29.2.71,9, *In primam infortiati partem* (Venice, 1593), fol. 143ra-va: "et est hic casus de eo quod practicatur Florentie ubi est statutum quod si ille cui delata est hereditas ceperet aliqua bona hereditaria, vel fuerit ingressus, etiam non tanquam heres: sed alio iure vel cause pretextu: ut si diceret quod essent sibi obligata pro dote materna, et quod nihilominus efficiatur heres, et teneatur omnibus creditoribus insolidum: et sibi nihil

The only remedy was a formal repudiation. His student, Alessandro Tartagni, fully agreed with him that unless one followed the safe route of first repudiating, and registering that act, the statute could preclude even a judicial decree of possession of maternal dowry.[44]

Still, it cannot be stressed too much that the 1415 statute represented an important softening of Florence's hard line regarding repudiation. Retention of paternal property in the name of the mother's dowry was now allowed, at least as long as she was alive. Realistically, the law meant that mothers and children did not have to abandon the paternal home if they wanted to repudiate. This statutory shift could have the effect of encouraging use of repudiation, as it no longer carried so high a potential "cost" in relation to the mother's dowry. This shift itself may have been the result of the increasing influence of trained jurists, such as Paolo di Castro, on the drafting and interpretation of laws in Florence. It may also have been possible to allow this exception to a strict alignment of repudiation and abstention because Florence had a successful and functioning tool with which it tracked people's use of repudiation.

Registration of Repudiations

Cessation of liabilities for inheritance, when they otherwise were so easily and automatically assumed, was extremely troublesome for a community such as Florence, where there was a very strong and extended statutory sense of mutual liability between fathers and sons. Following the first devastating outbreak of the Black Death of 1348, numerous inheritances were left vacant or passed through several hands in fairly short order, often ending up with distant relatives of the original holders.[45] Legislators and jurists confronted unprecedented situations.[46] Repudiation, along with other devices, proved very useful in such changing and confusing circumstances, but it also raised

---

proficiat confectio inventarii quod ergo remedium habebit filius. Si non vult hereditatem patris et tamen vult dotem maternam, ad quam hereditas patris est obligata, etiam bona sunt hypothecata, certe remedium est quod primo et ante omnia repudiet palam hereditatem paternam, et ubi est statutum quod debeat fieri repudiatio in consilio publico communis ad obviandum fraudibus, et hoc facto poterit petere iudicem et cum eius authoritate occupare bona hereditaria: et non nocebit sibi statutum: debet ergo intelligi statutum quando occuparet etiam authoritate curiae, antequam repudiaret expresse: secus si postea."

[44] Tartagni to C. 6.31.1, *In primam et secundam codicis* (Venice, 1570), fol. 157vb: "Dicit etiam Pau. de Ca. hic quod quandoque statuta provident quod qualitercunque occupet, etiam si dicat pro dote materna intelligatur esse heres, tamen adhuc secundum eum non debet intelligi dictum statutum, de eo qui iudicialiter occupasset, quia alias statutum impediret iustam exactionem dotis."

[45] David Herlihy, *The Black Death and the Transformation of the West*, ed. Samuel K. Cohn, Jr. (Cambridge: Harvard University Press, 1997); Daniel L. Smail, "Accommodating Plague in Medieval Marseille," *Continuity and Change* 11 (1996): 11–41.

[46] Note, for example, Bartolo da Sassoferrato's role in clarifying one implication of Florence's intestate inheritance statute in 1351, as per Kuehn, *Law, Family, and Women*, 243–44.

problems. In 1355, these and other issues were addressed in a new redaction of Florence's statutes, some of which were greatly emended by recent legislation.

Helping precipitate this process of statutory emendation was the concession to Florence by Emperor Charles (1346–1378) in March 1355 of the right to enact its own statutes.[47] Of course, Florence already had statutes, so this imperial legitimizing of legislation was essentially pro forma. Concurrently, and more directly motivating concerns with repudiation was a growing sense of the deleterious effects of deceptive practices on trade and social relations. The Florentine chronicler Matteo Villani reported an effort of August 1355 to ease the process for creditors intent on finding their debtors' assets by compiling a register of all *beni immobili* in the city and contado.[48] The project was quickly abandoned in view of its difficulty and enormous scope, especially, said Villani, because changes of ownership were so frequent in a city that "abounds with commerce and trades and crafts" ("abonda di mercatantie e di mestieri e d'arti").

On 10 July 1355, a *provvisione* was enacted in Florence that addressed fraud in regard to both emancipation of children and repudiation of inheritance.[49] For both legal institutions, the remedy proposed was a public registry of acts providing a central source of information for creditors (who might also be kin). Registration of emancipation, which in both civil law and statutes dissolved liabilities between fathers and children (mainly sons, in reality), was subsequently written into the revised statute on the obligations of sons and fathers.[50] Registration of repudiations was similarly inserted into the statute on the obligations of heirs. But there were some telling and subtle differences in the treatment of emancipation and repudiation. Anyone who emancipated or was emancipated had fifteen days (if in Florence), a month (if in the contado or distretto under Florentine rule), or two months (if outside Florentine Tuscany) to notify the Mercanzia of the emancipation. The Mercanzia was the international merchants' court that also had general oversight of all the Florentine guilds.[51] Lodging registration

---

[47] Matteo Villani, *Cronica con la continuazione di Filippo Villani*, 2 vols., ed. Giusseppe Porta (Parma: Fondazione Pietro Bembo, 1995), 1: 583–84.

[48] Ibid., 697–98.

[49] ASF, Provvisioni registri 42, fols. 88r-v, in which the priors are described as "multorum fraudibus occurrere cupientes." On the effects of this law and a subsequent one of 1421 for emancipation practices in Florence, see Thomas Kuehn, *Emancipation in Late Medieval Florence* (New Brunswick: Rutgers University Press, 1982), 35–48.

[50] Compare the 1325 version (Statuto 1325, liber 2, rubrica 44, De obligatione filii emancipati, 119) with that of 1355 (ASF, Statuti 16, liber 2, rubrica 26, De obligatione filii familias et qualiter pater pro filio conveniatur, fols. 78v-79v, and rubrica 28, De obligatione filii emancipati, fol. 80r).

[51] Guido Bonolis, *La giurisdizione della Mercanzia in Firenze nel secolo xiv* (Florence: Seeber, 1901), which is still valuable but now updated in important ways by Antonella Astorri, *La Mercanzia a Firenze nella prima metà del Trecento* (Florence: Olschki, 1998).

of emancipation with that body indicates a primary concern with the contractual liabilities between fathers and sons and the contractual abilities of the sons.

Those involved in repudiations, on the other hand, were ordered to register their activities in the councils of the commune and the popolo in the presence of the priors and the gonfaloniere di giustizia – in effect, in the presence of the chief executive body of the city. Those living within Florentine jurisdiction, in or out of the city, had one month to register (two by the more generous 1415 statute); those living elsewhere had two months (four in 1415).[52] As repudiation affected succession and thus family lines, it seemed a matter for city government and not a market-oriented court like the Mercanzia.

Otherwise, the results sought were the same. There would be books kept registering the names of the parties, the notary who officiated, the dates of the act and of the notification. These were to be legible and organized.[53] They were intended to be available for consultation by anyone concerned to learn of the true legal exposure of his debtors (something weakly analogous to credit reports nowadays). Those who registered acts were assessed a fee, so there was a modest cost attached (one florin to the Signoria for each repudians). And for both emancipation and repudiation, failure to notify the appropriate body led to the same result: "Otherwise such repudiation or abstention may be presumed fictitious and simulated and done to defraud creditors and in no way may they work to the benefit of those repudiating or abstaining."[54]

These registers were indeed established and used. They survive essentially intact. Judging from the numbers recorded in them and their consistent quality, Florentines generally obeyed such registration laws. Economic or political disruptions might temporarily derail the process, but it was quickly restored. The new government of late 1494, for example, following the departure of Piero de' Medici in the wake of the invading army of Charles VIII of France, having reorganized governing institutions and rights to office, hastened to affirm that the new administrative council would accept the notifications of repudiations previously handled in the councils of the popolo and commune.[55] As much as possible, a smooth transition ensued and no gap of any consequence occurred in the registries. When the Medici returned to

---

[52] The modestly less urgent need to register urban repudiations (versus urban emancipations) may indicate less concern with or fear of short-term market effects of repudiation, which, after all, ostensibily took property from someone as opposed to bestowing new capacities and possibly property on them, as emancipation did.

[53] ASF, Provvisioni 42, fol. 88r: "Et ipsam scripturam sic clare per alfabetum vel alio modo fieri facere quod sit facile cum expedierit sibi de aliquo reperire."

[54] Ibid.: "Alioquin talis repudiatio seu abstinentia presumaretur fictitia et simulata et in fraudem creditorum facta, et in nullo prosint ipsi repudianti seu abstinenti." For emancipation, there was the slight variation that it "nullius sit efficacie vel momenti."

[55] ASF, Provvisioni registri 185, fol. 12v (22 December 1494).

Florence in 1512, the Signoria decreed that notification of repudiations would occur in the usual manner before the new *balìa* impaneled in that time of crisis.[56] Less than four years later, as the military and diplomatic situation became more heated and chaotic, and the Medici scorned the work of citizen councils, a law passed recognizing that sporadic meeting of the councils had led to a situation in which many repudiations could not be registered within the required time period, despite the good intentions of the parties. An extension was granted to all those in the past six months who now came in and paid the fee during the term of the present council.[57]

Ultimately, in fact, these registration procedures survived the constitutional change from republic to principate. The abolition of the republican magistracies in 1532 was accompanied by the establishment of the Consiglio dei Dugento, which took over a number of functions of the old Consiglio del Popolo.[58] Among these were the registration of repudiations, emancipations, recollection of dowries by wives of men verging on bankruptcy, and grants of Florentine citizenship. Registration of these acts from 1534 to 1781 also survives in Florence's state archive.[59]

Registration was hardly a device unique to Florence, but it was one Florentine legislators would rely on, less notably and less successfully, in some other instances.[60] It was also a device that was supported by jurists, as seen in the following example from Baldo degli Ubaldi's *consilia*. Two women had repudiated inheritance from their father and followed local statute in having their action reported to the town executive council.[61] However, there was also a recent addition to the statute. It ordered a summoning of creditors to various legal acts that potentially affected their claims, and these two women had fallen afoul of this requirement. Baldo faced the argument that it was unjust to void the repudiation and treat these women as heredes. They seemed to have followed all requirements, and the town council had heard and approved of their repudiation. But in Baldo's eyes, following

---

[56] This measure is recorded in its essentials in the registry volume then in service: RE 28, fol. xli verso (formerly fol. 1), 19 September 1512.

[57] ASF, Provvisioni registri 202, fols. 58r-59r (21 February 1515/6).

[58] Furio Diaz, *Il granducato di Toscana: I Medici*, in *Storia d'Italia*, ed. Giuseppe Galasso, vol. 13 (Turin: UTET, 1976), 50–53.

[59] ASF, Consiglio dei Dugento, 175–225. The registers were kept, as during the republic, in a parallel series of volumes, one for emancipations with dowries inserted near the end, and the other for repudiations and citizenship. The fondo as organized, unfortunately, does not separate them into distinct subsets or even indicate distinctions in the inventory.

[60] As in 1458 regarding arbitration agreements intended to last a number of years; see Kuehn, "Multorum Fraudibus Occurrere," 318, 325–32.

[61] Baldo, cons. 76, *Consilia*, 6 vols. in 3 (Venice, 1575; reprint ed., Turin: Bottega d'Erasmo, 1970), vol. 2, fol. 18ra-b. It is not possible from the printed text to determine where this case arose.

those formalities was not enough. He ended up reluctantly arguing against the women,

> considering the statute's words, and holding always to the truth, it seems correct to say that this law is tough, if by rational interpretation it cannot be reduced to natural equity.[62]

Baldo was content to let the proper registration of repudiation protect the women, but the legislative change did not allow him to leave the matter with repudiation alone, as the creditors had clear privileges as defined by the statute.

As a safeguard for the community in general, for an estate's creditors in particular, registration served as an inducement to use repudiation. In that light, it is noteworthy that the legislation roughly coincided with measures of 1349 that encouraged branches of Florentine magnate lineages, politically disenfranchised by their magnate status, to separate from their kin. However, in those instances the requirements were highly symbolic (to adopt new insignia and a new cognomen) and aimed at renouncing solidarity in arms and acts of vengeance. They did not touch on basic filiation or importantly on the transmission of inheritances.[63] In seeking official separation from their kin, Florentine magnates alleged as one strong reason a desire to escape financial burdens arising from kin experiencing difficulties.[64] In that case, separation was at least akin to emancipation, if not repudiation.

Debts and Liabilities

One important rationale to restrict the operation of both repudiation and emancipation was to retain as much extended liability as possible in the cases of fugitive bankrupts (*cessantes et fugitivi*). They presented such a problem that an entire block of statutes came to deal with them by the time of the 1415 redaction.[65] The controlling feature in obligations here was the time at which a debt was contracted. If that moment preceded the son's emancipation, the later emancipation did not remove him from possible liability (personal as well as financial). As debts in all likelihood preceded any repudiation, it too did not free sons from debts of their *patres cessantes et fugitivi*. We can see this determination even in practice in Florence. The lawyer Antonio Strozzi (1455–1523), in a *consilium* endorsed by many others (he said), argued that both the emancipations and the repudiations of the

---

[62] Ibid., fol. 18rb: "consideratis verbis statuti, salva semper veritate, videtur dicendum quod sit dura ista lex, si per sanam interpretationem ad naturalem equitatem reduci non potest."

[63] Christiane Klapisch-Zuber, *Retour à la cité: Les magnats de Florence, 1340–1440* (Paris: Éditions de l'École des Hautes Études en Sciences Sociales, 2006), 210–12.

[64] Ibid., 326.

[65] Statuta 1415, vol. 1, liber 3, rubrica 2, 521–22, is the central statute, but not the only one. There is also an entire "Tractatus de cessantibus et fugitivis."

sons of Luca Capponi did not free them from the obligations of their *cessans* father (here for return of a dowry).[66] Thus, though these sons had utilized both forms of protection, they were not going to be protected when their father had fled from his obligations, to the point of public knowledge of his default.[67]

The presumptions regarding fathers and sons, however, did not similarly operate between mothers and children, nor between fathers and daughters. For fathers and daughters, dowry and marriage constituted effective exemption from liability.[68] In principle, the married daughter took the dowry as her portion, left her father's house, and entered her husband's. Her daily involvement with her father was effectively at an end. By extension, the passage of property in inheritance to daughters could not seem so automatic. Angelo degli Ubaldi handled a hypothetical case that gravitated about that issue. A daughter, sole heir to her mother, grew up and married after twenty years. Meanwhile, her father had possessed her mother's property and enjoyed its use and revenue. Paternal creditors argued that her silent acceptance of her father's control and enjoyment of the mother's *hereditas* for so long a time implied both a tacit *aditio* of the estate on her part and exposure of it for paternal debts. The problem was that statutory law did not allow a woman to obligate herself for anything or to anyone without her husband's consent, and there was no evidence of his consent to a tacit *aditio*. Angelo termed this problem "dubius et delectabilis." It was the complication of the husband's consent that Angelo seems to have found delectable, for there was in contrast no doubt that, if the father held the property for some time before the girl married, her acceptance of the maternal estate was presumed.[69] But if her acceptance could not be presumed until after marriage, then she could not be obligated without her husband's consent.[70]

Yet more tellingly, her *aditio* might not be presumed, for she did not possess the maternal estate; her father did. He had no right to it unless she had repudiated, which was not in issue here. After briefly examining

---

[66] ASF, Carte strozziane, 3rd series, 41/14, fols. 98r, 101r-9v; and see Kuehn, *Emancipation*, 143–44. The telling phrase is: "Filii autem talium debitorum cessantium et alii masculi descendentes per lineam masculinam tenentur et obligati sunt, sicut parentes eorum, creditoribus, et pro dictis debitis capi et detineri possunt, non obstante aliqua renuntiatione vel abstinentia hereditatis, vel non obstante aliquo iure disponente filium pro patre conveniri non posse."

[67] Ibid., fol. 101v laid out three forms of cessantes: "notorie," those pronounced as such by the court of the Podestà or Mercanzia, and those given sindaci by a court to examine one's records and liquidate assets.

[68] Kuehn, *Emancipation*, 42.

[69] Angelo cons. 318, *Consilia* (Frankfurt am Main, 1575), fols. 223ra-va.

[70] Ibid., fol. 223ra: "Ex quo concludo quod ex quo illo tempore tunc filia incipit obligari, cum tempus totum decurrit, et obligari non potest sine viri consensu, non habemus de dicta praesumptione tractare, cum nec vera agnitio eam obligare potest, ut superius est expressum."

arguments on both sides of the issue, including the meanings of the *iura antiqua* of the *Digest*, Angelo found that

[n]owadays, because a son remains heir and is bound for debts, it seems to me harsh and unjust that a son be taken to have accepted an estate as a result of [his father's] possession for a very long time, as he gained no benefit in the intervening period but he only lived and took refuge with his father, unless we tolerate this injustice from the fact that the person of the father and of the son is reckoned to be the same.[71]

The treatment of father and child as *una persona* worked with sons, not with daughters. It was also the case that fathers did not figure as heirs to their wives; their children did. Thus, the daughter in this case could seek restitution of the fruits of the maternal estate consumed by her father. She had not accepted the estate, and her father had used it in full knowledge that it did not belong to him.[72]

Lines of Juristic Interpretation

Two Florentine lawyers, Alessandro Bencivenni (1385–1423) and Tommaso Salvetti (1390–1472), devoted commentaries on the statutes of 1415, including the pivotal statutes regarding inheritance. Drawing on ius commune and on consilia written in Florentine cases before and after 1415, they sought to erect an interpretive framework around these statutes by examining their terms in light of the reigning jurisprudence of ius commune.[73] These were very practical manuals aimed at the needs of practicing attorneys and notaries in Florence. Their lengthy treatments of the statute on heirs' liability are testimony to the difficulties it raised.

It was the younger man, Salvetti, who gave eloquent expression to their common point of departure in a preamble to his discussion of the statute. The point was that "this statute forcefully departs from the ius commune." The result (a juristic interpretive commonplace) was that "therefore it must be construed strictly lest in total it encompass inequities, as it takes away rights

---

[71] Ibid., fol. 223rb: "Sed hodie, quia filius remanet heres, et oneribus alligatur, quod ex possessione temporis longaeva filius intelligitur agnovisse, durum et iniquum mihi videtur, cum nullum commodum ipse percepit medio tempore, sed solum confluxerit et decurserit ad patrem, nisi hanc iniquitatem toleramus ex eo, quia persona patris et filii eadem censenda est." He quarreled with extending Bartolo's view of the presumption of possession by a tutor to fathers, because tutores had to render accounts, while fathers were subject to no accounting for their administration of their sons' property.

[72] Ibid., fol. 223va: "contra heredes [patris] agere poterit ad restitutionem duarum partium fructuum perceptorum per patrem de hereditate praedicta, eo quod tempore vitae patris dicta hereditas non pertinuit ad patrem, nec ad filiam, quae non agnovit, et scivit, et scire debuerit pater hereditatem suam non esse."

[73] For an illuminating discussion of the sorts of interpretive devices these men wielded, see Umberto Santarelli, "La gerarchia delle fonti secondo gli statuti emiliani e romagnoli," *Rivista di storia del diritto italiano* 33 (1960): 49–164.

of dowry, of repudiation, and of inventory, which must all be safeguarded in ius commune."[74] He and Bencivenni were at pains time after time to point out where the statute parted company with ius commune. Above all, they held to what they had learned from ius commune about the many ways one could hold property by a right other than as heir.

One device, by which these jurists sought to salvage as much as possible of the meaning and effect of ius commune, was the elaboration of a *ius familiaritatis*, by which one could reside on and use property without being its owner or even legal possessor. A *familiaris* was not an heir and could not be sued as heir. Bencivenni's treatment skirted different legal terms related to ownership (including *possessio* and *detentio* or *tenuta*) to come to the precise sense of the *familiaris* as one who neither "possessed" nor "held."[75] He simply enjoyed use of property of another. The prime example was the emancipated son who continued to reside with his father.[76] His cohabitation was not a right but flowed from a "familiar patience or confidence or even an explicit gratuitous concession."[77] A related concern was to protect a son's right to his mother's dowry, statutory concession of which Bencivenni labeled "noviter introductum."[78] Salvetti relied on what he had learned from the long-lived Florentine jurist, Filippo Corsini (1334–1421), who had personally advised him that the statute's desire to protect creditors was not compromised by rental (*conductio*) "nor habitation by right of familiarity, especially children with their mother...lest a cruel separation of blood result, which the laws abhor."[79] He went on to invoke a 1403 case of another Florentine lawyer,

---

[74] BNF, Fondo principale, II, iv, 434, fols. 60r-79r, at 60r-v (hereafter Salvetti): "et maxime quia hoc statutum fortiter exorbitat a iure communi, demum ut huiusmodi possessorem vel debitorem obligare creditoribus etc. non obstante quod pretendat possidere pro iure matris et non obstante repudiatione vel beneficio inventarii. Et ideo debet stricte intelligi ne in totum contineat iniquitatum speciem cum tollat iura dotis, repudiationis, et inventarii, que omnia salva esse debent de iure communi." On strict interpretation and other interpretive tropes of medieval jurists, see especially Mario Sbriccoli, *L'interpretazione dello statuto: Contributo allo studio della funzione dei giuristi nell'età comunale* (Milan: Giuffrè, 1969).

[75] BNF, Fondo principale, II, iv, 435, fols. 16v-22r (hereafter Bencivenni), at fol. 17r: "ratio est quia quidam sunt detentores tenentes pro aliquo suo iure ut commodatarius vel possidens ex proprio decreto et etiam tenens pro iure dominii.... Quidam vero sunt detentores simpliciter non possessores sed ipsi presentant se possidere vel se dominos esse, sed nec possident quia alius possidet.... Quidam vero sunt qui nec possident neque tenent usum tamen in re habentes sed non firmiter, ut puta habitatores et familiares." On these notions of property, see the classic work of Paolo Grossi, *Le situazioni reali nell'esperienza giuridica medievale* (Padua: CEDAM, 1968), and his collected studies, *Il dominio e le cose: Percezioni medievali e moderne dei diritti reali* (Milan: Giuffrè, 1992).

[76] Bencivenni, fol. 17r; Salvetti, fol. 61v.

[77] Salvetti, fol. 62r: "patientia et seu confidentia familiari vel etiam expressa concessione gratuita."

[78] Bencivenni, fols. 20v-21r; Salvetti, fols. 64r-65v.

[79] Salvetti, fol. 62v: "nec habitatio iure familiaritatis, maxime filii cum matre...et ne dura separatio sanguinis inducatur, quam iura aborent."

Ricciardo del Bene (d. 1411), and his own conclusions in several cases "that when one resides by virtue of mere familiarity he is not considered legally liable if in truth he holds these goods in his own right and freely has them in payment."[80] Still, for anyone who was heir, both Bencivenni and Salvetti thought the safest course was to repudiate in order to remove any suspicion that he or she acted as heir.[81]

These commentaries thus display an evident professional bias against the features of Florence's statute that departed from *ius commune*. The revision of 1415 conceding maternal dowry rights to sons and grandsons living with their mother or grandmother gave recognition, in effect, to a *ius familiaritatis*. The impact of jurists' opinions was, at the least, to buy some time for a dead man's wife and children to remain in his house and develop some way to meet or avoid his debts, as long as they also took advantage of legal devices such as inventory or repudiation.

Salvetti also gave eloquent testimony to how clever Florentines could be in trying to get around this statute. As its harsh terms were aimed most directly at adult male heirs, there was some utility in passing the bulk of the property to other sorts of persons.

> Very often I issued consilia and advised many testators that they establish as heir a woman or a small grandchild or other who could not be seized for debts; and that they command their son to be content with what he had during their life, such as an emancipation gift or expenses for study or a wedding and so forth; and then, because the hereditas is not handed to that son, he is not faced with the consequences of the statute, which seeks to hold liable him to whom the hereditas devolves by testament or on intestacy.[82]

Such maneuvers did not cancel debts, but they put the hereditas in the hands of those who either had more legal protections (a woman could not be imprisoned for debt) or more time before they had to face full liability (a youngster). These steps succeeded only through intergenerational cooperation; they could not simply be mandated by a testator.

Obviously, both attorneys drew the conclusion that the statute essentially precluded use of inventory by those over eighteen, as it did not prevent their

---

[80] Ibid., fol. 63v: "quod quando mere familiaritatis causa atesserit, quod non intelligatur obnoxius, si atinens re vera ea bona iure proprio et libere habuit in solutum."

[81] Bencivenni, fols. 16v, 17r-v, 18r-v, 19r, 10v; Salvetti, fols. 66v-67v, 68r, 70r-v, 71v.

[82] Salvetti, fol. 64r: "Ego autem sepissime consilia dedi et praticari feci a pluribus testatoribus quod instituerint feminam heredem vel nepotem parvum vel alium atinentem qui non possit capi, et filium iusserint contentum esse eo quod habuit in vita, ut in premio emancipationis vel pro studio vel quod nuptiis et similibus, et tunc, quia hereditas non defertur ei filio, non habet sibi obstare statutum, cum velit illum affici cui hereditas deferretur ex testamento vel ab intestato."

liability to creditors. An inventory came attached as a condition or limitation to aditio, which was why the statute rejected inventory.[83]

On a related practical problem, Bencivenni and Salvetti agreed the Florentine statute did not apply to clergy or ecclesiastical institutions. As Salvetti put it, an ecclesiastical institution was not generally subject to statutes; the problem was when abstention by a cleric or institution put property into the hands of laymen. He concluded that several jurists had advised that a cleric's repudiation in favor of his brothers was valid, even if not registered, but that repudiation by an institution, such as the hospital of Santa Maria Nuova, had to be registered so that the next in line by intestacy could learn of it and exercise the option to accept the estate.[84] Bencivenni noted that ecclesiastical institutions were generally treated in civil law as equivalent to minors, with extra legal protections.[85]

Both jurists had to respect the statute's intent to prevent fraud. Precluding fraud was, after all, the goal of ius commune in regard to repudiation every bit as much as it was the goal of the much more aggressive statutory law.[86] One problem that arose in practice came from attempts of some Florentines to claim a portion of an estate despite their repudiation of it. That is, some tried to claim their "legitimate portion" (*legitima*) anyway. Legitima was a quota due to children or other necessary heirs, even if the bulk of the estate went elsewhere.[87] As we saw in the first chapter, and as these jurists knew, a repudiating heir could not seek his legitima.[88] In fact, Bencivenni was contradictory about the matter. At one point, he declared that a son or other descendant could seek legitima without being heir, as legitima was owed him by law of nature. However, later, considering the consequences if one heir repudiated but then tried to claim the estate through a clause of substitution for his brother, Bencivenni took a harder line, denying that a repudians could seek legitima.[89] Salvetti, in contrast, did not equivocate: "Whether a repudians can seek legitima nowadays, [the answer is] no, because he has it by hereditary right, and one cannot have part of an estate when he may have it all."[90]

---

[83] Salvetti, fol. 70r.
[84] Salvetti, fol. 76r.
[85] Bencivenni, fol. 18v.
[86] Salvetti, fol. 63r.
[87] Bencivenni, fol. 17r: "Sed nunquid filius vel alius descendens vel ascendens cui defertur hereditas potest petere legitimam vere nec in bonis defuncti absque eo quod sit heres, dic quod sic, quia dicta legitima petitur tanquam sibi debitum iure nature, non ut heres, quia ille qui non percipit ex bonis defuncti ultra sic debitum iure nature non dicitur heres, ut scribit F<ranciscus> de Aretio in l. defuncti C. si in frau. patro."
[88] Bencivenni, fol. 20v; but on 17r he seems to say the opposite; Salvetti, fols. 76v-77v.
[89] Bencivenni, fol. 20v.
[90] Salvetti, fol. 76v: "Legittimam an posset petere repudians hodie non, quia illam habet iure hereditario ... et de hereditate non potest quis habere partem cum habeat totam.... In uno tamen casu potest habere legitimam et hereditatem obmictere si habet substitutum vulgarem

Whether or not repudiation precluded legitima, it did not preclude some other modes in which a son indeed followed in his father's footsteps. Repudiation did not prevent a son from acting in the place of his father in making peace – formally ending a feud with others by an act of peace (*pax*). A son who repudiated the patrimony of a father matriculated in a guild also still enjoyed the privilege and honor his father had had in the guild, because that was not something hereditary (although Bencivenni did not indicate why it was not).[91] The same could be said of the privileges and honors of citizenship, as we will see.

Legislation, Fraud, and the Misuse of Repudiation

Registration of legal acts did not prevent abuse, especially if the registries were not consistently kept. In 1410, the officials of the Mercanzia found it necessary to rebuke their notaries for the slipshod manner in which they kept the emancipation registry. Perhaps for that reason in part, the Signoria in 1421 initiated a separate, second required registry of emancipations, thereafter kept in parallel with the repudiation registry (with the occasional mistaken entry of one or the other in the wrong book).[92]

Legislative concern with fraudulent use of legal devices certainly did not end in 1355. Continued economic and fiscal problems in the fifteenth century called forth a host of laws intended to promote or protect the markets and civic revenues. These ranged from major fiscal measures, such as the establishment of the public fund for dowries in 1425 and the institution of the catasto in 1427, to pieces of legislation protecting creditors.[93] Examples of the latter include an enactment of 1408, at the behest of the Mercanzia, to register business partnerships so as to keep partners from being totally bankrupted by the actions of one of them. Another law of 1467 inserted

---

et est gravatus legatis.... Veritas est quod non est heres proprie, quia sibi non convenit nomen heredis ut subcedat in universum quod defunctus habuit, tamen habetur heredis loco quo ad quedam."

[91] Bencivenni, fol. 20v.

[92] On all this, see my *Emancipation*, 37–39, and "Multorum Fraudibus Occurrere'" 315–16.

[93] On these institutions, see Julius Kirshner and Anthony Molho, "The Dowry Fund and the Marriage Market in Early Quattrocento Florence," *Journal of Modern History* 50 (1978): 403–38; Molho, *Marriage Alliance in Late Medieval Florence* (Cambridge: Harvard University Press, 1994), 27–79; David Herlihy and Christiane Klapisch-Zuber, *Les toscans et leurs familles* (Paris: Fondation Nationale des Sciences Politiques, 1978), 28–30, 45–46; Elio Conti,, *L'imposta diretta a Firenze nel Quattrocento (1427–1494)* (Rome: Istituto Storico Italiano per il Medio Evo, 1984); Molho, "L'amministrazione del debito pubblico a Firenze nel quindicesimo secolo," in *I ceti dirigenti nella Toscana del Quattrocento* (Florence: Papafava, 1987), 191–207; id., "Fisco ed economia a Firenze alla vigilia del Concilio," *Archivio storico italiano* 148 (1990): 807–44; Nicolai Rubinstein, *The Government of Florence under the Medici (1434 to 1494)* (Oxford: Oxford University Press, 1966), esp. 88–104.

the Signoria into the process of apportioning a bankrupt's assets among his creditors (at a moment when one spectacular bankruptcy was beginning to reverberate through the city).[94] Continual economic and fiscal problems called forth such periodic attempts to close loopholes in response to never ending attempts by Florentines to find such loopholes and crawl through them, to the detriment of their creditors and the city's government.

Repudiation of inheritance became the object of some particular concern in the middle decades of the Quattrocento. The measures enacted pursued a number of threads consequent on repudiation – unclaimed estates, mothers' estates, and fiscal liabilities.

Unclaimed Estates

A law of 1439 ordered that all *hereditates iacentes* (unclaimed) from the past three years, that were not formally accepted within four months, were to be considered "renuntiate." Anyone accepting such a hereditas had one month from that date to give notice to the councils and have it inscribed in the same books used to record repudiations. In future, all other hereditates iacentes were to be considered renounced three years from the date of death. The law was not to be construed to harm the rights of minors or to prevent creditors from seeking judicial remedy to make a potential heir commit one way or the other sooner than three years. Nor did this law claim to stand in the way of one passed the previous November, mandating payment of fiscal obligations from hereditates iacentes.[95] It was quite probably such fiscal obligations that then may have encouraged the spreading problem of vacant estates.[96]

On the face of it, this law was terribly flawed and posed serious problems. The statute on heirs' obligations gave them fifteen days, if they were present on the estate. Ius commune generally gave one year. Here three years were allowed. This law also resulted in tacit repudiation, whereas the statute on heirs' liabilites resulted in tacit aditio – not to mention the confusion of enrolling such aditiones in the books of repudiations (though none appear there). This law needed fixing only two years later. The new law of 1441 declared that estates of minors were exempt from the law of 1439. In effect, that exemption meant that minors could not be forced to act about an estate during their minority, as ius commune had protected them, and that they had four years to deliberate after reaching adult age. The new law also exempted estates coming from women (mother, grandmother, sister, aunt) from the three year rule enacted in 1439.[97]

---

[94] On these see Kuehn, "Multorum Fraudibus Occurrere," 317–19. For a brief but lucid presentation of Piero di Cosimo de' Medici's role in precipitating a financial crisis, see Christopher Hibbert, *The House of Medici: Its Rise and Fall* (New York: Morrow, 1975), 103–4.
[95] ASF, Provvisioni registri 130, fols. 87r-v (12 June 1439).
[96] See John Najemy, *A History of Florence, 1200–1575* (Oxford: Blackwell, 2006), 256–61.
[97] ASF, Provvisioni registri 132, fols. 168r-v (17 August 1441). The passage is: "Quod lex et provisio de qua supra fit mentio ullo modo, forma, iure vel causa conprehendat aliquem pupillum

Legislation, Fraud, and the Misuse of Repudiation 73

The exemptions established in 1441 were minor problems compared to the one provoking the next legislative correction. In July 1445, the councils noted that

> often it happens that, not withstanding said law, many to whom said hereditates devolve, after three years and four months, nevertheless accept them by public instrument, and under this pretext they exchange monte credits, extract payment from the estate's debtors, and collect the income from the estate's assets; and later, when confronted by the estate's creditors, they say that by force of the said law they are understood to have repudiated and so said aditio was not valid. And it seems absurd and inconvenient that they want to enjoy the benefits and not the burdens, against the intent of said provision and all right of law.[98]

In future, all who did a formal aditio after three years and four months would be considered true heirs to the estate and held liable for all debts and duties and could not allege any tacit repudiation. Those clever Florentines had taken a law designed to reassure creditors and turned it into its opposite, a device that hurt creditors. The key was the time permitted. That was what allowed strategizing, or indeed was the strategy.[99] The fundamental statute had recognized the possible exploitation of time limits implicit in its allowance of a mere fifteen days. The legislation of 1439 had failed to appreciate that.

In the end, the law of 1439 was so fundamentally flawed it was totally thrown out. After addressing a number of related issues, the magistrates in April 1477 decided that so many lawsuits and other difficulties had resulted, confounding the basic statute on liabilities of heirs, that it was best just to abrogate the law of 1439. Not only were they desirous of eliminating opportunities for fraud, they were also highly reluctant to see anyone pronounced an heir merely by failure to appear in court to answer a creditor's summons, which might be the consequence of a too liberal application of the statute.[100]

---

   aut adultum durante sibi minori etate et annis quatuor postea immediate futuris.... Item non conprehendat ut supra nec si extendat ad aliquam hereditatem matris aut avie seu sororis carnalis ex eodem patre sive matertere vel amite."
98 ASF, Provvisioni registri 136, fols. 91v-92r (10 July 1445): "sepe accidit quod non obstante dicta lege [of 1439] plurime ad quos deferentur post triennium et quatuor menses nichilominus adeunt dictas hereditates per publicum instrumentum, et sub hoc pretextu permutant credita montium, exigunt a debitoribus hereditariis, et fructus percipiunt ex substantia hereditatis, et deinde conventi a se contra illos dicentes se intelligi repudiasse vigore dicte legis et dictam aditionem non valere, quod quidem videtur absurdum et inconveniens, ut velint sentire commoda et non onera, contra mentem dicte provisionis et omne iuris debitum."
99 The importance, indeed necessity, of time for social and familial strategies, is a point cogently made by Pierre Bourdieu, *Outline of a Theory of Practice*, trans. Richard Nice (Cambridge: Cambridge University Press, 1977), 6.
100 ASF, Provvisioni registri 168, fols. 24r-25v (15 April 1477): "et informati quod dicte tres provisiones [1439, 1441, 1445] circa hereditates iacentes facte fuerunt ad petitionem aliquorum civium quibus et dispositio et mutationes proprie plurimum proderant et fuerunt causa multarum litium et expensarum propter eorum dubitates, quas tollere cupientes et addere

The right of the heir to decide to accept or reject an estate was upheld against any rule to force a decision, one way or the other. As for hereditates iacentes, they were to remain, it seems, a problem well beyond any legislative fix.

Games Kin Play

The abrogation of the law concerning hereditates iacentes was in fact part of a wave of legislative emendations addressing a number of different judicial problems and interpretations, beginning in March 1477.[101] The first enactment began with rhetorical flourishes and classical references aimed at the central statute in the Florentine scheme of intestate inheritance. The legislation proclaimed that it wanted to provide justice, "which preserves and enriches cities" ("que civitates conservat et auget"). Its means of doing so was to ensure that testaments be observed – a forceful statement of the moral weight of testaments – in regard to what testators left to women.[102] It was a long and difficult, even potentially sensitive matter.[103] The legislators

---

aliqua statuto ordinario communis Florentie sub rubrica de heredibus et hereditate debitoris conveniendis nequa fraus possit in damnum alterius committi per quod statutum provideatur.... Quod stante firmo dicto statuto de heredibus et hereditate debitoris conveniendis in omnibus suis partibus, dum limitatione tamen infrascripta, dicte tres provisiones de hereditate iacente disponentes ... a principio earum usque in finem intelligantur ex nunc ex toto revocate et penitus abrogate et anullate sint et esse intelligantur, nec amplius citendantur aut observentur."

[101] Note here the observations of Andrea Zorzi, "Ordinamenti e politiche giudiziarie in età laurenziana," in *Lorenzo il Magnifico e il suo tempo*, ed. Gian Carlo Garfagnini (Florence: Olschki, 1992), 147–61, at 154–57; and the parallel and contemporary legislative concerns investigated by Antonella Astorri, "Note sulla Mercanzia fiorentina sotto Lorenzo dei Medici: Aspetti istituzionali e politici," *Archivio storico italiano* 150 (1992): 965–93, at 971–80.

[102] ASF, Provvisioni registri 168, fols. 1r-4v (18 March 1476/7). Beyond asserting a general concern that the statute "observetur inviolabiliter absque aliqua sinistra aut mala interpetratione prout iacet et scriptum est ad unquem," the law addressed a clause in the statute on intestacy that ordered women to remain content with what was left them in a will by a testator whose descendants would exclude those women on intestacy (by the earlier terms of the same statute). The "maior et clarior" interpretation now offered was that it did not matter if the testator did or did not have sons or male relatives who by terms of the statute excluded those women: "dummodo talis testator ... habeat tales coniunctos ex linea masculina qui excludat filias feminas et descendentes earum de successione ab intestato secundum formam supradicti statuti."

[103] Lauro Martines has it that in March 1477 Lorenzo de' Medici was specifically targeting the Pazzi in retaliation for wresting the papal alum mining monopoly from him nine months earlier. The immediate target was the estate that seemingly was to fall to Beatrice Borromei, wife of Giovanni de' Pazzi. Repudiations from years before had left the property to her, until the legislators stepped in (Lauro Martines, *April Blood: Florence and the Plot against the Medici* [Oxford: Oxford University Press, 2003], 106, and citing some of Lorenzo's letters regarding motive). Indeed, it seems that repudiations by Giovanni, Carlo, and Lodovico d'Antonio Borromei of their father, added to the repudiation by the monastery of San

did not stop there, however. They advanced two interesting enactments concerning repudiation. The first began by noting a general tendency for fraudulent activity to take the form of forestalling creditors through hidden legal acts that lodged ownership of property with others.[104] Specifically mentioned were secretive gifts to children or other kin and formal repudiations in which the property was actually held under pretext of *fideicommissum* or some other legal right. The law bemoaned that creditors were deceived. Women lost their dowries. People withdrew from trade ("si ritraggono dal trafficare") or were too afraid simply to buy or sell pieces of property. A situation thus described by the *provvisione* with terms like "dannoso" and "non honesto" cried out for remedy. The one hit upon was overly ambitious. Every alienation of landed property or any *immobilia* was to be reported to the gabelle officials, who already collected duties on contracts and seemed the logical ones to keep records of land transfers.[105] Provisions in wills, codicils, gifts in view of death (*causa mortis*), which otherwise remained unknown while the owner was still alive and could always change his or her mind, were also to be reported, as well as all alienations of property over the previous ten years on which some obligation (that is, part of the purchase price) was still outstanding. Such acts not notified within the requisite time limits were null and void. Recognizing to some degree the magnitude of the recording task they were demanding and the mountain of information it could generate, the lawmakers ordered that one notary of the gabelle be deputed to this alone.

Such a monumental undertaking, it seems, was bound to fail. As the law itself mentioned repudiation, which was already registered, one can see why

---

Salvatore of Settimo, may have positioned the property nominally to Pazzi's wife (RE 19, fols. 11 [4 October 1464], 14 [10 November 1464], and 41 [26 September 1465]). Bartolomea and Giuliano di Giuliano di Piero Borromei also repudiated their father ([RE 19, fol. 205 (17 August 1470)]). Lack of timely repudiation to Beatrice's benefit would pass the property to creditors, including the city, according to the new law of 1477. If, on the other hand, the law of October 1476 (to be discussed) seeking to draw out tax-shirking heirs or land them in the speculum was designed to ensnare the Pazzi, it is worth noting that only one Pazzi repudiation took place during that intense burst of repudiating activity at the end of the year (Jacopo Pazzi's repudiation of Piero di Domenico Lamberteschi [RE 20, fol. 162 (20 December 1476)]).

[104] ASF, Provvisioni registri 168, fols. 4v-5v (20 March 1476/7): "secondo il ricordi di sani cittadini provedere a molte fraude le quali si commettono per fare occulti molti contracti pe' quali e beni inmobili di qualche cittadino sono alienati o obligati o in modo legati che non se ne può disporre liberamente et nondimeno per essi così occulti sono tali cittadini giudicati possessori di tali beni et è loro creditto buono somme." On this law, see Kuehn, "Multorum Fraudibus Occurrere," 320-21.

[105] On this form of tax and Florentines' modes of evasion, see Charles M. de La Roncière, "Indirect Taxes or 'Gabelles' at Florence in the Fourteenth Century: The Evolution of Tariffs and Problems of Collection," in *Florentine Studies: Politics and Society in Renaissance Florence*, ed. Nicolai Rubinstein (Evanston: Northwestern University Press, 1968), 140-92.

it was thought that registration would solve the problem. But repudiation was something on the minds of these legislators in another way.

Nine days later, as those priors came to the end of their two-month term of office, they issued another *provvisione* that in fact proposed three distinct revisions to portions of the second book of the city's statutes. These problems, like that of property left to women in wills, had been reported to them from the courtrooms of Florence. Judges had issued variant rulings and consulting jurists had run across difficulties and uncertainties in interpreting statutes. Two revisions of statutes they proposed led to clarification regarding the obligations of unemancipated sons and the dowry rights of wives of fugitive bankrupts (*cessantes et fugitivi*). A third revision involved repudiation, which had led to problems regarding mothers' estates.

A factor at work here was the increasingly common practice of repudiating the paternal estate but accepting the maternal (at a time of escalating dowry values). There was general awareness of the practice. When a Savonarolan partisan, Domenico Cecchi, penned his vision of reforms for Florence in 1496, he lamented the fact that large dowries were destroying families and that when a widow had a large dowry it might force repudiation of the father's estate.[106] What the legislators found in 1477 was a disturbing pattern that they tried to fix:

[I]n law there is dispute whether estates of women left on intestacy or by testament can be repudiated at any time after a year, provided they were not entered into by public instrument by anyone else; and although the jurists decide in different ways, still the common opinion holds that it can be repudiated, and in this way decisions are produced by which creditors are much defrauded, because many to whom hereditates of women belong, after ten or fifteen years and more, when they had contracted a large debt with creditors, renounce the estates of said women, which are commonly almost always lucrative, and very often they secretly bargain with their brothers or sisters or others to whom such a repudiated hereditas devolves by intestacy or by testament. If they have not been repudiated after a year from the date of transmission by him to whom they are transmitted and have not been reported in the palace of the Signori and the other three councils, as must be done with other repudiations, then after one year all rights of said hereditas will belong to the creditors for satisfaction of all their credits, as if they had been entered into by those to whom they devolved and had not been repudiated; and the same terms will be observed by anyone who may be bankrupt at the time of repudiation or who became bankrupt within one year after said repudiation for four months.[107]

---

[106] Umberto Mazzone, *"El buon governo": Un progetto di riforma generale nella Firenze savonaroliana* (Florence: Olschki, 1978), 190.

[107] ASF, Provvisioni registri 168, fols. 12v–13v (29 March 1477): "Et quia de iure disceptatur an hereditates mulierum delate ab intestato sive ex testamento alicui possint elapso anno quandocunque repudiari cum per publicum instrumentum non fuerint adite. Et quamvis varie sententiant doctores, tamen communis opinio tenet quod possit, et in hanc partem feruntur sententie ex quo creditores multum defraudantur, quia multi ad quos spectant alique

Legislation, Fraud, and the Misuse of Repudiation 77

The role of the jurists, who followed ius commune into results harmful to creditors, is one interesting revelation of this law, which nonetheless retained a respect for ius commune. Notably, it did not shorten the period of deliberation to less than a year. It was simply intent on making one year an effective and closed limit. It was very aware of the sorts of collusion that could transpire among kin around a repudiation – perhaps because some of the legislators had tried it themselves?

A few months later, July 1477, the Consiglio del Cento carried the concern with procedural delays and the potential for fraud such strategizing allowed to a new level. The immediate desire was to bring lawsuits to quick resolution and preclude deceptive practices ("ad abbreviandum lites et tollendum subterfugia") that were occurring when heirs looked to the division of property. Parties were variously denying that there was common property to be divided or resolutely refusing to propose arbitrators to oversee the division or agree on those proposed as arbitrators. While it might seem that active merchants would be inclined to move quickly to separation of holdings and individualized ownership, so that the woes of one person did not bring down the rest, it was also the case that Florentines were desirous of patrimonial unity and continuity, at least delaying the inevitable.[108] The Cento fashioned a complicated piece of legislation that, while setting time limits and alternative modes of selection of arbitrators, also had enough holes in it that it probably had little effect. Still, this enactment too indicates that there was awareness that delay meant confusion and confusion allowed for fraud.[109]

Taxing Repudiators

Most Florentine citizens had one insistent creditor in the fifteenth century – the government. They tried to take advantage of time to avoid its demands, as the government admitted in a law of 1476. Thirty years before, another law had established that anyone not paying his taxes and loans to the government

---

hereditates mulierum post decem vel quindecim annos et ultra, cum multum debitum contraxerunt cum creditoribus renuntiant hereditatibus dictarum mulierum que communiter sunt lucrose fere semper et persepe occulte paciscuntur cum eis sive fratribus sive sororibus sive aliis ad quos talis hereditas repudiata defertur ab intestato seu ex testamento alicui masculo. Si non fuerint repudiate ultra annum a die delationis per eum cui sunt delate, et non fuerint notificate in palatio dominorum et aliorum trium consiliorum prout de aliis repudiationibus debet fieri, pertineant elapso dicto anno ad creditores omnia iura dictarum hereditatum pro satisfactione eorum creditorum in omnibus et per omnia et ac si per tales quibus deferebatur et non fuerant repudiate, ut supra, adite fuissent; et idem observetur in similibus hereditatibus que intra dictum annum repudiarentur ab aliquo qui esset cessans tempore repudiationis vel cessasset intra dictum annum post dictam repudiationem per quatuor menses." Here also see Kuehn, "Multorum Fraudibus Occurrere," 321–23.
[108] See Bartolomé Clavero, "Dictum beati: A proposito della cultura del lignaggio," *Quaderni storici* 86 (August 1994): 335–63, at 336–37.
[109] ASF, Consiglio del Cento, Registri 2, fols. 19r-20r.

could not hold office.¹¹⁰ But, as the legislators and advisers noted in 1476, numerous heirs long delayed paying duties owed by a deceased other than their father. Their officeholding rights were not derived from such a person, so they did not face having their names inscribed in the list (*speculum*) of delinquent taxpayers.¹¹¹ The Signoria and councils enacted that anyone who was heir, until he had repudiated and notified them of it, as long as he did not also abstain from that estate in reality, was liable for all obligations to the city arising on a nonpaternal estate, as if the debts were his own. Anyone who came forth by the end of December (it being October 19), or thereafter within three months of the de cuius's death, and who repudiated with proper notification would avoid being added to the *speculum*. The notary of the *speculum*, monte officials, or others with oversight of finances were expected "diligenter inquirere" into these estates and place in the *speculum* any names that came to their attention. No heir who failed to pay the estate's duties would be allowed to hold office. Heirs could face a fine of 500 florins, a quarter of which would go to the person who turned them in (*notificator*), and be fully treated as a debtor in the *speculum*.¹¹²

One effect of this law was a flurry of repudiations and registrations at the end of December 1476 – showing us both that Florentines took this law seriously and that they largely procrastinated as long as they could (strategizing to the end?). Presumably, those Florentines who repudiated an hereditas, and thus its fiscal obligations, retained their officeholding rights (as long, of course, as they met their own obligations).

The previous law of 1446 had affirmed the link between fiscal obligations and capacity to hold office, and the law of 1476 had brought the relationship closer. The capacity to hold office flowed from fathers to their sons, as long as fiscal obligations were met. But what of repudiation? It severed the successoral link between fathers and sons, which could include the fiscal obligations that coincided with officeholding rights. In a precursive way, the issue came before the councils in April 1482. Luca di Salvestro degli Albizzi sought legislative indulgence in view of his repudiation of his father's hereditas, which had left him *sine onere*. Monte officials were directed to assess Luca a fitting fiscal contribution, not less than what his father's had been, and have his name entered in the *prestanza* registers. By these means, Luca would then have met, in his own name, the fiscal tests for officeholding eligibility.¹¹³

Sons who repudiated their father's inheritance, thus breaking the continuity in fiscal obligations and officeholding, were given a period of months

---

¹¹⁰ ASF, Provvisioni registri 137, fol. 60r-v (6 May 1446).
¹¹¹ See Anthony Molho, *Florentine Public Finances in the Early Renaissance, 1400–1433* (Cambridge: Harvard University Press, 1971), 104–5.
¹¹² ASF, Provvisioni registri 167, fols. 164r-65r (19 October 1476).
¹¹³ ASF, Provvisioni registri 173, fols. 18v-19v (26 April 1482).

to arrange to have fiscal obligations and accounts set in their own names. Once they had done so, but not before, they were eligible for office. As a number of their fathers were, in fact, in debt to the city, having failed to meet their obligations (and such debts being a good reason to repudiate an estate as damnosa), the sons were being given the opportunity to start with a clean slate of their own. But they were also being "caught" – the commune hoped – so they met tax duties and did not manage both to hold office (because not inscribed in the *speculum* in their own names) and not pay taxes (that fell on the deceased and repudiated father).[114] It was assumed, of course, that the repudiation was otherwise registered and valid.

Inheritance thus emerges as another arena in which it is true to say that "although modern liberal paradigms have taught us to think of homes as private and streets as public, and of sex, marriage, and family as aspects of 'private life,' thinking in this way obscures our understanding of late-medieval society."[115] Too much rode on inheritance, for the heirs and legatees, but also for so many others, to permit all calculations regarding it to be merely private. The impact of repudiation on fiscal revenues and officeholding eligibility seems to be an area of sensible interest for a government. Problems of fraud, continuities in markets, and the passage of titles across generations likewise seem to be subjects of clear interest to governors and legislators. In these regards, Florence was not alone among the cities of Tuscany or the rest of north and central Italy. Florence may have been unique, however – only extensive research on a number of other cities will demonstrate this – in attempting to discipline repudiation for civic purposes while allowing it legal play for patrimonial (family) purposes.

Judging from the legislative record, Florence's rulers were more successful in affecting behavior when the goal of that behavior was more clearly in their control. Eligibility for public office was an effective stick to wield. Eligibility was checked every time (that is, every few months) offices were filled. The broader goal of safeguarding creditors from fraudulent use of repudiation was not so easily met. Voiding an act like repudiation – for failure to register or for continued possession of property – could only occur whenever it finally, if ever, came to light. The less direct or overt the inheritance connection – hence the problem with maternal estates and *hereditates iacentes* – the harder it was to bring deceit and fraud to light. Time might work to the benefit of those who simply hid their actions as best they could.

The constant legislative concern with fraudulent practices is also revealing of the character of Florentine "civil society" in the era in which power fell increasingly into fewer hands, ultimately those of the Medici. Katherine Lynch, drawing on the ideas of Robert Putnam, has argued that in Western

---

[114] As per Strozzi in ASF, Carte strozziane, 3rd ser., 41/14, fols. 192r-97v.
[115] Shannon McSheffrey, "Place, Space, and Situation: Public and Private in the Making of Marriage in Late-Medieval London," *Speculum* 79 (2004): 960–90, at 986.

Europe, under the impetus of Church teachings and other initiatives, there arose a valuative and practical space of social interaction that was outside the domain of kinship and family.[116] Voluntary associations, as of craftsmen or neighbors, or for charitable goals, took their place alongside kin structures in Western European cities. Habits of association utilizing what Putnam characterizes as "weak ties" (those with family members and close friends being, in contrast, "strong ties") made for better government and stronger economies.[117] A civic cooperation, solidarity, and public-spiritedness results, the proving ground for which, according to Putnam, was the urban communes of northern and central Italy. There one sees the precocious development of governmental institutions, guilds, confraternities. There a complex economy grew and credit was invented. But there too – and this is the problem raised initially in this chapter and elsewhere throughout this book – citizens (at least those of Florence) were doing their best to skirt laws and creditors, mocking or at least undermining trust and credit.

To use Putnam's influential terminology, repudiation of inheritance could be said to have reasserted the strong vertical prerogatives of family over the civic, horizontal (and "weak") ties of credit. To employ another terminology, repudiation could seem to be a tool in the service of an "amoral familism" maximizing short-term household advantage and assuming others would do likewise, rather than acceding to outside claims and demands.[118] Thus, repudiation furnished occasions when outside authorities (legislative bodies, courts of law) had to step in.

---

[116] Katherine A. Lynch, *Individuals, Families, and Communities in Europe, 1200–1800: The Urban Foundations of Western Society* (Cambridge: Cambridge University Press, 2003), 212–21. Her sense of the Church's role in restricting the domain of kinship runs parallel to that of Jack Goody, *The European Family: An Historico-Anthropological Essay* (Oxford: Blackwell, 2000), who points to the ecclesiastical stance on adoption and close marriage as restricting inheritance and family continuity.

[117] Robert D. Putnam, *Making Democracy Work: Civic Traditions in Modern Italy* (Princeton: Princeton University Press, 1993), esp. 86–91, 174–76. But note also the cogent critiques of his concepts offered by Florentine historians: Gene A. Brucker, "Civic Traditions in Premodern Italy," *Journal of Interdisciplinary History* 39 (1999): 357–77, reprinted in his *Living on the Edge in Leonardo's Florence*, 22–42, and Samuel K. Cohn, Jr., "La storia secondo Robert Putnam," *Polis* 8 (1994): 315–24. A volume of essays grappling with Putnam's approach is in press: Nicholas Terpstra, Mark Jurdjevic, and Nicholas Eckstein, eds, *Sociability and Its Discontents: Civil Society, Social Capital, and Their Alternatives in Early Modern Europe* (Brussels: Brepols).

[118] Edward Banfield, *The Moral Basis of a Backward Society* (Chicago: Free Press, 1958). Putnam largely accepts Banfield's characterization for the less civic and less wealthy south of Italy, in contrast to the north (*Making Democracy Work*, 88, 91). Banfield's work has been criticized for failing to take the observed behaviors as an effective adaptation to conditions, but more so for the assumption that a society should rest on an absence of self-interested motivation. See William Muraskin, "The Moral Basis of a Backward Sociologist: Edward Banfield, the Italians, and the Italian-Americans," *American Journal of Sociology* 79 (1974): 1484–96.

There are several ways to look at repudiation in this context. First, what of the perfectly licit and sincere repudiation? There were too many debts on the estate. The legalities were all appropriately attended to. Could we not say that there the strong ties of kinship had failed in some sense, making the cut off of weaker ties of credit necessary, inevitable, or at least plausible? Even other strong ties might be undermined, as obligations falling on estates were highly likely to involve the claims of kin. At the same time, repudiation may have been an act to save what was left of family, to meet some demands, and to remain in touch with more distant kin, who fell next in line as heirs.[119]

What of the sneaky and deceitful uses of repudiation that called forth so much sustained legislative attention? Were these not immoral, leave alone amoral? Were these not a betrayal of trust and destructive of credit, economic and social? Clearly, they had that quality in the eyes of the legislators. For those who exploited repudiation in that manner, it was something else perhaps. It was a way to stay in the game and score points in relation to their neighbors. It was a means of recovering, on the stage where they had some control, the losses and uncertainties arising from wars, diseases, weather, and all else that undercut earning or ate up income. The repudians, neither heir nor stranger, neither owner nor outsider, could exist in a marginal condition, for whatever time he could manage. The failed law of 1439 only gave more time and uncertainty to play with in regard to the hereditas left iacens. Ingenuity and cleverness, as well as secretiveness, marked these deceptive practices. In a city that notably spawned a literature of private account books and family records and a narrative tradition of tales of trickery, deceptive use of repudiation fit in nicely.[120]

---

[119] Note comments by David I. Kertzer, "Urban Research in Italy," in *Urban Life in Mediterranean Europe: Anthropological Perspectives*, ed. Michael Kenny and David I. Kertzer (Urbana: University of Illinois Press, 1983), 53–75, esp. at 60–62.

[120] For a revealing analysis using a tale of Boccaccio, see John A. Marino, "Economic Idylls and Pastoral Realities: The 'Trickster Economy' in the Kingdom of Naples," *Comparative Studies in Society and History* 24 (1982): 211–34.

3

Repudiation and Inheritance

Inheritance in Florentine Family Records

Florentine sons knew that their futures depended in large part on what their fathers left them – not just houses, lands, and other tangible assets, but kinship and patronage connections, political rights and business opportunities, and the elusive sense of esteem and status captured in terms such as *onore*, *onestà*, *vergogna*, or *fama* that graced so much of Florentine discourse. For their part, daughters too knew that their dowries (which were generally, if not strictly so in legal terms, their inheritance share) set their futures as wives or as nuns, as did those same social ties and qualities their brothers looked to. In the poorer families, there was less to expect on the death of one's parents, less to bind the generations to each other. Still, for them too inheritance could be important.

In comparison to other Italian communities, notably in contrast to Venice, Florence went to an extreme to emphasize the masculine and patrilinear (agnatic) nature of kinship in inheritance. That linearity left Florentine women with, formally, a more restricted sphere of legal agency, while it also obscured their role in the transmission of lineage identity. Thus, ties of neighborhood and patronage figured more obviously in Florentines' self-constructions than did the useful ties with cognatic kin, about which Venetians seem to have been more open.[1] Mechanisms of linear inheritance, and means to avoid them (namely repudiation), may well have carried more meaning and utility in Florence than many other communities.

There was no shortage of advice in Florence as to gaining and preserving wealth and honor. And in accord with a theme prominent in the era of plagues, there was also no shortage of advice on how to prepare for death

---

[1] The literature on women and families in Florence and Venice is vast. A nice overview with many references is E. Igor Mineo, "Stati e lignaggi in Italia nel tardo medioevo: Qualche spunto comparativo," *Storica* 2 (1995): 55–82.

and see to one's affairs.[2] Quite often, this advice was contained in family account books and diaries, overtly addressed by the author to his sons. This was a genre of vernacular writing that peculiarly flourished in Florence, though it is also found elsewhere.[3]

There is perhaps no more eloquent testimony to the Florentine sense of inheritance of property, name, status, and honor, than the pages of Giovanni di Pagolo Morelli's *Ricordi* dedicated to sketching out his ancestors. He gave account of Morello di Giraldo, about whom more was known than about any Morelli before him because of what he had inherited ("le redità de' suoi passati") and his own skill in gaining more. There was Pagolo di Bartolomeo, who, due to inheritance, had to contend with lawsuits and other demands arising from the usuries of Calandro Morelli. In his own case, as Giovanni was left at a young age without a father, he recorded in great detail the seven hardships that befell such fatherless children and threatened their inheritance and future standing in the community.[4]

Beyond the undoubted dangers of rapacious kin and guardians using the opportunity to plunder the inheritances of youngsters left fatherless, Morelli saw a consistent danger in the inevitable expenses of settling a deceased father's estate. Expanding on the fourth of the seven hardships fatherless children faced,[5] he explained,

---

[2] Alberto Tenenti, *Il senso della morte e l'amore della vita nel Rinascimento (Francia e Italia)* (Turin: Einaudi, 1957).

[3] On *ricordi* in Florence, see Christian Bec, *Les marchands écrivains: Affaires et humanisme à Florence, 1375–1434* (Paris: Mouton, 1967); P. J. Jones, "Florentine Families and Florentine Diaries in the Fourteenth Century," *Papers of the British School at Rome* 24 (1956): 183–205; Richard Goldthwaite, *Private Wealth in Renaissance Florence* (Princeton: Princeton University Press, 1968); Gian Mario Anselmi, Fulvio Pezzarossa, and Luisa Avellini, *La "memoria" dei mercatores: Tendenze ideologiche, ricordanze, artigianato in versi nella Firenze del Quattrocento* (Bologna: Patron, 1980); Claudia Bastia and Maria Bolognani, *La memoria e la città: Scritture storiche tra Medioevo ed età moderna* (Bologna: Il Nove in Italia, 1995); Angela Cicchetti and Raul Mordenti, *I libri di famiglia*, vol. 1: *Filologia e storiografia letteraria* (Rome: Edizioni di Storia e Letteratura, 1985); Christiane Klapisch-Zuber, "Albero genealogico e costruzione della parentela nel Rinascimento," *Quaderni storici* 86 (1994): 405–80; Anthony Molho, Roberto Barducci, Gabriella Battista, and Francesco Donnini, "Genealogia e parentado: Memorie del potere nella Firenze tardo-medievale, il caso di Giovanni Rucellai," *Quaderni storici* 86 (1994): 365–403; Leonida Pandimiglio, "Libro di famiglia e storia del patriziato fiorentino: Prime ricerche," in *Palazzo Strozzi: Metà millennio, 1489–1989*, ed. Daniela Lamberini (Rome: Istituto della Enciclopedia Italiana, 1991), 138–58; Fulvio Pezzarossa, "La memorialistica fiorentina tra Medioevo e Rinascimento: Rassegna di studi e testi," *Lettere italiane* 31 (1979): 63–90; Giovanni Ciappelli, "Family Memory: Functions, Evolutions, Recurrences," in *Art, Memory, and Family in Renaissance Florence*, ed. Giovanni Ciappelli and Patricia Lee Rubin (Cambridge: Cambridge University Press, 2000), 26–38.

[4] Giovanni di Pagolo Morelli, *Ricordi*, in *Mercanti scrittori: Ricordi nella Firenze tra Medioevo e Rinascimento*, ed. Vittore Branca (Milan: Rusconi, 1986), 101–339, at 123, 141, 165–81.

[5] The first was being fatherless; the second motherless; the third subject to bad guardians.

The fourth loss that the ward receives...is the many expenses that arise after the father's death, as principally the funeral, where great damage can occur. Next, the return of the dowry, because whether the mother or wife of the testator remarries or not, she wants her dowry in her own hands and she wants its proceeds free and clear.[6]

These expenses would arise on any estate, whether or not the father died when his children were young and are prime forms of "circumstantial credit."[7] They are also the kinds of charges that might render an estate damnosa and lead to its repudiation. An example on this score was Michelangelo, who, on the advice of his father, repudiated his uncle, Francesco (as did his father and brothers), in order to avoid his aunt's claim for her dowry. He took a moment, then, from his artistic labors in Rome in the summer of 1508 to repudiate the estate before a Roman notary, and two days later he enclosed the notarial documents in a letter to his brother in Florence. Two weeks later, the Florentine Signoria received notice of all the Buonarroti repudiations.[8]

Beyond such circumstantial credit lay numerous overt debts that constantly threatened the well being of any household. Gene Brucker has remarked on the staggering frequency of business losses and failures that emerge in various Florentine sources. By his estimation, about a score of merchants annually were declared bankrupt by the court of the Mercanzia and had their assets seized. Creditors "usually began to clamor for their money at the first sign of difficulty. Often a merchant's death precipitated a massive rush of his creditors to collect from his embattled heirs."[9] Brucker concludes that uncollectible debts were probably the largest single factor behind business failures in Florence. All these debts rode on a layer of trust, which in turn rested on the ties between parties to transactions. Guilds served to ensure some degree of trust and credit "in a society that had grown too large to generate it through personal ties alone."[10] Records of guilds such as Florence's wool guild are replete with judgments and confiscations for unpaid debts as requested by creditors, who were often also employers of the debtor.[11] The catasto is full of examples of Florentines who listed debts as

---

[6] Morelli, 176.
[7] Daniel Lord Smail, *The Consumption of Justice: Emotions, Publicity, and Legal Culture in Marseille, 1264–1423* (Ithaca: Cornell University Press, 2003), 144.
[8] The proceedings are briefly described in Ross King, *Michelangelo and the Pope's Ceiling* (New York and London: Penguin, 2003), 77. Michelangelo's letter is in *The Letters of Michelangelo*, 2 vols., trans. and ed. E. H. Ramsden, vol. 1: *1496–1534* (Stanford: Stanford University Press, 1963), 46–47. Registration is in RE 26, fol. 157 (11 August 1508).
[9] Gene A. Brucker, *Renaissance Florence* (New York: Wiley, 1969, reprint ed., Berkeley and Los Angeles: University of California Press, 1983), 74–75.
[10] John Najemy, *A History of Florence, 1200–1575* (Oxford: Blackwell, 2006), 41.
[11] Ibid., 159; Franco Franceschi, *Oltre il "Tumulto": I lavoratori fiorentini dell'Arte della Lana fra Tre e Quattrocento* (Florence: Olschki, 1993), esp. 187–88, 228, 280–85.

assets only to declare that the debtors had fled, died, had nothing, or simply would not pay. Such debts were often written off as lost.[12]

On an aggregate level, according to figures developed by Charles de La Roncière, debts thoroughly consumed assets for the lowest 30% of Florence's taxpayers. Debts ate up 40% of the patrimony of the next 20% of households.[13] Debt was also heavy in households with younger heads, whose deaths would thus be doubly tragic.[14] Yet even fairly well-to-do households could carry a significant burden of debt which, while it did not necessarily consume all assets, could still cripple social standing. Florentine courts of the Mercanzia and Podestà faced a continual load of litigation involving debts.[15] Outstanding obligations, generated by business dealings or family matters, including weddings and funerals, could complicate or even threaten inheritances.

For many Florentines, the opening of an account book was occasioned precisely by inheritance, typically from one's father. Matteo di Niccolò Corsini, on his return to Florence from London in 1361, drew up a list of all "our old possessions."[16] Thus, he set out as his starting point all that he had inherited before undertaking patrimonial management himself. Lapo di Giovanni Niccolini likewise initiated his *ricordi* with an account in detail of his father's testament and the subsequent division of the patrimony among the three brothers. His own testament followed, and soon thereafter he gave a recounting of his brother's death and his will.[17] Francesco di Matteo Castellani, with the advantage of being sole male heir to a very wealthy father, inherited landed property that his father too had inherited. But his father also died when Francesco was only twelve years of age, and mounting fiscal pressures ate at his patrimony during his minority.[18] When in 1436 he temporarily lost "our house along the Arno that contained the blessed memory of my father" ("la nostra chasa lung'Arno <che> murò la benedetta memoria di mio padre") for back taxes, Castellani repurchased the property and a family farm at Antella through a San Gimignanese, who was not

---

[12] Franceschi, 76, for examples.
[13] Charles de La Roncière, "Pauvres et pauvreté à Florence au 14ᵉ siècle," in *Études sur l'histoire de la pauvreté (Moyen Âge-16ᵉ siècle)*, ed. Michel Mollat (Paris: Publications de la Sorbonne, 1974), 661–765.
[14] David Herlihy and Christiane Klapisch-Zuber, *Tuscans and Their Families: A Study of the Florentine Catasto of 1427* (New Haven: Yale University Press, 1985), 304.
[15] Laura Ikins Stern, *The Criminal Law System of Medieval and Renaissance Florence* (Baltimore: Johns Hopkins University Press, 1994), 79–86; Samuel K. Cohn, Jr., *The Laboring Classes in Renaissance Florence* (New York: Academic Press, 1980), 191–92.
[16] *I ricordanze dei Corsini*, ed. Armando Petrucci (Rome: Isituto Storico Italiano per il Medio Evo, 1965), 6.
[17] Christian Bec, ed., *Il libro degli affari proprii di casa de Lapo di Giovanni Niccolini de' Sirigatti* (Paris: SEVPEN, 1969), 60–70.
[18] Giovanni Ciappelli, *Una famiglia e le sue ricordanze: I Castellani di Firenze nel Tre-Quattrocento* (Florence: Olschki, 1995), 65–71, 99.

subject to the crushing civic duties he faced. As he prefaced his account, he had "seen how much loss resulted, to lose said goods by such a sale," ("veduto quanto danno mi risultava, di perdere per tale vendita detti beni") for taxes.[19] In an interesting variant, the well-known diary of the apothecary Luca Landucci opens with his apprenticeship but also quickly moves to record his father's acceptance of his mother's (Luca's grandmother) inheritance, more than a year and a half from her death.[20] Because he had already long begun in business, Landucci never indicated when his father died and what he himself inherited.

Florentine fathers were entrusted with the task of assembling and maintaining a patrimony to hand on to their children, or to close kin in the absence of direct descendants. Maintaining the patrimony demanded close attention not only to monetary and commercial transactions of one's own but also to one's children's education, career, and marital choices. Ideally, the energies and loyalties of all members of a household were marshaled behind the task of gaining and maintaining, and therewith preserving and transmitting, family wealth and honor. In fact, this ideal was more likely to be realized in elite families, whereas in less affluent families sons had to operate with a certain autonomy from their fathers. The threat of a partial or total disinheritance was much more effective when there was in reality something substantial to lose.[21]

Moderate use and careful investment were the keys for the truly expert manager of family property, the *massaio*.[22] In keeping with a society in which wealth was vitally gained in inheritance, it was even thought – at least by the fourteenth-century collector of proverbial wisdom, Paolo da Certaldo – that preservation of wealth was the highest domestic virtue. Because inherited wealth was not gained by one's efforts, it might more easily be spent; thus, its careful preservation was indicative of true virtue.[23] His sentiments

---

[19] Francesco di Matteo Castellani, *Ricordanze*, vol. 1: *Ricordanze A (1436–1459)*, ed. Giovanni Ciappelli (Florence: Olschki, 1992), 64–65.

[20] Luca Landucci, *A Florentine Diary from 1450 to 1516*, trans. Alice de Rosen Jervis, ed. Iodoco del Badia (London: J. M. Dent & Sons; New York: E. P. Dutton, 1927; reprint ed., 1969), 1.

[21] See Christiane Klapisch-Zuber, "La vie domestique et ses conflits chez un maçon bolonais du xve siècle," in *Le petit peuple dans l'Occident médiéval: Terminologies, perceptions, réalités*, Actes du Congrès international, Université de Montréal, 18–23 octobre 1999, ed. Pierre Bogliani, Robert Delort, and Claude Gaurard (Paris: Publications de la Sorbonne, 2002), 485–98, at 495–96. Franceschi, *Oltre il Tumulto*, 314, notes that laborers in wool found their *fideiussores* only about ten percent of the time among their kin, concluding that for these folk "l'ambito familiare tende a ridursi a quello dei parenti più prossimi."

[22] Giovanni Rucellai, *Zibaldone quaresimale*, ed. Alessandro Perosa (London: Warburg Institute, 1960), 16. See also Ruggiero Romano, *Tra due crisi: L'Italia del Rinascimento* (Turin: Einaudi, 1971), 143–48.

[23] Paolo da Certaldo, *Libro di buoni costumi*, in *Mercanti scrittori*, 1–99, at 12–13: "Molto è bella chosa e grande sapere guadangniare il danaio, ma più bella chosa e magiore è saperlo

were echoed two centuries later by Francesco Guicciardini.[24] The celebrated fifteenth-century humanist, Leon Battista Alberti (more properly, one of his dialogic characters, Lionardo), stressed the importance of such virtue when he said it was more important that one know how to suffer poverty than to descend to begging or being enslaved to riches. But the shame of poverty, of loss, colors this entire statement.[25] In fact, Florentines often bolstered such "virtue" with legal clauses in gifts, wills, and other transactions designed to prohibit alienation of vital properties outside the *casa*, whether that meant the household itself or a wider circle of agnatic kin.[26]

One problem was that the presence of more than one son would result in fragmentation of the patrimony across generations. Over time, different branches of a family could face very different material circumstances.[27] Florentines such as Francesco Castellani and Lapo Niccolini kept tabs on uncles and cousins and their continued possession or loss of patrimonial properties.[28] That process began with their own divisions with their brothers, perhaps none of which was more closely charted than that of Ugolino di Niccolò Martelli with his six brothers and half-brothers. One interesting facet of their division, and indicative of the weight of debts and obligations on an estate, was the provision, "per oservare equalità tra lloro," to split proportionately every other debt that had not yet come to light.[29] But such

---

spendere chon misura e dove si conviene. E sapere ritenere e guardare quello che t'è lasciato dal tuo patrimonio o dai altri parenti è sopra le dette virtudi, però che quello che l'uomo non guadangnia è più agevole a spendere che quello che guadangnia con sua faticha e con suo sudore e solecitudine."

[24] Francesco Guicciardini, *Ricordi diari memorie*, ed. Mario Spinella (Rome: Riuniti, 1981), 151; English trans. Mario Domandi, *Maxims and Reflections of a Renaissance Statesman* (New York: Harper & Row, 1965), 50.

[25] Leon Battista Alberti, *I libri della famiglia*, ed. Ruggiero Romano and Alberti Tenenti (Turin: Einaudi, 1969), 65; English trans. Renée Neu Watkins, *The Family in Renaissance Florence* (Columbia: University of South Carolina Press, 1969), 67–68.

[26] Thomas Kuehn, *Emancipation in Late Medieval Florence* (New Brunswick: Rutgers University Press, 1982), 62; id., *Law, Family, and Women: Toward a Legal Anthropology of Renaissance Italy* (Chicago: University of Chicago Press, 1991), 238–57; id., "Vicissitudini di un patrimonio fiorentino del xv secolo," *Quaderni storici* 88 (1995): 43–61. Generally J. P. Cooper, "Patterns of Inheritance and Settlement by Great Landowners from the Fifteenth to the Eighteenth Centuries," in *Family and Inheritance: Rural Society in Western Europe, 1200–1800*, ed. Jack Goody, Joan Thirsk, and E. P. Thompson (Cambridge: Cambridge University Press, 1976), 192–327.

[27] Ciappelli, *Una famiglia e le sue ricordanze*, 41; Francis William Kent, *Household and Lineage in Renaissance Florence: The Family Life of the Capponi, Ginori, and Rucellai* (Princeton: Princeton University Press, 1977), 127–36.

[28] Ciappelli, *Una famiglia*, 112.

[29] Ugolino di Niccolò Martelli, *Ricordanze dal 1433 al 1483*, ed. Fulvio Pezzarossa (Rome: Edizioni di Storia e Letteratura, 1989), 172. The division was not equal, as the sons from Niccolò's second marriage were younger, so they got more but also faced seven ninths of the debts.

divisions did not mean that the different branches of a lineage lost touch with each other or ceased to be involved in, or at least aware of, each others' affairs. Divisions, while responding to social as well as legal rationales, were not indicative of any growing privatization or individualism.[30] In the case of the Martelli, there was even a moment of marked individuation by Carlo that was quickly defused by outside interference. Carlo Martelli bought a palace from the Boni family, in his name and those of other Martelli, but later he had a falling out with his kin. He was unable to take possession of the palace because Lorenzo de' Medici stepped in and alleged exorbitant financial claims against him. Carlo had to declare a large fictitious debt to his brother in order to get access to the house. Lorenzo de' Medici had thus forced him to return in some way to dealing with his kin.[31] This is just one example (repudiation will supply many more) of Florentines' willingness to exploit legal devices in clever ways.

There was a genuine sense of urgency behind all the advice about using and preserving wealth. Alberti captured it in one way, when he began his *Libri della famiglia* with a reminder of all the once-great-and-wealthy Florentine lineages that had fallen on hard times, some disappearing altogether.[32] Outsiders were one clear source of danger to a family. They could not be trusted; their tricks, deceit, and thievery were a constant menace. Even friends were not always faithful. Francesco Castellani, for example, bemoaned the fact that Neri di Gino and Agostino Capponi had interfered in division of a property at Castelvecchio between himself and Michele d'Alberto Castellani. The cost to him was such that he refused to ratify the resulting arbitration agreement.[33] Here two friends had stepped in, ostensibly to help the Castellani brothers, although Francesco failed to see things in that light. Ordinarily, a network of friends and partners could vitally supplement kin, and mutual expectations of gain might adequately serve to prevent cheating and allow trust to grow over a long term.[34]

Threats from within the family also had to be measured. Disobedient, unruly, ungrateful, profligate children or spouses were at times an even greater danger than outsiders to a provident paterfamilias. Lapo Niccolini's complaint about his son Niccolaio and his wasteful ways was only one such.[35] Much conventional advice was aimed at rooting out vice from within the family, keeping wives and children obedient, while seeking

---

[30] See Brenda Preyer, "Planning for Visitors at Florentine Palaces," *Renaissance Studies* 12 (1998): 357–66.
[31] F. W. Kent, *Lorenzo de' Medici and the Art of Magnificence* (Baltimore: Johns Hopkins University Press, 2004), 82.
[32] Alberti, *Libri della famiglia*, 3. See also Kuehn, *Law, Family, and Women*, 162–63.
[33] Castellani, *Ricordanze*, 1: 153–54.
[34] See Ricardo Court, "*Januensis ergo mercator*: Trust and Enforcement in the Business Correspondence of the Brignole Family," *Sixteenth Century Journal* 35 (2004): 987–1003.
[35] Niccolini, *Libro di ricordi*, 136–37.

the good of the household as a whole.[36] The head was to be the prince of the family, carefully watching and assessing each member, "thus providing for the health, peace, and honor of the entire family." And his first concern was to keep the family united, stifling any internal discord.[37]

The repeated warnings about internal discord, coupled with other evidence, shows that in fact such discord within families arose at times and could be quite destructive.[38] Sons could disappoint fathers, and fathers sons. Most obviously destructive were the sorts of conflicts that could erupt among brothers, who had to share or divide the same patrimony.[39] Managing and disposing of a patrimony were vital to family well being and unity and often figured at the heart of family conflicts.

Estate Planning

One way to prepare for death, and thereby also try to keep some control over one's heirs, was to devise a last will and testament. Advice to that effect was common in the era of plagues. Paolo da Certaldo, for example, put it plainly: "Always keep your testament made, and if it should happen that you want to add or remove something, you can make another and annul the first."[40] When such advice is coupled with other admonitions, as those of the Church to see to charitable uses of property and to offer monetary penance for one's sins (whether in purchasing masses, making restitution for usuries, or other immoral forms of gain), and with the noted horror of ancient Romans regarding intestacy (still enshrined in the texts of ius commune), it can seem that the most important, if not in fact all, inheritances devolved by means of a written testament.[41]

A testament by its nature worked an alternative, more individualized scenario to the general inheritance rules of intestacy. In practice, some

---

[36] Kuehn, *Emancipation*, 64–67.
[37] Leon Battista Alberti, *De Iciarchia*, in *Opere volgari*, vol. 2, ed. Cecil Grayson (Bari: Laterza, 1966), 185–305, at 273–74.
[38] Kuehn, *Emancipation*, 67–71; id., "Honor and Conflict in a Fifteenth-Century Florentine Family," *Ricerche storiche* 10 (1980): 287–310.
[39] Kuehn, *Law, Family, and Women*, 37, 48–50.
[40] Paolo da Certaldo, *Libro di buoni costumi*, 24.
[41] Important here are the following: Samuel Kline Cohn, Jr., *Death and Property in Siena, 1205–1800: Strategies for the Afterlife* (Baltimore: Johns Hopkins University Press, 1989); id., *The Cult of Remembrance and the Black Death: Six Renaissance Cities in Central Italy* (Baltimore: Johns Hopkins University Press, 1992); Steven Epstein, *Wills and Wealth in Medieval Genoa, 1150–1250* (Cambridge: Harvard University Press, 1984); E. D. English, "La prassi testamentaria delle famiglie nobili a Siena e nella Toscana del Tre-Quattrocento," in *I ceti dirigenti nella Toscana del Quattrocento*, ed. Riccardo Fubini (Florence: Papafava, 1987), 463–72; Salvatore I. Camporeale, "La morte, la proprietà e 'il problema della salvezza': Testamenti e ultime volontà a Siena dal 1200 al 1800 (considerazioni di storia e storiografia)," *Memorie domenicane* 108 (1991): 381–404.

testaments did little to that scheme, naming as heirs those who would have been heirs by intestacy anyway, adding perhaps only a charitable bequest or funeral instructions. Others worked extreme and complicated variations with numerous legacies and bequests, clauses of substitution and much more.[42] Generally, testators hoped to take advantage of devices not available with intestacy. They could fix the form of their funeral and burial site, memorial masses, and charitable or compensatory provisions for the good of their soul; they could establish bequests (*legata*) to specific persons or institutions of discrete amounts or objects; they could name their heirs (indeed, had to for a will to be valid); they could establish substitutions to their heirs; they could set up conditions or restrictions on the use or disposition of property. To take a few examples, in his testament of 26 January 1412, Jacopo di Vannozzo Bardi not only named his son, Vannozzo, as his heir; he also included a specific bequest of his house on Piazza de' Mozzi to his son (and any future sons and male descendants in the male line to the third degree). If this direct line were to fail for lack of legitimate male descent, the house then went to Jacopo's brother, Simone, and his male descendants "so that said house may perpetually remain among the sons and descendants of said Simone, and so that the aforesaid may have full effect, he prohibited alienation of said house for one hundred years."[43] This combination of fideicommissary substitutions with the prohibition of alienation became the essence of entailed estates that became increasingly common among Florentine patrician lineages.[44]

A more elaborate example from around the same time is the testament of Lorenzo di Totto Gualterotti, who had only recently changed his family name, and, as the terms of the testament show, still considered himself a Bardi.[45] He named five sons as his heirs, substituting them to each other (in fact, one would later repudiate his brother).[46] But he added deeper layers of substitution, should it happen that all five died without legitimate male issue. In that case, he left any daughters, beyond other legata for their dowry, an additional 700 florins (each). If there were any illegitimate sons of his sons,

---

[42] For one outstanding example of interest for its slant on usury, see Lawrin Armstrong, "Usury, Conscience, and Public Debt: Angelo Corbinelli's Testament of 1419," in *A Renaissance of Conflicts: Visions and Revisions of Law and Society in Italy and Spain*, ed. John A. Marino and Thomas Kuehn (Toronto: Centre for Reformation and Renaissance Studies, 2004), 173–240.

[43] ASF, NA 9042, fols. 9r-12r (26 January 1412): "ad hoc ut dicta domus perpetuo sit penes filios et descendentes dicti Simonis, et ad hoc ut predicta plenius effectum habeant, prohibuit alienationem dicte domus hunc ad centum annos."

[44] See Kent, *Household and Lineage*, 136–49.

[45] The Bardi were one of the largest magnate lineages, which eventually saw several branches embrace the legal fiction of renaming and separation. As the clauses of Gualterotti's testament reveal, that fiction did not obliterate all traces of kinship, a point emphasized by Christiane Klapisch-Zuber, *Retour à la cité: Les magnats de Florence, 1340–1440* (Paris: Éditions de l'École des Hautes Études en Sciences Sociales, 2006), 334–35.

[46] RE 13, fol. 82 (20 June 1438).

subsequently legitimated, they became heirs with the duty to pay 700 florins to each daughter. If there were no bastards either, then his heirs were to be Filippo and Andrea di Giovanni d'Andrea Bardi, while their brother, Paolo, was to receive a bequest of 300 florins. If Filippo and Andrea died without legitimate sons, the heirs became the descendents of Pietro Bardi da Vernia for one third, descendents of messer Bindo Bardi for another, and those of Aghinolfo Bardi for the remaining third.[47]

There is sentiment expressed in such wills that cannot be extracted from intestate successions. It is possible to surmise much about feelings regarding kin, for example, in these substitutions. Such feelings could be the generative force behind testaments. Yet, as will become clearer when we examine repudiations, many estates continued to pass in intestacy. Intestacy did not leave behind as much in the way of paper records (though inventories for benefit of heirs can be found), and certainly it could not furnish intriguing glimpses into the thoughts and emotions of testators. But intestacy was a real functioning device of property transmission – and not merely for the humble. Important and wealthy Florentines, Cosimo de' Medici among them, died intestate. They did so not just because death caught them too soon, before they could get around to it. In fact, some of them may have disposed of their property well in advance of death by means of gifts, fictitious sales, dowries, and other devices. The point is that intestacy was not necessarily an accident (death catching someone before making a will). One could deliberately choose to die intestate.

Clearly, some Florentines found intestacy more useful than testaments.[48] For one thing, testaments, or at least features within them, were also subject to challenge, more so than intestacy ever could have been. They were open to dispute on numerous formal grounds or substantively for being "undutiful" (*inofficiosum*).[49] Testamentary inheritance provoked problems generally for two reasons. For one thing, the testament did not render certainty against some presumed uncertainty in intestacy regulations. Far from ensuring "that a person's intentions were impervious to subsequent legal dispute," testaments were the objects of repeated lawsuits in the surviving records of courts, lawyers, and jurists.[50] Rather, by layering a testator's possible

---

[47] NA 9042, fols. 3r-6v (26 June 1411). A slightly different later version is in ibid., fols. 34v-39r (25 February 1416).

[48] Ann Crabb, *The Strozzi of Florence: Widowhood and Family Solidarity in the Renaissance* (Ann Arbor: University of Michigan Press, 2000), 40, notes that within the one wealthy Florentine lineage she studied "more people died without wills than with them."

[49] See Julius Kirshner, "Baldus de Ubaldis on Disinheritance: Contexts, Controversies, *Consilia*," *Ius Commune: Zeitschrift für Europäishce Rechtsgeschichte* 27 (2000): 119–214, at 124–27.

[50] Epstein, *Wills and Wealth*, 13, who nonetheless notes that the jurist Martino da Fano was able to compile a list of ways in which a testament might be challenged. Cohn, *Death and Property*, 129, more simply notes that sixteenth-century Sienese "testators attempted more

multiple (and conflicting?) intentions over intestacy rules, the testament could generate untold forms of uncertainty, notably in relation to legal mechanisms to interpret and validate a testator's intent. Secondly, such uncertainty became the focal point of dispute and litigation from those heirs who saw themselves overly disadvantaged by testamentary terms, and from the potentially wider group of people and even institutions implicated in a testament, with its various bequests, executors, guardians, substituted heirs – all posed against those named heredes universales.[51]

A will could greatly complicate the relatively simple scheme of succession in intestacy. Executors might step in; legacies had to be settled; conditions met; debts and obligations on the estate paid off. A wealthy and powerful man like Cosimo de' Medici faced numerous expectations from individuals and institutions, especially ecclesiastical, such that intestacy may well have appeared an acceptable escape. Comments of other Medici, who also often took the path of intestacy, indicate that they believed they shared a common love and trust and that testaments were unnecessary among them.[52] Giovanni di Matteo Corsini, himself facing grave financial difficulties in the 1420s, well understood the situation when he and another Florentine, Lippozzo di Cipriano Mangioni, were summoned to the sickbed of Giuliano di Bartolo Gini. In their presence, Giuliano informed his son, Benedetto, "that he did not want to make a will for good reason, but he wanted that, if God summoned him, said Benedetto would do certain things after his death." Corsini wrote down what these were, and he and Mangioni were witnesses. This was a sort of will, but unofficial, if not outright illicit. Gini's death would officially result in intestacy, which would mean that no outsider or more distant relative could allege any valid interest (other than contractual debts) in the disposition of his affairs.[53]

The implication in Corsini's account is that Gini's finances were in fact in a bad way. It was necessary to keep some properties or objects out of public

---

carefully than before or afterward to foresee and forestall future lawsuits." In contrast, note the position taken by Lloyd Bonfield, "Developments in European Family Law," in *The History of the European Family*, vol. 1: *Family Life in Early Modern Times, 1500–1789*, ed. David I. Kertzer and Marzio Barbagli (New Haven and London: Yale University Press, 2001), 87–124, esp. 118–20.

[51] Natalie Zemon Davis, *The Gift in Sixteenth-Century France* (Madison: University of Wisconsin Press, 2000), 30–31, suggests that the possible use of testaments to disinherit could make the patrimony seem more gratuitous for the heirs, who then would be bound by the sort of reciprocity accompanying gifts to accept the testament's terms. There may have been something to the moral weight of the testament and estate succession generally. But it is also the case that disinheritance was extremely rare, only available for cause, and very difficult to uphold if challenged. On this, see Kirshner, "Baldus de Ubaldis on Disinheritance."

[52] Note Dale Kent, *Cosimo de' Medici and the Florentine Renaissance: The Patron's Oeuvre* (New Haven and London: Yale University Press, 2000), 242.

[53] Corsini, *Ricordi*, 125–26: "che non voleva fare testamento per buona cagione, ma ben voleva che, se Dio il chiamasse a ssè, ch'el detto Benedetto faciesse dopo la morte sua queste cose."

notice. Corsini himself had no incentive to draw up a will. Instead, he had "from regard to my miserable state and it seeming to me better to leave my sons the house than leave them without it, because it is the support of the family," deeded over to his sister his house in Florence and later his farm at Castello.[54] Thus, he sought to keep his creditors at bay. In fact, the house he deeded over to his sister was already part of a deceptive strategy. He had sold this dwelling a few years before for 700 florins, at which point his three sons had been present to give surety that they would not try to press claims as heirs. At the same time, the sons took the inheritance of their mother, which removed it from their father's hands ostensibly. Two months later, Corsini bought another house, but he first had it stated in the contract of sale that it belonged to Luca di Matteo da Panzano – and three weeks after that had it declared to be his sister's.[55] In either event, it was not overtly legally identified as his and thus supposedly not exposed to his creditors. Posting notice of such skullduggery in one's private account books was one thing; putting it in a public notarized document such as a testament was something else. In a more simple manner, when Lapo Niccolini recorded the passing of his cousin Giovanni di Niccolaio in the plague of 1417, he revealed that there was no testament, as nothing remained of his property but debt ("del suo non rimase nulla se non debito"). His wife and her 900 florin dowry also quickly departed, leaving "the children sleeping on straw, with nothing" ("i decti filgliuoli in sulla palglia, sanza nulla").[56] There was perhaps no reason for someone with nothing to compose a will.

The clauses and restrictions in a will did not necessarily bind the hands of the heirs, if they chose not to be so bound. As J. P. Cooper perceptively remarked in surveying elite inheritance practices throughout early modern Europe, "even the strictest entails needed family cooperation, if they were to be effective. Unless there was cooperation, there were endless opportunities for litigation provided by the need to conjecture and interpret the intentions of dead ancestors."[57] Repudiation was part of an arsenal of choices available to heirs. Repudiation and aditio alert us to the undeniable point that the inheritance process involved the combination of intent of the deceased and intent of the heirs. Strategizing took place on both sides.

The degree to which a testament controlled property and heirs after death was a matter of active interest to Florentines. Consider simply a couple of

---

54 Corsini, *Ricordi*, 131: "per rispetto del cattivo mio stato e parendomi meglio lasciare a' miei figluoli casa che non lasciargli sanza essa, perch'è i ritenimento della famiglia." The farm's ownership had to be hidden as it was "il principale podere dela posesione e venduto quelo guasto ongni cosa."
55 Corsini, *Ricordi*, 127.
56 Niccolini, *Libro di ricordi*, 134–35. Her dowry claim was settled in a subsequent arbitration (142).
57 J. P. Cooper, "Patterns of Inheritance and Settlement by Great Landowners," 297.

stories current in Florence in the period. Paolo da Certaldo told the tale of a Giovanni Cavazza, a wealthy man with two daughters, both of whom he married to noble young men, and upon whom he lavished his goods until he left himself "impoverito," at which point his daughters and sons-in-law ceased to deal with him. The lesson in that turn of events was never to make children the owners of one's property while still alive. But Giovanni Cavazza also got his revenge. He announced that he was going to make a testament, and in the course of a dinner he showed his children a locked chest containing the large sum of 2,000 florins, which he had in fact borrowed from a friend. He told them they would have it all as his heirs as long as they treated him well for the rest of his life, which, of course, they did, bringing him clothing and food and spending time with him. Cavazza then drew up a will leaving various sums to friars and priests, setting funeral instructions, and obligating his daughters and sons-in-law, as his heirs, to carry out the bequests before they could get the keys to the chest from the friars. Following his death, after an honorable life at his children's expense, the heirs eagerly paid out the bequests, obtained the keys, and opened the chest, only to find a club and a brief "testament" proclaiming that Giovanni had been "killed" by it.[58] Cavazza thus shamed his children for how they had treated him when they knew he had nothing left.

Another example, among the *novelle* of Franco Sacchetti, is the story of Basso della Penna, who was abandoned by wife and children when on death's door. His revenge too took the form of a testament, in which he placed a simple bequest that every year on the feast day of San Jacopo in July a large basket of pear halves be left out in a designated place for the flies to devour. The flies were the only ones who had not abandoned him at the moment of death (nothing is said of the notary who presumably drafted this will). If his children failed to do this every year, they would be disinherited and his property go to religious uses. The resulting annual action brought shame ("grande reprensione") to his family. Sacchetti drew the lesson that "such is our love that not only do sons put their lives before their fathers but a good part of them desire their fathers' death to be freer."[59] For both these old men, as long as they had some property (or seemed to, given Cavazza's deception), a testament was a means of control in this life, at least as much so as after it.

Testamentary devices of this sort were not mere literary fictions. Consider briefly the codicil that Paolo di Lapo Niccolini added to his testament in 1450. He left to Bartolomea, wife of Matteo da Romagna, who had wetnursed Paolo's son Jacopo, "the inheritance of the house where I live or where my

---

[58] Paolo da Certaldo, *Libro di buoni costumi*, 78–79, 93–95.
[59] Franco Sacchetti, *Il Trecento Novelle*, ed. Antonio Lanza (Florence: Sansoni, 1984), novella 21, 43–44: "tale è il nostro amore che non che li figliuoli mettessino la vita per li loro padri, ma gran parte desiderano la morte loro per essere più liberi."

family may live" ("la redità della casa ove habito o dove habitasse la mia famiglia"). If she chose to live elsewhere, he left her for life quantities of grain, oil, and wine to be paid every October.

And in case said heirs do not provide said items in said time and manner, I will and bequeath that said Bartolomea may enter into possession (*tenuta*), without the ruling of any court or judge, of one of my farms that is called La Torre in the Val di Pesa in the parish of Campoli, popolo of San Gaudenzo, and have its fruits for life, and thereafter it may return to my heirs; or she may enter into possession of a house in Florence in the popolo of San Simone... and the rent of said house may be hers all her life, intending that it remain at the discretion of said monna Bartolomea, if my heirs do not observe this.[60]

Reference to courts and judges, while also asserting that Bartolomea need not wait on them, put some teeth in this obligation on the heirs. Obviously, Niccolini had some affection or felt a debt of gratitude toward this woman.

If testaments such as these were to work after the testators' deaths, it was because the testament cleverly set up a framework in which there was some other interested and sufficiently powerful party (in both *novelle* ecclesiastical persons or bodies, in Niccolini's the legatee herself) to blow the whistle on heirs who failed to conform. Even then, the whistle might only lead to a lawsuit that the heirs might win. The testament was not going to work on the strength of the desires of a dead person alone. The testament was a collaborative effort. As Thomas Cohen has found, after following a particularly complicated Roman situation, even in the making "some wills are the product of several minds."[61] Beyond the testator, there were present kin (in many cases), witnesses and notary (in all cases), and the result was often a congeries of their wishes and experiences.

Obligations of Heirs

To be sure, testators' stated desires carried legal and moral weight. It is interesting how often Florentines seem to have shouldered in good faith, if at times reluctantly, the burdens of legata in testaments. At least when faced with fiscal officials, in order to argue for indulgence in setting tax

---

[60] NA 690, fols. 379v–80v (14 November 1450): "et in caso decte heredi non dessino le decte cose al decto tempo et modo, voglio et lascio che la decta Bartolomea possa entrare in tenuta ipso iure sanza il braccio d'alchuna corte o giudice in uno mio podere che ssi chiama la Torre, posto in val di Pesa nel pioveri di Campoli, popolo di San Godenzo, et de quello avere le rendite tutto il tempo della sua vita, et poi sia delle decte mie heredi ovvole entrare in tenuta in una chasa posta in Firenze nel popolo di San Simone, nella quale sta a pigione monna Chaterina figliuola fu di ser Cambio Salviati et danne fi. quatordici l'anno, et decta casa sia sua la pigione tutto il tempo di sua vita intendendo che a sua electione stia della decta Bartolomea non observando decti miei heredi."
[61] Thomas V. Cohen, *Love and Death in Renaissance Italy* (Chicago: University of Chicago Press, 2004), 98.

assessments, a number of Florentines obligingly revealed how they faced the burdens of legata (none quite as silly as leaving a basket of fruit for the flies). Three sons of Betto di Zanobi reported an obligation, shared with cousins, that arose from their grandfather's testament to make an annual contribution to a Florentine hospital.[62] Pierfilippo di messer Giannozzo Pandolfini had a legatum in his father's testament to pay annually one and one-fourth florin to the monks of the Badia and one from his mother's for the same amount.[63] Yet the same source also indicates that some legata were not faithfully discharged, whether from lack of motivation or lack of funds. In 1480, Sandra, widow of Piero di ser Cristofano da Laterina, reported that she had an annual obligation of four florins to the hospital of Santa Maria Nuova from her father-in-law's will, which had accumulated over years to a sum of 200 florins charged against her dowry, because her late husband had not paid the yearly installments to the hospital.[64]

Of course, Florentines had reason to pose as dutiful heirs to officials who had the power to lighten their tax burden. Yet there is plenty of other evidence to corroborate the impression that they often tried to meet the wishes of the deceased. Certainly, we can find plenty of legal evidence in the notarial archives that Florentines discharged obligations laid on them by testaments whose terms they accepted. For example, in 1379 Piero di Bernardo of the rural parish of San Donato in Poggio, described as poor and needy ("pauper et egena persona"), provided a legal receipt to the testamentary heirs of Piero di Vanni di Rinaldo that they had paid him fifteen *lire* in accord with a charitable bequest.[65] A woman to whom a modest dowry (30 florins) had been left likewise acknowledged receipt of the funds.[66] Alessandra Strozzi advised her son, Filippo, to act quickly on his brother's testamentary provisions for his soul, leaving the rest of his bequests to be done "at leisure."[67] Such bequests might so burden an estate that it was no longer lucrative for an heir and instead became the object of repudiation.

---

[62] Catasto 1014, fol. 140v. Another example is in ibid., fol. 106r.
[63] Catasto 1022, fol. 415v.
[64] Catasto 1014, fol. 264v: "One addare ongni anno allo spedale di santa Maria Nuova fi. quatro di sugello, e quali sono per uno incharicho che ser Cristofano lasciò per suo testamento che in perpetuo detti fi. 4 si debbono paghare al detto spedale, che quando ebbi a ripigliare la mia dota ne truovi debito chon detto spedale circha a fi. dugiento perchè Piero mio marito nonna aveva paghati fi. quatro l'anno."
[65] NA 9386, fol. 141r (12 November 1379).
[66] NA 15220, 28 March 1385. The testator was Lippo di Giovanni di ser Lippo; the woman one of the daughters of Cambino di Giovanni, of the popolo of Santa Maria Alberighi, to whom dowries were directed.
[67] Alessandra Strozzi, *Selected Letters of Alessandra Strozzi*, trans. Heather Gregory (Berkeley: University of California Press, 1997), 84 and 85. In the event, "leisure" was around five years; at least it was only at that point that Alessandra expressed her approval of the news that all the will's terms had been met (ibid., 109).

A salient example of a burdensome testament is that of Giovanni di Bernardo di Antonio da Uzzano. He fell heir not only to his father but to his uncle, Niccolò, one of the wealthiest and most politically prominent Florentines of the first third of the fifteenth century. Instead of the great wealth he might have expected, however, Giovanni faced mountains of debt and dwindling fortunes, in part because his uncle's death exposed the lineage to political reprisals, including crushing fiscal demands in the difficult years of the 1430s and 1440s, but mainly because Niccolò's will had so burdened his estate with legacies that even his brother, as his heir, had faced heavy expenses to meet them. Giovanni da Uzzano repudiated his father only six days after his death in October 1440. The family business was already in bankruptcy. Had Giovanni not been able to safeguard patrimonial assets in his mother's dowry and receive the inheritance of his paternal grandmother, he would have been in very straightened financial circumstances indeed. Giovanni's treatise on trade and business practices was one fruit of his difficulties.[68]

Other obligations fell on heirs simply by virtue of succession itself, testate or intestate, without having to take the form of legata or otherwise having to be spelled out. They simply came due in the course of events. One of the most common was the obligation to return a dowry. At times, testators put this obligation in the form of a legatum to the woman to whom it was to be returned or offered the alternative of remaining for life in the testator's home during chaste widowhood.[69] They thereby added more immediate moral and legal weight to that important and primary obligation. There are countless notarial texts acknowledging receipt of a dowry and absolving the payer from any further claims concerning it.[70]

At marriage, the husband or his father or someone else on his behalf would legally acknowledge reception of his wife's dowry. This event was, in fact, more frequent than marriage itself, as multiple kin might similarly acknowledge the dowry and obligate themselves, in a secondary manner, for

---

[68] Bruno Dini, "Nuovi documenti su Giovanni di Bernardo di Antonio da Uzzano," in his *Manifattura, commercio e banca nella Firenze medievale* (Florence: Nardini, 2001), 209–26 (original in *Nuova rivista storica* 64 [1980]: 378–95). The repudiation is in RE 13, fol. 176 (12 October 1440).

[69] Julius Kirshner, "Materials for a Gilded Cage: Non-Dotal Assets in Florence, 1300–1500," in *The Family in Italy from Antiquity to the Present*, ed. David I. Kertzer and Richard P. Saller (New Haven: Yale University Press, 1991), 184–207; Isabelle Chabot, "Widowhood and Poverty in Late Medieval Florence," *Continuity and Change* 3 (1988): 291–311, and "'La sposa in nero': La ritualizzazione del lutto delle vedove fiorentine (secoli xiv-xv)," *Quaderni storici* 86 (1994): 421–62; and for Venice, Stanley Chojnacki, "Getting Back the Dowry," in his *Women and Men in Renaissance Venice: Twelve Essays on Patrician Society* (Baltimore: Johns Hopkins University Press, 2000), 95–111.

[70] For example, NA 9036, fol. 26r (1405), where following the death of Bartolo di Luca of Settignano, his widow made a quitclaim to her son Luca and by way of him to her other son, Lorenzo, for her dowry of 130 *lire* paid to Bartolo back in 1384.

its return to the bride or her heirs on the dissolution of marriage.[71] At the end of the marriage, the wife, if she were the survivor, would seek return of the dowry, or her heirs (in all likelihood children), if she were the deceased, would seek it at some point. Something like a third of notarial acts of quitclaim (*finis*) for a debt – at least for some notaries – revolved around return of the dowry.[72] Much less visible were the countless obligations entered into over the course of a long and busy life in which one pledged oneself and one's heirs to the observation of various contractual terms or to guarantee various arrangements, including even the dowries of others. To unearth all of these would be a task as vast as investigating most of the legal realm we would describe as private law.

As one example, two brothers were awarded a house by an arbitrator. The other party was ordered "in law and fact to defend, authorize, and expedite by all means" ("de iure et de facto defendere, auctorizare et disbrigare in modis omnibus") the new owners' claims against those arising from any person, place, commune, or corporation. Further, if a suit arose against these brothers or their heirs, the other party and his heirs had to appear within five days of receiving notice and take on the role of principals in the suit, including its expenses, and keep the brothers unharmed. If they should lose the suit, the other party or his heirs had to compensate the brothers or their heirs for the value of the house. The other party or heirs then could not argue that the loss of the property was in any way the fault of the heirs. Note how in every case the heirs were implicated in the legal language. While it may be true that such circumstances were unlikely to arise, it is also true that property ownership was contested even decades after an event, and then such clauses could come into play and heirs could find themselves facing legal demands that were unanticipated and all the more onerous for that fact. Of course, were one to take on the overt role of guarantor (*fideiussor*, *mallevadore*), it was much more likely.[73]

---

[71] Against twenty-one betrothals (*sponsalia*) and thirty marriages (*matrimonia*) in one volume, and eighteen and twenty respectively in another, one notary recorded forty-seven dotal receipts (*dotes*) and twenty-five respectively (NA 9040 and 9038). An example of multiple recourse to this act is that of Benedetto di Marco Strozzi and his brother Carlo, who later supported his pledge to return the dowry (NA 9040, fols. 222v [10 December 1425] and 239r [11 April 1426]).

[72] This by a quick count of acts of *finis* in NA 9038 and 9040. In the first were seventy-seven *fines*, fifteen to women for dowries and a further six to heirs. In the second, 114 *fines* included thirty-seven to women, most regarding dowries, and another twelve to heirs.

[73] Ugolino di Niccolò Martelli's *ricordi* provide several examples in which he had to make payments against the hereditas iacens of Bino di Niccolò because he had gone surety for him (Martelli, *Ricordanze*, 157). Also on the law here, see Julius Kirshner, "A Question of Suretyship in Trecento Florence," in *Renaissance Studies in Honor of Craig Hugh Smyth*, ed. Andrew Morrogh (Florence: Giunti Barbera, 1985), 129–45.

That likelihood explains another good example. Giovanni Tornabuoni gave various properties to his grandsons, children of his son Lorenzo, on which he imposed the restriction that, if he or Lorenzo sold or obligated any goods, even those not included in the gift, the gift did not prejudice the sale or alienation. In other words, the property included in the gift was available to Giovanni or Lorenzo to guarantee their performance of other debts or obligations. The condition was, on face of it, duplicitous – a gift that yet was not. But it also recognized a very common state of affairs in sales and other transactions. A seller guaranteed title and delivery to the buyer and pledged redemption if, for any reason, the buyer was bothered or evicted (*ratione molestationis et evictionis*) from the property as a result of a claim arising against the seller. That warranty commonly passed to the seller's heirs. The effect of the conditional gift was that, if a buyer of some property from Giovanni or Lorenzo as his heir, were evicted, he could not move against the donated property, even though it had seemingly been posed as his remedy in such a situation. Two prominent Florentine lawyers struck down Tornabuoni's gift in an opinion for the court, when a suit arose, noting, as they did so, that Tornabuoni's maneuver was a way for this Medici partisan to cover some assets in the aftermath of the expulsion of Piero de' Medici in 1494.[74]

Examples of contractual and testamentary clauses later coming into play can be found. An exact statistical examination of them will require a long lifetime of a very patient scholar. Clearly, the desires of the deceased, perhaps especially with regard to bequests to Church bodies or charity in general, were given serious consideration and honored in many, if not most, instances. But that does not mean that Florentines were not aware of the expenses and problems attendant on inheritance. There is a particularly trenchant bit of advice in a letter of Alessandra Strozzi to her exiled son Lorenzo. Noting the approaching demise of Jacopo di Leonardo Strozzi, she warned her son that he was likely to be left in charge of Jacopo's affairs.

If he hasn't left you anything, take my advice and don't accept anything [offered by anyone else], and if he has left you in charge you should refuse to do it. Things to do with inheritance are very risky and can lead to a lot of trouble and aggravation and you don't want to get involved in that. Above all make sure you don't let yourself become legally liable for anything or to anyone, no matter who wants it, because you know if you accept liability you do so personally. Do the clever thing where this is concerned and let this warning be enough.[75]

Her warning anticipated that her son would be executor rather than heir or legatee, but the possibilities for liability were much greater for the heir. It

---

[74] ASF, Carte strozziane, 3rd ser., 41/12, fols. 147r-52r.
[75] Strozzi, *Selected Letters*, 100 and 101.

was not that great a step from refusing to act as executor (or guardian) to repudiating the inheritance.[76]

That such savvy advice came from a woman is also worth noting. Clearly, a woman such as Alessandra Strozzi could be astute about business and legal affairs, although in her case the exile of her husband and sons propelled her to a more active role in household management than was typical of Florentine wives and mothers. Yet this was also a woman who had direct experience with inheritance issues, being involved in a long dispute with siblings and nephews over her brother's estate (a dispute she ultimately lost). In fact, only about a year and a half before giving Lorenzo her advice, she indicated to her other son, Filippo, that she was carefully deliberating whether to accept the estate of her recently deceased third son, Matteo.[77] Repudiation entered her consciousness, and she was fully aware of the burdens and debts that could accompany an estate.[78]

Repudiations in Florentine Family Records

Repudiation was designed in law to avoid financial difficulties. It was employed often for its expressed legal purpose to escape from liability on a debt-ridden estate. Luca Boschetto, in an exemplary study of the Alberti family and especially Leon Battista, has uncovered the use of repudiation to that effect, following the family's repatriation to Florence in the 1430s, when family fortunes began to turn sour.[79] Maria Serena Mazzi and Sergio Raveggi followed the tracks of a contadino who repudiated his father's paltry estate and went to Florence to work in wool manufacture.[80] We will add many more examples before we are done.

But beyond its financial purposes, repudiation was also one of a number of tools to maneuver inheritances around. It was related to the slightly different practice of renunciation (*rinunzia*) by which sons or daughters who had entered or were about to enter a monastery or convent, renounced their rights to a portion of an estate (father's or mother's usually). Luca da Panzano recorded the renunciation of February 1418/19 by Fruosino di Bernardo Quercitani, who was emancipated in order then to give his mother's dowry to his brother Simone.[81] Bartolomeo Masi noted that his brothers in religious

---

[76] On guardianship and for examples of guardians bowing out, see my "Social Processes and Legal Processes in the Renaissance: A Florentine Case from 1452," *Quaderni fiorentini per la storia del pensiero giuridico moderno* 23 (1994): 365–96.
[77] Strozzi, *Selected Letters*, 89.
[78] In the event, there was no repudiation, at least by the testimony of the registry.
[79] Luca Boschetto, *Leon Battista Alberti e Firenze: Biografia, storia, letteratura*, Ingenium vol. 2 (Florence: Olschki, 2000), 60–61.
[80] Maria Serena Mazzi and Sergio Raveggi, *Gli uomini e le cose nelle campagne fiorentine del Quattrocento* (Florence: Olschki, 1983), 307–15.
[81] ASF, Carte strozziane, 2nd ser., 9, fol. 12r.

life, Matteo and Romolo, both renounced their shares.[82] Marco di Giovanni Strozzi in 1499 carefully had Giovanmaria renounce his portion of paternal and maternal estates in favor of his two brothers before departing for the Badia of Settimo.[83]

Renunciation by clerical children was a practice disallowed by Roman law, although it was countenanced by canon law.[84] The practice was a close parallel to the statutory limitation of daughters' shares to the dowries they had or would receive, which was also contrary to Roman law.[85] Above all, such renunciations were preemptive steps to prevent loss of a portion of the estate. It was not driven by fear of debt supposedly but by filial piety. It happened before death, whereas repudiation came after it.

When Florentines took note of repudiation, they did so matter-of-factly. There are not many such records in *ricordi* and diaries. Those who kept such records had generally accepted the inheritance left them; it was the basis for their accounts. Unlike possible emancipations, for which fathers were necessarily around and thus could keep records, the keeper of an account book was not around to record a repudiation of what he left behind. Repudiations noted in accounts were generally those by other kin. An exception is the early record (1316) of Francesco and Alessio Baldovinetti, who made note of their repudiation of their father's estate. However, this record was also more than a bit duplicitous. These two sons, who had previously been emancipated, had ten days earlier received the "houses and lands and debts" as a gift from their father, just before his death.[86] Technically, the property they held was not hereditas. The hereditas itself was then effectively nothing, so there was every incentive to repudiate it. As this blatant attempt to be heirs in all but name occurred prior to the first statute redaction of 1325, perhaps these two were able to get away with it in the absence of a forceful statutory position on the liabilities of heirs. At least the account book does not reveal any particular trouble on that score.

Another example from a few years later shows the consequences of heavy debt. The considerable fortune inherited by Lapo di Valore dei Ciurianni in 1299 had become a crushing burden of debt, more than 4,500 florins, at

---

[82] *Ricordanze di Bartolomeo Masi calderaio fiorentino dal 1478 al 1526*, ed. Giuseppe Odoardo Carozzini (Florence: Sansoni, 1906), 248, 264–65.

[83] ASF, Carte strozziane, 4th ser., 353, fol. 142v. Here, however, within two weeks this son had returned home "e non volle fare professione per amore non gli piaque l'oserva frate."

[84] Cooper, "Patterns of Settlement," 266.

[85] On which, see my "Person and Gender in the Law," in *Gender and Society in Renaissance Italy*, ed. Judith Brown and Robert C. Davis (New York: Longmans, 1998), 87–106.

[86] Gino Corti, ed., "Le ricordanze trecentesche di Francesco e di Alessio Baldovinetti," *Archivio storico italiano* 112 (1954): 109–24, at 114, 115: "Memoria che dí vi di settembre '316 donò Borghino a Francescho e Dalesso le case e le terre e debiti. Faciela ser Michele Dini.... "Memoria che Franceschо e Dalesso rifiutorono la redità di Borghino nel 1316 a dí 16 di settenbre. Fece la charte ser Michele Dini."

his death thirty years later. His son, Valorino, began his entries in the family accounts with his repudiation of his father's estate, left to him as sole son and heir by testament. In fact, he then emancipated his young sons, to whom the property fell as next in line, and had them accept their grandfather's estate. Arrangements were made in subsequent years to settle outstanding debts. Valorino and later his sons paid off all these commitments within ten years, but the repudiation had bought them time and the limitation on the claims that accompanied benefit of inventory for minors.[87]

Almost two centuries later, Bartolomeo Masi recorded the repudiation by his uncle of his grandfather's estate. His grandfather had not been well off, having been reduced to living in a house belonging to his wife and her sister. Bartolomeo's notation thus implicitly explained away the repudiation as a wise economic step.[88] Paolo di Lapo Niccolini calmly found that his son Lodovico, at his death in 1479, owed 2,000 florins on his wife's dowry and had a number of other creditors. He repudiated Lodovico's estate, which did not absolve him from the obligation to repay a dowry for which he had stood surety, but it may have effectively limited his exposure to business debts of his son.[89]

Other Florentines, as the legislative history alerts us, were not so above board in their dealings. *Astuzia, furberia, scaltrezza,* and other terms were used to describe behavior in and out of the markets in many cities, including Florence.[90] These terms generated a powerful ambivalence. On the one hand, they were negative, non-Christian, destructive of good social and economic order, of the sorts of *fede* and *fiducia* on which markets and broader social relations were based. It was from this perspective that Alessandra Strozzi cautioned her son, Filippo, to "do the right thing" when accusations arose against him. Not rendering debts to others can lead to one's damnation, she cautioned.[91] From her distanced position, her concern was for her son's reputation ("buona fama") and his soul. But from his position, while *fama* and salvation were not inconsiderable elements, the positive side of cunning, deceit, and double-dealing was more prominently in view, perhaps. Filippo Strozzi, like other Florentines, Francesco Guicciardini and Matteo Palmieri

---

[87] ASF, Manoscritti 77, fol. 5r. In general on this account book and family, see the perceptive essay of Isabelle Chabot, "Reconstruction d'une famille: Les Ciurianni et leurs *Ricordanze* (1326–1429)," in *La Toscane et les Toscans autour de la Renaissance: Cadres de vie, société et croyances: Mélanges offerts à Charles M. de La Roncière* (Aix-en-Provence: Publications de l'Université de Provence, 1999), 137–60. She notes that "les liens de la dette constituent le fil rouge qui relie entre elles les trois premières généations de rédacteurs" (148).

[88] *Ricordanze di Masi,* 8–9.

[89] Ginevra Niccolini di Camugliano, *The Chronicles of a Florentine Family, 1200–1470* (London: Jonathan Cape, 1933), 171; RE 21, fol. 88 (21 July 1479).

[90] Here note John A. Marino, "Economic Idylls and Pastoral Realities: The 'Trickster Economy' in the Kingdom of Naples," *Comparative Studies in Society and History* 24 (1982): 211–34.

[91] Strozzi, *Selected Letters,* 104 and 105.

among them, not to mention Niccolò Machiavelli, understood that honesty was not always useful, while dishonesty sometimes was.[92] The need to be secretive of some affairs, the need to keep separate sets of books, the need, in short, to deceive, was well known.[93] It was a weapon one could brandish for oneself and had good reason to fear from others. Repudiation of inheritance leant itself easily to deceptive practices.

The strategizing that might lay behind repudiation and simultaneous legal maneuvers was revealed in Luca di Matteo da Panzano's comments on the doings of his cousin, Totto d'Antonio di messer Luca.

I record how said day [11 December 1414] Totto d'Antonio di messer Luca repudiated the estate of monna Maria, daughter of the late Nofri Busini and wife of Antonio, and then I also hear from Totto that Antonio had emancipated him....

And the same day he emancipated Mea, and she accepted the estate of monna Maria her mother in the presence of messer Rosso d'Andreozzo [Orlandi], and many other contracts on this day appear through the hand of ser Antonio Pierozzi, and then Mea took possession of the house in Florence....

I record how on 11 December 1414 Mea, daughter of Antonio di messer Luca da Panzano, emancipated and not married, or married and not gone to her husband, accepted the estate of monna Maria her mother, not withstanding her father Antonio being alive. And this was done in truth to defend the goods of her father Antonio because the affairs of his bank stood badly.[94]

Here property was maneuvered into the hands of a young woman on the verge of marriage, arguably as dowry, but in any case not in the possession of her father or brother. However, Totto da Panzano's repudiation of his mother's estate was not, in fact, registered with the Signoria, whereas his emancipation and his sister's were duly recorded, in compliance with the law,

---

[92] Kuehn, *Emancipation*, 39–40.
[93] For one parallel example of deceit in service of a reasonable family goal, see Anthony Molho, "Deception and Marriage Strategy in Renaissance Florence: The Case of Women's Age," *Renaissance Quarterly* 41 (1988): 193–217.
[94] ASF, Carte strozziane, 2nd ser., 9, fol. 3v: "Richordo chome detto dì Totto d'Antonio di messer Lucha rifiutò l'eredità di monna Maria figliuola fu di Nofri Busini e donna fu d'Antonio sopradetto, e dipoi senti anche da Totto detto che Antonio di messer Lucha l'aveva mancepato. E di tutto disse esserne roghato di detti due chontratti fatti di detto mese....

"E a dì sopradetto mancieppò la Mea et detto dì la Mea prese l'eredità di monna Maria sua madre a presencia di messer Rosso d'Andreaozo, e molti altri contratti in questo dì apare tutto per mano di ser Antonio Pierozzi et prese di poi la tenuta della casa di Firenze la detta Mea, carta per mano di ser Antonio Pierozzi.

"Richordo chome a dì xi di dicembre 1414 la Mea figliuola d'Antonio di messer Lucha da Panzano emanceppata et non è maritata, o maritata non n'era ita a marito, prese l'eredità di monna Maria sua madre, non istante vivento Antonio suo padre. E questo si fe' in verità per difendere i beni d'Antonio suo padre perchè fatti del suo bancho istavano male, fune roghato ser Antonio di Nicholaio di ser Pierozzo, notaio fiorentino."

before the Mercanzia.⁹⁵ It seemed more pressing to enshrine the sweeping immunity from liability worked by emancipation against Antonio's financial problems than to establish his separation from maternal property, which was not liable for the bank's debts and destined for Mea's dowry in any case. Two months later, Luca penned an entry in his accounts detailing his reluctant guarantorship of a sale by Mea of a house. Antonio had begged him to do so, but Luca was leery of Antonio's financial woes.⁹⁶

We should not be overly surprised to find such devious maneuvers on the part of Florentines. We have already seen from the legislative history that they took advantage of repudiation to exasperate both creditors and lawgivers (not mutually exclusive categories). This is all part of the agonistic nature of social relations in Florence, most especially evident because of the deeply personal nature of credit. The economic landscape of Florence was marked by a "prevalence of uncollectible debt" that generally involved friends, neighbors, and relatives.⁹⁷ With Luca da Panzano, we see the interesting example of a man extending credit to a relative in need and at the same time exposing a reluctance, even a fear that this credit would only be lost, as Antonio's creditors had lost theirs.

Paolo Niccolini's father, Lapo, had reason to regret when one female cousin (not nearly as accommodating as Mea) sued him over a house he had purchased from the brother whose intestate inheritance she had taken. Lapo claimed in his accounts that the brother had in fact entrusted the house to him in the midst of the plague of 1417 so that it not "leave our family."⁹⁸ The sale had been a clever maneuver, now called into question by the sister.

Bernardo Machiavelli, himself a doctor of laws and father to Niccolò, famed author of *The Prince*, was an acute observer of kin and neighbors.

---

⁹⁵ ASF, Mercanzia 10819 bis², fol. 267r.
⁹⁶ ASF, Carte strozziane, 2nd ser., 9, fol. 5v: "Richordo chome insino a dì xiii di febraio 1414 [1415] io sodai per la Mea, figliuola d'Antonio di messer Lucha et per Antonio predetto, una vendita per loro fatta a Jachopo di Gilio Gilii d'una chasa posta nela via di l'Anghuillaia nel popolo di Santo Apolinari di Firenze per prezo di fiorini setteciento cinquanta d'oro, la qual casa n'aveva presa la tenuta la Mea predetta. Et non volli sodare non istante che Antonio di messer Lucha me ne preghasse e stetti ostinato assai di inperò che ne da Jachopo Gilii et anche Antonio detto mai me dissono di detta vendita inperò ch'arei rimediato con qualche parente e amico, pure perchè fatti d'Antonio andavano male cho' chreditori suoi in rovina sodai, funne roghato ser Ghuido di messer Tommaxo, notaio fiorentino per fiorini 750."
⁹⁷ Cf. Ronald F. E. Weissman, "The Importance of Being Ambiguous: Social Relations, Individualism, and Identity in Renaissance Florence," in *Urban Life in the Renaissance*, ed. Susan Zimmerman and Ronald F. E. Weissman (Newark: University of Delaware Press, 1989), 269–80; id., *Ritual Brotherhood in Renaissance Florence* (New York: Academic Press, 1982), 26–41; Thomas Kuehn, "*Multorum Fraudibus Occurrere*: Legislation and Jurisprudential Interpretation Concerning Fraud and Liability in Quattrocento Florence," *Studi senesi* 93 (1981): 309–50; id., *Emancipation*, 39–40.
⁹⁸ Niccolini, *Il libro degli affari*, 136.

He had opportunity to record details of several repudiations of inheritance in the 1470s and 1480s. In one instance, in 1477 he served as witness when Boninsegna di Guido Machiavelli declared himself satisfied of his claims on his mother's 500 florin dowry, because he repudiated his father's estate in 1456.[99] The following year (1478) Machiavelli noted that the same Boninsegna accepted the estate of his brother Piero Amadio. Whereas Boninsegna had repudiated his father's estate in 1456, in 1458 Piero Amadio and Pietro Pagolo, the other two sons, had accepted and split it. These two had died back in 1463, so Boninsegna had waited for fifteen years to cash in on the estate of one of his brothers.[100] On paper, Boninsegna was his brother's heir, not his father's, even though he was in possession of some of his father's holdings by that less direct route. In the next year, 1479, when Guido di Pietro Pagolo died, leaving a testament in favor of his uncle, Boninsegna effectively became heir to the other half of his father's estate. Ironically, Boninsegna too was at death's door. He rose from his death bed long enough to meet a notary at the door to his house and accept Guido's estate. The next day Boninsegna died, leaving two sons and a widow with a 1,063 florin dowry claim against his estate.[101]

A further irony here was that six years later Boninsegna's son Battista, in turn, repudiated his father.[102] Previously, Battista's mother had taken properties assigned by the Magistrato dei Pupilli (in 1482) and others assigned by the court of the Podestà (in 1483) for her dowry. In sum, these amounted to 939 florins (still more than 100 florins short of the nominal value of her dowry) and seemingly left very little else in the hereditas.[103] As these various repudiations, acceptances, and dowry settlements affected ownership of patrimonial properties, notably around Bernardo Machiavelli's holdings in Sant'Andrea in Percussina, he had reason to maintain some record of them.

Another example shows that sometimes the heir, not the father, was the source of problems for an estate. In 1500, Giovanni Rinaldeschi died. His son Antonio, a hotheaded young man with a penchant for gambling, who the following year was executed for an act of sacrilege, quarreled with his stepmother and sisters over the estate. He filed suit before the Podestà; they countersued in the Mercanzia. Giovanni Rinaldeschi had charged his son's debts against the estate, making it an unprofitable proposition for Antonio, who repudiated his father but advanced a claim for his mother's dowry.

---

[99] Bernardo Machiavelli, *Libro di ricordi*, ed. Cesare Olschki (Florence: Le Monnier, 1954), 66–67; RE 16, fol. 209 (19 July 1456). His repudiation covered one third.
[100] Ibid., 68–69.
[101] Ibid., 95–97.
[102] As it indeed was: RE 22, fol. 117 (3 February 1486); and was his brother Piero's repudiation of Boninsegna: RE 23, fol. 27 (20 May 1489).
[103] Machiavelli, 216–17.

In November, the parties reached a settlement through arbitrators, with a second settlement with a half-sister coming the following April.[104]

As these examples show, passage of property could be a long and complicated process. Just how extremely complicated it could be emerges from the example of Giovanni di Filippo di Giovanni Corbizi, who, in October 1512, came forward to ratify a property settlement involving his kin. It took the notary several pages to record the journey the property rights in question had taken, beginning back in 1430, when Giovanni's grandfather had received his wife's 500 florin dowry. In 1457, this grandfather, also named Giovanni di Filippo Corbizi, had been found by the Florentine Mercanzia to be debtor of Raimondo Mannelli for 1,799 florins. So it is not so surprising that, following his death in 1473, Giovanni's son, Filippo, quickly repudiated the paternal estate, and Giovanni's wife (Filippo's mother) accepted as her dowry a farm at Montici and a small house (*domuncula*) and two shops in Florence in Borgo degli Albizzi.[105] Ten years later, Filippo's young sons, heirs by virtue of their father's repudiation, accepted the grandpaternal estate with benefit of inventory.[106] When their grandmother passed away in 1490, she left a testament naming her son (Filippo) as heir and his sons (there were then four) after him.

In 1502, Filippo died intestate, leaving five sons (one illegitimate) and a widow. Three sons (Bernardo, Roberto, and Antonio) repudiated the estate of their predeceased brother (confusingly he had been named Giovanni and then the name was reused for the younger sibling with whom this account began). One also repudiated his fifth of the grandmother's.[107] The three others accepted their fourths of her estate, and later the remaining brother also repudiated the father and accepted the grandmother. In 1503, Filippo's widow, for her 1,300 florin dowry, received half the farm that the grandmother had held for her dowry, while two of the brothers died that year as well.[108] In 1504, Roberto and Antonio, as the remaining brothers and in Giovanni's name, accepted the estate of one deceased brother.

Now there appeared on the scene Raimondo Mannelli's heir, who quickly gained a court sentence against them for the 1,799 florins decreed as a debt

---

[104] Elements of this set of events are discussed in William J. Connell and Giles Constable, *Sacrilege and Redemption in Renaissance Florence: The Case of Antonio Rinaldeschi* (Toronto: Centre for Reformation and Renaissance Studies, 2005), 29–30 and n. 38. The repudiation is registered in RE 25, fol. 48 (5 June 1500).

[105] RE 20, fol. 81 (1 February 1474).

[106] In 1487, their grandmother gave her illegitimate grandson the house she had claimed in 1473.

[107] See RE 25, fol. 136 and 137 (9 November 1502). Antonio again repudiated his father on 29 December (ibid., fol. 141).

[108] And Niccolò repudiated Bernardo (ibid., fol. 165 [9 September 1502]), the same day Roberto repudiated his father's estate for the second time.

almost fifty years earlier. He took the farm and small house, though only after a judicial reversal of the sentence of 1457, a re-reversal on appeal, and a *retentio* by the heirs against the properties for the value of the grandmother's dowry and improvements made to these properties at her expense. Finally, in 1506 the Mannelli heir sought police help (*bracchium militare*) to expel the Corbizi. He declared he was prepared to pay the 500 florin dowry and compensate the improvements (the sum for which was fixed by judicial sentence at 200 florins in 1507). The other brothers had issued their quitclaim on these sums in 1510. Giovanni in 1512 was only finally ratifying their actions directly in his own name.[109]

The entire document is revealing of the number and types of different claims that could accumulate over time on any one piece of property. We see how one and the same estate was repudiated and accepted, and how heirs turned their backs on a paternal estate but grabbed hold of a maternal one. The very situation ("intermingling" in the repudiated paternal estate by right of the mother's dowry) that the Florentine statute both set up and seemingly feared was a reality, here and in other instances.[110] It is also instructive that in the end the judicial interventions in favor of the Mannelli claims were decisive.

Conclusion

The few explicit statements about repudiation that have emerged from the pens of Florentines show a willingness to use a device that might avoid debts and problems. There was no negative attitude toward repudiation as shameful or disrespectful to the deceased, who had probably not been an effective manager or steward. Whatever fear or concern may have been expressed by communal authorities about the use of repudiation did not carry over to those who found it a useful legal tool to maintain family assets. There was so much emphasis in inheritance practices and strategies on keeping property in the hands of family over time that repudiation, in overtly and deliberately breaking the continuity of transmission, even if to avoid liabilities and problems, had to seem ambiguous.[111] It was one generation's rejection of its predecessors, or one child's rejection of his or her father, and thus not an optimal solution. As Charles M. de La Roncière has posed, what characterized a true man was an aptitude for social interaction and reponsibility

---

[109] NA 9653 (1512–13), fols. 41r-46r (25 October 1512).
[110] As another example for the moment, Querino and Giovanni di Pietro de' Fighinelli, who had repudiated their father but accepted their mother's 200 florin dowry, sought a decree of *tenuta* from the court of the Podestà: ASF, Podestà 4437, fols. 50v-51v.
[111] Beatrice Gottlieb, *The Family in the Western World from the Black Death to the Industrial Age* (New York and Oxford: Oxford University Press, 1993), 204–5.

in regard to the family.[112] Repudiation was a responsible, if not inherently attractive, option.

In the course of the fourteenth and fifteenth centuries, jurists came to elaborate dimensions of the civil law's *fideicommissum* into a means to construe preservation of property within a family.[113] Thus legally arrayed, the *fideicommissum* was capable of increasing prominence in inheritance strategies. This coincided with and encouraged a reemphasis on inheritance and social connections in a more vertical mode (across generations in a direct line, if possible) rather than in a horizontal linkage to kin and patrons throughout the city. Samuel Cohn has tracked an increasing tendency of Florentines to look to preservation of patrimonies in successive generations and to set clauses to preclude alienation. In so doing "almost invariably, they favored the property rights of the family stock and lineage (*in stirpe*) over those of the individual (*in capite*)."[114] Linked with such practices was the genealogical tendency of Florentines to neglect relationships forged through women, who contributed, as mothers, to the preservation of other lineages.[115] As inheritance practices tended to an even more aristocratic concentration of patrimony into the hands of a single male heir, younger sons too were, if not forgotten, subordinated to group solidarity.[116] This process set in for Florence by the second half of the fifteenth century, as Medici political ascendancy defined routes of access to power and wealth.[117] Yet even the antithesis to Medici rule, the Great Council that followed Piero de' Medici's exile in

---

[112] Charles M. de La Roncière, "Une famille florentine au xive siècle: Les Velluti," in *Famille et parenté dans l'Occident médiéval*, ed. Georges Duby and Jacques Le Goff (Rome: École Française de Rome, 1977), 227–48, at 242.

[113] Cooper, "Patterns of Settlement," 280; Mario Caravale, "Fedecommesso (storia)," *Enciclopedia del diritto*, vol. 17 (Milan: Giuffrè, 1968), 109–114.

[114] Cohn, *Cult of Remembrance*, 196; see also 172–80; id., *Death and Property*, 70.

[115] Klapisch-Zuber, "Albero genealogico."

[116] Renata Ago, "Giochi di squadra: uomini e donne nelle famiglie nobili del xvii secolo," in *Signori, patrizi, cavalieri nell'Italia centro-meridionale nell'età moderna*, ed. Maria Antonietta Visceglia (Bari: Laterza, 1992), 256–64; Raffaella Sarti, *Europe at Home: Family and Material Culture, 1500–1800*, trans. Alan Cameron (New Haven: Yale University Press, 2002), 59; Maria Carla Zorzoli, "Della famiglia e del suo patrimonio: riflessioni sull'uso del fedecommesso in Lombardia tra cinque e seicento," in *Marriage, Property, and Succession*, ed. Lloyd Bonfield, Comparative Studies in Continental and Anglo-American Legal History 10, ed. Helmut Coing and Knut Wolfgang Nörr (Berlin: Duncker & Humblot, 1992), 155–213.

[117] Anthony Molho, *Marriage Alliance in Late Medieval Florence* (Cambridge: Harvard University Press, 1994), 334; R. Burr Litchfield, *Emergence of a Bureaucracy: The Florentine Patricians, 1530–1790* (Princeton: Princeton University Press, 1986), 30–41; David Herlihy and Christiane Klapisch-Zuber, *Les toscans et leurs familles* (Paris: Fondation Nationale des Sciences Politiques, 1978), 520; Giovanna Benadusi, *A Provincial Elite in Early Modern Tuscany: Family and Power in the Creation of the State* (Baltimore: Johns Hopkins University Press, 1996), 128–32; Judith C. Brown, *In the Shadow of Florence: Provincial Society in Renaissance Pescia* (Oxford: Oxford University Press, 1982), 41–41; Richard Goldthwaite,

1494, based officeholding eligibility on a direct line of father and grandfather.[118] Funerals too gave expression to a family-based model of governance rooted in patrilines.[119] As Gianna Pomata has nicely put it,

in the preceding centuries, when in most Italian cities the political structure was not yet stably dominated by a single family or small group of families, the competition for power among factions gave great political value to the creation of extended networks of kinship by means of marriage alliances. In this context the spreading of *parentado* was crucial for the family's acquisition or preservation of political power. Hence the multiplication of the *casato*'s collateral branches by the marrying off of all sons. The establishment of the oligarchic power of a few families, in contrast, favored a vertical vision of the family, limited to the *casato*'s main branch.[120]

With such strong emphasis on family, repudiation could well be something other than an individualistic assertion in contrast to family prerogatives.[121]

At the least, the desire to keep property in the family would at times run into changing family demographics and thus generate practices that were less rigidly exclusionary of cadet lines and women.[122] The hereditary system was not and could not be rigid in order for it to function.[123] In that light, repudiation can be taken as just one of several useful legal means of flexibility. While repudiation could forestall some obligations, dowry rights and other property inherited through women could hold some people and assets together, at least for a while, against debts and financial failure laid to the account of male relatives, especially one's father. Dowry was discriminatory in usually leaving women with less wealth than their brothers inherited and in subjecting them to effective male power and control in many situations, but it was also an investment in a woman. Perhaps for that reason Florentine law notably preferenced sons over daughters not only in inheritance to their fathers (in fact other agnate males also preceded daughters there) but also

Private Wealth in Renaissance Florence: A Study of Four Families (Princeton: Princeton University Press, 1968), 171–72.

[118] Jill Burke, *Changing Patrons: Social Identity and the Visual Arts in Renaissance Florence* (University Park: Penn State University Press, 2004), 18.

[119] Sharon T. Strocchia, *Death and Ritual in Renaissance Florence* (Baltimore: Johns Hopkins University Press, 1992), 125, 132, 178–79.

[120] Gianna Pomata, "Family and Gender," in *Early Modern Italy, 1550–1796*, ed. John A. Marino (Oxford and New York: Oxford University Press, 2002), 69–86, at 76.

[121] See Manlio Bellomo, "La struttura patrimoniale della famiglia italiana nel tardo medioevo," in *Marriage, Property, and Succession*, 53–69, for a sense of family prerogative in inheritance from the perspective of a legal historian.

[122] See Gianna Lumia-Ostinelli, "'Ut cippus domus magis conservetur': La successione a Siena tra statuti e testamenti (secoli xii-xvii)," *Archivio storico italiano* 161 (2003): 3–51, at 41.

[123] See Isabelle Chabot, "'Biens de famille': Contrôle des ressources patrimoniales, *gender* et cycle domestique (Italie, XIIIième – Xvième siècles)," in *The Household in Late Medieval Cities: Italy and Northwestern Europe Compared*, ed. Myriam Carlier and Tim Soens (Leuven: Garant, 2001), 89–104.

to their mothers.[124] *Testamenta, legata, aditiones, repudiationes, donationes causa mortis, fideicommissa*, and so much more allowed inheritances to be tailored to fit, including being avoided in total. Consider the strategies of Lapo di Giovanni Niccolini, with seven sons from two marriages. Though he foresaw difficulties from one son of the first marriage, Biagio, and ultimately he and his brother, Giovanni, did fall into financial difficulties, Lapo emancipated the sons of his first marriage and settled portions on them by means of emancipation gifts. The younger sons of the second marriage were his testamentary heirs. The older son, who had entered a monastery, received only a token bequest in the will, and he dutifully repudiated his mother's estate so that his share fell to his brothers.[125] Here then an array of devices – a testament, emancipations, a repudiation – formed a coordinated strategy of inheritance, playing itself out over time, that still almost floundered on future financial problems.

Repudiation can be seen as in line with, not in opposition to, family solidarity and its needs. Repudiation, if anything, posed that not the repudians but the *repudiatus* (to coin a word) was an individual (in an anthropological sense of being outside social connections). The one who had failed to maintain property was not the continuator of a patrimony and thus fell to some extent outside the realm of full social or familial personhood.[126] It was the deceased who had riddled the patrimony with debts and left it untenable, ostensibly, as continued family possession. In the case of Antonio da Panzano, it was even a living person who used repudiation (albeit to his dead wife) to maneuver property around himself and his financial problems. He was still trying to be a good manager for the sake of the family. Boninsegna Machiavelli's repudiation of his father, whose property then went to his two brothers, can also be seen as one in which the repudians was burdened with debt of his own and kept himself away from the paternal estate in consequence. He took advantage of the two salient features of repudiation – the avoidance of debt and the direction of property to the next in order of succession. The Corbizi example is so revealing. Employing repudiation at several points and anchoring property claims to dowries, the son and grandsons struggled to hold on to family properties and, through those, to a sense of continuity of generations, even to the grandfather who left them facing that debt to the Mannelli that would ultimately defeat them.

It is false to conclude that family and individual were always in opposition. As Francis William Kent noted almost thirty years ago, "a heightened

---

[124] Here one can now find a succinct and critical presentation of the issues in Isabelle Chabot and Anna Bellavitis, "A proposito di 'Men and Women in Renaissance Venice' di Stanley Chojnacki," *Quaderni storici* 118 (April 2005): 203–38, esp. 211–14, 218–24.
[125] Niccolini di Camugliano, *Chronicle*, 120–24, 144–45; RE 10, fol. 60 (26 August 1423).
[126] On these themes and for some of the rich anthropological literature, see my *Illegitimacy in Renaissance Florence* (Ann Arbor: University of Michigan Press, 2002), 4–6.

and assertive sense of personal capacity and achievement could live quite comfortably with a sense of lineage, which anyway had probably never converted individual kinsmen's successes into an impersonal clan property."[127] Repudiation was a dimension of family strategy. In that regard, it was no less a family strategy than the testament drawn up by any one paterfamilias who was attempting to make his expanded will into the will of his successors, and thereby restrict their freedom through his own expansive freedom of ownership and testation.

But it would also be false to conclude that what Florentines valued and strove for in the fourteenth, fifteenth, and early sixteenth centuries amounted to some form of "amoral familism." Florentines continually built partnerships and social alliances, while also using ties of kinship and neighborhood. Much rested on trust, and that trust was betrayed with perhaps stunning regularity; but what is also astounding is that Florentines kept getting back into partnerships and relying on trust and credit. Trickery and deceit, whether using repudiation or some other legal device, were not prized as optimal behaviors. They were coping strategies in a world in which government, law courts, and other institutions were weak in regard to enforcement and yet powerful enough to have considerable financial impacts and to gather and store some forms of information, like the registry of repudiations.

---

[127] Francis William Kent, *Household and Lineage*, 288–89. Note Crabb's distinction between "familial individualism" and "familialism" (*Strozzi*, 233).

4

Profile of Florentine Repudiation and Inheritance

The surviving registry of repudiations for the republican period (to early 1534) is the central source for this study. The registry provides data from which to recover a chronological overview of repudiation activity; the relationships between repudiator and repudiated, including the shifting incidence of females in each category; and the frequency of repudiations by Florentines and other Tuscans subject to Florence. The registry also provides some basis to discuss whether repudiations concerned all or only part of an estate, were consequent on intestacy or testamentary succession, and how much these factors varied by wealth and status (namely place of residence and possession, or not, of a family cognomen).

The Registry and Its Data

Florence's registry of repudiations consists of twenty-nine volumes, two of which are in fact indexes to some of the others. The twenty-seven effective volumes cover the period from 8 August 1365 to the final registered repudiation on 20 February 1534, during which a total of 11,317 repudiations of inheritance were recorded.[1] As the legislation establishing the registry of repudiations was passed fully ten years before the first surviving record (10 July 1355), I presume that the first ten years were lost. The somewhat haphazard state of the first couple of surviving volumes supports this presumption.

Repudiations are also not the only matters recorded in these pages. Satisdations of new citizens crop up repeatedly in the first volume and thereafter once in a while for several more volumes. From time to time across just about the entire span of the registry, "repudiations" of guild membership also appear. These occurred in the first volumes more frequently, but one can

---

[1] Some were duplicated or repeated acts on different dates.

still run across them even into the late fifteenth century.[2] The repudiations themselves were occasionally recorded out of order. On the one hand, some repudiations were allowed by extension or exemption, as that by Gianna di Francesco di Ghinozzo Pazzi of her brother Francesco by a *provvisione* of 13 June 1491,[3] or that granted to Bartolo di Piero di Bartolo Ligi in 1514.[4] On the other hand, some were removed for failure to pay the requisite registration fee.[5] These may not have counted in Florentine law courts, but they count in the data used in this study.

Appendix 1 offers a fairly typical example of registration of repudiation. The text is, in fact, a little legal narrative. It reports that the priors were assembled to do business on a given date, that the communal herald reported to them the details of a repudiation, and that in return the requisite fee had been deposited. The details of the repudiation vitally included the name of the repudiating party, the name of the deceased whose hereditas was refused and the relationship to the repudians, the name of the notary before whom the repudiation had occurred, and its date.[6] The text in Appendix 1 in fact offers some other bits of useful information – the place of residence (here in the form of a city parish), the fractional share of each heir (here amounting to the totality of the hereditas), and the fact that it came by intestacy.

From time to time, the entries in the registry yield even more information, though in much too spotty a fashion to furnish any statistical results. Fairly constant in the best days of registry record keeping were notations establishing how an estate had devolved to the person then repudiating it. Giovanni di Niccolò Benci established that he stood to inherit from his uncle Dorato as a consequence of a fideicommissum in his grandfather's testament.[7] Others told how repudiation by others had landed the estate in their laps (and could there be any doubt why they, in turn, were repudiating?). Brancazio di Niccolò Rucellai fell heir to his brother Piero thanks to repudiation by Piero's daughter (a repudiation that seems to have restored the statutory agnatic

---

[2] Two examples: RE 11, fol. 125r (24 September 1432), when Lorenzo di Piero Lenzi foreswore his membership in the Arte di Cambio; and ibid., fol. 81r (18 May), when Antonio di Jacopo da Monte declared he was leaving the Arte di Corazai.
[3] RE 23, fol. 143 (15 June 1491). Also by Lionardo di Tommaso Altoviti on the same day and through the same enactment.
[4] RE 28, fol. 62 (21 October 1514); also for Lorenzo di Francesco Guidetti (RE 28, fol. 64 [9 November 1514]), Carlo di Filippo Cappelli (RE 28, fol. 88 [22 January 1516]), Giuliano di Bettino di Sante (RE 28, fol. 91 [12 March 1516]), Piero di Luca di Maso and Roberto di Rinaldo Bardi (RE 28, fol. 98 [9 August 1516]).
[5] A total of 21: RE 15, fol. 55; 21, fol. 27; 27, fols. 31 and 104; 28, fols. 14, 78, 80, 83 (2), 126, 144 (2), 157 (2), 158; 29, fols. 19, 24, 25, 36, 70.
[6] The process is further described and another example given in Thomas Kuehn, "Law, Death, and Heirs in the Renaissance: Repudiation of Inheritance in Florence," *Renaissance Quarterly* 45 (1992): 484–516.
[7] RE 25, fol. 158 (26 May 1503).

inheritance pattern).[8] Lattanzio di Bindo Guasconi came to repudiate the estate of his uncle, Jacopo di Niccolò, as a result of prior repudiations by Jacopo's sons.[9]

When in 1394 Jacopo di Giovanni di Lippo repudiated the estate of his brother Francesco, he stated that it was for the half now fallen to him by repudiation of his brother's other heir, the Florentine hospital of Santa Maria Nuova.[10] In the year following a plague, naming the hospital as heir was probably excited by pious and moral concerns. The case is an example of another feature of the use of repudiation in Florence. From time to time the repudiating party was an institution – occasionally a guild or a neighborhood association, but usually a convent or monastery, which was the recipient of property less by volitional charity than by virtue of the fact that the institution in question in fact harbored among its members an inheriting son, daughter, brother, or other. The institution could move to accept or reject such an estate or portion. The Badia Fiorentina repudiated Filippozzo di Giovenco Bastari's share destined for his son Giovenco; similarly, the Annunziata rejected what one mother left her daughter.[11] Repudiation by an institution left the property to flow back to the next of kin, who, of course, had the prerogative to accept or reject.

One interesting feature of the registries is that from time to time we run into Florentines or other Tuscans acting unlawfully. Despite rules of ius commune, Giovanni di Giusto di Barone and his brother Altobianco repudiated their still-living father.[12] Piera di Ghino Rondinelli repudiated her mother, who was still alive but had remarried.[13] Lorenzo di Francesco Spinelli effectively excused his repudiation of Carlo di Jacopo Spinelli by noting that, though Carlo was still alive, he was in exile by a decree of October 1477.[14] Others tried to retain a legatum when they used repudiation. Francesca di Giovanni di Francesco Arnoldi repudiated what her husband, Piero di Niccolò di Brancazio Rucellai, had left her, but stipulated that she reserved her right to a bequest.[15] Piero di Jacopo Bischeri repudiated his father's estate yet accepted a legatum of 600 florins.[16] In contrast to these, other estates

---

[8] RE 21, fol. 116 (11 January 1480). See also RE 24, fol. 85 (19 February 1497); 26, fol. 36 (14 March 1505).
[9] RE 11, fol. 108 (13 March 1432). Also RE 13, fol. 13 (30 June 1436).
[10] RE 4, fol. 122 (28 April 1394).
[11] RE 13, fol. 68 (26 February 1438); 16, fol. 6 (22 May 1450). Also RE 2, fol. 16 (4 October 1379); 4, fol. 8 (28 June 1390); 5, fol. 68 (23 January 1396); 7, fol. 24 (23 December 1404); 9, fol. 237 (1 October 1420); 10, fol. 236 (20 October 1427); 15, fol. 112 (28 April 1447); 16, fol. 85 (27 January 1452); 27, fols. 96 and 97 (11 March 1512); 29, fol. 21 (4 February 1523); 29, fol. 78 (23 April 1529); 29, fol. 119 (30 June 1533).
[12] RE 9, fol. 133 (23 July 1418).
[13] RE 20, fol. 216 (20 March 1477).
[14] RE 21, fol. 17 (31 October 1477).
[15] RE 21, fol. 62 (4 December 1478).
[16] RE 20, fol. 156 (6 December 1476).

seem to have been especially toxic. Piero di Graziano's hereditas, for example, was repudiated in short order, first, by Lorenzo di Giovanni di Bici de' Medici, then by Giovanni di Michele di Torello, Graziano di Bernaba, and Michele di Bernaba.[17]

Information as to occupation of repudians or deceased was given generally as an aid in identifying the persons. It is too inconsistent to exploit systematically. It is interesting, nonetheless, to note the range of occupations, from nobles and great merchants to humble "laboratores terrae," that recur in the registry. Given the prevalence of credit relations at all levels of society, repudiation proved useful to persons in all walks of life. Other information is necessarily consistent to a high degree – such as gender of the parties and their relationships to each other. Important insights result from examining these bits of information.

Chronology of Repudiations

Beyond the varying degrees of sloppiness in the first volumes, consistency was undercut by the low volume of business in general (See Table 1.)[18] Gaps in the record for 1368–71 and 1374–76 also speak to spotty record keeping and preservation.[19] Not surprisingly, activity was low in the tumultuous year of the Ciompi Revolt, 1378 (twelve entries, with only two coming after June). It was under the more egalitarian post-Ciompi regime that activity picked up in 1379, 1380, and 1381. The return of oligarchic control early in 1382 led to a brief break in registrations (between 4 December 1381 and 16 March 1382), but it was probably no accident that the following year, 1383, saw the highest total for registrations in a year to that point (sixty-one). As Florentine politics became mildly more stable, as power and wealth in Florence progressively fell into fewer and fewer hands, repudiation from that point became an ever more consistent feature of Florentine life. These were also the very years in which figures such as Angelo and Baldo degli Ubaldi were resolving some of the most pressing practical legal questions revolving around repudiation. That development too tended to encourage recourse to the institution, as

---

[17] RE 9, fols. 245, 246, 249 (12 and 30 December 1420, 28 January 1421).
[18] Given the incredible fall off in emancipations when registry was begun with the Signoria in 1421, after having been the exclusive preserve of the Mercanzia since 1355 (cf. Thomas Kuehn, *Emancipation in Late Medieval Florence* [New Brunswick: Rutgers University Press, 1982], 82–83), the Signoria's participation in repudiation registry may well have meant low levels of registered activity from the start.
[19] There are no entries between 19 May 1369 and 27 February 1370, nor between that latter date and 7 July 1371. Eliminating the one entry from 1370 means the entire series has been lost for over two years between May 1369 and July 1371. It would appear to be a loss of records that accounts for these low figures; it hardly seems likely that there was no activity, even if in the following years the levels of activity remained low. 1374 effectively ends in March and there are no registered repudiations from 1375, leaving again a gap of almost two years between 28 March 1374 and 14 February 1376.

TABLE 1. *Repudiations, Year by Year*

Year	Number	Year	Number	Year	Number
1365	17	1397	46	1429	63
1366	37	1398	49		
1367	46	1399	56	Decade Total	774
1368	19				
1369	6	Decade Total	492	1430	69
				1431	65
Decade Total	125	1400	89	1432	73
		1401	83	1433	62
1370	1	1402	59	1434	56
1371	9	1403	47	1435	70
1372	17	1404	69	1436	71
1373	16	1405	52	1437	65
1374	10	1406	49	1438	89
1375	0	1407	57	1439	75
1376	23	1408	53		
1377	25	1409	40	Decade Total	695
1378	12				
1379	34	Decade Total	598	1440	75
				1441	79
Decade Total	147	1410	45	1442	84
		1411	45	1443	68
1380	43	1412	51	1444	80
1381	28	1413	58	1445	69
1382	27	1414	44	1446	85
1383	63	1415	73	1447	78
1384	67	1416	65	1448	57
1385	51	1417	73	1449	59
1386	35	1418	108		
1387	45	1419	94	Decade Total	734
1388	40				
1389	59	Decade Total	656	1450	90
				1451	97
Decade Total	458	1420	78	1452	57
		1421	66	1453	72
1390	57	1422	71	1454	58
1391	53	1423	93	1455	49
1392	48	1424	94	1456	42
1393	39	1425	72	1457	55
1394	56	1426	75	1458	54
1395	37	1427	83	1459	77
1396	51	1428	78		
				Decade Total	651

Chronology of Repudiations

Year	Number	Year	Number	Year	Number
1460	66	1490	120	1520	61
1461	76	1491	102	1521	47
1462	62	1492	98	1522	66
1463	69	1493	114	1523	50
1464	55	1494	74	1524	47
1465	59	1495	88	1525	91
1466	79	1496	85	1526	38
1467	56	1497	142	1527	79
1468	78	1498	109	1528	111
1469	56	1499	93	1529	44
Decade Total	656	Decade Total	1025	Decade Total	634
1470	65	1500	103	1530	44
1471	56	1501	95	1531	86
1472	74	1502	69	1532	61
1473	63	1503	80	1533	63
1474	48	1504	83	1534	10
1475	52	1505	98		
1476	162	1506	71	Decade Total	264
1477	139	1507	85		
1478	98	1508	87		
1479	94	1509	74		
Decade Total	851	Decade Total	845	Grand Total	11,317
1480	108	1510	83		
1481	101	1511	69		
1482	85	1512	71		
1483	86	1513	101		
1484	95	1514	78		
1485	95	1515	71		
1486	88	1516	85		
1487	93	1517	61		
1488	96	1518	78		
1489	110	1519	58		
Decade Total	957	Decade Total	755		

did continued high mortality rates. Florence's population, which had fallen precipitately after the first plague of 1348 (from perhaps 120,000 to 40,000), experienced ups and downs despite immigration from rural areas, under the impact of wars and successive recurrences of epidemics to a low point around the time of the first catasto (1427), when the city's population was only about

37,000. Proportionally similar losses struck the rural areas and smaller cities subject to Florence's rule.[20]

Growth in repudiations at the end of the fourteenth century brought the average to almost fifty per year in the 1390s. The first seven decades of the fifteenth century saw remarkably consistent use of repudiation, with somewhere between sixty and seventy per year, with a peak of seventy-seven per year in the 1420s (a decade of war, a plague, and increasing state activity in the form of the Monte delle doti, the catasto, and other measures).

The 1470s saw a shift. Repudiations increased almost 30% over the 1460s, and they continued to increase over the next two decades: 11.4% in the 1480s, and another 8.2% in the 1490s. This pattern coincided with a demographic one in which population levels were recovering. The decade of the 1470s was, not accidentally, also the period of the greatest legislative and administrative interest in repudiation. It also began a period in which mounting economic woes, followed by the turbulence of the 1490s, raised the fears of people regarding debts and rapidly reversing fortunes.[21] Whether ditching obligations or hiding assets, Florentines seem to have found repudiation most useful at that time.

In the 1500s, repudiation activity began to decline – down 17.6% in the century's first decade, then 10.7% in the next, and a further 16% in the 1520s to an average of sixty-three to sixty-four repudiations per year, a level of activity comparable to the first decade of the fifteenth century. This was the period in which the registries themselves became more terse and there were notable lapses in the Signoria's activities, including recording repudiations, which called forth legislative exemptions, and extensions from the statutory deadlines to register. For its part, population probably declined during the years of Medici exile, 1494–1512, recovered some after their return, 1512–27, and then was held in check by wars and economic factors until mid-century, when it was close to 60,000.

Within this large scale chronological picture – establishment, upsurge, downturn – there are also some noteworthy year-to-year fluctuations. Political and military events influenced repudiation acitivity – for example, the spike of activity in 1513 (101 repudiations, up from seventy-one in 1512),

---

[20] The most recent treatment of Tuscan population history is the English edition of David Herlihy and Christiane Klapisch-Zuber's monumental study, *Tuscans and Their Families: A Study of the Florentine Catasto of 1427* (New Haven: Yale University Press, 1985), 60–92. It is the source for this and subsequent demographic observations. A broader demographic canvas, sketched mainly with an eye for plague mortality is Samuel K. Cohn, Jr., *The Black Death Transformed: Disease and Culture in Early Renaissance Europe* (London: Arnold, 2003), in which, for Florence, note 32, 88, and 200–219.

[21] Raymond de Roover, *The Rise and Decline of the Medici Bank, 1397–1494* (Cambridge: Harvard University Press, 1963), 358–75; L. F. Marks, "La crisi finanziaria a Firenze dal 1494 al 1502," *Archivio storico italiano* 112 (1954): 40–72.

following the destructive siege of Prato and return of the Medici to Florence the previous year or the almost doubling of registrations (from forty-four to eighty-six) in 1531 after the end of the siege of Florence herself. Yet repudiations were most markedly affected by shifts in mortality. If we had no other device for tracking epidemics in this period, the registry of repudiations would provide a very useful tool for spotting them. The epidemic of 1393, for example, resulted in a 44% increase in repudiations in 1394 (from thirty-nine to fifty-six), while that of 1400 led to an increase of 59% over 1399 (eighty-nine to fifty-six) and in 1401 a total that was still 48% higher than 1399 (eighty-three). The mortality of 1417 was marked by a jump from seventy-three repudiations to 108 in 1418 (48% increase), and a similar increase from seventy-one to ninety-three (31%) marked 1423. The same sort of increases proclaim the epidemics of 1437, 1449, 1468, 1495–99, and 1527.[22] The only known epidemics that did not show an increase in the annual total of repudiations were those of 1457 and 1464.

Use of repudiation also responded to legal developments. Adoption of the revised statutes of 1415, now allowing for repudiation with retention of paternal property for maternal dowry, seems to have promoted use of repudiation. In 1414, there were forty-four repudiations; in 1415, there were seventy-three. For the first five years of the decade, there were 243 repudiations, a total which predicted a decade's output in line with the 1390s, instead the second five years of the 1410s saw 413 repudiations. Again, this total was spiked by the 1417 epidemic, but the level of activity for that decade was essentially the new threshold for subsequent decades across the next century.

A conjunction of legislative actions, political turmoil (the Pazzi conspiracy of 1478 and the resulting war), and disease coincided with the most feverish period of repudiations in the second half of the 1470s. It seems safe to say that two elements were at work at different points. The figures for 1478–81 probably reflect the effects of plague and war. Repudiations in those years averaged 100 per year, as opposed to the average of sixty per year for 1470–75. The high figures for 1476 and 1477 can clearly be ascribed to the law of 1476, which set a deadline of 31 December 1476 to register repudiations or pay fiscal duties owing on certain estates. We will examine this activity more closely in the next chapter.

---

[22] The figures are as follows: 1437, sixty-five repudiations, versus eighty-nine in 1438 (37% increase); 1449, fifty-nine repudiations, versus ninety in 1450 (up 53%) and versus ninety-seven (64% over 1449) in 1451; 1468, seventy-eight repudiations, versus fifty-six in 1467 (39%); 1527, seventy-nine, versus 1528 111 (41%). 1495–99 witnessed leaps from eighty-eight and eighty-five per year to 142 (second highest annual total in the entire registry) in 1497 (67% increase over 1496), with 1498 seeing 109, 1499 ninety-three, 1500 103, and 1501 still ninety-five.

Repudiating Florentines and Tuscans

In compiling a statistical table of relationships, I have stuck with the Latin terms employed in the registry, but I have also elided some of them in minor categories for which few instances occurred. (See Table 2.)[23] The overwhelming majority of relationships in play in repudiations, described in terms of the de cuius's relationship to the repudians, were male (over 95%). Of those, the dominant relationship was paternal. Sons and, occasionally, daughters repudiated fathers' estates in almost 75% of all repudiations between 1365 and 1534.

Across the decades, there was a steady upswing in the percentage of repudiations in which paternal patrimonies were rejected. In the 1370s, paternal repudiations were 61.9% of repudiations; in the 1380s, they were 69.2%; in the 1390s, 73.5%; and in the 1400s, 80.6%. In the 1410s, they were 84.1% and account for all the numerical increase in repudiations from the previous decade.[24] A case can be made that the revised statute of 1415 had an effect. For the rest of the fifteenth century, at least 80% of repudiations were aimed at paternal estates; then, fairly precipitately, the rate at which fathers' estates were repudiated fell to around 73% for the next three decades, even as the overall level of repudiation activity rose. That new activity came from repudiations of estates of persons other than fathers during the time that the overall frequency of repudiations fell across the first decades of the Cinquecento.

More specifically, the number of repudiations involving estates of brothers, uncles, and cousins (*patruelis*) picked up enormously. From the 1460s to the 1470s, repudiations of brothers almost tripled, repudiations of uncles rose sixfold, of cousins eightfold. Put another way, brothers' estates went from being the object of less than 4% of repudiations in the 1440s to 8% in the 1480s, ascending continually to over 25% when the registry was closed. The corresponding rates for uncles went from around 1% to over 5% in the 1480s and close to 12% in the 1510s. The increase for cousins was also sharp.

---

[23] Consanguineus, cognatus, affinis, and consobrinus have all been grouped under a single heading, consors, also found in the registry. Maritus has been labeled by the semantic equivalent, vir. Given the few instances in which an avus or avia was maternal, rather than paternal, no distinction was drawn, so as not to clutter the chart needlessly with minor categories. Similarly, under nepos were also included the few clear instances of a nepos ex filia or of a grandson, as the semantic range of that term covered all those relationships. Under frater are several other terms – germanus, frater uterinus. Amita includes patrua. Patruelis has been employed not only when the text used it but as a catchall term for patrilateral cousins when a relationship was posited by a single cognomen. One reason the category of unknown relationships shrinks over time is Florentines' increasing use of a family name, allowing recovery of a vague cousinship where one was not so easily recoverable earlier.

[24] For the 1420s 82.3%; in the 1430s 82.7%; the 1440s 87.9%; in the 1450s 87.3%; in the 1460s 87.7%.

TABLE 2. *Relationship of Deceased to Primary Repudiator*

Male

Decades	Pater	Frater	Patruus	Avus	Filius	Patruelis	Vir	Unknown	Nepotis	Avunculus	Consobrin	Socer	TOTAL
1360s	71	8	4	1	3	5	8	6	0	0	2	0	108
1370s	91	11	3	0	3	5	5	8	2	0	1	0	129
1380s	317	29	5	4	6	10	12	31	3	1	1	0	419
1390s	362	38	7	4	6	12	11	24	1	0	2	0	467
1400s	482	26	7	4	9	7	9	21	0	0	2	0	567
1410s	552	33	11	2	5	7	5	16	1	1	2	0	635
1420s	637	36	7	7	9	9	8	26	2	1	0	0	741
1430s	575	25	12	7	4	6	7	13	1	0	1	1	652
1440s	645	12	8	13	7	4	1	14	2	0	0	0	706
1450s	568	19	8	8	3	2	4	7	1	0	0	0	620
1460s	575	24	8	10	2	3	5	5	0	0	0	0	632
1470s	616	68	50	10	7	24	3	15	1	1	1	0	796
1480s	697	118	49	13	1	22	3	8	3	1	1	0	916
1490s	757	117	71	14	5	11	3	9	5	1	1	0	994
1500s	547	152	86	9	4	10	1	6	5	1	3	0	824
1510s	437	139	89	9	4	23	3	15	7	2	1	1	730
1520s	360	130	62	9	11	26	1	6	5	3	3	0	616
1530s	148	68	21	4	5	4	2	3	4	0	0	0	259
TOTAL	8437	1053	508	128	94	190	91	233	43	11	21	2	10811

(continued)

121

TABLE 2 (continued)

Decades	Mater	Avia	Soror	Uxor	Amita	Patruelis	Unknown	Matertera	Filia	Neptis	Sclava	Noverca	TOTAL	MALE & FEMALE TOTAL
1360s	10	1	2	2	0	0	2	0	0	0	0	0	17	125
1370s	8	1	1	3	0	0	5	0	0	0	0	0	18	147
1380s	22	0	6	1	2	1	6	1	0	0	0	0	39	458
1390s	13	1	4	1	0	0	5	0	1	0	0	0	25	492
1400s	18	1	3	3	0	2	2	0	1	1	0	0	31	598
1410s	10	1	2	0	1	0	6	0	1	0	0	0	21	656
1420s	14	5	2	2	1	0	9	0	0	0	0	0	33	774
1430s	31	2	1	1	0	0	4	0	2	1	1	0	43	695
1440s	18	0	3	1	1	0	5	0	0	0	0	0	28	734
1450s	24	0	1	1	1	0	3	0	0	0	0	1	31	651
1460s	16	2	2	0	4	0	0	0	0	0	0	0	24	656
1470s	38	4	5	0	4	2	2	0	0	0	0	0	55	851
1480s	27	6	1	1	4	1	0	0	0	0	0	1	41	957
1490s	17	2	5	0	1	1	5	0	0	0	0	0	31	1025
1500s	17	4	0	0	0	0	0	0	0	0	0	0	21	845
1510s	11	6	0	0	6	1	1	0	0	0	0	0	25	755
1520s	11	2	2	0	0	1	2	0	0	0	0	0	18	634
1530s	1	2	0	0	0	0	1	0	1	0	0	0	5	264
TOTAL	306	40	40	16	25	9	58	1	6	2	1	2	506	11317

One hundred seventy repudiations disclose secondary relationships. Either a repudians repudiated two separate estates at the same time (as father and uncle, for example), or one of a group of repudiantes in the same act stood in a different relationship to the deceased (e.g., son and grandson). One hundred thirty-two of the 170 covered the four categories of brother, uncle, grandfather, or cousin.

That political fortunes or more wide-ranging economic interests were behind repudiations of relatives such as brothers and uncles can perhaps be confirmed by a simple correlation. One measure of wealth and status employed by historians of Florence is the existence of a family name, a cognomen. Those with a cognomen repudiated their fathers only 58% of the time they used repudiation, in contrast to 84.5% of repudiations for those lacking a family name. (See Table 3.) More than a third of repudiations of those with cognomen were thus aimed at other than paternal relationships, versus the 15.5% for those without a name. That statistical comparison alone may be highly indicative of the degree to which humbler folk, of the city and the countryside, inherited almost solely from their fathers. Those with last names repudiated paternal uncles, brothers, cousins, even mothers at significantly higher proportions.[25] They also repudiated estates of various women at a higher rate – 6% of their repudiations as opposed to 3.6% for those lacking a family name. Whether their goal was to dodge a liability or to direct property to others, those with more means and status looked in more directions more frequently.

Brothers and uncles also appeared more frequently in the ranks of those repudiated precisely at the point that repudiations with multiple repudiators (most often brothers acting together) also became more frequent. Between 10 and 20% of repudiations always involved more than one repudiator – ranging from a high of 20% in the 1360s to a low of 11.5% in the 1430s. (See Table 4.) In the 1470s, however, the percentage rose above 20% and peaked at close to 30% in the 1520s. In those decades, from time to time, groups of brothers and other kin numbering as many as twelve, came forward to repudiate an estate. Statutory crackdowns in the 1470s may have made such group avoidance of liability more pressing. Still, it is important to note that Florentines' concerns with estates of brothers and uncles were mirrored in a collateral grouping of brothers and cousins as repudiators.

Most of the additional repudiantes were brothers, which is to be expected, as the set of male siblings in a system of partible inheritance came to the same hereditas at the same moment. But others joined in repudiations too. Paolo di Zanobi di Paolo da Ghiacceto was joined by his sons when he repudiated his father (their grandfather).[26] Geri d'Ubertino di Gherardo Risaliti

---

[25] Uncles: 9.1% to 1.7%; brothers: 17.3% to 4.5%; cousins: 4% to .3%; mothers: 3.7% to 2.1%

[26] RE 23, fol. 56 (17 December 1489).

TABLE 3. *Relationship to Repudians*

Relationship	Frequency	Percentage
With a Cognomen		
unknown	59	1.4
amite	20	.4
avi	66	1.6
avie	28	.7
avunculi	9	.2
consortis	12	.3
femine	11	.3
filie	2	.0
filii	37	.9
fratris	731	17.3
matris	157	3.7
nepotis	31	.7
neptis	1	.0
noverce	1	.0
patris	2455	58.0
patruelis	171	4.0
patruelis femine	6	.1
patrui	387	9.1
sclave	1	.0
soceri	1	.0
sororis	19	.4
uxoris	8	.2
viri	22	.5
Total	4235	100
Without Cognomen		
unknown	174	2.5
amite	5	.1
avi	62	.9
avie	12	.2
avunculi	2	.0
consortis	9	.1
femine	47	.7
filie	4	.1
filii	57	.8
fratris	322	4.5
matertere		1.0
matris	149	2.1
nepotis	12	.2
neptis	1	.0
noverce	1	.0
patris	5982	84.5
patruelis	19	.3

Relationship	Frequency	Percentage
patruelis femine	3	.0
patrui	121	1.7
soceri	1	.0
sororis	21	.3
uxoris	8	.1
viri	69	1.0
TOTAL	7082	100

repudiated his brother Rosso, accompanied by several cousins, Jacopo di Mariotto, Antonio di Tommaso, Ubertino di Simone, and Stefano di Girolamo Risaliti.[27] The notaries' offices were crowded in 1513, when twelve Altoviti repudiated Giovangualberto d'Ubaldo Altoviti and ten Scarlatti repudiated Carlo d'Antonio Scarlatti.[28] These and many other acts grouped cousins in the repudiations of uncles or other cousins.

What lay behind this shift from fathers to brothers, uncles, and cousins? Some of it has to be due to legislation, notably that of 1476, which encouraged repudiation of estates of relatives other than fathers. Yet it was also the case that more estates were coming from indirect lines or that repudiation of such estates was more necessary on other grounds. Inheritance practices emphasizing linearity, often tied to fideicommissa, meant that uncles, brothers, and cousins without direct heirs were more likely to employ or themselves be subject to a substitution in fideicommissum that directed property to collateral paternal kin.[29] The more property came to such kin, the more opportunity they had to repudiate it. Conversely, it may also have been the case, manifest at least when the rate of repudiation of fathers' estates fell after 1500, that it was harder to reject what was left by one's father, which may have carried its own clauses of substitution. Clauses attached to fideicommissa that forbade alienation *extra familiam* of key assets – stipulations that were elaborated by jurists and upheld by courts – may well also have lowered the risks of accepting a debt-ridden paternal estate. One could hold the property against creditors, if one could stand behind such clauses.[30]

The elaboration of fideicommissa that endeavored to hold family property intact and undivided was a relatively late phenomenon in the world of

---

[27] RE 23, fol. 88 (20 April 1490).
[28] RE 28, fol. 25 (22 April 1513) and fol. 34 (21 June 1513).
[29] One example was Giovanni Benci's repudiation of Dorato (RE 25, fol. 158 [26 May 1503]).
[30] J. P. Cooper, "Patterns of Inheritance and Settlement by Great Landowners from the Fifteenth to the Eighteenth Centuries," in *Family and Inheritance: Rural Society in Western Europe, 1200–1800*, ed. Jack Goody, Joan Thirsk, and E. P. Thompson (Cambridge: Cambridge University Press, 1976), 192–327, at 265. And see my "*Fideicommissum* and Family: The Orsini di Bracciano" *Viator* (in press).

northern and central Italian cities – arriving around the 1490s and after.[31] Prior to that point, fideicommissa provided patterns of substitution predicated on egalitarian division of estates; clauses prohibiting alienation of important properties might keep them within a family, if in many hands. Repudiation furnished a means to eliminate some of those hands. Conversely, the drop off in numbers of repudiations from the 1510s may indicate a more extensive use of testaments to hold property in undivided ownership, both reducing the number of heirs in a position to repudiate and the number of estates that were so small or impoverished as to deserve repudiating.

Gender Analysis

Overall, between 1365 and 1534 estates of women were repudiated only 4.5% of the time. (See Table 2.) Women undoubtedly held less property and were not in position as easily to run up debts and obligations in Florence, so it stands to reason that there was both less to repudiate and less to inherit. In the 1360s and 1370s, when women's estates were about 10% of those repudiated, their estates may only have represented complications more easily disposed of. After the 1380s, women's estates were consistently a modest portion of those repudiated, between roughly 3 and 6%.

The other side of the ledger regarding gender and repudiation is the degree to which women were the repudiating parties.

Table 4 shows that women were slightly more frequently repudiated than repudiating (only 4.1% of all repudiantes). Their involvement with repudiation was relatively higher at the beginning of the registry period, but by the 1460s they were consistently less than 4% of repudiantes.

Among repudiations of women's estates are a number of curious instances in which men or, once in a while, women repudiated women either distantly or not overtly related to them. Francesco di Rinaldo di Bardo Magnesi, for example, repudiated Diana, widow of Buonaccorso di Niccolò Torelli, and Cesare di Benedetto di Biagio da Certaldo repudiated Lisa di Pera Nerli, widow of Ciallo di Dino.[32] There is no relationship retrievable from the names alone in these instances. What tends to demarcate them is that they largely hail from outside Florence and involve seemingly humble folks. In the small society of a rural village, there was either close friendship or an undisclosed kinship behind such inheritances, whatever else accounted for

---

[31] Franca Leverotti, "Strutture familiari nel tardo medioevo italiano," *Revista d'historia medieval* 10 (1999): 233–68, at 11–15, which represents a theoretical and methodological position derived from her exhaustive study of the Lucchese countryside, *Popolazione, famiglie, insediamento: Le Sei Miglia lucchesi nel xiv e xv secolo* (Pisa: Pacini, 1992). Also Bartolome Clavero, "*Dictum beati*: A proposito della cultura del lignaggio," *Quaderni storici* 86 (August 1994): 335–63.

[32] RE 13, fol. 106 (22 December 1438); RE 1, fol. 214 (17 September 1377).

Gender Analysis

TABLE 4. *Gender of Repudiantes*

Decade	Males	Females	% Female	Multiple Acts	Total
1360s	140	17	.108	25	157
1370s	162	19	.105	26	181
1380s	520	47	.083	82	567
1390s	588	33	.053	94	621
1400s	671	34	.048	76	705
1410s	772	24	.030	111	796
1420s	861	42	.047	101	903
1430s	744	53	.066	80	797
1440s	864	29	.032	117	893
1450s	755	33	.042	99	788
1460s	769	26	.033	111	795
1470s	1094	61	.053	179	1155
1480s	1254	46	.035	209	1300
1490s	1386	47	.033	252	1433
1500s	1204	26	.021	204	1230
1510s	1113	36	.031	201	1149
1520s	899	31	.033	187	930
1530s	334	7	.021	50	341
TOTALS	14,130	611	.041	2204	14,741

the repudiation.[33] Only a few of these drew Florentines, such as Arrigo di Filippo Rucellai, who in 1394 repudiated what had been left him by India d'Ugo d'Arrigo Ricasoli, widow of Giannozzo di Neri Vettori, or Lisa, wife of Ridolfo Peruzzi, who repudiated Gapa, wife of Marco Gigoli.[34]

Otherwise, Florentines repudiated their mothers about 60% of the time when they repudiated inheritance from a woman, which contrasts with the 78% for repudiation of fathers when repudiating the estate of a male. In total, only 306 mothers were repudiated, against 8,437 fathers. Small percentages mark repudiations of estates of grandmothers, sisters, aunts, and even wives. In some instances, remarriage played a role in repudiation. Checco di Checco had occasion to repudiate his mother, who had remarried.[35] In reverse, Gostanza di Lorenzo di Giovanni repudiated her daughter from her

---

[33] Further examples: Filippo di Bartolomeo di Girello and Marco di Giovanni of Gangalandi from Ginevra d'Antonio del Peccha, wife of Bellotto d'Andrrea of Artimino (RE 10, fol. 225 [24 July 1427]); Cristoforo di Lorenzo from Dalma di Falchino, widow of Barozzo di Bono (RE 4, fol. 34 [27 April 1391]); Antonio di Lodovico di Simone da Fighino from his aunt Lorenza, widow of Giovanni di Lorenzo of Castel San Giovanni (RE 19, fol. 42 [5 October 1465]).

[34] RE 4, fol. 115 (25 February 1394); 10, fol. 195 (19 November 1426).

[35] RE 6, fol. 84 (28 April 1402).

first marriage, Maria di Niccolò di Battista di Jacopo.[36] In neither of these did remarriage attenuate a maternal bond when it came to inheritance (financial viability and repudiation being different matters).

When repudiating, women rejected their fathers' estates a relatively low 47.5% of the time. (See Table 5.) This is not surprising. As their brothers stood to inherit the paternal estate on intestacy, and were really little less likely to gain it by testament, daughters would not have been in position to inherit from their fathers, except in the absence of brothers. One could also assume that, if daughters inherited from fathers, there was corresponding pressure on them from male relatives to repudiate, although we also have to recognize that repudiations by their brothers, cousins, or uncles could land an estate in their hands.

Another figure that stands out is that, although women's estates were only 4.5% of those repudiated, women repudiantes repudiated estates from women 13.5% of the time. They repudiated their mothers at a higher rate than men did (7.3% versus 2.5%). While women repudiated fathers and uncles at a lower rate than their male kin, they repudiated sons and brothers at a higher rate. And many more husbands than wives were repudiated (all these estates, especially from husband to wife, requiring a testament for such to occur), indicating not only the trends in economic power (putting wealth in the hands of men to be distributed to others) and demography (leaving young wives to outlive their husbands), but also the degree to which husbands sought to bind their widows to their household and children.[37]

If we subdivide the female repudiantes by marital status, we learn that widowed women, beyond accounting for all the repudiated husbands, did little other repudiating (most of that being fathers, brothers, and mothers). Married women overwhelmingly repudiated fathers, sometimes brothers and mothers. The remaining women, who include not only the generally younger cohort of those not married but also those for whom we have no firm designation of marital state, were naturally more directed at repudiating fathers and brothers.[38]

As managers of property, as well as nominal owners of it, women were as liable to debts as their brothers. But the result of laws, customs, and ideology was that women held much less property and were less involved in the

---

[36] RE 29, fol. 109 (21 June 1532).
[37] Cf. Julius Kirshner, *Pursuing Honor While Avoiding Sin: The Monte delle doti of Florence* (Milan: Giuffrè, 1978); Christiane Klapsich-Zuber, "Le complexe de Griselda: Dot et dons de mariage au Quattrocento," *Mélanges de l'Ecole Française de Rome* 94 (1982): 7–43, translated in *Women, Family, and Ritual in Renaissance Italy*, trans. Lydia G. Cochrane (Chicago: University of Chicago Press, 1985), 213–46; Isabelle Chabot, "Widowhood and Poverty in Late Medieval Florence," *Continuity and Change* 3 (1988): 291–311.
[38] In total, married women account for 139 repudiations (eighty-six being of paternal estates), widows for 140 (twenty of fathers, eighty-nine of husbands), and others for 279 (159 of fathers).

TABLE 5. *Gender and Relationships to Deceased*

Relationship	Frequency	Percent	Female Totals
Men			
Unknown	218	2.0	
Amite	24	.2	24
Avi	122	1.1	
Avie	37	.3	37
Avunculi	10	.1	
Consortis	21	.2	
Femine	50	.5	50
Filie	2	.0	2
Filii	70	.7	
Fratris	989	9.2	
Matris	265	2.5	265
Nepotis	40	.4	
Noverce	2	.0	2
Patris	8171	76.0	
Patruelis	186	1.7	
Patruelis femine	8	.1	8
Patrui	493	4.6	
Sclave	1	.0	1
Soceri	1	.0	
Sororis	33	.3	33
Uxoris	16	.1	16
TOTALS	10,759	100	438
Women			
Unknown	15	2.7	
Amite	1	.2	1
Avi	6	1.1	
Avie	3	.5	3
Avunculi	1	.2	
Femine	8	1.4	8
Filie	4	.7	4
Filii	24	4.3	
Fratris	64	11.5	
Matertere	1	.2	1
Matris	41	7.3	41
Nepotis	3	.5	
Neptis	2	.4	2
Patris	265	47.5	
Patruelis	5	.9	
Patruelis femine	1	.2	1
Patrui	15	2.7	
Soceri	1	.2	
Sororis	7	1.3	7
Viri	91	16.3	
TOTALS	558	100	68

turbulent economy of material or monetary (as opposed to symbolic) credit. Women were highly susceptible to the needs of kin. Their repudiations responded more often to family imperatives than just to economic factors. This is not to say that they could not perceive the need for repudiation when faced with a debt-ridden estate. Men who repudiated their mothers (over 60% of female estates men repudiated) released the estate to siblings, including sisters. Women who repudiated estates of fathers, husbands, and brothers (collectively the target of 75% of repudiations by women) were releasing them to agnatic male kin. In their repudiations, as in their wills, women were subtly expressing their affective and patrimonial ties to a range of persons.[39]

Geography of Repudiation

The one fairly consistent bit of information in the registry is the place of residence of the repudians.

Table 6 discloses locations of repudiators in three categories, within Florence itself, any location outside the city (from nearby places such as Sesto or Prato to more distant locales like Pisa, Venice, or Rome), or no designation at all. Many of the latter were, in fact, probably Florentine, as the recording notaries did not feel compelled to give neighborhood locations for such well-known families as Medici, Alberti, Soderini, and so forth. Entire areas of Florence's dominion, notably cities such as Pisa and Arezzo, whose relationship to Florence was spelled out in treaties, escaped the registration requirement and various statutory peculiarities. Only an occasional repudiation of a Pisan or Aretine, probably someone with active business interests in Florence, appears in the registries.

Repudiations from the contado, distretto, and foreign parts grew as a portion of registered repudiations from the 1390s through the 1420s – an era in which Florence was militarily and diplomatically engaged in expanding and consolidating her dominion.[40] There were, in consequence, more people and property there to become involved in repudiations, and possibly the sort of fresh disruption of agricultural and commercial patterns that could turn credits sour and call forth repudiation. After the 1420s, repudiations from

---

[39] See Merry E. Wiesner, *Women and Gender in Early Modern Europe* (Cambridge: Cambridge University Press, 1993), 109; Isabelle Chabot, "Seconde nozze e identità materna nella Firenze del tardo medioevo," in *Tempi e spazi di vita femminile tra medioevo et età moderna*, ed. Silvana Seidel Menchi, Anne Jacobson Schutte, and Thomas Kuehn (Bologna: Il Mulino, 1999), 493–523, at 520–21.

[40] See William J. Connell and Andrea Zorzi, eds, *Florentine Tuscany: Structures and Practices of Power* (Cambridge: Cambridge University Press, 2000); Samuel K. Cohn, Jr., *Creating the Florentine State: Peasants and Rebellion, 1348–1434* (Cambridge: Cambridge University Press, 1999); Gene Brucker, *The Civic World of Early Renaissance Florence* (Princeton: Princeton University Press, 1977).

Partial Repudiations

TABLE 6. *Locations of Repudiations*

Decade	Unknown (%)	Florence	Contado/Elsewhere
1360s	13(.104)	71(.568)	41(.328)
1370s	6(.041)	95(.646)	46(.313)
1380s	27(.059)	272(.594)	159(.347)
1390s	15(.030)	222(.451)	255(.518)
1400s	18(.030)	243(.406)	337(.564)
1410s	24(.037)	259(.395)	373(.569)
1420s	53(.068)	287(.371)	434(.561)
1430s	54(.078)	298(.429)	343(.494)
1440s	58(.079)	329(.448)	347(.472)
1450s	57(.088)	321(.493)	273(.419)
1460s	91(.139)	293(.447)	272(.415)
1470s	151(.177)	427(.447)	273(.320)
1480s	290(.303)	342(.357)	325(.340)
1490s	212(.207)	568(.554)	245(.239)
1500s	199(.236)	457(.541)	189(.224)
1510s	209(.277)	374(.495)	172(.228)
1520s	169(.267)	307(.484)	158(.249)
1530s	67(.254)	112(.424)	85(.322)
TOTALS	1713(.151)	5277(.466)	4327(.383)

outside Florence declined. Repudiation, at least in the pages of the registry, became more and more a Florentine activity. Other factors were also at work, such as the spread of sharecropping arrangements (*mezzadria*) that left rural families in possession of nothing to inherit or repudiate. Many repudiations carrying no overt designation of residence in fact involved Florentines, so the proportion in the table is no doubt understated.

Partial Repudiations

The registries were much less consistent, unfortunately, regarding two other matters. Both at the beginning of the registry, when record keeping was more sporadic and in the more uniformly minimal records of the early sixteenth century, there was no systematic attempt to determine if the estate being repudiated had devolved by testament or intestacy, or if the repudiation concerned the entirety of the estate or only a portion.

As a result, on both these issues the resulting tables have been truncated, leaving out the first two and the last four decades.[41] The decades with the

---

[41] Testate/intestate indications were given only four times in the 1360s, six in the 1370s; six, two, three, and one respectively for the 1500s, 1510s, 1520s, and 1530s. For the same decades, indications of partial repudiations were five, three, two, one, zero, and zero.

TABLE 7. *Partial Repudiations*

Decade	Half	Other	Total	Percent of Repudiations
1380s	30	19	49	.107
1390s	22	18	40	.081
1400s	31	32	63	.105
1410s	41	40	81	.123
1420s	76	77	153	.198
1430s	109	94	203	.292
1440s	99	162	261	.356
1450s	112	157	269	.410
1460s	76	135	211	.322
1470s	55	117	172	.202
1480s	63	101	164	.171
1490s	41	80	121	.143

best coverage of these matters were the 1440s and the 1450s. Past that period, all conclusions on these matters have to be couched tentatively.

What the registry data shows is that partial repudiations were a significant portion (20% or more) of all repudiations from the 1420s through the 1470s, rising to over 40% in the 1450s. (See Table 7.) These are those repudiations in which the repudians revealed that the repudiation covered only a portion (such as half or a third). In addition, the registry allows us to determine that brothers, for example, might repudiate the same estate separately and on different dates; but these have not been retrieved for the purposes of assembling the table. The flurry of statutory regulations and adjustments in the 1470s may have discouraged such a piecemeal approach to avoiding obligations on estates, and thus account for the dropoff in such repudiations from the 1480s; but the statistics may also simply be the result of increasing terseness in the records. As the number of multiparty repudiations increased, one would expect the number of partial repudiations to decrease. We also cannot recover the motives behind such repudiations. Whether a brother simply acted on his own, without reference to his sibling, or, quite the opposite, collaborated with his brother by repudiating his share to leave it all to the other, can only emerge from other records.

Intestate Succession

Intestacies can be known only when so indicated. Indication of intestacy or testament was not strictly necessary for repudiation and certainly not for registration, which is most apparent in the total lack of concern to take down such information after 1500. The figures that emerge show that in the 1440s and 1450s well over 60% of repudiated estates had passed in intestacy.

TABLE 8. *Intestate Successions Repudiated*

Decade	Unknown	Intestate	Testate	Total	% Intestate
1380s	366	58	34	458	.127
1390s	399	54	39	492	.110
1400s	457	103	38	598	.172
1410s	438	182	36	656	.277
1420s	436	292	46	774	.377
1430s	313	323	59	695	.465
1440s	237	449	48	734	.612
1450s	179	435	37	651	.668
1460s	320	311	25	656	.474
1470s	604	203	44	851	.239
1480s	738	201	18	957	.210
1490s	845	161	19	1025	.157

(See Table 8.) In the 1430s and 1460s, the proportions were well over 40%. Against a growing sense that testamentary inheritance became normative, these percentages give pause.[42]

Intestacies were about equally likely to come from outside Florence (47.3%) as from inside (43.6%). Still, while more intestacies came from outside Florence (1,314 to 1,211), fewer repudiations did (4,327 to 5,277). While, in the 1440s and 1450s, 60% or more of Florentine repudiations were to intestate hereditates; these in turn amounted to only 45% of intestate estates repudiated. In sum, the figures seem to indicate that intestacy (or repudiation thereof) was slightly more common in rural areas, or at least outside Florence. This finding could indicate that intestacy, to some degree, correlated with relative lack of wealth (and perhaps literacy too). In contrast, in those same decades only 5.2% of repudiations were clearly testamentary by overt admission at the time of registration.

It may well be that repudiation could exaggerate the proportion of intestacies. It may have been easier to repudiate an intestate estate, which came without express desires regarding not just heirs but legatees, charities, and funeral arrangements. When the de cuius did not express his or her will, it may have been easier for the volition of the heir to find expression. Also, once heirs refused a testamentary inheritance, if it contained no clauses of substitution, it thereafter devolved in intestacy.

---

[42] Samuel K. Cohn, Jr., *The Cult of Remembrance and the Black Death: Six Renaissance Cities in Central Italy* (Baltimore: Johns Hopkins University Press, 1992), 11, notes that few wills survive from before the thirteenth century. Steven Epstein, *Wills and Wealth in Medieval Genoa, 1150–1250* (Cambridge: Harvard University Press, 1984), 13–14, after noting that wills were not the only device to convey property, mentions gifts *inter vivos* and *causa mortis* but does not mention intestacy.

Conclusions

The 168 years of the registry of repudiations break down into four periods. From the beginning to about 1383, the registry was in flux. The total number of repudiations was, relatively speaking, low, and the format for registration was not standardized. The registry itself was not even solely given over to repudiations, and there were notable gaps in the record, beyond the missing first ten years. From the mid-1380s to the end of the 1470s, repudiation settled into a fairly stable pattern. Certainly, its registration format became fairly uniform, recording potentially useful information regarding repudiantes and the hereditates they were rejecting. That information has allowed us to see, to some degree, how prevalent intestacy remained among Florentines and Tuscans, how widespread the use of repudiation was in the contado and distretto, and how frequently repudiations were employed on partial shares of an estate. It was also during that period that, as they became comfortable with repudiation in inheritance practices, Florentines found ways to abuse the institution and circumvent the intentions behind legislation to fix firmly and openly ownership and obligations on inherited property.

A third stage of repudiation's use opened with the aggressive regulation of 1476, which led to an intense burst of activity. Rates of repudiation rose and remained at more elevated levels until just after the turn of the century. Repudiations were also aimed more widely about the family tree. Up to the 1470s, paternal estates were the clear targets of repudiations over 80% of the time. Thereafter, estates of brothers, paternal uncles, and paternal cousins came to figure increasingly in repudiations. Women came to be less frequently the repudiators or the objects of repudiation. Repudiation also became increasingly a Florentine phenomenon. That this was an era of war and growing economic difficulties, culminating for Florentines in the French invasions and the collapse of Medici power, may only have impelled a greater need for repudiation to protect family wealth.

A final period, 1500 to 1534, was marked by minimal entries, little more than the necessary names and dates. Gaps in the record arose for political reasons, as the Signoria became a less vital organ of state and sat less consistently, or as war made travel and business too difficult. Legislative extensions and exemptions papered over the political failings. Meanwhile, the tendency to aim repudiation toward estates of brothers, uncles, and cousins became more marked. Fideicommissa, employing patrilateral substitutions and prohibitions of alienation of vital, significant family properties, came into wide favor in the ranks of the wealthier citizens. There was a consequent lineal intergenerational emphasis in inheritance practices. Property come sideways, as it were – that is, from brothers, uncles, cousins – was now a greater probability perhaps, reflected in increased repudiations of such estates. But always, a repudiation by one party only opened things up for the next in line. The nephew who stood aside from an uncle's estate may only thereby have directed it to his brother or to his own children, if he had any.

As Stephen Wilson has stated for nineteenth-century Corsica, "there was no inheritance, no transfer of property from one person to another, but rather a continuous cycle endlessly matching family to resources."[43] Where and for whom that match was made was a problematic process in which repudiation figured in shifting ways. It is that match to resources that must next concern us.

---

[43] Stephen Wilson, *Feuding, Conflict, and Banditry in Nineteenth-Century Corsica* (Cambridge: Cambridge University Press, 1988), 142.

5

Repudiations and Household Wealth

As the legal excuse for repudiation was that an estate was *damnosa* and not *lucrosa*, one begins with the presumption that repudiated hereditates were of little real value and riddled with outstanding debts and obligations. Given the nature of the commercial and agricultural economy of Tuscany, in which credit was multiform and ubiquitous, it seems a safe presumption. In a unique account of a repudiation, Maria Serena Mazzi and Sergio Raveggi traced the fate of a *contadino* whose meager estate was repudiated by his son in 1443. The son moved to Florence and worked in wool shops until succumbing to the plague.[1] This was not a rich family. Their debts were real and assets few.

Still, the statutory record, if nothing else, alerts us to the fact that poverty and misery (and probably in relative, not absolute, terms) were not the only factors at work behind repudiations. There was deliberate maneuvering of property ownership. There were strategies in play. These required resources. The intent was to avoid debts, to be sure, but such strategies were not necessarily linked to misery.

Understanding the uses of repudiation in Florence requires coming to grips with economic factors, insofar as that is possible. Fortunately, Florence's archives provide means to get at the family situations behind repudiation, at least for a representative sample of Florentine citizens.

1427 Catasto

Perhaps the most widely known archival source unique to Florence is the catasto, the first and most complete version of which, that of 1427, was magisterially analyzed by David Herlihy and Christiane Klapisch-Zuber. Also

---

[1] Maria Serena Mazzi and Sergio Raveggi, *Gli uomini e le cose nelle campagne fiorentine del Quattrocento* (Florence: Olschki, 1983), 307–315.

important for our purposes will be the last catasto, that of 1480.[2] The typical catasto declaration was, in fact, an additive process, which Herlihy and Klapisch-Zuber describe. The head of household submitted a statement, but neighbors were also interrogated and the final entry was an adjusted one. Householders reported their real assets and sums owed them, both by the city, if they held shares of the public debt, and by individuals. They also quite sensibly tried to claim every debt they owed, which lessened their taxable balance. Some debts were even listed as unrecoverable. The householder had incentive to disguise assets and to exaggerate debts. In Florence and, to a lesser degree, in Pisa, dependents were deductible charges against assets.[3] In fact, only the initial catasto of 1427 was systematic and thorough in comparison to later efforts; but all of them are useful for a variety of purposes.

The catasto furnishes us with the possibility of correlating repudiations with these surveys of household wealth. If nothing else, analysis of catasto data can allow us to substantiate the legal presumption that poverty or debt lay behind repudiation. The frustration lies in actually pinning particular repudiated estates to the households presented in the catasto. Florentine society was certainly not static. The purposes of the catasto and the repudiation registry were not the same. Above all, the catasto was predicated on households, the registry on individual heirs. It is not always possible to find the latter in the former, even after a lapse of only a few years.

The premier point of comparison is the 1427 catasto, rendered digital and now online searchable.[4] It proved possible to locate Florentines (only the citizens' *campioni* are available) who repudiated estates in and around 1427. In fact, I tried to track those who repudiated between 1424 and 1435 – the earlier point set by the plague of 1423, the later justified on the sense of economic and political turmoil over the period, culminating in the triumph of Cosimo de' Medici in autumn of 1434. This seems a reasonable interval in which to hope that the catasto evidence does not vary much from the household situation at the moment of repudiation although it must be conceded that in Florence wealth was sufficiently volatile to force us to exercise proper caution in analysis.

Household information was available only when the identification of a household head or member with a party to a repudiation (as repudians, repudiated, or sibling or child of one) was certain.

---

[2] In fact, as Molho, *Marriage Alliance in Late Medieval Florence* (Cambridge: Harvard University Press, 1994), 361, points out, the survey of 1480, as well as those of 1441, 1445, and 1451, were not full catasti.
[3] For examples from 1427 in translation, see Gene Brucker, ed., *The Society of Renaissance Florence: A Documentary Study* (New York: Harper & Row, 1971), 6–13.
[4] *Florentine Renaissance Resources: Online Catasto of 1427*, ed. David Herlihy, Christiane Klapisch-Zuber, R. Burr Litchfield, and Anthony Molho (www.stg.brown.edu/projects/catasto).

The result yielded 136 households of repudiators and/or repudiateds in the 1427 catasto and another 271 in that of 1480. Within the cluster that thus emerged, some households were singular examples of unique or less frequent forms of repudiation. There is no attempt here to wrest statistical conclusions from anomalies, such as that of Riccardo Spinelli, who in 1430 became the unique instance of a Florentine who repudiated an inheritance left by a slave (Caterina, who belonged to Tommaso di Giovanni Fini).[5] Repudiations of distant kin or unrelated persons were too few to draw generalizations.

The catasto evidence largely involves repudiations of paternal estates. We have catasto reports from fathers whose estates were later repudiated, and we have declarations from sons, or their brothers, who repudiated fathers (the former coming generally after 1427, the latter before). Those two groupings are presented in Table 9.

The presence of two very wealthy households among those repudiated so skewed the averages that alternative figures discounting such outliers have also been offered. These two households were those of Luca di Piero Rinieri, worth 33,717 florins in 1427, repudiated by his son Guglielmo on 8 May 1428, and that of Giovanni Barbadori, repudiated by his son Antonio on 24 July 1431, worth 31,773 florins in 1427. Both were sizeable households, eleven and eight persons respectively, so rejection by one family member only left that share to others (though in neither case is the repudiation said to have been only of a specified portion of the whole). These were households that clearly could sustain debt payments. Rinieri may simply have avoided charges on his son's behalf by repudiating him. Antonio Barbadori may have yielded his claims in favor of his brothers.

I have also broken out households with assets totaling less than 400 florins, as well as distinguishing those repudiated after 1 January 1431 in order to see how, if at all, growing fiscal crises, as delineated in Anthony Molho's study of the Florentine public debt in the period, may have affected the growing number of repudiations in those years.[6] There is an interesting contrast between the average household wealth of those repudiating before 1431 of only 540 florins (just a bit more than half the average household wealth in Florence) and the average of 1,237 florins (more than double) for those households that saw a repudiation in or after 1431. Mounting fiscal and financial pressures may have driven these later repudiations. It is quite likely that the fairly healthy domestic accounts had declined markedly some four to five years later. One suspects that the 1427 level of wealth fell

---

[5] RE 11, fol. 112r (23 December 1430). Spinelli in 1427 was listed as a household of one, age seventy, with gross assets of 1,673 florins. He was hardly in need of whatever meager remains this slave left him, seemingly by will (but how could a slave legally make a will?). The relationship would seem to have rested on an elderly man's need for household help, which may or may not have included companionship.

[6] Anthony Molho, *Florentine Public Finance in the Early Renaissance* (Cambridge: Harvard University Press, 1971).

TABLE 9. *Households and Repudiation, 1427*

	#	Bocche	Wealth	Av. Casa	Av. Capita
Households of Fathers Repudiated					
Pre-1431	17	81	42356	2491.53	522.91
	(16)	(70)	(8639)	(539.94)	(123.41)
1431–35	43	261	83719	1946.95	320.76
	(42)	(253)	(51946)	(1236.81)	(205.32)
Totals	60	342	126075	2102.25	368.64
	(58)	(323)	(60585)	(1044.57)	(187.57)
( ) = without outlier					
Households under 400 florins					
	34	154	3616	106.35	23.48
Households Repudiating Father or Brother					
Entire	24	96	29327	1221.96	305.49
Partial	22	90	17779	808.14	197.54
Totals	46	186	47106	1024.04	253.26
Households Repudiating Brother					
	6	22	23410	3901.67	1064.09
	(5)	(15)	(11014)	(2202.8)	(734.27)
Households under 400 Repudiating Father					
	25	84	2678	107.12	31.88
Households Repudiating Mothers					
	6	26	7363	1227.17	283.19

precipitately for these families. Taken in their entirety, however, more than half these households experiencing a repudiation had assets worth less than 400 florins. For these families, the image of the repudiator fleeing debt and obligations seems to hold true.

Bolstering the impression of fiscal hardship behind repudiations is a bit of anecdotal evidence from a subsequent catasto, that of 1457. In that year, Politto di Jacopo di Simone dal Orna reported to catasto officials that

> the catasto of [14]27 was in [the name of] Simone di Giovanni d'Orna, my grandfather, and father-in-law of said monna Piera, my mother; since then my grandfather died in [14]35 and then the gabella del uno took all our property and left us dependents with nothing. And Jacopo my father renounced it because of the large debt it had, and still I have not affirmed his catasto because I was a small child.[7]

[7] ASF Catasto 788, fols. 891r-93v: "Il chatasto di 27 in Simone di Giovanni d'Orna mio avolo, e suocero dela detta monna Piera mia madre; di poi detto mio avolo morì ne [14]35 e alorra la ghabela del uno prese ogni nostro bene e lasciò i consumatori sanza nulla. Et Jachopo mio padre lo rinugiò per debitto grande degli avea, e però non sodare il chatasto suo perchè ero

The cycle of repudiations had continued, in fact, because Politto had already repudiated his father some four years earlier in 1453.[8] The devastation to the patrimony from taxation had not been made good almost twenty years later.

Perhaps unsurprisingly, those who could afford to repudiate the entire paternal estate had a higher average worth (1,222 florins) than those who gave up partial shares of their patrimony (808 florins). Even prior to repudiation these sole heirs did not have to share with others. These averages also warn us – true for all these figures – that the problems of obligation and debt, when they drove a repudiation, were relative. An estate with no assets and no debts was no more burdensome in theory than one with 1,000 florins in assets and an equal amount of debt. In fact, the latter might be more burdensome, as there was substance to distribute to those debts, and thus effort to be put in.

In their study of the 1427 catasto, Herlihy and Klapisch-Zuber compared levels of wealth to ages of household heads. Within a typical life cycle, a young Florentine head of household of twenty-five years of age would face the highest level of debt – consistent with just starting out in marriage and occupation – but could expect increasing fortune to age fifty, before seeing some diminution of wealth from age fifty-five – at which point he would be establishing dowries for daughters and some funding for sons' educations or businesses. The pattern in the countryside varied, with heads of household growing progressively richer up to their deaths.[9] As Herlihy and Klapisch-Zuber note, there were seeds of generational conflict in this situation in which fathers held wealth in their hands and sons under their authority.[10] With the lessening of mortality in the fifteenth century, this tendency then contributed to increasing need for the expression of vertical solidarity between fathers and sons.[11]

How, if at all, did this pattern contribute to levels and types of repudiations in the course of the fifteenth century? What little that can be concluded is that the ages of fathers repudiated were on average past the pivotal age of fifty-five, when they were probably on the downward side of their lifetime wealth. In 1427, the average age of fathers repudiated (using the age as reported in the catasto only, making no adjustment to the time of repudiation) was 57.31 years. Sons who repudiated their fathers were on average, in 1427, 31.3 years of age. The comparable averages for 1480 were 63.23 and 35.34 years of age

---

picholo fanciullo." Jacopo repudiated his father on 29 November 1435, and his brother did the same on 20 December (RE 11, fols. 227 and 229).

[8] RE 16, fol. 124 (28 April 1453).

[9] David Herlihy and Christiane Klapisch-Zuber, *Les toscans et leurs familles* (Paris: Fondation Nationale des Sciences Politiques, 1978), 494.

[10] Ibid., 500, 606–9.

[11] Ibid., 520.

respectively. But the figures for 1427 probably also reflect the mortalities of 1417 and 1423, which shortened fathers' lives and propelled their sons into inheritance at earlier ages. In comparison, the households later in 1480 were more stable and long lasting.

Herlihy and Klapisch-Zuber found that average household wealth for Florence and its Tuscan possessions was around 200 florins. But wealth was not distributed evenly; rather, the concentration of wealth was "highly skewed." Average household wealth in Florence was 1,022 florins. Keeping in mind that the catasto did not attempt to measure all wealth but only what went beyond the necessities of life (by deducting owned habitation and individual "mouths"), one confronts the fact that in Florence 14% of households were reported as having no taxable assets, while debts served to obliterate assets completely for the lowest 30% of Florentine households. For the next 20%, debts swallowed 40% of their assets (households with average wealth between sixty and 210 florins).

Against those figures, we find that households of those who opted to repudiate estates of mothers were relatively well off (1,227 florins on average). Those that repudiated brothers were even better off (3,901 florins, removal of one outlier makes the average still a hefty 2,203). These figures argue for seeing repudiations of brothers and mothers, at least for the period of the 1420s and 1430s, as less a matter of avoiding debts and losses and more a matter of maneuvering property to the hands of siblings in need of a dowry or of assets to start out in an occupation or as a householder. Again, the catasto records the assets of those who repudiated; the estates they repudiated do not emerge to view.

When a son repudiated his father, the catasto can only reveal the financial picture in one household. That is not the case when repudians and repudiated were not part of the same household. We have only a handful of such instances in 1427, although each of them is interesting. Ubaldino di Bindo Guasconi reported assets of 439 florins (415 taxed) as a sole householder. He was dead by 16 May 1430, when Lippaccio Bardi and his brothers, Geronimo and Carlo, repudiated Ubaldino's estate. Lippaccio, as head of household consisting of six mouths, reported assets of 18,224 florins. Francesco di Benedetto Bardi later, 21 February 1432, also repudiated Ubaldino's estate, to which his claim was reported to be only one-twelfth, so one imagines that what was left of it by Ubaldino's death was hardly worth endangering the considerable assets of some Bardi households.[12] On the other side of the wealth pyramid, Giovanni di Lapo Mazzei repudiated his brother Piero, who showed assets of only nineteen florins, against Giovanni's 684 for his modest household of three.[13]

---

[12] RE 11, fols. 46r, 103v; Catasto 975, fol. 650; 64, fol. 54.
[13] RE 11, fol. 54; Catasto 81, fols. 266 and 415.

Antonio di Adovardo Gianfigliazzi held 2,203 florins, yet in 1431 he repudiated his uncle, Lorenzo, who had reported 2,429 (though reduced to 668 for tax, both by dependents and debts).[14] While uncle Lorenzo may have been wise to list every debt he could to lower his taxable assets, the repudiation by his nephew points to a reality behind the accounting. Lionardo d'Antonio Nobili, with 1,174 florins to his credit in 1427, repudiated (8 March 1431) his brother Filippo, who had held 1,224 florins in his household of four.[15] These repudiations seem geared to place assets back in the hands of surviving daughters as dowry (had there been sons, the nephew and brother would not have been in line of succession). In fact, it seems Filippo d'Antonio Nobili was not dead when his brother repudiated his estate, for less than a year later (19 February 1432) he surfaced in the registry repudiating one-fourth of the estate of Filippo d'Antonio di Guccio, whose brother Roberto had appeared in the 1427 catasto, with assets of 1,880 florins for a family of nine.[16] Finally, Jacopo di Niccolò Guasconi's estate, reported as worth 2,590 florins in 1427, was repudiated on 13 March 1432 both by his son, Niccolò, for his half, and by Lattanzio di Bindo Guasconi, whose estate was valued at 3,167 florins in 1427.[17] Lattanzio must have also accepted his share of his brother Ubaldino's estate, for we have no registry of a repudiation by him of his brother. As there nominally were assets in these estates (according to the catasto), debt alone may not have been the reason for repudiation. Conditions certainly could change rapidly, such that a lucrative estate might be impoverished in a matter of months. And it has to be conceded that some otherwise lucrative estates may have been overly burdened with testamentary bequests and rendered unattractive to the heir(s).

The Catasto of 1480

A similar analysis can be worked with the 1480 catasto, which has also been digitized by Anthony Molho.[18] The 1480 data cannot be simply compared to that resulting from 1427, however. In 1480, Florentines were asked to report only their lands and houses and holdings in the city's dowry fund. Business assets and liabilities, holdings in the funded public debt, and other assets were not reported. So the household assessments in 1480 were only partial. The 1480 census of heads of household shows a modest level of population growth in comparison to 1427, though in a possibly smaller

---

[14] RE 11, fol. 71; Catasto 75, fols. 50 and 212.
[15] RE 11, fol. 74; Catasto 74, fols. 32 and 53.
[16] RE 11, fol. 103; Catasto 74, fols. 32 and 82.
[17] RE 11, fol. 108; Catasto 78, fols. 90 and 128.
[18] Whom I cannot thank enough for graciously sharing his database with me.

TABLE 10. *Households and Repudiation, 1480*

	#	Bocche	Wealth	Av. Casa	Av. Capita
Households Repudiating Father					
Entire	99	478	42575	430.05	89.07
Partial	34	184	18360	540.00	99.78
Totals	133	662	60935	458.16	92.05
NN	31	139	5462	176.19	39.29
FN	34	169	11807	347.26	69.86
LS	12	41	5341	445.08	130.27
S	19	91	7732	406.95	84.97
HS	37	222	30593	826.84	139.43
Households Repudiating Brother					
	67	405	53070	792.09	131.04
Households Repudiating Paternal Uncle					
	24	135	18278	761.58	135.39
Households Repudiating Mother				-	
	12	70	9086	757.17	129.8

number of households.[19] Yet it also discloses a reasonably stable level of wealth in land and a stable pattern of investment belying notions entertained by historians of a flight of investment from trade to land.[20] Within the terms of the 1480 catasto itself, 2,847 *case* were reported with holdings of less than 100 florins, controlling less than 1.5% of taxable assets. In contrast, 477 *case* (being 5.7% of all *case*) reported more than 1,500 florins in assets, possessing more than 35% of total value.[21]

Against the 1480 catasto, I attempted to locate Florentine households involved in repudiations between 1475 and 1485.

Household wealth of repudiating parties shows some interesting variations by relationship to the deceased. (See Table 10.) The average wealth in the twelve *case* when a mother was repudiated was 757 florins. The sixty-seven who repudiated a brother (which include the burst of activity at the end of 1476) reported average household wealth slightly higher, 792 florins. In 1480, there were more than enough instances also to determine that households whose heads repudiated an uncle had an average wealth of 762 florins.

---

[19] Molho's figures show 37,246 persons distributed across 9,821 households in 1427, but 40,874 persons in 8,414 households in 1480. He concludes that the shifting number of households (between 7,500 and 8,100 in 1458, around 7,500 in 1469) was the result of shifts in government policy as to whom to count (*Marriage Alliance*, 362–63).
[20] Ibid., 364.
[21] Ibid., 85.

When a partial repudiation of a paternal estate occurred, the average household wealth was only 540 florins. When (one assumes) the entire estate was renounced, the average value was an even more modest 430 florins. As the partial repudiations carried greater value, we might conclude that these partial repudiations were more about leaving the property in others' hands than about avoiding debts and obligations. But by the same logic, the higher average values of mothers' or brothers' repudiated estates argues that there was more strategizing in regard to these hereditates than to those of impoverished fathers.

We can further break down these paternal repudiations by status designations devised by Molho in light of this catasto: households with no family name (NN), those with a family name but no particular political or social status (FN), and those more prominent households of lower status (LS), middling status (S), and high status (HS). The averages of wealth in households with repudiations correlate with these five status designations by and large. Average household wealth of only 176 florins for those with no name or status (NN), to 347 florins for those with a name (FN), 445 florins for those of low status (LS), 407 florins for those of middling status (S), and 827 florins for those of high status (HS). While 827 florins was a level of some wealth, it was also far below the 1,500 florin standard of the wealthiest 500 *case* in 1480.[22] Levels of wealth impelling repudiations were clearly relative. But they were no less compelling for that. We can take one peculiar, but nonetheless revealing, set of instances. In 1484, Barone di Francesco Balducci repudiated his maternal grandfather, Beltramone Tosinghi. On face of it, one wonders why. Barone, part of a household of four, had assets worth only 348 florins in comparison to the 626 florins reported to be in the hands of Tosinghi's daughter, Madalena, in 1480.[23] But Madalena had, in fact, already repudiated her father's estate three years earlier.[24] Madalena was twenty-nine in 1480, a widow with a child. She was not bothered by repudiating the paternal estate, even though it devolved to her nephew. In all likelihood, she would have had a dowry of her own and some patrimony to manage for her child.

Again in 1480, there are a number of instances involving repudiations of brothers or others likely to be in different households, situations in which we have an idea of wealth on both sides of a repudiation. First, we have a couple of unique cases. Piero di Gherardo Gherardini repudiated the estate of his mother, Ginevra di Giovanni Banchelli (17 August 1484).[25] In 1480, Piero's

---

[22] In a table of the wealthiest households by the results of the 1427, 1458, and 1480 catasti (*Marriage Alliance*, 375–410), Molho gives 499 1480 households, the lowest in value having 1,460 florins.

[23] RE 22, fol. 17 (24 January 1484); Catasto 92, fol. 167; 93, fol. 450.

[24] RE 21, fol. 187 (17 May 1481).

[25] RE 22, fol. 45; Catasto 34, fols. 465 and 259.

assets were valued at 772 florins for his household of ten, while his mother, listed separately, had assets worth 494 florins. Piero Gherardini's repudiation of his mother probably allowed her property to go to his own children, bypassing him. In 1481, Andrea di Nastagio Guiducci repudiated his father's estate. The year before he had reported himself living separately with no landed assets, whereas his father had reported 253 florins for a household of three.[26] Possibly, Andrea faced debts that he kept separately from his father's estate and other heirs. Giovanni di Giuliano Comi repudiated his brother Bastiano in 1484, even though Bastiano in 1480 had 341 florins, while Giovanni and his brothers, Agostino and Domenico, divided in two households, had only 126 florins among them. By getting out of the way, Giovanni let Bastiano's property go to his brothers.[27]

Seven cases speak to levels of wealth of nephews and uncles. On average, the nephew's household was worth 487 florins more than the uncle's.[28] Perhaps it is no wonder there was a repudiation in such cases, especially when the uncle's household included several others, women mainly, who could otherwise use the assets.[29] In twenty cases, we can compare assets of brothers on opposite ends of repudiations. Here, in contrast to the nephew-uncle situation, the average disparity in wealth is only 92.6 florins, which makes sense for those sprung from the same household.[30] In three cases, the repudiated brother in 1480 held more than the repudians; in one case, they were even. The one consistency is that the repudians resided in a larger household (an average of five persons, versus 2.2 in the households of the repudiated brothers). On the one hand, some of these repudiated brothers seem to have been in relative poverty and thus ripe for repudiation. On the other hand, some repudiations again allowed other brothers or one's own children to emerge as heirs. Consider these cases. Francesco and Filippo di Niccolò Mori repudiated their brother Giovanni, as did their nephew Bartolo. These repudiantes had 288, 441, and 1,050 florins respectively, while the deceased had 281 for his household of four. In effect, male heirs by statute (this was an intestacy according to the registration) stepped aside, seemingly leaving this property to be managed by a mother for daughters.[31] The same might be said for Bonifazio di Niccolò Ruggieri's repudiation of his brother Zanobi in 1484. Though Zanobi's modest assets of 198 florins

---

[26] RE 21, fol. 194 (28 June 1481); Catasto 61, fol. 464 and 1010, fol. 291.
[27] RE 22, fol. 42 (13 August 1484); Catasto 27, fols. 139, 165, 415.
[28] Nephews held 899.4 florins, their uncles 412.3.
[29] In one case, when Giovanni di Simone Acciaiuoli repudiated his uncle Dardano, there was in fact at least one son to accede to his patrimony (presumably laid out in a testament), so repudiation kept it all in the household of Dardano (RE 20, fol. 180 [24 December 1476]; Catasto 54, fols. 310 and 419).
[30] The averages are 432.5 florins for repudiantes, 339.9 florins for the deceased brother.
[31] RE 21, fols. 168, 173, 181 (20 December 1480, 24 January and 20 March 1481); Catasto 61, fols. 240, 380, 436, and 1010, fol. 13.

in fact compared favorably to Bonifazio's 238, Zanobi left behind a child in need of a dowry.[32]

The 1480 catasto also allows us to inquire more deeply into the rush of repudiations at the end of 1476. This flurry of activity bound to legislation deserves a closer look. Up to 1 December 1476 there had been only forty-two repudiations registered since 1 January. Even though the bill threatening loss of officeholding privileges had passed in October, until the last month of the year activity was in line with that in the previous year. By the middle of the month, matters had changed only a little: eighteen more repudiations through 15 December. By Christmas, there were fifty-one more. After one each on 28 and 30 December, forty-eight were enrolled on 31 December.

Through 2 December, twenty-four repudiations were designated as involving residents outside Florence. Thereafter, only nine were so designated, and one of them involved a Florentine of some status. It was the Florentines who clogged the Palazzo Vecchio at the end of 1476. They were wealthier, or at least more politically interested. Through 2 December those Florentines who have emerged from the 1480 catasto had an average patrimony of 712 florins (nine instances). The thirty-seven Florentine repudiations recorded on or after 19 December carried a slightly more modest average value of 663 florins. We can further distinguish these folks by Molho's categories. Before 19 December there were five households of "high status" (average wealth 791 florins), two of "low status" (average wealth 542 florins), and two of no status (one with a family name, one without, their average wealth 685 florins). From that date, thirty-seven households discernible in the catasto break down as follows: seventeen of high status with an average wealth of 817 florins, four of middling status worth an average of 682 florins, four of low status averaging 945 florins, twelve of no status worth an average of 392 florins. In general, as one would expect of those with potential political interests, these were people of substantial, if not spectacular, fortunes. Covering the fiscal obligations of others was not going to threaten their political privileges, if all it took was a simple repudiation.

As these repudiations at the end of 1476 occurred before the catasto, we generally know the household wealth of the repudians, not the repudiated. In only three cases can we tell what the value of the repudiated estate may have been from the catasto, but in each instance it was relatively low. Jacopo d'Andrea Pazzi did not head a 1480 household, having fallen victim two years earlier to the failure of the conspiracy against Lorenzo de' Medici that bears his family's name, but the estate left him by testament from Piero di Domenico Lamberteschi, which Pazzi had repudiated at the end of 1476, was worth only ten florins in 1480, according to the entry for Piero's "heirs."[33]

---

[32] RE 22, fol. 28 (7 April 1484); Catasto 39, fol. 173, and 40, fol. 474.
[33] RE 20, fol. 162; Catasto 34, fol. 484.

Giovanni di Simone di Michele Acciaiuoli and his brothers Francesco and Zanobi were in possession of real estate valued at 775 florins in 1480, when the holdings of their uncle Dardano (repudiated) were worth 522, and there were others in line to inherit that sum. Similar was the case of Niccolò d'Antonio Alberti, worth 1,738 florins in 1480, who repudiated his uncle Simone, worth 482 to his unspecified "heirs."[34]

In keeping with the terms of the law that drove them to repudiate, these Florentines rejected estates left them by different sorts of people. Prior to 19 December the sixty repudiantes had refused estates from fifty-one fathers, three brothers, three mothers, one paternal grandfather, one maternal grandmother, and one sister. Fathers thus were 85% of those repudiated. After 19 December, the situation was greatly changed. Fathers fell to less than one-third of those repudiated, while collateral relatives (brothers, uncles, cousins) came to over two-fifths.[35]

It would seem, as the law of 1476 said, that Florentines delayed repudiations on those estates for which it was easiest – those not falling directly from their fathers. Faced with the threat of loss of officeholding privileges for the sake of such estates, they moved under legislative pressure to clarify their relationship to such estates, repudiating relatives other than their fathers at a rate about three times greater than before the law of 1476 forced their hands. This is not to say that all repudiations in the final two weeks of December 1476 were driven by the new law. Some, such as those from the contado, may have occurred anyway, or were only minimally coaxed out by the obvious availability of the Signoria for such work at that point. But most of it, continuing into the high levels of repudiation activity in 1477, must have been strictly in response to the law.

Motivations

Close examination of the catasto declarations themselves shows more intimately what sorts of factors were at work in repudiations. As each situation was unique, we could get bogged down in many (admittedly fascinating) microhistories, if we let ourselves. A handful of instances from one gonfalone in 1480 can illustrate some of the nuances derivable from this source.

We can begin with an example of repudiation between brothers. Nerozzo di Piero di Filippo del Nero repudiated his brother Carlo on 20 March 1483. Back in 1480, the two had reported that they held their property, a "possessione" in the commune of Fabbrica, near Pisa, in common "pro non diviso." They had purchased it years before (because they also reported it

---

[34] RE 20, fol. 180 and Catasto 54, fols. 310 and 419; RE 20, fol. 190 and Catasto 50, fols. 535 and 623.
[35] Specifically, thirty-two fathers were 31.4% of the total; twenty-one brothers were 20.6%, twenty uncles 19.6%, thirteen paternal cousins 12.7%, six mothers 5.9%.

out in 1458 and 1469) from Piero de' Rossi. Nerozzo, the elder (age fifty-seven), was married and with children of his own and housed the son of his brother Filippo. Carlo, age forty-five, was unmarried and listed no children in reporting his corresponding half of the assets (690 florins each).[36] When Carlo died, his brother thus repudiated Carlo's half into the hands of his sons and nephew. His ownership and use of the property was unaffected by the repudiation, but his liability was no greater, directly at least, than it had been before.

Repudiations of fathers were, in contrast, more straightforward. Lutiano di Niccolò Bardi's catasto report is revealing. At age fifty, with a wife and three children, he claimed a podere worth 257 florins. He also said, "I find myself in a perilous situation and recommend myself to you [the catasto officials], because from the past catasto to the present I have been left poor, as I do not make enough to live on."[37] It does not appear there was much money to be found among these folks, who otherwise were part of one of Florence's oldest, wealthiest, and most eminent lineages.

Piero di Carlo Canigiani repudiated his father in 1475. In 1480, Piero said he was sixty-five, with six sons and three daughters. One girl was in a convent and another, age eleven, had a modest monte dowry. The oldest boy was sixteen. Piero had bought a house for 485 florins in 1465, but as it was his habitation, it was not computed among his taxable assets, which were a very humble twenty-one florins.[38] He lacked sufficient assets to absorb debts from his father's estate. Niccolò di Giovanni Banchi repudiated his father's estate in 1477. In 1480, he reported assets (two farms) worth 691 florins, in addition to his home. Terming himself "infermo e vechio" at age seventy-two, Niccolò disclosed that he had taken in the widow of Prierozzo Banchi and her eighteen-year-old daughter.[39]

Francesco d'Archangelo di Bernardo Cavalcanti, who repudiated his father in 1479, was only about thirty and his brother Salvadore twenty-nine in 1480. Salvadore reported that he had lived with and worked for Filippo di Federigo Federighi but had returned to live with his brother. Otherwise, Salvadore reported only how a portion of six shops in the Mercato Vecchio had been sold by his father in 1469 to his brother (Salvadore's and Francesco's uncle) for 110 florins to use as dowry for Bicie, their sister. For his part, Francesco reported that he held a house in the popolo of San Giorgio on which his father had suffered loss and expended legal effort. Their father, Archangelo, had been forced to rent out most of the house to

---

[36] Catasto 993, fols. 359r-60r, 365r-66r; RE 21, fol. 275 (20 March 1483).
[37] Catasto 993, fol. 92r: "truovomi in chalamità grande e racomandomi a voi perché da chastasto in qua sono stato lasciato per miserabile, perché non richoglio tanto posso vivere." RE 20, fol. 138 (26 May 1476).
[38] Catasto 993, fol. 212r-v; RE 20, fol. 121 (27 September 1475).
[39] Catasto 993, fols. 165r-66r; RE 21, fol. 14 (21 October 1477).

Stefano Corsellini, except for a room for himself, in which Francesco then lived with his recently returned brother. Though the house had been awarded to him in a lawsuit, he was assessed 128 florins on the portion rented out.[40] One has to wonder, in view of Francesco's possession of his father's modest asset, if Florence's statute would have considered him heir despite the repudiation. His catasto statement does not indicate that he had asserted a right of maternal inheritance.

Repudiation did not always resolve one's financial problems. At least that is what some Florentines told catasto officials. One such was Bastiano di Francesco di Pasquino, who repudiated the paternal estate in 1480.[41] Bastiano was only ten years old, but he had been orphaned, along with his little sister, when his father died of plague in 1479. The sole asset he could claim was his mother's dowry, worth 135 florins. The only property against which that dowry could be capitalized was the house his father had bought on the Costa San Giorgio from Jacopo di Niccolò Paganelli in 1477 for 180 florins. Two factors, however, prevented simply taking possession of the house. First, forty florins were still owed to Paganelli from the purchase price, and thus no instrument of sale had been executed. Second, Bastiano's stepmother occupied the house, presumably exercising thereby her own dowry claim. In consequence, and because he had repudiated his father's estate, he and his sister did not live in the house, although his intention clearly was to press a suit ("fare il piato") and advance his claims against his father's second wife. Obviously, all these claims and intentions were expressed through his guardian.

Young Bastiano's problems with inheritance were echoed throughout the catasto, including for those who repudiated others than fathers. Nanna, widow of Cristofano di Piero d'Arrigo di ser Orsino, reported that she had a bequest from her husband's will. He had wanted his heirs to sell various *beni mobili* to raise the sum of 200 florins, which was to be used to buy *immobili*, revenues and use of which were to go to Nanna for her life. In fact, the heirs had not been able to extract money from debtors and purchase the required *immobili*, and until they did they were bound to pay her twelve

---

[40] Catasto 993, fol. 276r (Salvadore) and 389r-v (Francesco); RE 21, fol. 103 (11 November 1479). From Francesco's: "E detto Archangiolo mio padre non fu sodo, se non di fi. 100 lar., che di fi. 50 lar., e suo mallevadore Giovanni Benizi che llo inghannò d'una scritta gli fece detto Archangiolo, che ssi chiamò debitore di detto Giovanni, e bisognò che detto Archangiolo paghassi e sopradetti denari sanza altro sodamento, e detto Archangiolo ebbe la sen<ten>tia chontro al palagio del podestà di fi. 100 lar., e fi. 25 lar. furono di spese nel 1478 l'aversario e Bartolomeo di Nicholaio di Ghino bichieraio, chome cessionario di Ghoro da Ghambassi. Considerate chome ne sto di detta chasa, vero è che Archangiolo mio padre l'à chomodo la magior parte a Stefano di Berto Chorsellini e riserbossi per se una camera nella quale abito. Tornasi mecho Salvadore mio fratello, e detto Stefano a stare in detta chasa insino a Ognisanti che viene, perché ò bisogno habitare per me e Salvadore mio fratello."

[41] RE 21, fol. 138 (6 May 1480).

florins every year.[42] Her husband's heirs were thus squeezed on two sides – facing an obligation to her but unable to realize obligations from the estate's debtors. Here is an example of how a testament could raise the level of debts on a patrimony.

And of course there were always a few estates that appeared in the catasto as hereditas iacens. One such was that of messer Niccolò di Guasparre di Giovanni da Terranuova, the sole asset of which was one-seventh of a farm, worth seventy-six florins. At the same time, two cousins, Vangelista and Nardo di Francesco di Giovanni di ser Niccolò, reported a patrimony worth 305 florins.[43] As possible heirs to messer Niccolò, these two were clearly in no hurry to claim that seventh of a farm. Similarly, back in 1457, Agnola, widow of Nozo di Tuccio di Marabottino Manetti, declared that she had no *sustanze* but that she was owed her 800 florin dowry against the unclaimed estate of her deceased husband. She had employed the services of a notary to initiate her suit for payment in the court of the Podestà of Florence, but the result was still in doubt at the point the catasto officials visited her.[44] As we have seen, the legislative misadventures concerning hereditates iacentes, it is likely that she waited a long time and possibly to little effect.

One element that emerges from the study of repudiations in conjunction with the catasto data is that repudiations of brothers and mothers perhaps tended to be matters of familial strategy in a positive way. That is, one person refused assets so that they could pass (or stay with) another, generally a sibling. Roughly one quarter of the repudiations traceable into the 1480 catasto involved brothers' or mothers' estates, although we have also seen that the 1476 legislation gave a different impetus to repudiate a brother. Repudiations of fathers, however, seem more often to have been negative – the avoidance of debts and obligations. The law of 1476 that threatened Florentines with loss of office for failure to meet fiscal charges on estates coming from kin other than fathers shifted the balance by adding

---

[42] Catasto 993, fol. 171r-v: "Uno lascio che lasciò Cristofano suo marito per suo testamento che lle sue redi vendessono de' suoi beni mobili tanti che faciessono la somma di fi. dugiento di sugello, e quali fi. 200 s'abbino a conperare beni immobili, e che la detta mona Nanna abbi gli usufrutti di detti beni durante la sua vita. E perché i detti redi nonnanno potuto conperare e detti beni immobili, perché nonnanno trovato da potere fare tanti danari che gli possano conperare, perché sanno a rischuotere da e debitori di detto Cristofano, e per detta chagione e detti redi si sono chonvenuti cho la detta mona Nanna di dare ogni anno a la detta mona Nanna per le dette chagioni fi. dodici larghi per insino a tanto che possino conperare tanti beni che faccino la detta somma di detti fi. 200 di sugello."

[43] Catasto 993, fols. 433r and 437r-v.

[44] Catasto 790, fol. 346r: "Debbo havere dalla heredità iacente del sopradetto Nozo per la drieto mio marito la dota mia, che è fiorini ottocento, cioè fi. 800, chome n'apare charta per mano di ser Antonio di Piero da Panzano, la quale à domando nella chorte del podestà di Firenze e essene chominciato il piato, et continuamente si segue, et per anchora non è diterminato, sicchè non posso anchora sapere chome io me n'abbia a chapitare."

substantially to the negative quality of some estates. The outburst of repudiation activity from that point can be taken as testimony to that.

Repudiation across Generations

A revealing way to get at a sense of the ways in which repudiation fit into family strategies is to follow the use of repudiation serially within a lineage. This is practically impossible to do with poorer families. Continuity was more tenuous in reality and harder to trace in the records. For them, financial factors were likely more immediate and overwhelming. Instead, I have isolated five lineages, all of "high status" by Molho's reckoning, and all sporting a number of households. These are the Alberti, Capponi, Rucellai, Salviati, and Spinelli.

One consistent element that emerges from the repudiations in these lineages is that repudiation was largely a device for the less wealthy and substantial branches. If we compare these names with those found in Molho's list of the wealthiest branches of all the various lineages of status in Florence, we find few of them represented there. Among the Alberti, for example, the line of Giannozzo di Tommaso, one of the wealthiest Florentines according to the 1427 catasto, saw repudiation only by a grandson, Benedetto di Francesco di Giannozzo, who with his three brothers repudiated another brother, Antonio, in 1484 and their mother in 1490.

But for other Alberti, repudiation became a useful device on several occasions. Riccardo d'Antonio di Riccardo in his youth, with his two brothers, repudiated his father (in 1445) and mother (in 1438). Matteo d'Antonio di Tommaso repudiated his father (in 1449); Niccolò d'Antonio di Niccolò di Luigi repudiated his uncle Simone (in 1476), who had repudiated his own father back in 1401 when the Alberti faced exile. Bernardo d'Antonio di Tommaso repudiated his brother (also in 1476). Filippo di Tommaso, who had reported a large fortune in 1427, was repudiated by his sons Francesco and Niccolò (in 1454).[45] This last instance and a relative rush of Alberti repudiations in the mid-Quattrocento were a tribute perhaps to the depth of financial crisis that began to hit the family from the mid-1430s. For them, under duress, repudiation was a device to help salvage as much as possible. The repudiations of the first decade of the fifteenth century coincided with the exile of most Alberti males for political reasons.[46] Otherwise, the Alberti lines represented in the repudiation registry were fairly obscure and modest.

Within the Rucellai, one finds no use of repudiation in the wealthy line of Giovanni di Paolo. The fairly well-to-do Brancazio di Niccolò di Brancazio twice repudiated his brother Piero (1478 and 1480), and his son likewise

---

[45] RE 8, fol. 86; RE 15, fols. 46, 195; RE 20, fols. 176, 190; RE 6, fol. 71; RE 16, fol. 150.
[46] Cf. Luca Boschetto, *Leon Battista Alberti e Firenze: Biografia, storia, letteratura* (Florence: Olschki, 2000), 3–19.

repudiated that uncle (1485). Years later, Brancazio repudiated his mother (1503).[47] Guglielmo di Cardinale was repudiated by his son Cardinale (1478) and his nephews (also in 1478).[48] Otherwise, only less known lines appear among the Rucellai in the repudiation registry.

For the smaller lineage of the Salviati, only Bernardo di Marco di Forese repudiated – his mother and brother, both in the rush at the end of 1476. Giovanni di Forese's son Lotto repudiated his brother (also in 1476), while the other two sons of Forese, Francesco and Filippo, repudiated their father (in 1476 and 1489 respectively).[49] Forse Salviati obviously gave birth to several possible lines in his sons. The lines through Marco and Giovanni seem to have grown from the inheritance, but Francesco and Filippo gave way to them.[50]

Among the Spinelli, there was a concerted and continuous effort to circumvent the inheritance of Carlo di Jacopo, who had been exiled. It was repudiated by his cousins (Lorenzo di Francesco in 1477, Lorenzo d'Antonio in 1478 and again in 1491), nephew (Girolamo d'Antonio in 1477), and even his father (in 1476).[51] Nanna di Lorenzo was repudiated by her brother Jacopo, along with three sons of Francesco and three of Antonio, and a couple of months later by another nephew. This same bunch also repudiated their paternal grandmother – all this occurring in 1490.[52] Three sons of Francesco di Domenico repudiated their father (in 1451 and 1456 and 1460), as did two sons of Lionardo di Francesco (in 1411).[53]

The estate of Giovanni di Piero di Angelo Capponi must have been rather poor, as at intervals his sons all seem to have refused it (Salvestro in 1449, Niccolò and Francesco in 1451, Gherardo in 1457, Donato in 1463, Filippo in 1467).[54] Luca d'Agostino's estate was rejected by his sons Galeotto and Simone (1492), Francesco (1492), and nephew Agostino di Bernardo (1492), whose estate, in turn, was refused by Francesco years later (1513).[55] Bastiano di Piero's was rejected three times by different sets of cousins in 1527 and 1528, as was the estate of Tommaso di Gino by his son, nephew, and daughter in 1529.[56] The combination of repudiations faces one with a sense of the broad agreement among such heirs – whether that agreement was that the state of the inheritance was poor or that it all should go to

---

[47] RE 21, fol. 59; RE 22, fol. 67; RE 25, fol. 172.
[48] RE 21, fols. 45, 50.
[49] RE 20, fols. 167, 168, 190, 206; RE 23, fol. 51.
[50] On this family, see Pierre Hurtubise, O. M. I., *Une famille-témoin: Les Salviati* (Vatican City: Biblioteca Apostolica Vaticana, 1985).
[51] RE 20, fols. 187, 235; RE 21, fols. 17, 27; RE 23, fols. 112, 154.
[52] RE 23, fols. 80, 92, 103, 104.
[53] RE 15, fol. 100; RE 16, fols. 69, 216; RE 18, fol. 97; RE 8, fols. 47, 50.
[54] RE 15, fol. 175; RE 16, fol. 10; RE 18, fols. 2, 219; RE 19, fol. 100.
[55] RE 23, fols. 175, 182, 183; RE 28, fol. 21.
[56] RE 29, fols. 59, 63, 66, 80, 81.

one set of hands. Certainly, such coordinated moves indicate a degree of communication among kin about such matters and a willingness to follow one repudiation with another and another, to strategize with and through repudiation.

All these families, as we noticed for those generally with cognomen, repudiated estates other than paternal with greater frequency. Isolating just two, we can see that the Alberti repudiated fathers in 48.3% of their repudiations, while Capponi rejected fathers even slightly less often (45.5%).[57] Conversely, these clans repudiated others in varying patterns. Capponi had concerns with estates of brothers and uncles; Alberti with mothers and cousins. The political exile of the Alberti in various combinations in the 1390s and early 1400s obviously affected the pattern of repudiations in this lineage.[58] It is also evident that generally members of the wealthier branches of these lineages were more likely to repudiate more distant or lateral relatives – brothers, uncles, mothers. Repudiation of the paternal estate was more likely to be an act of some financial desperation of the less well-heeled.

To put the matter another way, other than the Alberti, who saw distinct deterioration of fortunes, rarely were any of the most prominent households involved in repudiations, certainly not as the household repudiated. In addition to Giovanni di Paolo Rucellai and his sons, we do not find such Florentines as Neri di Gino Capponi or his son or grandson, or Giovanni di Mico Capponi or his son, Francesco d'Alamanno Salviati, or Tommaso di Lionardo Spinelli among the repudiated. Lorenzo d'Antonio Spinelli appeared only among the numerous Spinelli who at various times repudiated Carlo di Jacopo Spinelli.

Truly lucrative estates were accepted. Truly impoverished estates were just as definitively rejected – some several times. Most were not such easy calls. There were some assets – reasons to delay or maneuver estates to others, even if only temporarily. The catasto can render a sense of the financial rationalities behind repudiation. It is much less well suited to disclose the nonmaterial interests and values that could impel aditio or repudiatio (except at odd moments) or simply complicate monetary calculations.

---

[57] Alberti repudiated fathers fourteen times, mothers five, brothers three, cousins three, and others four times. Capponi repudiated fathers twenty times, brothers nine, uncles eight, cousins four, grandfathers three.

[58] See Susannah Foster Baxendale, "Exile in Practice: The Alberti Family In and Out of Florence, 1401–1428," *Renaissance Quarterly* 44 (1991): 720–56; Thomas Kuehn, "Family Solidarity in Exile and in Law: Alberti Lawsuits of the Early Quattrocento," *Speculum* 78 (2003): 421–39.

6

Repudiation as an Inheritance Practice

Examination of the data culled from the registries of repudiation of inheritance kept by the Florentine Signoria has already told us a great deal about repudiation in practice. What the registry entries in fact reported was that a legal action had been undertaken before witnesses and a notary acting as a judge to repudiate an estate. These acts of repudiation were written down in clean formal copies for the party or parties and entered in abbreviated form in the notary's book (*imbreviatura*). In essence, these acts stated that the heir knew he was heir to a named deceased and considered the share of the hereditas that fell to him to be more harmful than profitable (*inutilem* and *damnosam* versus *lucrosam*), in consequence of which he repudiated and abstained. In all, a fairly neat and simple procedure.

Even if the registries were consistently and thoroughly informative, it would still be necessary to pursue acts of repudiation of inheritance in the notarial sources in order to understand other dimensions of the family dynamic behind these acts. Parties, having found a notary to record a repudiation, might also undertake other acts at the same time. Notaries also could elicit information that was not elicited by those keeping the registers (as regarding intestacy or testacy). There is, in short, no substitute for looking at these notarial acts. The results of this effort are reported here, beginning with data gathered into Table 11.[1]

---

[1] The sample of 457 repudiations was gathered from different notaries across the lifespan of the signorial registry. The intent was to make this sample as representative as possible of the entire body of repudiations. If there is any distortion in this sample, it would reflect the bias in record survival in that the papers of Florentine notaries were somewhat more likely to survive than did those of notaries from the contado and distretto. But urban notaries can also be found working in rural areas and some of the inhabitants of outlying villages came to Florence for their legal needs (especially for an act such as repudiation, in which they faced a requirement to register it in Florence), so any distortion on that score is reasonably small.

TABLE 11. *Notarial Repudiations*

Decade	Intestate	Testate	Unknown	# of Repudiators	Partial
to 1370	2	1	3	10	1
1370s	2		1	3	2
1380s	2	3		5	2
1390s	10	6	1	23	3
1400s	14	5	2	24	9
1410s	5	4	2	11	1
1420s	28	6	2	42	11
1430s	15	5	1	27	9
1440s	21	4	3	37	22
1450s	16	2		20	13
1460s	6	3	4	13	9
1470s	5	4	32	47	3
1480s	37	5	52	135	8
1490s	27	6	35	93	7
1500s	32	3	6	51	6
1510s	5	3	2	11	4
1520s	11	3		20	6
1530s	7	3		11	2
Totals	246	65	146	583	118

Relationship of Primary Repudiator to Deceased from Notarial Repudiations

Decade	Patris	Patrui	Fratris	Matris	Other
1360s	4			2	
1370s	2			1	
1380s	2				3
1390s	10		3	1	3
1400s	7			7	7
1410s	5	1	2	2	1
1420s	28		2	4	4
1430s	16				4
1440s	23	1			4
1450s	16				2
1460s	9		1		1
1470s	23	3	9	1	5
1480s	66	4	16	4	4
1490s	46	3	7	2	10
1500s	30	4	3	1	3
1510s	5		3		2
1520s	4	2	6		2
1530s	3		4		3
Totals	299	18	59	23	58

The Data

Notarial acts of repudiation both confirm and modify what we have found from the registries. First, as to the relationship between repudians and de cuius, we find the same sort of distribution as in the registries. Estates left by fathers were far and away the most frequent object of repudiation. Only toward the end of the period, in the early sixteenth century, did repudiations of paternal estates slip to 50% or less. Repudiations of maternal estates also dropped off then. Repudiation of what was left by a brother, however, increased noticeably from the second half of the fifteenth century, which is also the period in which there were more rejections of uncles' estates.

More importantly, where registration data were less consistent, notarial information confirms our impressions. First, there was a similarly high proportion of repudiated estates passing in intestacy. Repudiation of intestacies might have arisen not only from a lack of preparedness on the part of the unfortunate deceased but also on the part of the heirs. Given the mere fifteen days allowed adult heirs in Florence to decide to accept or repudiate, repudiation might well have seemed a prudent response in a tight time frame when records and accounts could not be retrieved quickly. Notarial practice in this regard, unfortunately, paralleled registration practice. A high proportion of repudiations by the end of the fifteenth century did not clearly state whether it was a testament or intestacy that put the property before the repudians. Some notaries employed a catchall phrase like "quomodolibet delata" (left by whatever means), others provided no indication.[2]

Secondly, about 20% of the repudiantes were designated as partial heirs (the other heirs not present). Only a portion of the inheritance was being renounced.[3] Notaries listed other coheirs when there were any or indicated the fraction of the estate belonging to the repudians before them. Hence, we can have much more confidence in these figures in proportional terms than we can have in those generated from the registry, where interest in this dimension of a repudiation was less vital. Still, by the sixteenth century, notaries too found it unnecessary to be precise and forthcoming about shares and coheirs. We must remain aware that, while 20% of those using repudiation were vacating their claims in favor of a coheir, potentially every repudians was stepping aside in favor of the next in line. One of the interesting results of

---

[2] NA 14715, fol. 22v (5 December 1469).
[3] To give just one example at the moment, in 1526 Antonio di Paolo d'Antonio di Domenico, a woolworker from Santa Maria del Campo of Florence, repudiated an estate left him in intestacy by his uncle, Jacopo d'Antonio. By rules of intestacy, he shared this equally with his cousin, Giovanni d'Andrea d'Antonio; but he noted that Giovanni had already repudiated his share in 1524. Had we encountered Giovanni's repudiation standing alone before a different notary, by the assumptions used here it would have been counted as a partial repudiation, and in this instance properly so in that the coheir took two years or so to repudiate. NA 16314, fol. 79r (7 March 1526).

The Data

TABLE 12. *Time between Death and Repudiation by Relationship to Deceased*

	Fathers	Mothers	Brothers	Others
Days	67		7	7
Months	35	2	20	11
Years	47	6	9	11
Totals	149	8	36	29

investigating the notarial acts is the way in which we can follow this process in some instances.

Notaries, however, left other bits of information not generally found in the registries. One of the more interesting was notation as to the interval between the de cuius's death and the repudiation, which was very relevant for statutory and common law. The interval was indicated either by giving the date of death or by reporting the number of days, months, or years that had passed. By and large, fourteenth-century notaries did not elicit and record dates of death or interval since the death, as opposed to noting, when necessary, the date on which a testament had been redacted.[4] Across the first six decades of the fifteenth century, intervals were indicated sporadically, usually when there was a more complicated matter of guardianship to be established or when former wards, now grown, renounced estates in their own names. Intervals were recorded as a general (though never universal) practice only from around 1460.

The results of the scattered references to temporal intervals or to dates of death are offered in Table 12. It was not possible to be too precise. According to the texts, repudiations occurred anywhere from one day to forty-six years (in a case in which the de cuius was a grandfather) after death. Frequently, notaries resorted to the more imprecise term "plures" (several) – several days, several months, several years. In no case was a number of days greater than fifteen used, so we can be safe as taking all references to days (even "several") as falling within the allowed statutory interval for repudiation of a father's estate. Once the number of days became greater than fifteen, the next marker was one month. By the same token, no notary used months with a value greater than six, so here similarly past that point the next marker was one year.

The table would seem to indicate that Florentines and other Tuscans were often in violation of the statute on inheritance by taking more than fifteen days to repudiate a father's estate. However, that conclusion is deceptive. For one thing, children who were underage at the time of their fathers' deaths

---

[4] An exception, though part of a more elaborate legal arrangement to be discussed below, is NA 9384, no. 109, 24 November 1376.

were unable to repudiate for themselves. A large number of those repudiating after a number of years (and notably of the twenty-seven instances when repudiation took place "several years" after the death) were the then grown sons.[5] Also, in instances in which the repudiating party was faced with property already repudiated by others (this affecting mainly instances of repudiations to uncles, cousins, or others), there was necessarily a longer interval between death and repudiation. For another thing, the statute specified fifteen days, or as soon as one learned of the death. There were a number of repudiantes who excused their delay on an absence that prevented them learning of a death, sometimes for years. The best example in that regard comes from 1440 when Monaco and Piero d'Antonio Monachi claimed that they had been under the impression that their father had died intestate. Instead, just four days before, they had learned that there was a will drawn up back in 1429, perhaps a year or so before Antonio's death. The testament had named Antonio's five sons as heirs. One had since died and another had entered the Franciscans, so there were only three left. These two then repudiated, presumably leaving it all to the remaining son.[6] One wonders what their relation to the property had been in the intervening ten years, as they did not claim to have repudiated previously. They used the will as an excuse to repudiate so long after Antonio's death.

While we do not have a large number of repudiations of maternal estates, what we have seems to indicate that Florentines were in no rush to repudiate their mothers' estates (largely consisting of their dowries). No one did so within only days; a couple took "several years"; others took five, six, seven, or ten years to reject their mothers' estates. This evidence contrasts with the statutorily induced haste with which they acted on their fathers' estates, as 45% had taken care of it within the allowed fifteen days and about two-thirds had by the half year point. There is also the problem that Florence's rather harsh statute, which ran clearly contrary to ius commune, did not necessarily apply outside the city. At least twenty-eight of the eighty-two repudiations of fathers that took place from one month to twenty years after the paternal death involved parties living outside the city of Florence – most of them contadini, but some Florentines residing in places such as Rome or Avignon. But then one must also allow that some contadini were quite capable of repudiating within fifteen days.[7] The evidence as a whole

---

[5] To break down the numbers further regarding fathers: of the other twenty who took years, two took one year; three took two; three took three; one took five; and three took six. The remaining eight took (one each) seven, eight, ten, twelve, thirteen, fourteen, sixteen, and twenty. Of the thirty-five who took a number of months, eight took "several"; eleven took one; seven took two; two took three; one took four; four took five; two took six.

[6] NA 686, fol. 417r-v (8 April 1440).

[7] For example, NA 14726, fol. 44v (3 May 1495).

Strategies 159

seems to indicate that the sorts of delays in repudiating complained of in legislation from earlier in the century were more infrequent later, although some examples of prolonged delays persisted.

Strategies

Reject or Accept?

For the most part, notarial repudiations survive as isolated acts, unaccompanied by other acts that could permit one to see them as part of some unfolding patrimonial strategy.[8] In a sense, that is not surprising. Having renounced rights, obligations, and possible assets, the once-and-no-longer heir did not have anything to do. The contrast is with acts like emancipation in which one gained rights and capacities and quite possibly assets or with aditio in which one took on assets along with legal consequences.[9] In those cases, subsequent acts to use new capacities or secure new assets were more likely.

We can say little about many of these instances. We know that in May 1377 Giovanni di Stefano di Vanni repudiated his half of the intestate inheritance left by his father (Appendix 2). We do not know whether his brother (for such we can strongly infer to be the coheir to a father) also found the estate of little value. We can say little more about the 1423 repudiation by Bastiano di Chirico di Ghiotto da Seciano, a resident in the popolo of Santa Maria Novella, of his father's entire testamentary estate. We can add only that his father had been dead but a few days.[10] A century later, 8 April 1533, we learn little more about the repudiation undertaken by a rural laborer from San Martino a Pagliariccio of the Mugello, Filippo di Buono di Michele. His brother Michele had already repudiated what their father had left them in intestacy at his death eight years before. Filippo did not set out any excuse about minority and coming of age to explain the eight years (Appendix 3).

A simple aditio need not say much more in itself. On 23 November 1400, the brothers Bernardo and Donato d'Ugolino Bonsi took their halves of their brother Piero's estate, left to them by his testament. They asserted their intent to do so with benefit of inventory. If they subsequently decided to use that benefit and renounce the inheritance after more careful consideration, they did not do so before the same notary (Appendix 4). In some instances in which estates were accepted, agents (*procuratores*) were appointed to see

---

[8] Which is not to say that there may not have been transfers in advance of death or other arrangements not obvious from the records surrounding a repudiation.
[9] Thomas Kuehn, *Emancipation in Late Medieval Florence* (New Brunswick: Rutgers University Press, 1982), 100–122.
[10] NA 9040, fol. 143r-v (20 December 1423).

to taking possession of property and, of course, there were some as well for which the inventory was quickly entered into the record to confirm the aditio.[11]

A unique document from 1412 may be a direct result of the legal arguments that were being made at that time (I will address this in the next chapter). In July 1412, Corso and Sandro di Zanobi de' Ricci had drawn up a charter that first explained that they had each separately accepted the thirds left them in intestacy by their father. Corso dated his aditio to 19 February 1393. He had taken his share almost twenty years before, at which time their brother Giovanni was still alive, but their other brother Guido had already passed away. Still, as they had not declared on what basis they had accepted the estate ("quo animo et qua mente") – whether in their own persons or by way of Guido, their dead brother, they now clarified that they had done so "initially and immediately in their own persons and by right of increase" ("primordialiter et immediate ex eorum personis et iure accrescendi"). They never intended to be or to be perceived as Guido's heirs (Appendix 5). This could only have been the sort of legal confusion apt to arise in a lawsuit, whatever the parties and interests at stake in it. The need for explanation of repudiation was much less obvious, as long as it had been properly performed and registered.

In order for some heirs to repudiate an estate other than their father's, if he were still alive, they needed first to be emancipated. In these instances, one has to wonder how directive and controlling the father was in guiding the decision to repudiate. A dozen instances have emerged, all but three from the fifteenth century. They include the emancipations by Francesco di Benedetto Norducci of his son and married daughter so that they could repudiate their sister's hereditas.[12] Francesco di Bettino Bettini emancipated two sons and then repudiated his mother's estate, which would have cleared it to go to the boys, who were now legally financially independent of him.[13] And one cannot help but note the following historically interesting event. On 15 April 1478, only eleven days before the plot to kill Lorenzo and Giuliano de' Medici by some of his kin unfolded in bloody fashion, Uguccione di Ghinozzo Pazzi emancipated his daughter Giovanna, who repudiated the estate of her mother Caterina di Francesco di Luca del Sena. Giovanna also made a gift of her own rights to a dowry to her brother Ghinozzo, should she die without issue.[14] Though Uguccione was not implicated in the conspiracy

---

[11] NA 13976, 15 March 1400; NA 679, fols. 181v-83v (5 July 1420), which relates to events in the Albizzi clan that we will discuss below.
[12] NA 4360 (1406-8), fol. 95r-v (7 December 1407).
[13] NA 10188 (1474-76), fol. 386v (17 March 1476).
[14] NA 14718, fols. 189r-v (15 April 1478). On the Pazzi Conspiracy, see now Lauro Martines, *April Blood: Florence and the Plot against the Medici* (Oxford: Oxford University Press, 2003).

(not that he might not have caught wind of it), he used repudiation to move property to his son while not having to emancipate him.

Guardianship

Heirs were not necessarily adults. Death never works in neat generational patterns, and certainly not in an era fraught with plagues, famines, and wars. Underage heirs were placed in guardianship (*tutela*). It was left to the guardians to determine how damnosa a hereditas was.[15] There were constant concerns and consequent legal safeguards relating to the way guardians managed property. The Florentine Giovanni Morelli, himself left in guardianship at a tender age, has left perhaps the most systematic sense of the potential disasters of guardianship. The best option was that a caring mother remained with the children and administered their property and saw to their needs. His own mother had left the house to remarry.[16] Other mothers, however, were not so "cruel." They figure as *tutrices* with other *tutores* in the repudiation of estates on behalf of their wards.

Margherita, widow of Biagio di Dino di Lottiere of Signa, was named by her husband in his will as guardian for their three sons. In November 1398, two years after his death, before a judge of the court of the Podestà, she produced an inventory that merely reported that the sons had the right to accept or reject what their father had left them. In the name of one, Dino, presumably the eldest, she repudiated his share.[17] In 1438, Francesco di Leonardo di Tommaso Serristori, said to be between the ages of seven and twelve, with the consent of his uncles as his guardians, repudiated his father's estate, which had been left to him in its entirety by testament. In fact, immediately following, one uncle, Bernardo Bischeri, sought from the estate money his father owed to the youngster as his salary in the family business.[18]

---

[15] On *tutela*, see Gigliola Villata di Renzo, *La tutela: Indagini sulla scuola dei glossatori* (Milan: Giuffrè, 1975); id., "Note per la storia della tutela nell'Italia del Rinascimento," in *La famiglia e la vita quotidiana in Europa dal '400 al '600: Fonti e problemi* (Rome: Ministero per i Beni Culturali e Ambientali, 1986), 59–95; Giulia Calvi, *Il contratto morale: Madri e figli nella Toscana moderna* (Bari: Laterza, 1994). For a case relating to this area of law, see my "Social Processes and Legal Processes in the Renaissance: A Florentine Inheritance Case from 1452," *Quaderni fiorentini per la storia del pensiero giuridico moderno* 23 (1994): 365–96.

[16] Giovanni Morelli, *Ricordi*, in *Mercanti scrittori*, ed. Vittore Branca (Milan: Rusconi, 1986), 101–339, at 175. His sense of abandonment by a remarrying mother inspired Christiane Klapisch-Zuber's provocative essay, "La 'mère cruelle': Maternité, veuvage et dot dans la Florence des xive-xve siècles," *Annales* 38 (1983): 1097–1109.

[17] NA 667, fol. 161r-v (16 November 1398). Other examples are as follows: NA 691, fol. 83r-v (13 August 1451), fol. 128r (12 November 1451); NA 689, fols. 3v-4r (9 July 1445); NA 687, fol. 147r (29 March 1441); NA 683, fols. 330v-31r (1 June 1430); NA 14725, fol. 13r (14 April 1492), fol. 97r-v (10 February 1493), fol. 100r (13 February 1493); NA 14724, fol. 117v (8 March 1491), fol. 127r (21 April 1491); NA 14718, fol. 236v (11 December 1478).

[18] NA 686, fols. 162v-63r (14 June 1438).

Another mother who conscientiously pursued her duties as guardian was Nadda di Paolo Falconieri, widow of Michele di Giovanni. Her husband had been dead only a week when she went to a notary and claimed her prerogative, in the absence of a testament, to be *tutrix* to her sons Antonio and Giovanni. Aiding her were two guild brothers of her husband (*lanifices*), Serafino di Giovanni Ceffini as her *mundualdus* and Salvestro di Lodovico Ceffini as her guarantor (*fideiussor*). Nadda then made a quick inventory, in which she found simply the boys' right to accept or repudiate their father's estate. The guardians then repudiated for them. Finally, Nadda nominated two notaries as her agents. Reference to her dowry leads one to believe that they were to determine and secure her dowry against the estate she had just repudiated for her boys. Her dowry was what was going to sustain her and her sons, along with the goodwill of friends like the Ceffini and her own natal clan.[19]

Heirs in Religious Life

Another category of repudiantes consisted of those Florentines in convents or monasteries. Notarial records give us more insight into their situations. Niccolò di Tollosino di Francesco de' Medici, after six months in the monastery of San Benedetto, at his father's behest, or at least in his presence and with his consent, repudiated his share of his mother's estate. He had already received 300 florins in cash and furnishings from Tollosino and expressed concern "lest his brothers be cheated of the estate of their mother" ("ne alii eius fratres frauderentur ab hereditate matris").[20] In effect, his "renunciation" was a gift to his father of this share, yet in return Tollosino also recorded his promise, in gratitude to his son, to give the monastery fifty florins.

The gift to the monastery is a reminder that inheritances falling to individual members of a convent or monastery were in fact communal property, depending on the rules of the order involved. The entire assembly had to repudiate such an inheritance or the abbot, prior, or other official delegated to act on behalf of the institution had to. The same was true for those hereditates or portions thereof that came to ecclesiastical institutions by testamentary

---

[19] NA 9038, fols. 26v-27r (7 July 1412).
[20] NA 14712, fols. 135r-36r (9 June 1462): "publice recognovit etc. quod iam sunt quinque anni et ultra usque in presentem diem ad eius manus pervenit de bonis rebus et iuribus dicti Tollosini eius patris etc. tot et tanta bona inter denarios et res mobiles que ascendant ad summam et quantitatem florenorum auri ccc et ultra etc. itaque videns et cognoscens quod ex habentibus et possessionibus dicti Tollosini eidem fuit plusquam satisfactus de eius portione et parte etc. et volens veritati locum esse et ne alii eius fratres frauderentur ab hereditate matris predicte eveniente causa mortis dicti Tollosini etc. et ideo appensate consulte et deliberatione omnes et id totum quicquid ad eum potuisset vel poterit quomodolibet pertinere et spectare ad eum de hereditate predicta dicti Tollosini et de eiusdem Tollosini bonis etc. renumptiavit etc."

disposition. To cite a late example, in 1528 Paolo d'Antonio Guidi, as syndic and *procurator* for the friars of San Marco, repudiated what a widow had left in intestacy to two sons who were friars there.[21] In effect, this half share would thus go by *iure accrescendi* to their brothers as coheirs. To come to a somewhat earlier and different example, in 1459 the monks of Santa Maria degli Angeli convened to repudiate the one-third share of the patrimony of Niccolò di Francesco de' Medici left them in his will, which had been redacted back in 1423. The monks also renounced any future inheritance from Tommaso di Francesco de' Medici, his brother. Instead they gave these repudiated shares, they said, to Tollosino di Tommaso [sic – Francesco] de' Medici, the same one who three years later would get his son to donate his maternal share to him.[22]

Monastic repudiations also figured in one of the most complicated and revealing series of events involving repudiation of inheritance to have surfaced in the notarial records. It all began on 15 October 1409, when Bernardo di Giovanni Guidalotti repudiated the estate of his mother, Cilia. Bernardo also had four sisters, who stood to inherit, along with his daughter, who fell heir to a fifth once he had repudiated the hereditas. So later that day, in another location and before other witnesses, but with the same notary, his sister Antonia, wife of Simone di Niccolò Brunelleschi, repudiated her fifth. Still the same day, same notary, but in a third location and with a third set of witnesses, Caterina di Tieri di Domenico di Tieri, married daughter of Bernardo Guidalotti's sister Piera, repudiated her now one-fourth share from her maternal grandmother. Three days later, in the Dominican convent of San Niccolò of Prato, the nuns (many of whom were scions of illustrious Florentine lineages) gathered, among them Bernardo's sister Caterina. The same notary was present to record their deliberations, which began with consideration of all the repudiations that had already occurred, including that by another of Bernardo's sisters, Angela, a nun in San Jacopo di Ripoli, before a different notary in the intervening three days. The convent, through Caterina, was now in line for half of Cilia's estate, with the other half falling to Bernardo's daughter Gostanza. In consideration of the fact Bernardo "is poor and has a marriageable daughter... and neither she nor her father have the means by which this same Gostanza may be dowered, unless the dowry and dotal rights of monna Cilia be left her or a way emerges by which they can be left to said Gostanza," Caterina asked her fellow nuns to repudiate that half, which they obligingly did. All this set the stage for the final step, later that day back in Florence, where Gostanza, with her father as *mundualdus*, accepted the entirety of the estate that all her relatives had serially rejected in its various parts.[23]

---

[21] NA 16315, fol. 236r-v (1 February 1528).
[22] NA 9040, fols. 154r-55r (8 March 1424).
[23] NA 9037, fols. 173v, 174r-76v (15 and 18 October 1409).

In just a few days, Bernardo Guidalotti had thus scurried across town, back and forth, and out to Prato and Ripoli, notary in tow, to record the legal acts that amounted to his sisters' and niece's acquiescence in his plan to use his mother's dowry as his daughter's. Undoubtedly, the plea of poverty alleged by one sister is to be understood in relative terms. Assembly of a sufficient dowry to marry her in a socially honorable and useful arrangement of *parentado* was not cheap.[24] The formulaic assertions in each of the several repudiations regarding the harmful and useless quality of the estate also ring hollow in the face of the equally formulaic assertion of the aditio that it was useful and lucrative.

Coheirs

The pattern of the Guidalotti – namely, repudiation by one or more heirs preparatory to acceptance by another – was not uncommon within the notarial records. Eighty-one times among the sample repudiations, one party's refusal paved the way for an immediate aditio by another or of a different estate by the same party. In other words, around one-sixth of all repudiations (by this evidence) were overtly part of a collaborative strategy to direct property to the hands of certain heirs. And this impression must leave out of account instances in which subsequent aditio happened not so immediately and before other notaries (making its recovery difficult). Gheri d'Antonio di Gheri, for example, accepted his mother's property because it came entirely to him, thanks to the repudiation by his brother.[25] Whether this result came from a coordinated strategy of the two brothers or simply Gheri's reassessment of the situation, we cannot definitively say, at least not without more information.

In another instance, Niccolò di Giovanni di Feo, from the contado near Ripoli, accepted the hereditas of his dead brother, Feo. The same hereditas had already been repudiated by the other brother, Domenico, so Niccolò was intestate heir in entirety. He then appointed as his agent a Florentine, Nero di Filippo di Nero, to whom he gave that hereditas in the name of his niece, daughter of Feo. As statutory law placed the brother before the daughter (it would not have placed him before a son), his gift was rectifying that and giving the paternal estate to the female offspring. A condition attached to the gift reveals a more refined intent behind it. In case the girl died before marrying, the estate would revert to Niccolò or his heirs.[26]

In what seems to have been an extension of marriage arrangements, Tinoro di messer Niccolò Guasconi repudiated both his daughter and his deceased wife, clearing the way for his other daughter the next day to

---

[24] See Anthony Molho, *Marriage Alliance in Late Medieval Florence* (Cambridge: Harvard University Press, 1994), 145–53.
[25] NA 668, fol. 47r (25 June 1400).
[26] NA 9040, fols. 156v–57r (13 March 1425).

accept her sister's estate. The beneficiary's husband, Bernardo di Giovenco de' Medici, then acknowledged receipt of her 600 florin dowry from his wife's maternal uncles, Niccolò and Bernardo di Domenico Giugni. Tinoro then repaid his brothers-in-law with shares in two shops.[27] In 1373, Piero di Nello Malegonelli emancipated his daughters Bartolomea and Simona so that the first could repudiate and then the second accept the estate of their mother. Bartolomea was already married (to Piero d'Andrea di Sante), so the estate may have furnished her sister with a dowry. Both girls then consented to two subsequent sales of property by their father, possibly also part of a plan to assemble cash for Simona's dowry.[28] Giovanni di Guido di Francesco Baldovinetti emancipated his son Francesco so he could give the boy his rights in Guido's estate by repudiating it, even as his brother Paolo, prior of San Casciano in the Mugello, accepted his half.[29] These sons, a monk and an emancipated son, would have protection from Giovanni's debts, as they were both no longer under his potestas.

Beyond emancipation, one way to use repudiation to avoid obligations, yet still retain control of property, was to follow it with aditio by minor children. Bernardo di Filippo de' Ciari repudiated the estate of his maternal grandmother Roba, wife of Matteo de' Ricci and daughter of Bindo Ricasoli, only to accept it for his five young children, to whom it fell after his repudiation.[30] Technically, the property was not his, though really under his day-to-day management. When Antonio di Turino Baldesi repudiated his uncle Bernardo in August 1494, he followed that three days later by accepting the same estate for his three-year-old Vincenzo, adding the express protestation that he was involved in his uncle's estate only *iure familiaritatis*, as it was his son's property.[31] Even as early as 1343, Tino di Faldino, of Santa Maria da Spagnola, emancipated his son Faldino so that, following his father's repudiation of his mother's estate, he could accept it for Faldino and assemble an inventory.[32]

In one of the most complicated of such maneuvers, Telda di Uberto degli Albizzi, widow of Ardingo di Corso de' Ricci, repudiated the estate of her brother Gianni, who had died the year before. Originally, Gianni's testament had nominated as heir his brother Giovanni, with substitution (if Giovanni died without heirs) to Telda. There was a further substitution after her that left half to the descendants of Baldassare di messer Francesco degli Albizzi and the other half to the descendants of Piero di Vanni degli Albizzi. Giovanni had died only a week before, when Telda repudiated as substituted heir to the

---

[27] NA 684, fols. 388v-92v (3 and 4 March 1434).
[28] NA 6184 (1372–77), fols. 41r-42v (2 January 1373).
[29] NA 14725, fols. 186v-87r (26 February 1494).
[30] NA 9040, fols. 103v-4r (30 June and 1 July 1423).
[31] NA 14726, fol. 16r-v (27 and 30 August 1494).
[32] NA 5239, fols. 6v-7v (17 December 1343).

entire estate. The next substitutions thus kicked in, so later the same day (in another location), Piero d'Uberto degli Albizzi and Alamanno and Tommaso d'Albizzo degli Albizzi accepted what Telda had declined. Next, Giovanni di Piero di Vanni degli Albizzi, as uncle and manager for his three nephews accepted the other half of Gianni's estate. It would be almost a year, however, before Baldassare took formal guardianship and conducted an inventory of Gianni's estate, which led to a repetition of the aditio.[33] Getting one's hands on the property and knowing what was there was a bit more problematic for a cousin. It is interesting that none of this could have happened without Telda's willingness to step aside from property that must have been worth something for her kinsmen, but that would have swelled the Ricci coffers had she taken it.

As the Florentine intestate inheritance statute effectively ruled out benefit of inventory for an adult, use of repudiation to maneuver an estate into the hands of an underage heir was an important option for Florentines. That way the estate fell to a minor, and the family could take advantage of a detailed survey of estate assets to limit liability. We have direct testimony that Florentines were willing to repudiate to put an estate into the hands of young heirs in order to make use of the benefit of inventory. Gerozzo di Cambio di Vieri de' Medici in 1495 repudiated his testamentary third from his mother, as did his two sons, Cambio and Alessio, and his brother Gabriele. Before a week had passed Gabriele went to the same notary and recorded that he had repudiated "because benefit of inventory established in law cannot help Gabriele by virtue of the statutes" ("quia benefitium inventarii a iure introductum ipsi Gabrielli prodesse non poterit ex facto statutorum"). Claiming to have better knowledge of his mother's estate now, "and considering also how his sons, who are of minor age and childhood, are not excluded from benefit of law and inventory according to the statutes" ("et considerans etiam qualiter dicti sui filii prope minorem et infantilem etatem non sunt exclusi ab benefitio legis et inventarii secundum formam statutorum"), he accepted the estate with benefit of inventory for them, as did his nephew, messer Matteo, again also with benefit of inventory.[34] Thus, Gerozzo and his sons abstained totally from the hereditas, while Gabriele held it for his sons. Similar logic applied when Tommaso di Lorenzo Soderini repudiated his half of the estate of his father, but his brother Raynerio, still less than eighteen years of age, accepted the entire paternal estate with benefit of inventory.[35]

Given how stealthy Florentines could be in hiding assets from tax officials and creditors, and in view of the diversified holdings of even modestly wealthy people, it could be very hard for someone, even one who grew up in

---

[33] NA 679, fols. 28r-30r (29 July 1419) and fols. 181v-83v (5 July 1420).
[34] NA 14726, fols. 67r-68v (20, 21, and 27 November 1495).
[35] NA 16318, fols. 86v-87v (18 June 1533).

the same household, to know what was there. Inventories could be incredibly detailed, room-by-room accounts of utensils and furnishings, among other things.[36] The painting *Taking of an Inventory*, attributed to Domenico Ghirlandaio's workshop, in the Oratory of San Martino di Buonuomini in Florence is a nice illustration of the process.

Women may have had particular need to invoke a right to inventory for their protection. Caterina di Napoleone de' Franzesi, widow of Antonio di Giovanni Gherardini, repudiated her son, Giovanni, who by his testament had named his mother his heir. Then her sister-in-law, Caterina di Giovanni Gherardini, wife of Bartolomeo Spinelli, accepted (1) her brother Catalano's estate, which the society of Or San Michele had passed on, after it devolved to them by substitution contained in a codicil to Catalano's will; (2) her nephew Giovanni, thanks to his mother's repudiation; and (3) her brother Antonio's estate, which flowed to her on intestacy and in the absence of aditio by his son. She then invoked her right to an inventory because of her doubts about the value of all these estates ("dubitans de viribus dictarum hereditatum"). The entire cycle of events concluded with a quitclaim (*finis*) between the two Caterinas regarding the 700 florin dowry Caterina Franzesi had brought when she married Antonio back in 1384. It seems clear from that text that all the men, Antonio, Giovanni, and Catalano, had succumbed to the plague that had struck Florence the year before (1417), which would explain why all their estates were simultaneously available.[37]

These examples, to which many more could be added, have to impress on us two things. One is the processual quality of inheritance. The deceased's death only began a period of deliberation, which might be brief (as Florence's statute sought) or long. Sometimes people even changed their minds, later accepting what they had first rejected, or even alleging new information, to reject what they had initially accepted. And rejection by one heir only tossed the deliberative onus to coheirs or the next in line.

The other point is that a portion of Florentine repudiations were about heirs maneuvering property into certain hands – to underage heirs who had benefit of inventory, to or away from heirs in religious life, to girls in need of dowries, to one only of a number of heirs (often brothers). The results of these maneuvers were not predictable from rules of intestacy or clauses of testaments alone. Had we not recovered the documents detailing events, as that set in motion by Bernardo Guidalotti, for example, we would have to assume that, in his case, he took the maternal estate in accord with the intestacy rules in force at the time, rather than entering the series of

---

[36] One can find a nice presentation on the subject of making inventories in Jill Burke, *Changing Patrons: Social Identity and the Visual Arts in Renaissance Florence* (University Park: Penn State University Press, 2004), 49–61.

[37] NA 9039, fols. 110r-12v (6 July 1418).

maneuvers to put it in the hands of his nubile daughter.[38] Similarly, we would have assumed Telda Albizzi's inheritance by substitution to her brother, Gianni, once the other brother passed away, instead of her generous repudiation so that the next substituted heirs, six male cousins, could inherit. Hers was an interesting concession to the agnatic male bias of inheritance in Florence, as usually embodied in testamentary substitutions, but curiously not her brother's.[39]

Trading Spaces
Repudiation of one estate was sometimes followed by acceptance of a different one by the repudiating party. Here, far and away most common was repudiation of the paternal estate and acceptance of the maternal. No less than 10% of the repudiations unearthed in the notarial archives fall into that category (forty-seven of 457), notably so from the mid-fifteenth century on. Again, the statute of 1415 had made this tradeoff of paternal estate for maternal a more attractive option. Fairly humble agricultural laborers as well as fairly well-to-do Florentines took advantage of this legal possibility.[40] Typically, the father's death was recent, or at least more recent than the mother's, when we have indication of interval since death.[41]

As law in Florence gave the husband of a predeceased wife a life interest in the property, unless he expressly stepped aside, effective inheritance and management by his children was not an issue until he too died.[42] The repeated combination of repudiation of paternal and acceptance of maternal estate draws attention to the fact that fathers' assets might well be burdened with real or performative obligations, while mothers' were unlikely to be so burdened, even if of less absolute monetary value. Pledging the return of the dowry against paternal assets, including the family's home, meant one could claim to remain there, while limiting losses to the value of the paternal estate. The son would not bear personal obligation for paternal debts, because he was not technically his father's heir. All of which alerts us to another utility of dowry, as a claim against the family's property that could be exercised

---

[38] See Isabelle Chabot, "'La sposa in nero': La ritualizzazione del lutto delle vedove fiorentine (secoli xiv-xv)," *Quaderni storici* 86 (August 1994): 421–62, at 451; and id., "La loi du lignage: Notes sur le système successoral florentin (xive-xve, xviie siècles)," *Clio: Histoire, femmes et sociétés* 7 (1998): 51–72.

[39] See Thomas Kuehn, *Law, Family, and Women: Toward a Legal Anthropology of Renaissance Italy* (Chicago: University of Chicago Press, 1991), 238–57.

[40] NA 14733, fol. 200r-v (28 February and 1 March 1486); Spinelli brothers in NA 16315, fols. 99v-100r (1 December 1527); Baldovinetti in NA 690, fol. 146v (29 March 1449).

[41] NA 14729, fol. 118r (26 September 1506) and NA 14728, fol. 138r (13 June 1502).

[42] Julius Kirshner, "'Maritus Lucretur Dotem Uxoris Sue Premortue' in Fourteenth- and Fifteenth-Century Florence," *Zeitschrift der Savigny-Stiftung für Rechtsgeschichte (Kan. Abt.)* 97 (1991): 111–55.

Strategies 169

for the good of the family (against outsiders) – beyond the evident utilities of transferring goods at marriage and certifying the honor of those involved.⁴³

An interesting example can serve to remind us of the varying obligations that could strike men and women in Florence, where the range of legal actions open to women was circumscribed and protected by forms of guardianship. At the end of August 1492, a few months after the death of Lorenzo de' Medici, whose enmity for his family had been evident at least since 1478, Filippo di Leonardo d'Uguccione de' Pazzi repudiated father and accepted mother. Leonardo had died in the aftermath of the failed attempt to kill Lorenzo in 1478, when Filippo was an infant. His mother, Bice d'Angelo Cavalcanti, had died in February 1477. Now turned eighteen, Filippo jettisoned the no doubt burdened paternal estate left in intestacy. Then, as his mother's heir, Filippo appointed Antonio di Bernardo Paganelli as his agent to obtain Monte credits of eighty-nine florins held in his father's name as part of his mother's dowry. The original credit had been almost 500 florins, but the remaining 409 were to go to Antonio Paganelli, who had compensated Giovanni di Sodo di Lorenzo, Filippo's former guardian, for expenses he had incurred in meeting Filippo's needs (food, clothing, and so on) during his youth.⁴⁴ In essence, after growing up, Filippo Pazzi found little value left in his mother's estate, but it was still better than being heir to his politically disgraced father. A few years later, when the Medici had been chased from town and the Pazzi could hope for political rehabilitation and economic recovery, Filippo would have had reason to pursue claims to paternal and grandpaternal property.⁴⁵ Yet it is also the case that what Filippo Pazzi did was not substantially different from the acts of Lorenzo di Cristoforo Giuntini of Montevarchi, who also repudiated father, accepted mother, and as heir appointed agents to see to his resulting property interest.⁴⁶ In the case of Giovanna di Francesco di Michele of Giogoli, married to Alessandro Bostichi, we can follow the same process a step further, as her *procurator*

---

⁴³ Here see Julius Kirshner, "Wives' Claims against Insolvent Husbands in Late Medieval Italy," in *Women of the Medieval World*, ed. Julius Kirshner and Suzanne F. Wemple (Oxford: Blackwell, 1985), 256–303; id., "Materials for a Gilded Cage: Non-Dotal Assets in Florence (1300–1500)," in *The Family in Italy from Antiquity to the Present*, ed. David I. Kertzer and Richard P. Saller (New Haven: Yale University Press, 1991), 184–207.

⁴⁴ NA 14725, fols. 45v-46r (31 August 1492).

⁴⁵ See Osvaldo Cavallar, "I consulenti e il caso dei Pazzi: *Consilia* ai margini della *In integrum restitutio*," in *Legal Consulting in the Civil Law Tradition*, ed. Mario Ascheri, Ingrid Baumgärtner, and Julius Kirshner (Berkeley: Robbins Collection, 1999), 319–62, and "Il tiranno, i *dubia* del giudice, e i *consilia* dei giuristi," *Archivio storico italiano* 155 (1997): 265–345.

⁴⁶ NA 14713, fol. 206r (3 March 1467). Similarly, NA 1209, fol. 128v (30 July 1400); NA 686, fols. 103v-4r (22 September 1437).

put her in possession of her mother's eighty-six *lire* dowry, which became in fact a list of tools, implements, and bits of furniture.[47]

Other repudiations worked variations on this theme. One finds instances of repudiating father and accepting grandfather,[48] repudiating father and accepting one or other grandmother,[49] repudiating father and accepting brother,[50] repudiating brother and accepting mother or others.[51] One woman accepted her father's estate but repudiated that of her son, who was prior of Santa Maria de Avena.[52] A set of brothers, with the one over eighteen acting as *tutor* for the rest, repudiated their father's but accepted their uncle's (for five-sevenths), which resulted in an inventory showing a credit of over 492 florins in the Monte.[53] Francesco and Simone di Girolamo di Piero del Guanto repudiated their brother's property but accepted the fideicommissum in their father's testament, which directed they be substituted if their brother died without issue. In essence, they were their brother's heirs, but they were claiming the property by substitution as their father's heirs.[54]

Declarations

In some of these repudiations, especially those in which one accepted the maternal estate, we also find explicit declarations to the effect that property was not held by claims through the one who had been repudiated. These reveal how aware Florentines were that they were skirting a grey area. The legal value of these *protestationes* is uncertain, except that we may assume that they were intended to function as notarized evidence in a court of law. These *protestationes*, however, were almost all the product of a single notary, ser Andrea di Cristoforo Nacchianti, who had a long career in Florence.

For one example, we can look to 30 December 1489, when Giovanni and Girolamo di Berlinghiero Berlinghieri repudiated what had been left them by their brother, Francesco, who had died a few days before.

The aforesaid Giovanni and Girolamo and each of them, in the presence of myself and the above named witnesses, said and expressly affirmed and proclaimed and do

---

[47] NA 9039, fol. 41r-v (30 January 1418). These parents were victims of the plague of 1417, it seems.
[48] NA 1208, fol. 21r (8 August 1397).
[49] NA 14716, fol. 94r (5 May 1473); NA 14717, fols. 108v-9r (23 September 1475); NA 14725, fol. 98r-v (12 February 1493); NA 691, fol. 162r (29 December 1451).
[50] NA 14719, fol. 137r (30 April 1480).
[51] NA 14719, fol. 3r (4 January 1479); NA 9902, fol. 753v (27 June 1515).
[52] NA 1757, fol. 115r (1 March 1401).
[53] NA 684, fols. 54v-55r (4 August 1431).
[54] NA 16317, fols. 322v-23v (27 June 1532). They found it useful thereafter to arrange an arbitration between them, but we do not have the resulting sentence of the arbitrators. See also NA 14723, fol. 244r (30 December 1489); NA 14727, fol. 8r (23 June 1497); NA 14726, fol. 9v (14 June 1494), fol. 16r (27 August 1494); NA 14725, fol. 147r (26 August 1493); NA 14724, fol. 183r (26 October 1491).

Strategies   171

proclaim that if in any way it appears that they or one of them stay, dwell in, or hold the goods or other things common among them or of one of them and the said late Francesco, their deceased brother, they intend to stay in these and to hold and possess them only as their share among themselves and in the part and portion belonging to them or to one of them, and that they do not intend [to possess] in any way the part or portion of said Francesco.⁵⁵

The key here, it seems, was the expression of "intent" to hold property by some other right than as heirs to Francesco, whom they had just repudiated. They had their own direct rights to the property. They hoped this distinction and the repudiation would have the effect of limiting the estate's exposure to Francesco's share alone.⁵⁶

In October 1478, Brancaccio di Niccolò di Brancaccio Rucellai repudiated his brother Piero, to whom he was testamentary heir. A month later, Brancaccio entered a *protestatio* that also took the form of an assurance to Francesco di Filippo di Vanni Rucellai, *tutor* to Piero's daughter, Alessandra, that he would not raise any lawsuits on his niece's behalf. Ten days later, Brancaccio protested that, though he and his brother had accepted what their father had left them in his will, he was still not his brother's heir but held the property by virtue of the fideicommissary substitution in his father's will that replaced him for Piero if Piero died, as he had, without sons.⁵⁷ A draper, Giovanni di Domenico di Zanobi del Marinella, repudiated his father in 1480 and then asserted that back in 1471 he had purchased a house for his father's use and that now reverted to him after his father's death. He was simply owner of it by purchase and not as his father's heir.⁵⁸

A common ploy invoked in these *protestationes* was the excuse of restitution of the maternal dowry. In 1464, Giovanni di Filippo di Bartolomeo

---

⁵⁵ NA 14713, fols. 193v–94r (13 January 1467): "Prefati Johannes et Jeronimus et quilibet eorum, constituti in presentia mei et testium suprascriptorum etc., dixerunt et expresse affirmaverunt et protestati fuerunt et protestantur quod si quomodo apparent etc. eos vel alterum eorum stare, habitare, vel tenere in aliis vel bonis communibus inter eos vel alterum eorum, et dictum condam Franciscum, fratrem eorum predefunctum, quod solummodo intendunt in illis stare illaque tenere et possidere pro ratha eorum inter alterum eorum et in parte et portione eis vel alteri eorum pertinenti etc. nec ut intendunt modo aliquo parte vel portione dicti Francisci."

⁵⁶ Another legally precise declaration was that of Tommaso di Neri Ardinghelli, NA 680, fol. 32r-v (6 May 1421): "non intendit sibi aliqualiter preiudicare in aliquo iure sibi quomodolibet quesito et seu competenti in bonis infrascripte domine Cilie vel hereditariis ipsius domine, et maxime ex forma et secundum formam et dispositionem et seu condictionem quoruncunque statutorum civitatis Florentie, et maxime statuti positi in secundo domini potestatis rubrica qualiter succedatur in dote et aliis bonis uxoris premortue."

⁵⁷ NA 14718, fols. 228r (28 October 1478), 235v (28 November 1478), 236r-v (8 December 1478).

⁵⁸ NA 14719, fols. 179v–80r (16 November 1480). Likewise Mariotto di Francesco di Piero protested that he had bought his house, after repudiating his father (dead twelve days) but accepting his mother (dead seven years) (NA 14726, fols. 179v–80r [15 March 1497]).

Baronci reported that his paternal grandmother had received in 1425 from the court of the Podestà, as payment for her dowry, a farm and other goods worth 270 florins. These holdings had later been judicially assigned to his own mother for her dowry. Giovanni thus claimed that he held these properties as sole heir to his grandmother and his mother and not by any right by way of his father, whom he had repudiated (Appendix 6). In a similar manner, Sandro di Goro d'Antonio of Castro Franco, now adult in the year since his father's death, repudiated his father, but his half-brother Francesco accepted. The brothers, seeking to avoid lawsuits and expense, assigned the surviving second wife, Sandro's mother, as restitution of her dowry, thirty-four florins, in the form of a share of a house in Montevarchi, where Francesco lived. As Sandro her son "can at any time go and stay in said portion of said house" ("posset aliquando ire et stare in dictis partibus dicte domus"), he thus protested that he did so "iure familiaritatis" and did not intend to be his father's heir. Lest there be any doubt, he repeated his repudiation.[59]

These *protestationes* show that strong doubts lingered when paternal property was held by some other title. Such claims could plausibly be contested, and the burden of proof fell precisely on the sorts of holders who had the notary draw up their declarations of right. Behind these acts lies the delicious paradox that, even as agnation and lineal descent were increasingly emphasized in inheritance practices, especially in wills, these combinations of repudiation of father and acceptance of mother tied the preservation of agnatic property to a female who was not agnate (the mother). Through her some portion or quota of the house could be held, even if the rest slipped to creditors.

A final complex of cases is interesting in its own right. Gerozzo di Francesco Bardi in 1424 repudiated his brother Andrea, likely a victim of the recent outbreak of plague. His deceased brother's *procurator*, Dego di Piero degli Spini, then released Gerozzo from any further claims regarding Andrea's estate. Then Tommaso di Bartolomeo Barbadori, as arbitrator between Dego degli Spini and Gerozzo's sons, Francesco and Bernardo, declared that Andrea's partial share in the house on Via de' Bardi, where Gerozzo and his sons lived, belonged to Francesco and Bernardo. No justification for the decision appears, but the effect of the arbiter's decision, paired with the repudiation by Gerozzo, was that the house now fully belonged to his family without it being in his name or being labeled part of the *hereditas* of his brother. The missing element, however, is that the sons were nowhere labeled emancipated, which they would have had to be to stand as parties in an arbitration, even if, as was the case here, they were said to operate with the consent of their father.[60]

---

[59] NA 14729, fol. 148r-v (28 May 1507).
[60] NA 681, fols. 132v (29 February 1424), 135v (6 March 1424), 138v (13 March 1424), 142r-44r (25 March 1424). Catasto 64, fol. 132r, reveals that Gerozzo was 74 in 1427 with total

Complications of Management

At times, Florentines faced such complicated patrimonial situations that one wonders if repudiation were not a tool to unravel some of the layers left by previous heirs and owners. Repudiations just initiated a series of acts and opened a window into these dense thickets of ownership and obligation that unfolded over time. For example, in 1430 Lippaccio, Girolamo, and Carlo di Benedetto di Lippaccio Bardi, all three underage and thus acting with the consent of their guardians (Andrea and Larione, their uncles), repudiated their nine-twelfths share of their maternal grandfather, Ubaldino di Bindo Guasconi. Then the uncles agreed to arbitration in Domenico di Zanobi Adimari,[61] who immediately determined that, as these brothers had divided their common holdings in September 1428, that settlement first needed to be restated and reconfirmed. Then Larione received an additional farm and, more importantly, the entire palazzo in Florence he currently shared with Andrea, but which they could not divide without destroying ("non poterant commode dividi quin destruerent"). Larione had to pay his brother the hefty sum of 3,150 florins to buy out his half interest. The palazzo would remain an identifying piece of property for the entire Bardi lineage, but it would be in the hands of a distinct branch.[62]

The arbitrator also detailed that in 1415 a prior arbitration judgment had considered that Ubaldino Guasconi owed Benedetto Bardi 300 florins as dowry for his daughter Lisa. Ubaldino had been ordered to pay that sum. It was also noted that in 1413 Bindo d'Ubaldino, as heir to his mother, having been emancipated, had accepted her property and given it to his father, who later in 1421 gave it and more to Lisa (to a sum of 400 florins), after having emancipated her. Guasconi's catasto declaration of 1427 showed him possessing assets worth only 439 florins, so it is not perhaps surprising that the four grandsons, as heirs to their mother, had accepted her estate, while these three now had repudiated her father. A few days later, Girolamo and Carlo deeded over to Lippaccio whatever rights they had from that arbitration and two gifts (700 florins in total), and Lippaccio ceded this interest to Andrea and Larione. This may have been in compensation for the expense of raising them. It may have been from a sense that two such wealthy and powerful Bardi adult males stood a good chance of actualizing these credits into cash or other real assets.[63]

---

wealth, almost all of it in real estate (beyond the house which was exempt by law), of 2,528 florins.

[61] On whose legal problems, see Kuehn, *Law, Family, and Women*, 101–26.
[62] Here note the apposite comments of Burke, *Changing Patrons*, 29, 39.
[63] NA 9041, fols. 3v-4r (11 April 1430), 5r-7v (21 April 1430). The 1427 catasto reveals that Ubaldino Guasconi was not wealthy, having assets worth only 439 florins (Catasto 975, fol. 650r).

The matter did not end there. The fourth brother, Francesco, who had not been present for any of the earlier dealings, in 1432 also repudiated his share of Ubaldino Guasconi's estate, which he said amounted to a twelfth share in his own name and three more twelfths that came to him by virtue of his brothers' repudiations.[64] The mathematics of the shares across these acts is muddled, but it seems that the four grandsons had effectively repudiated the entire estate.

In 1505, Francesco di Piero di Lorenzo Cresci repudiated his half of his father's estate but accepted the entirety of his mother's, then entering arbitration with his half-brother Raffaele. The arbitrators' judgment two months later determined that Francesco had petitioned against the underage Raffaele to see Piero's books and determine how much his mother's dowry was worth. The arbitrators found that Francesco's mother's dowry was worth 1,350 florins, but also that Piero had emancipated Francesco and used part of his mother's dowry to dower his sister. The arbitrators assigned certain hereditary properties that were "minus dampnosa" to Raffaele.[65] The rest was Francesco's.

Then there was the case of Francesca di Zanobi di Maso di Valore, widow of Baschiere di Franceschino Tosinghi, who repudiated her husband, who had left her his heir in his will. She repeated this repudiation three months later, but this time also

with this declaration placed and made in the beginning, middle, and end of the present act that the same lady by the aforesaid terms or any of them does not intend nor want to renounce any legacy and bequest made to her by said Baschiere in his testament, but she ratified, accepted, and affirmed the legacy and bequest and everything bequeathed by said Baschiere she held firm, fixed, and agreeable.[66]

In all likelihood, the legatum was concerned with the return of her dowry, possibly also with standard widowhood rights. However, a testament in favor of a wife also argues that the union was childless, as the husband almost certainly would have named any children as his heirs and, had he not, the will would certainly have been challenged. There may well have been more than a dowry specified in the will. This widow was securing property rights while dodging the deleterious dimensions of allowing herself to be termed heres.

---

[64] NA 9041, fol. 64r (13 February 1432).
[65] NA 14729, fol. 28v (22 April 1505).
[66] NA 9040, fols. 163r (25 July 1424), 167r-v (19 October 1424).: "cum hac protestatione tamen in principio, medio, et fine presentis actus apposita et facta quod ipsa domina per predicta vel aliquid predictorum non intendit nec vult renuntiare alicui legato et relicto sibi domine facto per dictum Baschierem in eius testamento, sed ipsum legatum et relictum et omnia sibi per dictum Baschierem legata ratificavit, adceptavit et emologavit et firma, rata et grata habuit." Her catasto (Catasto 79, fol. 426r) discloses assets worth 370 florins, all in real estate.

This woman's desire to retrieve a legatum even in the face of a repudiation was not unique. In 1409, Giovanni di Luca di Duccio, repudiated his father, but "knowing that his father in his testament had bequeathed him arms and the right to bear arms . . . he accepted said bequest."[67] As a social and civic honor, akin to the right to hold office, the right to a coat of arms and to bear arms in the city was something that might be inherited despite repudiation.

Unclaimed Estates

As we have seen, estates that saw neither aditio nor repudiatio, remained iacentes and were a particular headache to legislators, judges, and jurists, as well as to creditors. It was not that such estates were uselessly inert. Some business went on. Claims were pressed and credits retrieved on occasion. For example, Ugolino Martelli, as guarantor of a sum provided to Bino di Niccolò Bini, had to pay off that credit and have his resulting claim posted against Bini's hereditas iacens.[68]

As the handling of an unclaimed estate could greatly influence any subsequent decision to accept or reject it, it is worth the effort to follow a few interesting examples that survive among notarial papers. In 1398, Giovanni d'Agnolo di Guido and Giovanni di Buono, as creditors of Bonaiuto di Ventura, went to the Florentine doctor of law, Ricciardo di Francesco del Bene,[69] sitting as a judge in his home. They explained that Bonaiuto had been dead four years and that it was still unclear if anyone would come forward as his heir, because his son Francesco had notably not accepted the *hereditas*. They put forth the name of Matteo di Duccio as a suitable person to take charge of this estate

so that future heirs of said Bonaiuto, if any will subsequently appear, not be harmed and so the creditors not be harmed and so that they can settle with their debtors, and mainly Antonio di Duccio di Betto, called Conte, of the parish of Santa Trinita of Florence and his heirs and property of the goods possessed for a certain debt or credit of 80 gold florins . . . from an arbitration set and issued between the said late Bonaiuto and others, as one party, and said Antonio, as the other party, on 25 September.

Del Bene concurred and dispatched a herald to summon the son Francesco and all other relatives to appear before him four days later. When no one appeared by the appointed hour, del Bene duly made Matteo di Duccio

---

[67] NA 9037, fol. 97v (26 March 1409): "sciens dictum eius patrem in eius testamento sibi Johanni legasse arma et ius ferendi arma . . . dictum legatum . . . acceptavit."

[68] Ugolino di Niccolò Martelli, *Ricordanze dal 1433 al 1483*, ed. Fulvio Pezzarossa (Rome: Edizioni di Storia e Letteratura, 1989), 157. This is an area of law and economic practice deserving of a full-length study.

[69] On whom, see Lauro Martines, *Lawyers and Statecraft in Renaissance Florence* (Princeton: Princeton University Press, 1968), 483.

executor of the estate with specific mandate to retrieve the 80 florins and make a complete inventory, which in fact showed only the (suspiciously convenient) 80 florin credit.[70]

One can see that various safeguards were built into this legal procedure. The appointed guardian presumably faced the same legal obligations that any guardian did for management of property, although here he was solely in control of property and not, as usually the case, also guardian of a person. The son Francesco and any other kin were given their chance for four more days, as they had already had four years to act. It was the relatively neutral and learned doctor of law, not a notary or a judge attached to a particular court, who presided.

Two years later, the same notary recorded another petition from creditors regarding a hereditas iacens, this time before the attorney Bartolomeo Popoleschi.[71] The de cuius, Antonio di Ghiere, had been dead several months, and it was uncertain that his son Ghiere would step forward as heir. The creditors' assertion to this effect gains weight from the fact that months earlier Ghiere had carefully taken title to his mother's estate only.[72] His neglect of the paternal estate would seem to have been willful. The same procedure was followed to the same conclusion: a guardian was appointed (this time one of the estate's creditors himself), an inventory compiled showing houses, furnishings, tools, and account books.[73]

It is not clear how large the claim of these creditors was. Some claims could be quite modest. Lucia, who had long acted as servant to ser Paolo di ser Andrea and been left an annuity of twenty-five florins in his will, went to the guild of judges and notaries to state her case that the estate, now left vacant by the death of ser Paolo's brother and heir, be assigned an executor so that she could collect what was due her. Again, the same process unfolded.[74] In this instance, however, in contrast to the first two, there is no indication that there was an identifiable heir waiting around and doing nothing.

A final example emerges from the catasto declaration of 1480 for the neglected estate of Giuliano di Nerlo, a humble spinner. This Giuliano was said to have spent more than five years in Florence's prison, the Stinche,

---

[70] NA 667, fols. 127r-29v (5 and 9 July 1398): "ad hoc ut futuri heredes, si qui in postero apparebunt, dicti Bonaiuti non ledantur et ut non ledantur creditores et ut possint exigi debitores, et maxime Antonius Duccii Betti, vocatus Conte, populi Sancte Trinitatis de Florentia, et eius heredes et bona bonorum possessorum pro quodam debito et seu credito florenorum ottuaginta auri . . . cuiusdam laudi lati et dati inter dictum olim Bonaiutum et alios ex parte una et dictum Antonium ex parte alia die xxv mensis Septembris [1393]."

[71] See Martines, *Lawyers*, 499.

[72] NA 668, fol. 47r (25 June 1400)

[73] NA 668, fols. 115v-19r (24 November 1400).

[74] NA 669, fols. 33v-35r (14 and 15 June 1401). This is the reverse of the sort of testaments analyzed by Giovanna Benadusi, "Investing the Riches of the Poor: Servant Women and Their Last Wills," *American Historical Review* 109 (2004): 805–826.

for debts of 400 florins. He escaped when the Stinche was opened in the chaos of the Pazzi conspiracy in 1478, but he died within a month. He was survived by his second wife, Tita, and his dowerless eighteen-year-old daughter, Dimitilla, by his first wife. Two small farms in the Mugello had been listed in his 1469 catasto declaration. The widow and her step-daughter were in court contesting these properties against each other, and the result was still in doubt. A notation reveals that Giuliano in fact had two sons, Nerlo and Francesco, who obviously had not claimed the estate.[75] The women could contest dowries and hope to reclaim them, while escaping the creditors who had been behind Giuliano's incarceration.

If nothing else, all the Florentine evidence makes us aware that there were indeed abiding issues of debt and obligation and the need to avoid them, and there were strategies of heirship – whether to become one, to whom, by whom. Florentines were certainly not merely passive recipients of the wealth and debts of the previous generation or of lateral relatives. The living still had to make their way in the world. Repudiation of inheritance, on its own or in conjunction with other legal devices, was useful to many of them. It gave them the possibility of altering their reality – at least on paper. We have to recognize that much lay outside the pages and remained fearfully uncertain and in flux. But we also have to see those pages as not only the essence of a fixed and neat history but as contributing elements to the flux, even while they bear traces or clues as to the mixture in which they first arose.

The law said estates passed in intestacy or by testament. Repudiation added another wrinkle. Some estates effectively passed by a combination of the two. Refusal of a testament set up an intestacy. Collaborative refusal of an intestate inheritance could result in a de facto single heir, such as would otherwise emerge only from the provisions of a will. Then there was the unclaimed hereditas. In a real sense, it was neither, and yet claims to it remained in force and it was managed in some form (enough to be given space in catasti).

Law also dictated that heirs could not lay claim only to part of an inheritance. It was all or nothing. But in fact, by claiming what was the mother's while refusing what was the father's, many Florentines managed to take only part of the whole, salvaging it from creditors. The wife/mother may, in one sense, have been only the most privileged creditor on her husband's property, but her claim nonetheless could result in a partial inheritance. It was not that the rules and maxims of law did not function, but their functioning was dependent on the manipulation people could devise.

Another element that emerges from these notarial texts is the familial context to repudiations of inheritance. These Florentines were not singular individuals acting on behalf of themselves or even for a self-regarding,

---

[75] Catasto 1001, fol. 209r.

self-sufficient household. If nothing else, the legal entanglement of their rights and claims with others precluded that. There were the claims they avoided (mainly those of outside creditors) and those they moved around. Whether their vision was horizontal (toward brothers, cousins, or others who could inherit) or vertical (toward children or future generations yet to come), they were always implicated with others. Were they not, then they were indeed poor and in debt to others, financially and symbolically.

Florentines' arrangements, however, did not always proceed smoothly. Creditors, of course, always had interests contrary to those of repudiantes, but some of them were also kin. Conflicts arose and came to courts.

7

Repudiations in Dispute

In 1399, a case came to court in Florence that posed a vital issue at the heart of that city's attempt to discipline the use of repudiation of inheritance through its statutes. Two brothers, Jacopo and Niccolò di Guido, were found to be in possession of their father's property fifteen days after his death, although they had legally repudiated the paternal estate. Specifically, they were in possession of a substantial house described as "quoddam palatium." Their father's creditors brought suit to recover against these sons on the strength of Florence's statute, which, as we have seen, held liable heirs in possession of the deceased's assets after fifteen days, despite repudiation.

Jacopo and Niccolò argued that they had the house not as heirs to their father but as heirs to their mother, for return of whose dowry, in the customary Florentine manner, the house had been pledged. Of course, the Florentine statute then in effect expressly precluded such a defense. It did not exempt possession on the basis of maternal inheritance. So these brothers offered a further argument that the house in question did not in fact belong to their father but to his brother (named Gaddo). However, the creditors too had another argument in their favor, as they claimed that Jacopo di Guido had acted as his father's heir when he sold another house his father had owned. That act of alienation seemed to rest on the prior claim to the title being alienated, and thus to be the act of an heir.

Florence's statute spelling out the liabilities of heirs had been intent on a physical separation of the heir from the property, as well as a legal separation by means of repudiation. Jacopo and Niccolò were not feigning such a separation; rather, they argued to excuse their presence on paternal property on other grounds. The creditors' claims seemed plausible, and one might assume – if one went no farther in investigating this case – that they won. They did not. Why they did not had a lot to do with the intervention of a leading jurist.

Consilia and Litigation

By the thirteenth century, some communities had made provision for legal experts, generally called *assessores*, to sit with judges and advise them as cases proceeded. Related was the practice of seeking a written opinion, a consilium, from a doctor of law on the legal issues that had arisen in a case. By the time, about 1270, the jurist Guglielmo Durante (d. 1295) assembled the first great manual of procedural law, the *Speculum iudiciale*, recourse to consilia had become a customary feature in most jurisdictions in Italy. The first substantial numbers of written consilia begin to survive from the late thirteenth century. By the fifteenth century, consilia were arguably in the forefront of doctrinal elaboration – for repudiation of inheritance and the whole host of civil law institutions.[1]

Consilia took two forms. One was the *consilium sapientis iudiciale*. The *doctor* (or *doctores*) was approached in the course of usual forensic procedure, either at the behest of both parties to a suit through the judge, or by the judge with the knowledge and approval of the parties. These consilia served the purposes of the court. The judge was typically obligated by local statutes to give sentence in accord with the consilium, unless he could present a cogent argument not to do so.[2] One corollary feature of *consilia iudicialia* is that they need not be thoroughly explanatory. It was more important that they set out clearly what the judgment was than that they fully justify it. It is not that they did not offer some justification, but their sentences did not have to be fully "motivated."[3]

In that regard, they could contrast pointedly with the other major type of consilium, the *consilium pro parte*. These consilia served the purposes of

---

[1] Luigi Lombardi, *Saggio sul diritto giurisprudenziale* (Milan: Giuffrè, 1967), 121–23.

[2] See the magisterial study of Guido Rossi, *Consilium sapientis iudiciale: Studi e ricerche per la storia del processo romano-canonico* (Milan: Giuffrè, 1958); but also Lombardi, *Saggio*, 124–30; Mario Ascheri, "'Consilium sapientis,' perizia medica e 'res iudicata': Diritto dei 'dottori' e istituzioni comunali," in *Proceedings of the Fifth International Congress of Medieval Canon Law*, ed. Stephan Kuttner (Vatican City: Biblioteca Apostolica Vaticana, 1980), 533–79; Ingrid Baumgärtner, ed., *Consilia im späten Mittelalter: Zum historischen Aussagewert einer Quellengattung* (Sigmaringen: Jan Thorbecke, 1995); Mario Ascheri, Ingrid Baumgärtner, and Julius Kirshner, eds, *Legal Consulting in the Civil Law Tradition* (Berkeley: Robbins Collection, 1999); Adriano Cavanna, "Il ruolo del giurista nell'età del diritto comune," *Studia et documenta historiae et iuris* 44 (1978): 95–138; Patrick Gilli, "Les *consilia* juridiques de la fin du Moyen Age en Italie: Sources et problèmes," in *Les élites lettrées et le droit en Italie au Moyen Age*, Journée d'études internationale du Centre historique de recherches et d'études médiévales sur la Mediterranée occidentale, Université Montpellier III, juin 2000, *Reti medievali* (http://centri.univr.it/RM/biblioteca/scaffale/Download/Autori G/RM-Gilli-Consilia.zip [accessed August 30, 2005]).

[3] Mario Ascheri, *Tribunali, giuristi e istituzioni dal medioevo all'età moderna* (Bologna: Il Mulino, 1989), 55–66 and more generally Fulvio Mancuso, *Exprimere causam in sentencia: Ricerche sul principio di motivazione della sentenza nell'età del diritto comune classico* (Milan: Giuffrè, 1999).

only one party to a suit, as the jurists were retained to craft legal arguments favorable to that party. Paradoxically, precisely because they were partisan, in order to be convincing, *consilia pro parte* had to give fairly full rationales, both bolstering the viewpoint adopted and laying out the weaknesses of the contrary view. For that reason, the best of them, exploring all the pros and cons around a point of law, were treasured by other legal practitioners as sources for their own arguments in turn.[4] Consilia in that way could have influence beyond their original case. They were not binding precedents, but they could be exhaustive, expressive, and persuasive bits of legal reasoning and citation on point in subsequent cases. Consilia compiled by their authors and others became the effective interpretation of statutes, the living commentary on them. Even when one finds more overt commentaries, as survive for Florence in the writings of Alessandro Bencivenni and Tommaso Salvetti, they are largely based on consilia.

Consilia were not thoroughly divorced from the academic setting and the more dispassionate jurisprudence of the lecture hall. Academic commentaries, especially since the time of the so-called post glossators, such as Jacopo d'Arena and Jacopo Bottrigari, and more so with the authoritative commentators like Bartolo da Sassoferrato and Baldo degli Ubaldi, addressed statutes and their interpretive problems. *Consulentes* turned to these in their opinions, whether to exploit, modify, or reject them. The move between jurisprudence and forensic practice was not always smooth and seamless, and it went in both directions, as major academic theorists were themselves deeply and frequently engaged in crafting consilia in cases, which was a lucrative source of income.[5] There was a complex and dynamic process at work.

No single body of law can ever be comprehensive. The amalgam that was the late medieval ius commune certainly never was. Nor was it necessarily in the interests of lawyers and judges that the law be coherent and free of ambiguities.[6] In Florence and other communities, the legal situation was further complicated by the insertion of local rules that attempted to govern the use of institutions of ius commune, such as repudiation. Particularly with regard to repudiation in Florence, the restriction of the period of deliberation to

---

[4] Lombardi, 130–40.
[5] See Lauro Martines, *Lawyers and Statecraft in Renaissance Florence* (Princeton: Princeton University Press, 1968); Osvaldo Cavallar, *Francesco Guicciardini giurista: I Ricordi degli onorari* (Milan: Giuffrè, 1991); id., "Lo 'stare fermo a bottega' del Guicciardini: giuristi consulenti, procuratori e notai nel Rinascimento," in *Consilia im späten Mittelalter*, 113–44.
[6] In general on law and forensic practice, see Mario Sbriccoli, *L'interpretazione dello statuto: Contributo allo studio della funzione dei giuristi nell'età comunale* (Milan: Giuffrè, 1969); Manlio Bellomo, *Società e istituzioni in Italia dal medioevo agli inizi dell'età moderna*, 3rd ed. (Catania: Giannotta, 1979); Lombardi, *Saggio*, 79–148; Julius Kirshner, "Consilia as Authority in Late Medieval Italy: The Case of Florence," in *Legal Consulting in the Civil Law Tradition*, 107–40.

fifteen days, the requirement to register all repudiations, and the problems raised by succession to political standing and rights of participation in the community raised serious legal questions. And beyond whatever uncertain consequences arose within the law itself, there were the ever-inventive practices of Florentines and their penchant to fall into competition and conflict with each other over material and symbolic resources. Some Florentines were willing to use the law for whatever advantage it might give them and for as long as it did. They were not obliged to see a suit to completion. If they did, they could still find their own accommodations beyond or outside the judgment.[7] Florentines kept their small legion of notaries and growing coterie of trained lawyers busy drafting documents, composing allegations (arguments offered in the course of litigation) and consilia, representing them before courts and administrative organs, which in turn were occupied with recording procedural steps, witness testimony and other evidence, and entering judgments.[8]

It was the *doctores consulentes* especially who attempted to work out accommodations that made sense of the ius commune, statutes, customs, culture in general, and the shifting practices Florentines used. Their attempts to do so in the form of consilia are at the heart of this chapter. These opinions allow a revealing venue in which to bring together the various threads we have been tracing to this point.

Florentine Repudiation Cases, 1350–1450

We can divide our examination of repudiation of inheritance cases in Florence into two broad periods: the first century or so during which Florence kept a registry of repudiations and the second period up to the fall of the Republic. In this first period, several formative elements were at work. There was, of course, the inception of the registry in 1355, which became more frequently used and better organized in time. The registry itself coincided with a much needed redaction of the city's statutes in the same year, and these were again greatly revised in 1415. So the basic structure of Florence's rules regarding repudiation and inheritance in general, along with much else, was under scrutiny and in flux in the period. This was also the period in which major academic figures worked. Bartolo da Sassoferrato died in 1357. Baldo and Angelo degli Ubaldi were in their prime up to their deaths in the plague year

---

[7] See Thomas Kuehn, *Law, Family, and Women: Toward a Legal Anthropology of Renaissance Italy* (Chicago: University of Chicago Press, 1991), 19–100. For Marseille, Daniel Lord Smail, *The Consumption of Justice: Emotions, Publicity, and Legal Culture in Marseille, 1264–1423* (Ithaca: Cornell University Press, 2003).

[8] Regarding legal procedure, see Pietro Sella, *Il procedimento civile nella legislazione statutaria italiana* (Milan: Hoepli, 1927).

of 1400. Major canonists such as Antonio da Butrio (1338–1408) and Pietro d'Ancarano (c. 1330–1416) further shaped the legacy of Giovanni d'Andrea (d. 1348). Many of these men were also active in Florence in the period, at least on occasion. Baldo degli Ubaldi taught in Florence for six years, 1358–64, and had consultative roles in Florentine cases for years afterward.[9] Angelo degli Ubaldi and Pietro d'Ancarano were resident as professors, and thus available as *consulentes*, in Florence for a number of years in the 1390s and, in d'Ancarano's case, after. Their teaching had further influence through their consilia and in the efforts of Florentines who were their students and who came to figure among the first consistently influential (in broad political terms) members of the legal profession in Florence. These included Filippo di Tommaso Corsini (1334–1421) and Lodovico di messer Francesco Albergotti (d. 1398), who made way for Paolo di Castro and others later. This formative period in Florentine law drew to a close about the point that Bencivenni and Salvetti (writing between the 1420s and mid-century) were able to shape commentaries on the statutes as revised by Paolo di Castro and Bartolomeo Vulpi da Soncino (c. 1359–1435).[10]

Case One: Repudiation and Rights to the Maternal Dowry

It was Angelo degli Ubaldi who took up the case of Jacopo and Niccolò di Guido, which addressed recurring features of repudiation in Florence – namely, the statutes' fifteen day limitation for heirs to decide to repudiate and the preclusion of rights to the maternal dowry to permit the repudiating heir to remain on paternal property.[11] Acting, it seems, in a judicial capacity, Angelo was asked to determine if Jacopo and Niccolò were to be considered their father's heirs, despite the fact they had repudiated. This was a central legal conundrum of the statute – prior to the revision of 1415 – which declared heirs liable if in possession of paternal property, not withstanding repudiation or claims to a maternal dowry. However, there were also the facts stipulated to by both sides that the palace had belonged not to Guido but to Gaddo, his brother, although Guido had lived with his sons right up to his death, and that Jacopo had sold a house from Guido's holdings. The sale could be taken as an act appropriate to an heir (*gestio pro herede*).

---

[9] Note Julius Kirshner, "Baldo degli Ubaldi's Contribution to the Rule of Law in Florence," in *Vi centenario della morte di Baldo degli Ubaldi*, Perugia, 13–16 September 2000, ed. Carla Frova, Maria Grazia Nico Ottaviani, and Stefano Zucchini (Perugia: Università degli Studi, 2005), 313–64.

[10] On these men, see Martines, *Lawyers*, 482, 498, 499–500; Jonathan Davies, *Florence and Its University during the Early Renaissance* (Leiden: Brill, 1998), 34n, 41n, 56n.

[11] Angelo's consilium was reproduced in editions of his consilia in print: Angelo degli Ubaldi, *Consilia* (Frankfurt 1575), cons. 386, fols. 277va-78ra. He dates this as March 1399, which, if Florentine style, as I assume, was really 1400 (if March 24 or earlier).

Angelo stated that the Florentine statute did not apply to Jacopo and Niccolò di Guido because various underlying requirements had not been met. It was only proper to require the conjunction of all these elements

> because said statute greatly exceeds the limits of common law, as it wants a possessor or holder obligated for satisfaction of debts, despite the fact that such possessor or holder claims to possess by right of his mother, even despite repudiation or benefit of inventory... and so it must be construed as strictly as it can so that in all ways it not result in any sort of inequity, as it would by removing rights of repudiation, of dowry, and of inventory, which are all maintained and must be by common law.[12]

He thus plainly opposed ius commune to the Florentine statute and asserted the rule of interpretation to restrict the latter as much as possible, to hold it as closely as possible to the terms of the common law that it so evidently "exceeded," in order to preserve the presumed greater justice and equity of the ancient and learned law, whatever the evident utility sought by the statute.[13] The legal line of fire was obvious to Angelo, but he still had to have factual elements in the case that played to it. Here he relied on the fact that the palazzo had not belonged to Guido, so his sons could not hold it as his heirs. The property they held was that of Gaddo, and that was not changed even if they erroneously had asserted in statements to third parties that they held Guido's property in compensation for his wife's, their mother's, dowry.[14]

As for the other issue, that Jacopo had sold a house, the problem was not just that his action could be construed as that of an heir. The sale occurred while he was yet in Guido's potestas, although he had been married and held the job of *mensurarius* or *campsor* "publice et notorie." Florentine fathers were liable for sons openly practicing a trade, unless they made a declaration eschewing their liability before the sons' guild, or they legally emancipated them.[15] Barring any such thing, Florentine statute clearly established mutual liabilities between fathers and their unemancipated sons. In this case, however, in the course of a later arbitration agreement between father and son (for which a prerequisite would have been Jacopo's emancipation), the house had been determined to be Jacopo's. Guido lived there "iure patris

---

[12] Ibid., fol. 277vb: "quia dictum statutum fortiter exorbitat a iure communi, dum vult possessorem vel detentatorem obligari ad satisfactionem debitorum, non obstante quod talis possessor vel detentor se possidere praetendant pro iure matris sue, etiam non obstante repudiatione vel beneficio inventarii... et ideo strictissime debet intelligi quanto plus potest, ut sic in totum et per totum non contineat omnem iniquitatis speciem, cum tollat iura repudiationis, iura dotis, et iura inventarii, quae omnia salva sunt et esse debet de iure communi." Jacopo and Niccolò in this case may be the Niccolò di Guido di Niccolò whose repudiation is recorded on 28 March 1379 in RE 2, fol. 6. There is no registration of a Jacopo di Guido.
[13] Sbriccoli, *L'interpretazione dello statuto*, 429–38.
[14] Angelo degli Ubaldi, *cons.* 386, ed. cit., fols. 277vb-78ra.
[15] See Thomas Kuehn, *Emancipation in Late Medieval Florence* (New Brunswick: Rutgers University Press, 1982), 42–44.

et sic familiaritatis."[16] Angelo degli Ubaldi argued that the vital distinction was that "holding is not possession, neither in spirit nor in fact" ("detentio non est possessio, nec animo, nec re"). As Jacopo had the property for his mother's dowry, which was intended to sustain the burdens of matrimony that had ended with her death, Guido was not entitled to any usufruct. He had no right in his own name to be there. His presence in the house had been gratuitous and generative of no legal result. The conclusion Angelo handed the judge was that in no way were these sons their father's heirs, and thus they were not liable to his creditors.

One wonders what would have been the outcome for law and repudiation practices in Florence had Angelo taken the opposite position. It is hard, admittedly, to see him turning his back on institutions of ius commune such as repudiation. But had he opted for a thorough protection of creditors' claims, dowries (two in this case) would have been lost – to women and to the men who married or inherited from them. Florentines would have found less use for repudiation, if it could not protect dowry rights. They would have been forced essentially to make all repudiations, in order to be upheld as valid, take the form of physical removal from paternal property. Protection of property otherwise obligated for return of dowry would have been out of their hands. Instead, Angelo's consilium anticipated the statutory change of 1415 and what we have seen become a longstanding practice with repudiating Florentines. They kept maternal dowry rights and thus stayed on paternal property, holding onto at least a portion of it.

Angelo's decision was also part and parcel of a general feature of law, by which dowry was the most significant and frequent form of shelter for defendants from claims to recover debts.[17] Angelo confirmed in two different ways in his consilium that one could hold rights on a hereditas without being heir. Jacopo had rights to his mother's dowry and he had an arbitrator's judgment giving him his father's property. In sum, it may be that Florentines' willingness to use repudiation, as reflected in the data from the registries showing increasing numbers of repudiations from the early fifteenth century, was the product of authoritative jurisprudential positions like that of Angelo.

Case Two: Registration

Rosello dei Roselli (fl. 1350s–1390s), who had come to Florence in the late 1380s from Arezzo, by way of Bologna,[18] was handed what on first sight might seem to have been an easy case. Rogerio, heir to Bengo, had repudiated the hereditas but had also, according to witnesses, at the same time expressed

---

[16] Angelo degli Ubaldi, *cons.* 386, ed. cit., fol. 278ra.
[17] See Smail, *Consumption of Justice*, 163, 201; and see also his "Démanteler le patrimoine: Les femmes et les biens dans la Marseille médiévale," *Annales: Histoire, sciences sociales* 52 (1997): 343–68.
[18] On him see, Martines, *Lawyers*, 498.

an intent to be Bengo's heir, and ultimately he had possession of the property. Roselli found that Rogerio was heir and obligated to creditors of the estate.[19] What is interesting is the path he took to get to that conclusion.

He began with the statute ordering registration of repudiations, which would be deemed fraudulent and rendered null if they were not registered. Against this, he posed from ius commune that aditio and repudiatio both worked through *animus*, the desire to be (or not be) heir. *Animus* was more than mere words, gestures, or deeds but was revealed in the combination of them. It was not enough only to declare one did not want to be heir, and it was not enough to act as if one were not heir.[20] The statute did not mandate registration of those who *said* they were repudiating; it said, "whoever repudiated," seeking expression of *animus* in word and deed. In its way, the registration, as an action that went beyond declaring intent to repudiate, was evidence of *animus repudiandi*.[21] Otherwise, if matters remained at the level of words alone, Rogerio could still try to possess the property as heir, as witnesses showed he had. The *mens et ratio* of the statute was to prevent creditors being defrauded by "occultas repudiationes." The statute clearly looked beyond words, while it also looked for them.

Roselli thus defended the rationale behind the statute. For him, in contrast to Angelo degli Ubaldi in his case, there was no issue of conflict between ius commune and ius proprium (the statute). Repudiation was perfectly licit and available to use. It was not to be used to defraud. Roselli confirmed this sense in another consilium, preserved in the same manuscript, in which it was posed that a certain Giovanni had repudiated, as he had not decided to accept a hereditas ("non deliberet aceptare").[22] Roselli responded negatively. Giovanni had only struck a tacit middle point, neither repudiating nor accepting. However, Giovanni, who was testamentary heir, later sued the intestate heirs (to whom the estate passed on his abstention from it) for satisfaction of a debt and he demanded possession of property and delivery of the revenues or fruits therefrom. Again noting the parallels between aditio and repudiatio, and invoking the rule applicable to both that he who wanted part wanted all, Roselli pointed out that an heir could not act against an estate unless he had repudiated. So Giovanni's judicial action, coupled with his ambiguous verbal position, was taken as equivalent to repudiation.[23] Along

---

[19] BNF, Magliabechiano xxix, 174, fols. 18v–19r.
[20] Ibid., fol. 18v: "facta ergo et verba non inducunt repudiationem sed animus declaratus per facta et verba."
[21] Ibid.: "Et sic posito quod petitio debiti ab hereditate, quam possem adire et repudiare, in dubio presumatur facta animo repudiandi, iste animus declaratus per istam petitionem debuit in consiliis notificari ex forma dicti statuti, quod cum non sit factum tanquam nullum impedimentum prestante, cum dicatur fictitia et simulata et sic non facta, ut no. Bar. ff quod vi aut clam l. i."
[22] Ibid., fols. 20v–21r.
[23] Ibid., fol. 21r.

with verbal evidence, actual abstention from the property or acting as other than heir, by suing the heirs, mattered.

Case Three: Liquidating Property for Debts

The consilia of Angelo degli Ubaldi and Rosello dei Roselli set the basic parameters of statutory interpretation of repudiation. There are no later citations to their opinions as dispositive in other cases but there were also no further cases on these issues, so far as I have been able to determine from surviving Florentine consilia. Florentines were able to use repudiation to avoid burdened hereditates, while protecting their rights to dowries or other rights they might have against the estate. A case that came before Filippo Corsini (1334–1421) and Lodovico Albergotti (d. 1398) provided the opportunity for a deeper and more nuanced investigation of the thin line between pursuing one's rights on the hereditas and acting as its heir.

In this instance, there are not even first names of the parties, making the historical reality of the case essentially indistinguishable from a hypothetical academic argument. It certainly is hard to tell whether this opinion was delivered to the court or to one of the parties. Most of the text was dedicated to arguing one position, which was developed in opposition to an opening assertion.[24] That assertion, based on the statute, was that Florentine law removed any and all exceptions, so any son found in possession of paternal property fifteen days after his father's death was liable to creditors. In the case at hand, sons had physically abstained but then handed the paternal house to a creditor as payment of his claim. The argument was that by that act they had acted like heirs and accepted the estate and thus were fully liable to all its creditors.

With the ringing declaration "contrarium credo verum," the consilium launched into a long defense of the view that they were not heirs and not liable. It began with the same interpretive position Angelo degli Ubaldi had invoked that such a statute must receive a restrictive reading lest someone suffer undeserved loss ("ne quis dampnum indebite patiatur"). Here that restrictive reading centered on certain words. "Tenerit" or "possederit" were not to be taken in broad and simple terms as indicating one held or possessed what had been the deceased's. What mattered was that one held for himself, in his own right ("pro se et sibi"). In this case, the sons had not held the house for themselves. They had simply delivered it to a creditor. Various civil law examples and parallels were cited in support.

Another line of argument was that the statute was designed to prevent fraud against creditors. It was hard to say a fraud was committed by delivering the property to a creditor, unless there were multiple creditors, some of whom effectively lost out to the one who received the house; but in that case

---

[24] Ibid., fols. 232r–33v. On these lawyers, see Martines, *Lawyers*, 482, 498.

they might also pursue their claims against the other creditor. It would be more harmful to demand that such repudiating heirs stay totally away from the property, which as vacant property would not then be available to the creditor.[25] To read the statute as obligating these sons was to reach an unjust understanding of it.[26] Another point was that it was absurd that someone who had interacted with the deceased and contracted various credits, having repudiated the estate as "dampnosam," was not otherwise able to pursue his credits. Heirs were frequently also creditors of the estate as claimants to a dowry, as creditors in their own right for funds loaned, or for uncompensated labor, for example. If they were not allowed both to repudiate and yet to seek what was owed them, then the statute intent on protecting creditors from fraud would have contributed powerfully to one class of creditors losing their assets and claims.[27] If a son had to fear being obligated on an estate for stepping in to deliver property to a creditor, then anyone else – grandson, nephew, or other agnatic, or cognatic relative – would have no less fear. The credit would never be paid.

It was true, as Cino da Pistoia had said, that sons who repudiated but later trafficked in paternal property were liable to creditors of their father. The "doctors declare and understand this to be the case, unless it is done by some other just reason in good faith and without fraud."[28] The statute in this regard was only supporting ius commune, for both forbade repudiation's use to defraud creditors, so it was proper to reduce the statute to the terms of ius commune.[29] The rights of the creditors, Corsini and Albergotti concluded, were as safe after the transfer of the house as before.

---

[25] Ibid., fols. 232v–33r: "predictum statutum fuit factum ad obviandum fraudibus que excogitabantur adversus creditores, quia unius hinc alius unde res occupabant eas excogitata fraude diversis modis et titulis defensabant ab ipsis creditoribus. Aliam utilitatem non percipio afferre statutum set que fraus commicti potest aut fraudari possunt creditores ex contractu locationis re ipsa aut secundum propositum conducentis non re ipsa ex ipso contractu, quia et si res steterit vacans de aliena re non satisfiet creditoribus cuius possessoris nunc dominus recuperavit ac locavit etc. ut in themate dicitur, licit tempore mortis defunctus possideret."

[26] Ibid., fol. 233r: "Nulla ergo fraus est vel esse potest, ergo statutum non potest trahi ad conductorem vel alium qui fraude caret, et non est capax fraudis quia sic traheretur ad iniquum intellectum, ut is qui non fraudavit et fraudis capax non est tanquam fraudator a lege comprehenderetur, quod fieri non potest."

[27] Ibid.: "Si defunctus dum vixit et traxisset et se obligasset ei quem postea instituit, vel ei qui successurus sibi fuerit ab intestato et obligasset bona sua; ut fit frequenter, mortuo debitore creditor qui non vult hereditatem debitoris ut sibi dampnosam, non poterit prosequi ypotecas si aliter suum debitum non videat consequtus possessor erit... et sibi obligabitur hereditati, precludetur ergo ius creditoribus consequendi sibi debita. Et cum statutum vult providere creditoribus et fraudibus que fuerint eis obviare, ipsos creditores enormiter ledet ac fraudabit, quod est absurdum intelligere voluisse legislatorem lege qua disposuit providere aliquos circumscribere."

[28] Ibid.: "doctores istud declarant et intelligunt nisi hec faciat ex aliqua iusta causa bona fide et sine fraude."

[29] Ibid., fol. 233v: "debemus maxime statutum quantum possumus ad ius commune reducere."

The Florentine statute rested within the wider orbit of ius commune. Both ostensibly protected the claims of creditors, and repudiating heirs would not be penalized for acting to deliver hereditary assets to creditors. Left out of account here was the problem of which creditors received delivery of assets and which did not. These were not issues before the jurists. They were, in fact, essentially factual issues that were usually settled in guild courts or by arbitrators. Also out of account was the larger problem (but one seemingly likely on a hereditas considered damnosa) of debts outweighing assets, meaning that some credits would go unsatisfied, even if all assets were liquidated. It was those unsatisfied creditors, also protected by the laws, who would have an interest and press a case to get a repudiating heir, who in any way handled a portion of the estate, held liable to them.

The creditors were rarely faceless strangers. They were business associates, friends, and kinsmen (as the consilium hinted, when it noted that creditors and heirs were not mutually exclusive categories). Their claims rested on contracts that could include dowries, gifts, bequests, and so forth. Yet we also have to weigh the social realities of debts and credits. Debt litigation was a public performance, declaring that a social-economic relationship in which credit had been extended was now changed into one in which credit was withheld. Repudiation would seemingly withhold the repayment of debt when a suit already indicated that credit was being withheld. Repudiation and its registration were part of an evolving system of debt recovery developing across the fourteenth and into the fifteenth century. Practices of evasion developed in conjunction with it.[30] What repudiation clarified, if known to others, was that the next in line of succession was also next in line to pay off the credits.

Case Four: Claims of a Repudians to Legitima

Legitima was the portion of a deceased's estate earmarked for "necessary heirs." It had to be provided to them even if the deceased had made a will otherwise directing the bulk of his property to recipients other than the necessary heirs. The will could be contested in court and overthrown as "unduteous" (*inofficiosum*) if it failed to furnish this minimal portion, usually a quarter or a third, depending on how many necessary heirs there were. The obligatory nature of the legitima made for the basis of a case that the canonist Pietro d'Ancarano and two Bolognese colleagues, Bartolomeo da Saliceto (d. 1412) and Floriano di San Pietro (d. 1441), dealt with in April 1410.[31] The excision of detail from the *punctus* of the consilium leaves some doubt as to whether the case was in fact Florentine.[32] But the resolute disposition

---

[30] See Smail, *Consumption of Justice*, 158–63, 184, 196, for astute observations about debt litigation.
[31] BNF, Landau Finaly 98, fols. 171r–72v, 175r-77r.
[32] Reference to Niccolò's business partner as "Titius," the Roman law equivalent of "John Doe," raises this possibility.

of the legal issues by three such prominent jurists, along with the survival of a copy in a Florentine manuscript, reassures that their collective opinion had weight and standing along the Arno.

The *punctus* laid out the following progression of legal events leading up to the jurists' intervention. Niccolò and Lorenzo had one son and three sons respectively, when their father passed away, leaving them as his testamentary heirs for one-third, to be equally divided. Included in this third were 1,000 florins owed by the father's business partner and previously assigned to his emancipated sons in an arbitration. The rest of the estate was directed to the grandsons in equal shares. As both sons and all the grandsons had been under potestas of the grandfather, his testament thus operated to provide equally for all persons under his authority rather than for two lines of descent. Each of the six (two sons, four grandsons) ended up with one sixth, but Niccolò's line of descent realized only one third, not half.

Subsequently, Niccolò and his son Benvenuto repudiated, but supposedly under the condition that they could still retrieve their legitima, a right that they alleged still fell to them on the grounds first that the testament had contained a substitution of them to the others, should they die before the testator or otherwise not become heir (thus hinting at possible repudiation), and second that, by including the 1,000 florin credit in the hereditas, the testament burdened them not only in their legitima but in the property they already ostensibly held. Niccolò and Benvenuto sued for the legitima. Lorenzo responded that Benvenuto was owed nothing, as his claims yielded to those of his father, and that Niccolò could not seek his legitima because he had repudiated.

Pietro d'Ancarano disallowed any pretense to legitima at the outset. It was in the power of the heir to preclude substitution by accepting the hereditas, which he had to accept in total; he could not take a legitima and repudiate the rest.[33] If there were not enough value left in an estate after satisfying bequests and other obligations, a judge could be asked to step in and supplement what was left to form a suitable legitima. If there were more than enough left for legitima, however, the heir could not accept it and repudiate the rest.[34] Repudiation with reservation of legitima was not allowed. It flew in the face of the testator's desire to substitute another if Niccolò failed to be heir. But there was another way to take the situation, which d'Ancarano opted

---

[33] Ibid., fol. 171v: "Ex sola vulgari substitutione filius non potest pretendere se gravatum, quia in potestate sua est dictam substitutionem excludere hereditatem, videlicet adeundo... unde cum adeundo possit totam hereditatem consequi non potest eam dividere acceptando legitimam et repudiando residuum, ut sic ipsum habeat substitutum."

[34] Ibid., fols. 171v-72r: "Si enim deductis legatis et aliis oneribus legitima non superest, iudex eam supplere debet; si vero superest legitima et etiam forte multum ultra non credo filium posse legitimam retinere et illud ultra repudiare et substituto locum facere, quis iste conatus institui et substitui et partem adire partem repudiare est contra iuris regulas ut sepius dixi."

for. This was that a repudiation that was conditional was invalid. By that route, Niccolò still had the option to accept the inheritance and seek judicial supplement to the legitima, if it was insufficient. Invalidating his repudiation was, it seems, a kinder conclusion, as it gave him a second chance to claim his portion of the patrimony.

Bartolomeo da Saliceto, who in his signature excused his brief effort "propter infirmitatem" (he would die within two years), set it out that a conditional substitution (*si heres erit*) did not transmit a legitima, so repudiation with a condition to retain a legitima was not valid.[35] He also agreed with d'Ancarano that, as the repudiation was not valid, Niccolò's portion did not devolve on the substitute heirs but was still open to his acceptance.

Neither of these jurists contested the assertion that the son's rights were superseded by the father's or tried to claim that the substitution passed claims to the son. As the testament set separate portions for the sons and grandsons, it seems that it could plausibly have been argued that the son's rights in the estate were distinct and not derivative from his father. Floriano da San Pietro did not touch on that issue either. He was intent, as were the others, on dismissing conditional repudiation and eliminating a distinction between legitima and its excess within one heir's share.

There was a coda to this case, one that did not, strictly speaking, involve repudiation. But it is eloquent witness to the clever legal maneuvers some were capable of, as well as the legal reasoning employed to cope with them. Briefly, Niccolò, with pretense to some property of his brother Lorenzo, emancipated his son Benvenuto and entered arbitration with him, by the result of which Niccolò was sentenced to pay his son 200 florins. Benvenuto then used that judgment to gain control (*tenuta*) by judicial decree of Lorenzo's goods as his father's. Lorenzo responded with appropriate legal proofs to block *tenuta*; but Benvenuto then sought to have Lorenzo compelled to arbitration with him by force of a statute that ordered arbitration for kin who had disputes, especially regarding the division of hereditas.[36] Lorenzo argued that the matter between them had been settled judicially and that he could not be forced to a compromise on the same issue. Floriano di San Pietro and Pietro d'Ancarano had little trouble marshalling arguments against Benvenuto.[37]

Thus, the opinions of these authoritative Bolognese jurists mounted another important piece in place regarding repudiation. It had to be total and unconditional. Legitima did not slip past it. That was a category that set a minimum to what an heir might claim, but it was not a special category of inheritable property subject to different rules. This too was a fundamental

---

[35] Ibid., fol. 172v. He also dismissed an exception for a *filia instituta*.
[36] On this, see Kuehn, *Law, Family, and Women*, 26–30.
[37] Landau Finaly 98, fols. 175v–77r.

issue for repudiation in practice. It was not, perhaps, an issue so easily resolved in juristic interpretation, however.[38]

These four cases from the late Trecento and early Quattrocento set parameters for repudiation that were in place by the time Florence's statutes received their final revision. Soon thereafter it was possible first for Alessandro Bencivenni, later for Tommaso Salvetti, to lay out an interpretive framework. The main sticking point, it was already clear, was the Florentine statute's seeming interference with other rights of possession than as heir. While the statute of 1415 conceded rights of sons or grandsons to dowry, other problems remained or would emerge from later practices.

As there were no systematic reissues of statutes after 1415, more weight shifted to the interpretive framework jurists worked out in consilia, which formed the basis for the commentaries of Bencivenni and Salvetti.[39] Effort also shifted to the legislative corrections offered at points in reaction to practices and to interpretive contradictions and uncertainties the lawyers brought to the attention of lawmaking panels. By the end of the Quattrocento, the two developments, juristic interpretation and legislative emendation, in conjunction with ever-evolving practices, and intense use of repudiation, produced a new spate of revealing cases and adjusted juristic perspectives.

Florentine Cases, 1450–1550

Legislation in the course of the Quattrocento was increasingly concerned with Florentines' sharp, clever, cunning, but fraudulent uses of repudiation. We have seen laws express concern about creditors' ability to reclaim their assets and their willingness to enter into further transactions at a time when, for a variety of reasons, commerce and economic activity in general seemed to be stagnating. The sorts of voluntary creditors who underwrote commercial activity were being scared off by ruses involving repudiation. As we have seen, Florentine jurists respected the statutory desire to prevent fraud, and they were no less sympathetic to legislative initiatives intended to bolster that resolve. The interpretive problem was that they also saw the Florentine statute as arising outside ius commune, thus needing a restrictive reading when in conflict with ius commune (as regarding rights to the maternal dowry) or a reading in light of ius commune (when in harmony with it, as in preventing fraud). Were interpretations along the first set of lines going to gut the law of all force along the second set? How far would seemingly legitimate claims of repudiating heirs be taken against the valid claims of

---

[38] BNF, Fondo principale, iv, 435 (Bencivenni), fols. 17r, 20v; Fondo principale, iv, 434 (Salvetti), fols. 76v–77v; and above, Chapter 2.

[39] As a prime example, Salvetti, fol. 60r-v, in the process of describing how the statute "exorbitat a iure communi" cites, in addition to *leges* of the *Code*, Angelo degli Ubaldi's consilium from our first case.

creditors? These were the problems that faced later Quattrocento jurists, as they had faced their predecessors. But contexts had changed, and so did juristic interpretation.

Case Five: Fraudulent Use of Repudiation

Bartolomeo Sozzini (1436–1507) was a jurist from an illustrious Sienese family very active in Florentine legal cases, especially during his sojourn as professor of law in Pisa from 1474 to the mid-1490s.[40] At some point during those years, he was asked by a court (perhaps that of the Podestà of Pistoia) to render an opinion in a case involving repudiation of inheritance. The sealed opinion survives in the papers of Sozzini's colleague and student, the Florentine jurist Antonio di Vanni Strozzi (1455–1523).[41] Unfortunately, the facts of the case have to be reconstructed with difficulty and much is left unknown from the internal evidence of Sozzini's consilium.

A man named Vincenzo di Domenico had abstained from his father's estate but had accepted his mother's dowry, a fairly common practice by that point. As his mother's heir, he had continued to live in his father's house. He claimed three-eighths of a farm his father had held in common with his nephews, as compensation for the dowry, and he won a judgment to that effect (an unequivocal public testimony to the nature of his claim). The house, however, was not in his name but had fallen in title to his paternal cousin, Michelangelo, after other cousins had also repudiated it. On an unspecified dowry claim, someone brought suit against Vincenzo on the grounds that he was heir to his father and in possession of his estate, largely because he lived in the house. Vincenzo's defense was that he had repudiated the estate of his father and was in possession only of the estate of his mother. The case resolved itself into the question of the status of Vincenzo's abstinence from the estate – was it valid or was it a sham?

Sozzini began stating his decision that one of them, either Vincenzo or his cousin, Michelangelo, had to be liable. Sozzini shunned scholastic pro-et-contra dialectic in favor simply of larding the text with arguments against Vincenzo. First, after obtaining his mother's dowry in the form of land, Vincenzo had taken possession of other pieces of paternal land. These additional paternal properties could not be alleged to have been compensation for the maternal dowry. So, said Sozzini, within the three years allowed him by law to change his mind following a repudiation, Vincenzo had indeed revoked his abstention and "intermingled" himself in the paternal estate. In fact, he

---

[40] On Sozzini, see Martines, *Lawyers*, 504; and now more thoroughly Roberta Bargagli, *Bartolomeo Sozzini, giurista e politico (1436–1506)* (Milan: Giuffrè, 2000).

[41] ASF, Carte strozziane, 3rd ser., 41/2, fols. 275r-78v (hereafter Sozzini). Another sealed copy is in 41/1, fols. 493r-95r. That it was addressed to the court seems clear from the fact that there is no attribution to a party by Strozzi, whose marginal notes dot the pages, and by the way the final sentences address the judge and offer him sentencing options.

had done so within little time ("parvo tempore") at all. According to the texts of the *Code* and the commentary of Bartolo (to D. 29.2.88), Vincenzo had made himself heir.[42] The fact that Vincenzo's father had bought the land in question and placed it to be worked by the same steward (*villicus*) who worked other land expressly obligated for the dowry did not make any difference. Lands that were Domenico's alone and that Vincenzo was found to possess could only be available to him as heir to Domenico. No other "iusta causa" could be construed for his continued presence on his father's estate, and therefore he had to be considered to have revoked his abstention. The same logic by which continued residence in the paternal home resulted in a presumption of right of inheritance also applied to continued use of paternal fields or vineyards.[43] Vincenzo had come into possession of the lands held in common by his father and cousins by means of a court sentence; he had not an equivalent sentence to put him in possession of the other assets his father had owned.

What seemed to work for Vincenzo was the argument that, following repudiation, the acceptance of the estate "cum benefitio inventarii" by his cousin Michelangelo precluded Vincenzo from revoking his repudiation and "intermingling." Indeed, as we saw in the first chapter, aditio by a coheir or next in line extinguished a repudians' possibility of changing his mind. Sozzini, however, claimed on the basis of the authority of the *Glossa ordinaria* that during the three-year period in which a suus heres could revoke his repudiation the next in line (*sequens in gradu*) could not enter into formal possession.[44] In taking this position, Sozzini put himself in opposition to Alessandro Tartagni da Imola, his own teacher, so he carefully assembled a host of citations on his side of the argument: several to the *Glossa*, to Bartolo da Sassoferrato, Angelo degli Ubaldi, and Paolo di Castro. Sozzini built a case that the *filius* was not cut off during the triennium by an aditio undertaken by the next in line.[45] To backstop all these citations, Sozzini then brought forth the principle that "in consulting and judging in doubtful

---

[42] Bartolo to D. 29.2.88, *Opera omnia*, 10 vols. (Venice 1585), vol. 3, fol. 156vb, defined "inmiscere quod est suorum est hereditatem iure acquistam per actum voluntatis declaratum acceptare vel agnoscere."

[43] Sozzini, fol. 275v, citing Baldo to *Si paterna* (C. 6.31.1). Sozzini here also noted the views of Paolo di Castro and his teacher Giovanni da San Severino "quod licet essent bona ypothecata pro dotibus maternis, si tamen non posset propria auctoritate ingredi, censetur se inmiscuisse ne presummatur deliquisse."

[44] *Glossa ordinaria* to C. 6.31.6 (Lyons 1568), vol. 4, cols. 946–47, seems simply to affirm that a *filius* had a triennium to reverse his decision; but Sozzini also invokes the gloss and the text at related points, as D. 38.7.2 and its gloss (Lyons 1568), vol. 2, col. 1349, where a suus who repudiated is said still to block others from the estate.

[45] *Glossa* to D. 29.2.71,9, vol. 2, col. 458, and Bartolo to same, *Opera omnia*, vol. 3, fol. 153va; contrast to Alessandro Tartagni to C. 6.31.6, *In primam et secundam codicis* (Venice 1570), fols. 159ra–60ra.

matters one should not retreat from the gloss," itself bolstered by four references to the commentaries of Baldo degli Ubaldi, a parallel construction in a consilium of Lodovico Pontano (d. 1439), and the ringing assertion that his was the reigning common opinion ("ista eius oppenio videtur esse magis communis").[46]

Having disposed of this line of argument, Sozzini moved to the heart of his attack – that Vincenzo's repudiation of his father's estate was in fact "fictitia et simulata." He went on to say, "That it was simulated emerges because later he possessed all the hereditary property or the greater part, even though he might possess some part by another title." A repudiation could be presumed to have been made in mala fide when the repudiator was later in possession of all the hereditary property, no matter who bought it – when anyone secretly trafficked in the property through another – when one was found immediately (*incontinenti*) to be in possession.[47] It was that quick repossession, said Sozzini, that really set in place the presumption of fraudulent intent: "for by reason of the closeness of the acts one reaches the presumption of simulation."[48] Baldo had proclaimed that one who supposedly repudiated but secretly reacquired title, as established by circumstances and timing, was guilty of fraud and simulation.[49] And in the case at hand, Sozzini found presumption of fraud in the fact that the estate had passed to a paternal cousin, "and thus by reason of consanguinity fraud is also presumed." Further presumption lay in the fact that Vincenzo had secretly gained two pieces of land, "from the hiddenness of which simulation is also argued."[50]

Sozzini then invoked the Pistoiese statute, noting that it ruled out a defense in terms of possession of mother's dowry (as had Florence's before 1415), which ius commune protected. So in terms of the statute it was easier to presume and demonstrate fraud, especially with the speed by which one cousin had moved to accept the estate after Vincenzo's repudiation. That quick acceptance was taken to be part of the deception; Michelangelo, the cousin, was heir. His acceptance legally kept Vincenzo from reversing his decision to repudiate, while in fact he took his father's land. Michelangelo, it seems, had acted as agent (*procurator*) for the minor cousins in settling the dowry debt with Vincenzo; but he had done so regarding an estate to which he was also an heir, and thus an interested and biased party. And his was the act of an heir. Sozzini concluded that Vincenzo was liable "tanquam heres"

---

[46] Sozzini, fol. 276r-v.
[47] Arena, *Super iure civili* (1541), fol. 246vb; Cino da Pisotia, *In codicem et aliquot titulos primi pandectarum*, 2 vols. (Frankfurt,1575; reprint ed., Turin: Bottega d'Erasmo, 1964)), vol. 2, fol. 390ra.
[48] Sozzini, fol. 276v.
[49] Baldo to D. 29.2.91, *Opera* omnia (Venice 1577), vol. 3, fol. 118rb.
[50] Sozzini, fols. 276v–77r.

for the dowries owed by his father, "and if rather it please the lord judging that the cousins be held liable, he may condemn them. And whatever way is chosen I do not think that he can make a mistake," though Sozzini also voiced his preference that Vincenzo be obligated because he was heir in first degree.[51]

The telling distinction in his discussion of fraud was between the public knowledge of repudiation established in written archives (notarial papers, the registry) and the hidden, secretive nature of Vincenzo's possession.[52] Jurists could be harsh on fraud, and perhaps more so with an institution by which a son turned his back on his father's property. But Sozzini had also delved into, or been presented with, very detailed information on what property was involved and how it was held and on the timing of events.[53] He saw before him a set of paternal cousins colluding to hold property away from a legitimate dowry claim. He did not look at the facts before him the way Angelo degli Ubaldi had looked at fairly similar facts, as much as a century earlier. Powerful presumptions and penchants to take acts as fraudulent were current, it seems. At least the next case adds to that sense.

Case Six: Simulated Repudiation

Antonio Strozzi, from one of Florence's wealthiest and most illustrious lineages, left behind volumes of papers (consilia and allegations, in original or copies, even just working drafts, by himself and some others). Among these is the draft of a consilium pro parte written for Angelo di Totto da Panzano. Angelo wanted to have his uncle Guerriante forced to arbitration with him, in accord with the Florentine statute mandating arbitration between close kin.[54] Guerriante's resistance to this procedural demand on him rested on the fact that the dispute between him and Angelo was about Angelo's father's estate – a patrimony that Angelo had repudiated and Guerriante had accepted, both by means of public notarized instruments.[55] As there was no question of fact in dispute, there was nothing to submit to arbitration, which was only supposed to consider matters of fact, not those of law.

The counterargument from Angelo, one that Strozzi had some difficulty framing in appropriate legal terms,[56] is enormously revealing of the mindset of some Florentines toward legal instruments such as repudiation. Angelo's claim was that the repudiation was a fake (*simulata*) from the start. It was

---

[51] Ibid. The cousins could not be heredes if he were.
[52] This distinction runs parallel to the one that Smail, *Consumption of Justice*, 213–25, found at work in late medieval Marseille.
[53] Ibid., 219–20.
[54] Kuehn, *Law, Family, and Women*, 26–33.
[55] No repudiation by Angelo di Totto da Panzano occurs among those registered in Florence.
[56] ASF, Carte strozziane, 3rd ser., 41/1, fols. 1711-73v, 174v. The difficulties emerge all too clearly in this draft, where a long passage is cancelled out (but still very legible) in favor of an even longer passage squeezed into the bottom margin and then carried over two sheets later.

never intended to deprive him of his father's property but merely to allow him the guise of not being heir to his father, so he could pursue claims on property his father had alienated for his mother's dowry. These were claims he would have no legal standing to pursue if he were his father's heir, for no doubt his father had sold or otherwise parted with the property "pro se et suis heredibus."[57] As heir, he would be bound by such a contractual promise; as repudians, he was not. He had acted in collusion ("in concordia et conventione") with Guerriante. The simulated contract was of no effect, he argued, and thus there were issues of fact remaining to be disposed of by an arbitrator.

To pursue the case this far leaves one bathed in peculiarly Florentine ironies. Some sort of fraud and fiction were at work here. Either these two, nephew and uncle, had conspired to claim back lost property, or Angelo was working both sides of a very crooked street – trying to have his repudiation against those who had the dowry and yet (or in preference) dropping it against his uncle. Strozzi was retained to argue in favor of the joint conspiracy of nephew and uncle. That story then served as the main prop to the argument that after repudiation Angelo possessed Totto's property; Guerriante did not possess the estate he had accepted. Angelo's possession had been continual and immediate.

Further, there was the evidence of a prior arbitration between Angelo and Guerriante from 25 March 1498, in which Angelo had acted as intestate heir to his father and Guerriante had contracted with him as Totto's heir. Strozzi claimed the notarial instrument was evidence of their intent.[58] Guerriante had not posed as his brother's heir, even though Angelo had already repudiated, so he must have considered the repudiation fictitious.

Hence the words of said arbitration prove against Guerriante that Angelo is heir of Totto, his father, not withstanding repudiation, and that the repudiation was faked and [intended] for a different effect than that Angelo truly be removed from the paternal estate: for such simulations are proven only by conjectures... and these conjectures are very urgent in my judgment.[59]

Another bit of evidence was a private record, which Strozzi described as barely legible, in which Guerriante described the events. Despite the illegibility of the piece, Strozzi claimed it was worthy of some judicial trust.

---

[57] Ibid., fol. 171r: "Sed ad hoc respondetur quod illud proceditur nisi instrumentum repudiationis esset simulatum, quia in veritate Angelus non renuntiavit hereditati paterne ut se illa privaret, et ad Tottum [Guerriantem?] perveniret, sed ut posset vigore dotis materne agere contra quedam bona alienata per Tottum eius patrem, ad que non posset agere si fuisset heres patris, quia teneretur de evictione."
[58] Ibid., fol. 172r.
[59] Ibid., fol. 172v: "Quapropter dicti verba compromissi probant contra Ghueriantem ipsum Angelum esse heredem Totti sui patris, non obstante repudiatione et illam repudiationem fuisse simulatam et ad alium effectum quam ut vere Angelus privaretur paterna hereditate: iste enim simulationes non probantur nisi per coniecturas... et iste coniecture sunt multum urgentes iudicio meo."

The conclusion was that Guerriante quite certainly could be forced, by terms of the statute about arbitration between kin, to enter an arbitration with Angelo. At the very least, there could be an arbitration as to whether, as Angelo maintained, the repudiation was *simulata*.[60] Once that arbitration was begun, however, if the charge to the arbitrators was broad, as it quite conventionally was, they might end up passing judgment on all issues between Angelo and his uncle.

The nature of the case was such that Strozzi did not have to address the issue of fraud perpetrated on creditors in the attempt to retrieve dowry properties. One wonders what his response would have been had that issue come before him, for this case and the previous one show Florentine lawyers being tough about feigned repudiations. Civic concerns with fraudulent use of repudiation may have rubbed off on these men. Florentines otherwise may have been disinclined thereafter to use repudiation quite as freely as they had (hence, perhaps, the declining frequency of repudiations in the registries after 1500).

Case Seven: Implied Aditio

Strozzi's contemporary and sometime colleague, Ormannozzo Deti (b. 1464), participated in a marvelously complicated case somewhere around or after 1500. It seems, from the length and care with which he argued one side, that his consilium entered into the case's proceedings *pro parte*. His use of the pseudonymous "Sempronius" as the name for one of the principals was designed to give his opinion a more abstract, hypothetical, if not theoretical, cast, and thus contribute to its persuasive quality.[61] Unfortunately, that leaves us grasping in vain for any sort of historical reality, in terms of persons and time.

The case facts that framed his intervention were the following: a testator with six legitimate sons left five of them twenty florins each as legitima and a further fifth of the estate each, but as legata, after other bequests and claims were settled. The sixth son, Sempronius, was named sole universal heir. A later codicil corrected the will in that the five not named heredes were each to receive one-sixth, not one-fifth, and that portion was to include the twenty-florin legitima. The legal problem was that, although these five were thus not technically heredes, they were in possession of paternal property after his death. By "censura municipali," any adult son in possession of paternal property fifteen days after his father's death was liable for debts, not withstanding any pretexts regarding maternal dowry or benefit of inventory. The municipal law implied aditio as heir.

Deti briefly rehearsed the negative argument. These five were not liable because the hereditas had not in fact been "delata" to them, they were in

---

[60] Ibid., fol. 173v.
[61] BNF, Magliabechiano xxix, 193, fols. 234r-37r, which is a sealed original (hereafter Deti). On Deti, see Martines, *Lawyers*, 488.

fact legatarii, not heredes.⁶² His arguments to the contrary began quickly and ran at length, ignoring the statute that created the situation. His attention instead was drawn to the meaning in ius commune of being an heres and to the language of the testament, a very particular contributing factor to the situation before him.

What was left to the five sons was referred to as *prelegata*. In general, prelegata were not separated from an hereditas and were thus calculated in the division of the estate among its heirs, though treated as a burden falling proportionately on each share.⁶³ According to the teaching of authoritative jurists (Bartolo da Sassoferrato, Paolo di Castro, Alessandro Tartagni), prelegata were treated as hereditas. Deti relied on such doctrinal support to claim that the five sons were in fact "instituted" as heirs by the testament and the codicil,⁶⁴ and thus "are considered instituted heirs equally with Sempronius" ("censeantur instituti heredes pariter cum Sempronio").⁶⁵

Perhaps the most interesting argument Deti could muster was that a legatarius receiving a *quota hereditatis*, even if not strictly a heres, was nonetheless liable for *debita hereditaria*; for hereditas, after all, "is nothing other than representing the deceased in all his rights" ("nihil aliud sit nisi representare defunctum in omnibus suis iuribus").⁶⁶ This argument, however, really only led up to the true core of his position:

[A]nd the aforesaid conclusion should be maximally expanded by any good judge, because this testament was conceived in fraud for defrauding creditors. But no one's fraud and deceit should be protected... nor may a title acquired by fraud free anyone from hereditary obligations... unless the statute that arose to guard against frauds and was conceived as most watchful lest creditors be defrauded is easily set aside, it is necessary that it not be allowed.⁶⁷

Such a strange testament seemed indeed designed to perpetrate fraud. Deti admitted that different wording would not have implied *universitatem et onera*, as the words "deducto ere alieno et legatis" did. One wonders as well if simple legata of large sums to the five sons may not have accomplished the testator's intent to leave only a small portion of his estate and one son exposed to creditors.

---

⁶² Deti, fol. 234r-v.
⁶³ See Max Kaser, *Roman Private Law*, 2nd ed., trans. Rolf Dannenbring (Durban: Butterworth, 1968), 320.
⁶⁴ Deti, fols. 234v-35r. For example, in examining the language of the codicil Deti said, "verbum relinquo adiectum universitati bonorum ostendit institutionem."
⁶⁵ Deti, fol. 235r.
⁶⁶ Deti, fol. 235v.
⁶⁷ Deti, fol. 236r: "et maxime amplectanda est supradicta conclusio a quocunque bono iudice quia istud testamentum fuit excogitatum per fraudem ad fraudandos creditores. Fraus autem et dolus nulli patrocinari debent... nec titulus in fraudem acquisitus liberat etiam ab oneribus hereditariis... alias statutum quod emanavit ad observandas fraudes et ne creditores fraudarentur tot vigilius excogitatum... faciliter evincatur, necesse est quod non est admittendum."

Deti implicitly gave the statute a strong interpretation, though he did not directly read it into the case. He did not argue that there was an implied aditio by the terms of the statute. Instead, he struck at what may have seemed a more disturbing prospect, were it not countered by arguments such as those he drew together from within ius commune. The testament, were it allowed to stand, had the potential to drive a huge hole through creditors' legal protections simply by not calling the heirs heirs. In a way, no legal argument could stop such a maneuver if the proper language were used and the appropriate legal effects and risks were embraced (such as some sort of effective inequality of heirs, which the testator here seemed intent on avoiding). Deti conceded as much when he looked at alternative wording.

Case Eight: Effects of Repudiation on Officeholding Rights

In Florence, as in most other Italian communes, sons largely inherited their political standing and citizenship from their fathers. It was possible for one to change citizenship and acquire rights to political participation and officeholding elsewhere, but even that could be completed only over a generation in most cases.[68] It was also possible, even without changing cities, for sons or grandsons to gain the sorts of wealth, patronage, and general civic visibility that could propel them into the ranks of the politically active citizens. But here too the process rested on links to paternal ancestors and prolonged stable participation in the city's affairs, at least in the more passive guise of taxpayer.[69]

---

[68] Here above all are the works of Julius Kirshner: "*Ars Imitatur Naturam*: A Consilium of Baldus on Naturalization in Florence," *Viator* 5 (1974): 289–331; "Between Nature and Culture: An Opinion of Baldus of Perugia on Venetiam Citizenship as Second Nature," *Journal of Medieval and Renaissance Studies* 9 (1979): 179–208; id., "*Civitas Sibi Faciat Civem*: Bartolus of Sassoferrato's Doctrine on the Making of a Citizen," *Speculum* 48 (1973): 694–713; id., "Paolo di Castro on *Cives ex Privilegio*: A Controversy over the Legal Qualifications for Public Office in Early Fifteenth-Century Florence," in *Renaissance Studies in Honor of Hans Baron*, ed. Anthony Molho and John A. Tedeschi (Dekalb: Northern Illinois University Press, 1971), 227–64; id., "Mulier alibi nupta," in *Consilia im späten Mittelalter: Zum historischen Aussagewert einer Quellengattung*, ed. Ingrid Baumgärtner (Sigmaringen: Jan Thorbecke, 1995), 147–75. Also William Bowsky, "Medieval Citizenship: The Individual and the State in the Commune of Siena, 1287–1355," *Studies in Medieval and Renaissance History* 4 (1967): 193–238; Diego Quaglioni, "*Civilis sapientia*": *Dottrine giuridiche e dottrine politiche fra medioevo ed età moderna* (Rimini: Maggioli, 1991), 127–44.

[69] See Gene Brucker, *The Civic World of Early Renaissance Florence* (Princeton: Princeton University Press, 1977), 80–84, 254–59, 503–4; Dale Kent, "The Florentine *Reggimento* in the Fifteenth Century," *Renaissance Quarterly* 28 (1975): 575–638; Francis William Kent, *Household and Lineage in Renaissance Florence: The Family Life of the Capponi, Ginori, and Rucellai* (Princeton: Princeton University Press, 1977), 166–70, 197–202; Lauro Martines, *The Social World of the Florentine Humanists, 1390–1460* (Princeton: Princeton University Press, 1963), 39–50; John M. Najemy, *Corporatism and Consensus in Florentine Electoral*

Inheritance of officeholding rights was certainly of enormous concern in Florence. Florentines proudly recorded ancestors' participation in guild and civic offices, most especially in the Tre Maggiori (i.e., the Signoria of eight priors and the gonfaloniere di giustizia, the Dodici Buonuomini, and the Sedici Gonfalonieri di Compagnia).[70] Loss of such rights by judicially imposed exile (as happened to members of the Alberti, Medici, Strozzi, Pazzi, and so many other lineages) could be a more compelling punishment for political misbehavior or simple failure than execution.[71]

As in any area in which inheritance could play such a defining role, repudiation raised problems. Antonio Strozzi faced a case of this sort in which he devised arguments on behalf of the sons of Benedetto Uguccioni.[72] Bernardo and Giovanbattista di Benedetto Uguccioni repudiated their father's hereditas on 6 March 1497.[73] They did not intend thereby to lose inherited rights to hold office, however. When their rights were challenged in the volatile political climate in Florence in those years, they commissioned Strozzi to frame their case. The solution he crafted was, or so he claimed, subscribed to by several other Florentine lawyers.

Two pieces of Florentine legislation proved relevant. One was an enactment of May 1446. In order to enforce payment of civic fiscal obligations, it established that no citizen whose name appeared in lists of those in arrears to the city could hold any office. If such a person's name were extracted from the purse containing eligible names, it was to be removed. If he attempted to take the office, he faced a 500 lire fine, unless he came forth within eight days and made good on his outstanding obligations.[74]

Such a debt-ridden citizen's estate would also have been a prime candidate for repudiation, but then the problem was whether a repudiating son could recover the political rights lost by the father. Strozzi's consilium reports that this contingency was dealt with definitively by legislation of 29 July 1482, at a time when the state of Florentine finances was of urgent concern. This

---

Politics, 1280–1400 (Chapel Hill: University of North Carolina Press, 1982), 292–98; Julius Kirshner, "Paolo di Castro on *Cives ex Privilegio*: A Controversy over the Legal Qualifications for Public Office in Early Fifteenth-Century Florence," in *Renaissance Studies in Honor of Hans Baron*, ed. Anthony Molho and John A. Tedeschi (Dekalb: Northern Illinois University Press, 1971), 227–64.

[70] See Gene Brucker, *Renaissance Florence* (New York: Wiley, 1969; reprint ed., Berkeley: University of California Press, 1983), 93–97; Martines, *Social World*, 45–46.

[71] See Randolph Starn, *Contrary Commonwealth: The Theme of Exile in Medieval and Renaissance Italy* (Berkeley: University of California Press, 1982); Christine Shaw, *The Politics of Exile in Renaissance Italy* (Cambridge: Cambridge University Press, 2000); Thomas Kuehn, "Family Solidarity in Exile and in Law: Alberti Lawsuits of the Early Quattrocento," *Speculum* 78 (2003): 421–39.

[72] ASF, Carte strozziane, 3rd ser., 41/14, fols. 192r–97v (hereafter Strozzi), a working draft to which he added at the end "subscripserant se plures advocati florentini."

[73] RE 24, fol. 89.

[74] ASF, Provvisioni registri 173, fol. 60r-v (6 May 1446).

legislation has not emerged in fact from the Florentine archive,[75] yet what has emerged from 1482 shows without doubt that the effects of repudiation on officeholding rights was very much an issue of moment. On 26 April 1482, Luca di Salvestro di Giovanni degli Albizzi, seeking what had previously been granted many others ("ut multis iam ante hac concessum fuit"), alleged his repudiation of his father's hereditas to seek political reinstatement.[76] The Monte officials were instructed to assess Luca according to the distribution of the previous November, and in no case less than what his father had been assessed. Once assessed, listed in the books in his own name, and paid up, Luca would be eligible for office.[77] Less than two months later, Bartolomeo and ser Chiaro di Giovanni di Niccolò del Chiaro sought similar concessions.[78] They received them, with the added precaution that the heirs of their great uncle, Lorenzo, who had been assessed along with their father, were to see their assessment appropriately adjusted downward.[79]

The act Strozzi described ordered that no one could hold office unless for the previous thirty years he had been carried in the tax registers as paid up and paying – in his own name or his father's, paternal grandfather's, brother's, or father's brother's. An heir who repudiated the estate for whose obligations he was previously included was to be accepted for office only once he had been newly assessed in the fiscal registers. If a repudians's name was drawn from the purses during a period in which he was *sine onere* (that is, not yet listed in his own name), it was to be removed from the purses for two years, provided later he took on *onera* in his own name. The proviso of reinscription in fiscal registers insured that repudiation alone did not save him from the political fallout of his father's fiscal lapses. One could conclude, Strozzi noted, that one who repudiated and remained unregistered for fiscal purposes for more than thirty years, in his own account or his ancestors', could not hold office, even if he proposed to pay off all the outstanding obligations.

The principal difficulty for Strozzi, in arguing for the officeholding rights of Benedetto Uguccioni's sons, lay in making sense of the 1482 law. First, the prohibition on a repudians holding office, because he was not assessed in his

---

[75] Neither the apposite volumes of the Provvisioni registri (173) nor the Provvisioni duplicati (202) yielded a law of 29 July 1482, leave alone the one in question. Nor did the register of the Consiglio del Cento (2) for those years, 1477–90. There is no balìa for that year. On fiscal concerns at the time and measures taken by the Seventeen Reformers of the Monte, see Alison Brown, "Public and Private Interest: Lorenzo, the Monte and the Seventeen Reformers," in *Lorenzo de' Medici: Studi*, ed. Gian Carlo Garfagnini (Florence: Olschki, 1997), 103–65.

[76] His repudiation is recorded in RE 21, fol. 233 (11 April 1482).

[77] Provvisioni registri 173, fols. 18v-19v (26 April 1482). The measure passed seventy-five to ten, indicating little principled opposition to reintegrating such a repudians into the officeholding class.

[78] Recorded in RE 21, fol. 236 (24 May 1482).

[79] Provvisioni duplicati 202, fols. 50v-51r.

own name and no longer included by virtue of the repudiation in his father's account, was deemed merely temporary. It was lifted once the repudians was "de novo descriptus." Before that point, he was *sine onere*, and no one without *onere* was eligible for office. In that regard, the measure of 1482 was in line with that of 1446 fixing officeholding as the privilege of those *supportantes onera*.[80]

In the case at hand, Strozzi said the sons of Benedetto Uguccioni were eligible for office, for they had been "descripti" for thirty years in the father's name or their own. Following repudiation of the paternal estate, they had had themselves enrolled in their own names for *onera* and *distributiones*. The problem was that they had not been included in an *accatto* or *balzello* of 1494. Strozzi argued that that absence from a fiscal list did not constitute a break in the continuity of fiscal obligations over thirty years; it did not tell against them, as it had not been an *impositio universalis*. The authorizing language in 1494 had informed fiscal officials that they were to assign imposts "to those citizens whom they will judge and will seem to them to be suited" ("a quelli cittadini che giudicheranno et parrà loro convenirsi"). They had rather wide discretion. To see such legislation as rendering various citizens ineligible for office was to arrive at an absurd result, as the law wanted to prevent pauperization of the officeholding class so that they could perform their roles in office.[81] The laws of 1446 and 1482 had looked to general, not restricted, levies.

It is interesting that here for the first time, and at one of only a few points in the opinion, Strozzi cited any texts of ius commune. Citizenship, in large part, and eligibility for office, just about entirely, were matters of statutory law. In any case, Benedetto Uguccioni had been listed in all fiscal distributions up to his death in 1496. His sons, after repudiation, had been re-enrolled in their own names and had paid their taxes in all impositions touching all citizens. The thirty year sequence of payments was established. To be missing from some special imposition did not disable them from office. Nor did repudiation, for all that it left them temporarily *sine onere*, meaning that the continuous support of fiscal burdens for thirty years was broken. Once

---

[80] Strozzi, fol. 194v. He dismissed from consideration measures from 1421, 1474, and 1504, apparently adduced in preliminary arguments, as inapplicable.

[81] Strozzi, fol. 195v: "Si ergo aliqui remanserunt quibus non fuit impositum tale balzellum, quasi non putarint officiales debere illis imponi, non possunt dici per hoc effecti inhabiles ad officia, neque est credendum quod dicta lex voluerit inhabilitare ad officia illos cives quibus non fuisset impositum balzellum, quia sequeretur absurdum quod, cum comiserit iudicio officialium eligendorum quibus civibus sit tale balzellum imponendum, potuissent dicti officiales inhabilitare ad officia illos cives quos voluissent et illos privare honoribus civilibus, quod non est dicendum quia de intentione legis illius fuit quod si officiales reperirent aliquos imponentes ad supportandum tale balzellum non imponentur illis civibus pauperibus, et sic voluit illos relevare a tali honere, non autem gravare quod fient si inhabilitarentur ad officia et sic inducta ad unum effectum operaretur contrarium."

they had been newly enrolled in their own names, the merely temporary incapacity was removed. They could have been *sine onere* for years, as long as they did not miss a general imposition on citizens.[82] In fact, Strozzi posed a hypothetical that someone repudiated and went three years *sine onere* before having himself listed in the fiscal registers, after which his name came up for office.

I think that he should have that office, although he was not listed in the past in all fiscal distributions, first because it is not to be presumed that the law wanted anyone to be obligated for the impossible, because it says that after the father's death some distributions or taxes were imposed that were not widely in use or were supported by law, as was done everyday, and a new distribution was ordered.[83]

The law of 1482 "badly" provided for repudiantes when it left them *sine onere* until "de novo descriptus."

Strozzi's assertion that several other lawyers agreed with him perhaps allows us to conclude that there was some real legal weight here and that the Uguccioni sons won. The law of 1482, by rendering repudiantes temporarily ineligible for office, was as intent on the city seeing its duties paid off as the larger inheritance statute, by rendering tacit aditio after fifteen days, was on seeing creditors have their money back. In both cases, however, a genuine repudiation with clear signs of a desire to abstain from the estate (or to be assessed separately) allowed one to carry on as householder and as citizen.

Case Nine: Divergent Actions by Brothers

Marco degli Asini (1484–1575) matriculated in the Florentine guild of lawyers and notaries in 1507. Thereafter, he had a long and active career in Florence, which came to include at least one interesting case involving repudiation.[84] It touched on a matter that, while a feature of repudiation practices throughout the period with which we have been dealing, became more common and pressing toward the end of the Florentine republic and the beginning of the Medici principate – the repudiation of an estate by one brother in favor of another.

Niccolò di Thoma Antinori crafted a will in which he gave one son, Giovanbattista, 3,000 florins in cash to be converted to *immobilia*: farms in the contado of Florence and Pistoia at Pontano with all their animals and tools. All these assets were subject to a fideicommissum substituting his brothers

---

[82] Strozzi, fol. 196v.
[83] Strozzi, fol. 197r-v: "Dico quod illud debet habere, licet non fuerit descriptus pro tempore preterito in omnibus distributionibus, primo nam non est presumendum quod lex voluerit obligari aliquis ad impossibile, unde ponit quod post mortem patris urguentur alique distributiones vel gravedines que non sunt amplius in usu vel per legem sunt sublate, ut quotidie fit et ordinata fuit nova distributio."
[84] On him, see Martines, *Lawyers*, 489. The sealed consilium is in BNF, Magliabechiano xxix, 193, fols. 257r-66v.

or other "consanguineos et consortes." Named as heredes, however, were the other two sons, Alessandro and Camillo. Giovanbattista died without issue, leaving his brothers and his widow, Fiammetta, to whom he had given 6,000 florins by a public instrument. Alessandro repudiated Giovanbattista's estate, whereas Camillo accepted it with benefit of inventory (indicating that Camillo was yet underage and able to take advantage of the inventory).[85]

Nothing in this case was as simple as that narrative might make it seem. In view of the fideicommissum in Niccolò's will, Alessandro and Camillo took the bona immobilia of their brother – Camillo taking the farms at Pontano, Alessandro the rest. Both brothers further entered an agreement with Fiammetta by which an annuity took the place of the one-time gift of 6,000 florins. Alessandro later died, leaving several sons: Niccolò, Lorenzo, Sebastiano, and Vincenzo (though this last soon died). Of these, Niccolò accepted his share of his father's estate. The other two abstained, but not without gaining possession, thanks to a judicial decree, of the immobilia from their grandfather that had been purchased for Giovanbattista. Niccolò had repudiated his uncle, Giovanbattista, at the same time his father had.[86]

The legal question was whether Alessandro, despite his repudiation of Giovanbattista, was in fact his heir by virtue of possessing his property fifteen days after his death, and as a result were his sons in turn exposed to Giovanbattista's debts? The position *pro* was that Alessandro was heir to half Giovanbattista's hereditas, because he had taken a legitima. His repudiation did not matter by the terms of Florence's statute. And if he were thus heir for half, then his "abstaining" sons, Lorenzo and Sebastiano, were liable each for a third share of that in turn.

The *pro* was only briefly posed, as was so often the case, to allow the advocate to expound the *contra* at length. Asini set out to limit the liability of these Antinori. First, he noted that the farms at Pontano were not at issue, because Camillo had taken them. Then, if Alessandro, who had repudiated Giovanbattista's property, held any of it, it was by fideicommissum and not as his heir because Camillo had accepted the same estate. As Asini put it, "Therefore said statute cannot take effect where one repudiated and the estate was accepted by a coheir or the next in line."[87]

Asini flexed his interpretive muscles and presented a large stack of citations to ius commune. He tried to maintain that

if we should say said statute is to be understood simply such that it would comprehend also him who is in possession by some singular title sought after his repudiation and after the coheir's or the next in line's aditio, then he would acquire a right for a third

[85] RE 29, fol. 104 (12 January 1532).
[86] Ibid.
[87] Magliabechiano 193, fol. 260v: "Igitur statutum predictum in eo qui repudiavit et hereditas in solidum per coheredem vel sequentem in gradu adita fuit locum habere non potuit."

person by means of his aditio, which in no way can be taken to have been the intent of the legislators.[88]

It was impossible that the repudians could be heir when the coheir had accepted, "because it is impossible for two to be heirs in entirety at one time" ("quia impossibile est duos in solidum eodem tempore heredes esse").[89] Although, as Asini reported, Ormannozzo Deti had written a consilium arguing the opposite. Asini's reference is too brief to determine if he was pointing to Deti's case we examined earlier. What is clear is that Asini declared what had been determined (*iudicatum*) in Deti's case had not been in line with his opinion, but with the one Asini was here advancing, as well as with an opinion of Lodovico Acciaiuoli (1471–1527), subscribed to by the late Antonio Malegonelli (1451–1506), and concordant with consilia by Domenico Bonsi (1430–1502), Antonio Cocchi (1451–1491), Baldassare Carducci (1458–1530), Bartolomeo Sozzini, and Francesco Pepi (1451–1513).[90] Against that imposing professional phalanx, he could only affirm that

Shaped by the laws and reasons set out above and by the authority of so many illustrious jurists, twice I held that opinion in cases, and although one is not to judge by precedent, according to the *lex Nemo* of the *Code, De sententiis*, yet what appears from the aforesaid is sufficient [to show] how said statute has been interpreted by jurists, from whose interpretation some other unlearned person should not depart.[91]

What may seem more convincing to us, however, is the logic of an immediately subsequent point. Given the statute's desire to prevent fraud of creditors by means of repudiation, it could be said that, as there was an heres in solidum who had accepted the estate, there was someone liable to the creditors and thus no fear of their being defrauded.[92]

The properties Niccolò Antinori had bought for Giovanbattista had been intended to pass to others by the terms of the fideicommissum; they did not carry beyond his life.[93] So if Alessandro held any of the property bought for

---

[88] Ibid., fol. 262r: "Alias si diceremus statutum predictum simpliciter intelligendum esse ita ut illum etiam, qui aliquo singulari titulo post repudiationem suam quesito et coheredis vel sequentis in gradu aditionem possiderit, comprehenderet ius quesitum tertio sua aditione mediante acquieret, quod nullo modo de intentione statuentium fuisse credendum est."

[89] Ibid., fol. 263r.

[90] On these men, Martines, *Lawyers*, 486, 488, 494, 495.

[91] Magliabechiano 193, fol. 264r: "Ego fictus iuribus et rationibus suprascriptis et authoritate tot clarissimorum doctorum bis ita consulendo tenui, et licet exemplis non sit iudicandum, l. nemo C. de senten. attamen satis est quod apparet ex predictis quomodo dictum statutum a iuris sapientibus interpretatum fuerit, a qua interpretatione alio non docto recidi non debet."

[92] Ibid., fol. 264v: "Item dato herede qui in solidum adivit, creditores non fraudantur, et data paritate heredum a principio, non consideratur quod in futurum alter ex eis non solvendo efficiatur."

[93] Ibid., fol. 265r-v.

Giovanbattista, in view of the fideicommissum and the contracts of purchase, and especially the repudiation, he could not be considered his heir. Camillo's aditio likewise precluded such a conclusion. And so Lorenzo and Sebastiano, similarly by virtue of the fideicommissum which persisted in the male line and by the contracts of purchase, could enter the same immobilia bought for Giovanbattista, and they would not do so as their father's heirs, in view of their abstention from Alessandro's estate.

This opinion could seem to have made a mockery of the Florentine statute holding heirs liable to creditors. Here a testator had succeeded (in contrast to Deti's opinion, though he was cited as the sole exception on the other side of the issue, and to have lost the judgment in any case), in finding a way to place a substantial portion of property away from creditors' claims by a clever combination of legal devices, the legatum and a fideicommissum attached to it. The protection of patrimony had overtaken protection of creditors. The forceful assertions of the statute reading tacit aditio into (in)actions was vitiated by subtle plays on words and a cascade of citations. The willingness of so many lawyers practicing in Florence, on Asini's testimony, to uphold such hereditary devices signaled an important legal shift. The tough line Sozzini had taken against the obvious collusion between Vincenzo di Domenico and his cousin, Michelangelo, and that Deti had taken against the unusual will leaving five sons legata had wavered in the face of less unusual testamentary terms and repudiations when, other than a property or two, abstention from the estate was accepted as real. Testators' intentions, broadly construed as protecting the integrity of family and patrimony, were invoked against creditors' interests. The perpetuation of family lines overrode protection of markets.[94]

Conclusions

Asini's consilium, in contrast to the clean and brief opinion of Angelo degli Ubaldi with which we began, is illuminating of general trends in jurisprudence to more prolix, complicated, citation-riddled, and simply longer case opinions. But, for our purposes, it also reveals a change in Florentine lawyers' approaches to use of repudiation. It seems more than a little disingenuous to say that Giovanbattista Antinori's possession of property under fideicommissum did not meet the statute's intent. His was not a life usufruct extinguished at his death, as was the annuity his wife accepted from his brothers. The preservation of important immobilia in the hands of male kin through future generations was an increasingly prominent goal of family strategy. It

---

[94] See J. P. Cooper, "Patterns of Inheritance and Settlement by Great Landowners from the Fifteenth to the Eighteenth Centuries," in *Family and Inheritance: Rural Society in Western Europe, 1200–1800*, ed. Jack Goody, Joan Thirsk, and E. P. Thompson (Cambridge: Cambridge University Press, 1976), 192–317, at 265.

is doubtful that Alessandro did not consider himself an heres, even though Asini insisted that in strict law he was not.

It is also interesting that the focus of the final consilium we have considered was the brother, rather than the father. Given the fideicommissum and the testament, it would be much harder for Alessandro to try to feign that he was not his father's heir. Yet it is also the case, as we saw in analysis of the registry data, that by the early sixteenth century repudiation of collateral estates – brothers', uncles', cousins' – became statistically more prominent. But it also may be that, as clauses of fideicommissa proliferated to manage disposition of property by testators, heirs like these Antinori were able to embrace them so as to maneuver property to particular hands.

What seems consistent in all these cases are two features. One is the constant juxtaposition of ius commune and statute law regarding repudiation. The other is the adaptability of Florentines in their inheritance practices to find ways – within the law or close enough – to further their interests. They taxed the ingenuity of lawyers and outfoxed legislators.

In general, as confirmed in Asini's opinion, fideicommissa, which typically linked a pattern of substitution among close lines of descent with the prohibition of alienation of the property outside the family, were being accepted as a licit way to hold property that had been repudiated.[95] By the twist that one became heir to the testator by substitution (rather than to the heir who had died or repudiated and was thus substituted for), it was possible for jurists to allow with fideicommissum what they could not allow, or only with great difficulty, with legitima and mere legata. The substitution linked the person to the patrimony of a *casa* instead of posing him as a successor to the *persona* of the deceased. But creditors who had dealt with the deceased thus lost someone to take his place and satisfy their claims.

---

[95] For an interesting survey of language in fideicommissa, see Maria Carla Zorzoli, "Della famiglia e del suo patrimonio: riflessioni sull'uso del fedecommesso in Lombardia tra cinque e seicento," in *Marriage, Property, and Succession*, ed. Lloyd Bonfield (Berlin: Duncker & Humblot, 1992), 155–213.

Conclusion

Repudiation of inheritance persists in modern law. The Italian national law code contains a right of *rinuncia all'eredità*. Provided one has not undertaken acts implying a tacit or presumed acceptance of the inheritance, one can move to declare a *rinuncia* within the brief allowed terms, if in possession. If not in possession, one can simply refrain from the property for ten years. Formal renunciation can take the form of a notarial action or a declaration before the local court handling probate. *Immobili* renounced must be reported in writing to the official with competence over the registry of real estate. No *rinuncia* is valid if conditional or covering only a part of the *eredità*, nor is it valid if it turns out that the renouncing heir is in fact hiding some portion of the estate in his or her possession. Renunciation can be revoked, provided no one else has entered on the estate and accepted it. Creditors' rights are protected in that they can petition a court to accept the estate in the name of the repudiating party in order to satisfy their claims on the goods in the estate.[1]

In all these provisions, we can spot legacies of the medieval law of repudiations – the notarial act, its completeness and unconditionality, the right of revocation, the concern with subterfuge and evasion, but perhaps most notably the requirement to register repudiation of *immobili*. But the present-day registration of real estate titles, while it has undoubted fiscal purposes, is intended to facilitate an active property market by fixing titles. It is not just about protecting existing claims, and *rinuncia* is not treated as primarily a matter of avoiding an estate's onerous obligations. It is simply a right heirs may exercise, for whatever reason.

The purposes of directing property to other heirs by way of repudiation have also changed. A South African insurance, financial services, and investment firm, Sanlam Limited, has carried on its website a hypothetical

---

[1] Giuseppe Alessi, *I tuoi diritti di ereditare* (Milan: Hoepli, 1992), 46–47.

describing the financial incentives for a wife to repudiate an estate, even in favor of her son. Here a decision to favor a husband's testamentary dispositions and advantage the son could also lead to a gift tax hitting the wife for the value of what she gave up. The aim of Sanlam's hypothetical is to advise the client, thinking of drawing up a will in a world where one's heir has a choice, that the heir cannot be asked to give up too much and that the way to adjust the holding is by means of an appropriate life insurance policy.[2]

Florentines' use of repudiation was driven by calculations of material utility and of the values, real and symbolic, of kinship. In the centuries we have examined, repudiation proved to be a flexible and useful legal device. Florentines found it a means not only to avoid financial or other burdens imposed on them as heirs during difficult times, but also to shift property among themselves so as to consolidate holdings, gather dowries, or obtain other utilities. They exploited legal loopholes to avoid taxes as well as the repayment of debts. They adjusted the rules of intestate succession or even testamentary substitutions. And they did so with the ready assistance of notaries and with or against the interpretations of doctors of law. They were able to deceive and defraud their creditors (some of whom might well be kin) and their government.

The tightening of inheritance into knots of fideicommissary clauses had, by the fourth decade of the sixteenth century, reduced the need for repudiation in comparison to earlier decades. The property of the social elite was bound up in substitutions that more greatly complicated matters than mere repudiation could. Peasants were increasingly reduced to tenant status, working and living by terms of contracts of *mezzadria* that also vitiated any meaningful use of repudiation.[3] Repudiations in the sixteenth century were more often aimed at collateral inheritances enmeshed in those knots of substitutions and prohibitions of alienation. Yet repudiation continued as a legal instrument, and its registration persisted in Florence until 1781.

Repudiation's utility changed as inheritance practices changed, but it also helped change them. Learned law favored division of property among all legitimate children, even as social dynamics demanded means to preserve estates over generations. Girls were regularly excluded or limited by statutes or recognized customs to an "appropriate" dowry, but division among sons remained a problem. Predilections to primogeniture, as Bartolomé Clavero

---

[2] Http://www.sanlam.co.za/eng/aboutus/sanlambusinesses/sanlamtrust/news/heir+apparently, (accessed 4 September 2003).

[3] Here note Paolo Malanima, *Il lusso dei contadini: Consumi e industrie nelle campagne toscane del Sei e Settecento* (Bologna: Il Mulino, 1990); Vito Caiati, "The Peasant Household under Tuscan Mezzadria: A Socio-economic Analysis of Some Sienese Mezzadri Households, 1591–1640," *Journal of Family History* 9 (1984): 111–26; Frank McArdle, *Altopascio: A Study in Tuscan Rural Society, 1587–1784* (Cambridge: Cambridge University Press, 1978); David Herlihy and Christiane Klapisch-Zuber, *Les toscans et leurs familles* (Paris: Fondation Nationale des Sciences Politiques, 1978), 109–36, 241–300.

has pointed out, did not gain real legal sanction until the seventeenth century. Availability of fideicommissum in law, coupled with substitutions of heirs, helped establish a form of primogeniture.[4] Repudiation was another legal instrument adaptable to that purpose.

Fideicommissary substitutions, like repudiation, were able to hold persons and property immune from creditors. Both institutions inevitably had economic effects. Indeed, by the eighteenth century reform-minded thinkers were raising serious protest against the deleterious effects of *fedecommessi*. Ludovico Antonio Muratori (1672–1750) dedicated an entire chapter of his *Dei difetti della giurisprudenza* (1742) to the subject, denouncing the harm to creditors and protesting the profits lawyers realized from lawsuits. Alfonso Longo (1738–1804) similarly denounced *fedecommessi* for strangling commerce while rewarding lazy heirs. He implicated repudiation in the process as a device hard-pressed first born heirs could use to avoid creditors.[5]

The social world, especially its familial component, that Florentines inhabited was undoubtedly different from ours. We cannot accept as adequate description of their world the dichotomy between the individual and the kinship group that informed the guiding sociological and economic discourse of modernity. The social world of Florence from the aftermath of the first outburst of plague in the fourteenth century to the definitive end of the Florentine republic, yields few individualistic qualities and comes off as an "uncompromisingly nonmodern world."[6]

Repudiation of inheritance cannot be read as an assertion of individual prerogatives over against those of lineage, any more than testaments can (despite Maine). Senses of lineage changed; but the role of the individual was still to fit into a transmission of property, claims, rights, and obligations that involved him or her inexorably with others. This is not to say that there were not some instances of repudiation in which the repudians was extracting himself from a web of kinship and obligation in a manner recognizable as individualistic. But it is to recognize that Renaissance Florence was not a society that placed an unalloyed premium on individuality.

Certainly in the law, persons remained distinct bearers of rights, titles, and obligations, yet they were also recognizable in society through public social and legal conventions. They were enmeshed in dense networks with

---

[4] Bartolomé Clavero, "Dictum beati: A proposito della cultura del lignaggio," *Quaderni storici* 86 (August 1994): 335–63, esp. 342–45. The key legal change was to replace the bias to division into legitimate shares (*favor legitimarum*) with a bias to the needs of family (*favor familiarum*).
[5] Ludovico Antonio Muratori, *Dei difetti della giurisprudenza*, ed. Arrigo Solmi, Classici del diritto 1 (Rome: Formiggini, 1933), chap. 17, "De i fideicommissi, maggioraschi, primogeniture, e sustituzioni"; Alfonso Longo, "Osservazioni su i fedecommessi," in *Il Caffè, 1764–1766*, ed. Gianni Francioni and Sergio Romagnoli (Turin: Bollati Boringhieri, 1993), 115–32, at 121.
[6] Anthony Molho, *Marriage Alliance in Late Medieval Florence* (Cambridge: Harvard University Press, 1994), 347.

others like them. A vital portion of these networks involved kinship, with expectations regarding rights, titles, and obligations. These rights, titles, and obligations were transacted in repudiations of inheritance. Analogous rights, titles, and obligations were vested in women's dowries, which were kept conceptually and legally distinct from the property of husbands, who otherwise could easily treat dowry assets as their own in day-to-day management.[7] Another way to see the matter is that individual identity and family identity overlapped enormously, though there were limits.[8] There were points at which the relationship between individual identity and family identity were not isomorphic.[9] Repudiation, along with emancipation and some other legal devices, provided a means to manage and adjust such discrepancies to the benefit of at least some of those involved.

Did repudiation contribute to economic difficulties in Florence in the fifteenth and sixteenth centuries? Florence stood in relative disadvantage in those years. Places such as Verona and Venice grew and prospered more so than Florence as the fifteenth century progressed.[10] Florence seems not to have shared as greatly in the general European economic recovery after 1460.[11] Certainly, legislative measures designed to stop deceptive legal practices in Florence, including use of repudiation, can provoke an affirmative response to the question. But so much else affected the Florentine economy in those years – not least the foreign and fiscal policies pursued by the Medici – that it is hard to lay too much blame on one legal institution. Repudiation's persistence also did not prevent the return of prosperity to Florence that historians find after 1540.[12] In times of prosperity, repudiation would be

[7] Note Isabelle Chabot, "'Biens de famille': Contrôle des ressources patrimoniales, *gender*, et cycle domestique (Italie, XIIIième-XVième siècles)," in *The Household in Late Medieval Cities: Italy and Northwestern Europe Compared*, ed. Myriam Carlier and Tim Soens (Leuven: Garant, 2001), 89–104, at 92.
[8] Ann Crabb, *The Strozzi of Florence: Widowhood and Family Solidarity in the Renaissance* (Ann Arbor: University of Michigan Press, 2000), 237.
[9] Any more than are physical bodies and legal persons today. See Alan Hyde, *Bodies of Law* (Princeton: Princeton University Press, 1997), esp. 28–31, 154, 182, 260–61; and broadly on bounded senses of property, Jennifer Nedelsky, "Law, Boundaries, and the Bounded Self," in *Law and the Order of Culture*, ed. Robert Post (Berkeley: University of California Press, 1991), 162–89.
[10] Here David Herlihy, "The Population of Verona in the First Century of Venetian Rule," in *Renaissance Venice*, ed. J. R. Hale (London: Faber and Faber, 1973), 91–120.
[11] Bartolomé Yun, "Economic Cycles and Structural Changes," in *Handbook of European History, 1400–1600*, 2 vols., ed. Thomas A. Brady, Jr., Heiko A. Oberman, and James D. Tracy, vol. 1: *Late Middle Ages, Renaissance, and Reformation* (Leiden: Brill, 1994), 113–45.
[12] See Eric Cochrane, *Florence in the Forgotten Centuries* (Chicago: University of Chicago Press, 1973), 56–66; R. Burr Litchfield, *Emergence of a Bureaucracy: The Florentine Patricians, 1530–1790* (Princeton: Princeton University Press, 1986), 6–7, 203–5. More generally, Domenico Sella, *Italy in the Seventeenth Century* (London and New York: Longman, 1997), 19–49; and Paolo Malanima, *L'economia italiana: Dalla crescita medievale alla crescita contemporanea* (Bologna: Il Mulino, 2002).

less attractive or necessary for heirs, but in times of adversity its enhanced utility may have exacerbated and prolonged problems. But one Florentine's problem was another's solution.

It is thus too simplistic to see repudiation as an instrument of some Renaissance era Tuscan version of "amoral familism," posing family and kinship (undoubtedly central to personal identity) as an inflexible primary resource and consequently holding a community in a situation of deprivation and negative reciprocity.[13] Having kin close at hand and valuing kin relationships does not mean that their moral weight was constant and taken for granted. It does not mean that Tuscans did not seek out and honor other commitments, ascribe moral weight to them, and try to act accordingly. We can be easily deceived by repudiation, which situates the historian firmly in a family context and a kinship-centered event (inheritance), forgetting that the debts charged against estates were often the result of interactions with friends, neighbors, partners, fellow guild members, and so on. Use of repudiation implied that the validity, if not urgency, of these debts was recognized, even if their repayment was postponed or passed to others. It is true, as we have seen, that some of these folk were capable of cheating and deceiving to a felonious degree, but they still had to respect approved forms of dealing by practicing calculated deceptions. We can perhaps go further to say that use of repudiation, even in its most deceptive forms, was not an expression of disdain for the law but, far from it, sprang from an appreciation and knowledge of the law. Repudiation was a property and family relationship resource that allowed Florentines to cope with contingencies and strive after valued interests (household prosperity and lineage continuity – *substantia* in synchronic and diachronic forms), while maintaining the public image of law-abiding active citizen and household member.

---

[13] Edward C. Banfield, *The Moral Basis of a Backward Society* (Glencoe: Free Press, 1958). For one critique, among many, see J. Davis, "Morals and Backwardness," *Comparative Studies in Society and History* 12 (1970): 340–53; and for a recent analysis of southern Italians animated by a different methodology, see Italo Pardo, *Managing Existence in Naples: Morality, Action and Structure* (Cambridge: Cambridge University Press, 1996).

Appendix 1

ASF, Ripudie d'eredità 13, fol. 14v
31 July 1436
Registration of Repudiation by Loisio, Teghiaio, Francesco, and Uguccione Pazzi

In dei nomine, amen. Anno incarnationis domini nostri Yhesu Christi millesimo quadringentesimo trigesimo sexto, indictione quartadecima, die trigesimo primo mensis Julii in consilio populi civitatis Florentie in palatio populi florentini in quo domini priores artium et vexillifer iustitie moram trahunt in sufficienti numero more solito congregato, et astantibus sex et ultra de officio dictorum dominorum priorum et vexillifere in dicto consilio personaliter constitutus Antonius Petri publicus approbator et preco communis Florentie publice palam alta et intelligibili voce, vice et nomine Loisii, Theghiaii, et Francisci et Uguccionis, fratrum filiorum olim Ghinozii Loisii de Pazis populi Sancti Petri Maioris de Florentia notificavit qualiter predicti quatuor omnes repudiaverunt hereditatem dicti olim Ghinozii patris eorum cuilibet eorum pro quarta parte ab intestato delatam et ab ea se penitus abstinuerunt per instrumentum inde confectum per ser Loisium ser Michaelis Guidonis notarium florentinum sub die sextodecimo presentis mensis Julii.

Qui Antonius preco predictus incontinenti de pecunia predictorum misit in capsa existentia in sala magna dicti palatii, in qua consiliarii dicti consilii conadunantur secundum ordinamenta fl. quatuor auri.

Acta fuerunt predicta Florentie in palatio suprascripto, presentibus Jacobo ser Francisci, Francisco Silvestri et Bartholomeo Laurentii approbatoribus communis Florentie testibus ad hec vocatis et habitis.

Appendix 2

Notarile antecosimiano 15218
14 May 1377
Repudiation by Giovanni di Stefano di Vanni

In dei nomine amen. Anno domini ab eiusdem salutifera incarnatione millesimo trecentesimo settuagesimo settimo, indictione quintadecima, die quattuordecimo et mensis Madii. Actum Florentie in populo Sancti Petri Celorum de Florentia, presentibus testibus ad hec vocatis et rogatis ser Dominicho ser Salvi Gai notario florentino, Jacopo Binogii, et Lodovicho Pugii populi Sancti Salvatoris de Florentia.

Johannes condam Stefani Vannis populi Sancti Michaelis Vicedominorum de Florentia, sciens dictum Stefanum eius patrem mortuum esse ab intestato et hereditatem dicti Stefani ad ipsum Johannem pro dimidia pertinere, et credens dictam hereditatem sibi fore potius dampnosam quam lucrosam, ab ipsa hereditate se abstinuit et hereditatem dicti Stefani pro quacunque parte sibi delatam repudiavit, dicens se nolle habere commodum vel incommodum dicte hereditatis, rogans me Niccholaum notarium infrascriptum de predictis conficere instrumentum.

Appendix 3

Notarile antecosimiano 16318, fol. 34r-v
8 April 1533
Repudiation by Filippo di Bruno

Item postea dictis anno, indictione et die octava mensis Aprilis. Actum Florentie et in populo Sancte Marie in Campo, presentibus testibus, videlicet Pierantonio Francisci Blasii de Diaceto et Dominico Luce de Casi, laboratoribus terrarum et ambobus de potestaria Diaceti vallis Senis comitatus Florentie.

Pateat omnibus etc. qualiter Filippus olim Bruni Michaelis Bruni, laborator terrarum populi Sancti Martini a Pagliariccio de Mugello lige Aretri comitatus Florentie, constitutus personaliter coram me notario etc., sciens qualiter dictus Brunus eius condam pater mortuus est et decessit iam sunt anni octo proxime elapsi vel circa ab intestato, relictis post se et eius mortem dicto Filippo et Michaele eius filiis masculis legitimis et naturalibus et nullis aliis relictis habentibus eos excludere ab eius hereditate vel cum eis concurrere, et sciens qualiter dictus Michael eius frater hereditatem dicti olim Bruni repudiavit et ab ea se abstinuit, et sciens qualiter hereditas dicti olim Bruni sibi delata ab intestato et potius eam esse inutilem et dannosam idcirco in predictis et omni meliori modo etc. dictam hereditatem sibi ut supra delatam et pro omni rata et portione que sibi quomodolibet eo defertur repudiavit et ab ea se abstinuit, nolens commoda et incommoda dicte hereditatis et ita expresse dixit et declaravit, rogans etc.

Appendix 4

Notarile antecosimiano 668, fol. 114r-v
23 November 1400
Aditio by Bernardo and Donato di Ugolino Bonsi

Item eisdem anno, indictione, die vigesimo tertio mensis Novembris. Attum Florentie in populo Sancti Pancratii, presentibus testibus ad hec vocatis et rogatis Bellozo Laurentii Bartoli, spetiario dicti populi, et Remisio Baldesis populi Sancte Trinitatis de Florentia et aliis.

    Bernardus et Donatus, fratres et filii olim Ugolini Bonsi, spetiarii populi Sancti Fridiani de Florentia, scientes et cognoscentes hereditatem Pieri condam eorum fratris et filii olim dicti Ugolini spetiarii eis, videlicet uterque ipsorum pro una dimidia ex testamento per ipsum Pierum condito publice scripto manu ser Antonii olim Pieri Chelli de Florentia notarii publici, vigore substitutionis de eis facte in testamento predicto, delatam esse et eis pro dictis partibus fore et esse potius lucrosam quam dampnosam, ideo ipsam hereditatem omni via iure modo quibus magis et melius potuerunt, dubitative tamen et cum benefitio inventarii et spe et animo conficiendi inventarium, secundum formam iuris et ut consequantur et habeant benefitium legis et inventarii, quod datur adeuntibus hereditatem cum benefitio inventarii, adiverunt, adprehendiderunt et in ea se inmiscuerunt, rogantes me Agnolum notarium infrascriptum ut de predictis publicum conficere instrumentum.

Appendix 5

Notarile antecosimiano 9038, fols. 26v-27r
7 July 1412
Clarification of Intention in Repudiation by Corso and Sandro di Zanobi Ricci

Item postea dictis anno et indictione et die. Actum Florentie in populo Sancti Petri Maioris de Florentia, presentibus testibus ad hec vocatis, habitis, et rogatis [27r] domino Roggerio comite de Antiglana de Perusio et legum doctore et dicti populi Sancti Petri, et domino Nicholao filio dicti domini Roggerii, et ser Johanne Andree dal Campo, notario et cive pisano et aliis.

Certum esse dicitur quod de anno domini ab eius incarnatione millesimo trecentesimo nonagesimo secundo, indictione prima, secundum consuetudinem florentinam et die decimanona Februarii, Corsus olim Zenobii de Riccis de Florentia, tunc populi Sancte Margherite de Florentia, sciens hereditatem dicti Zenobii patris sui sibi ab intestato pro tertia parte delatam esse ipsam hereditatem pro dicta tertia parte ab intestato adivit et apprendidit et in ea se inmiscuit, prout hec et alia in publico instrumento dicte aditionis inde rogato et scripto manu ser Pieri Roggerii notarii florentini plenius et latius continetur. Et certum esse dicitur etiam quod Sander filius olim dicti Zenobii de Riccis et frater dicti Cursi, etiam sciens hereditatem dicti olim Zenobii sibi Sandro ab intestato pro tertia parte delatam, ipsam hereditatem dicti Zenobii eius patris pro dicta tertia parte ab intestato adivit et in ea se inmiscuit, de quibus et aliis latius constare dicitur publicum instrumentum per ser Bernabam Antonii Durelli olim notarii florentini. Et cum hoc sit quod tempore quo dicti Cursus et Sander dictam hereditatem sic adiverunt adhuc vivebat dominus Johannes, eorum frater carnalis et filius olim dicti Zenobii, et iam mortuus erat Guido, eorum frater et filius olim dicti Zenobii. Et cum hoc sit quod tempore dicte aditionis dicti Corsus et Sander in eorum aditione non declaraverunt quo animo et qua mente dictam hereditatem adirent, an ex ipsorum propriis personis iure acceptandi, an mediante persona dicti Guidonis eorum fratris ex iure transmissionis. Et volentes dicti Corsus et Sander declarare quo animo et qua mente et intentione et quo iure adiverunt dictam hereditatem ad omnem dubitationem tollendam, constituti in presentia mei, notarii Francisci infrascripti et testium predictorum, ad eternam rei memoriam et vel quibuscunque pateat animus et intentio ipsorum que fuit et est confessi fuerunt, dixerunt, asseruerunt, et declaraverunt se ipsos Corsum et Sandrum adisse hereditatem dicti eorum patris, videlicet quilibet ipsorum pro tertia parte ab intestato, primordialiter et immediate ex eorum personis et iure accrescendi et ex eorum personis immediate et iure accrescendi quelibet ipsorum pro dicta tertia parte ab intestato in dicta hereditate se inmiscuisse et immediate ex eorum personis et iure accrescendi fuisse et esse heredes, videlicet quilibet eorum pro tertia parte ab intestato dicti olim Zenobii, dicentes et protestantes quod per predicta vel alia per eos vel aliquem eorum facta vel gesta ipsi Corsus et Sander non intendunt neque intendiderunt, neque voluerunt vel volunt modo aliquo adisse vel adire hereditatem dicti olim Guidonis eorum fratris vel heredes esse dicti olim Guidonis. Rogantes me Franciscum notarium infrascriptum ut de predictis etc.

Appendix 6

Notarile antecosimiano 14713, fol. 24r
6 August 1464
Protestatio by Giovanni di Filippo Baronci

Item postea eisdem anno, inditione et die sexto mensis Augusti. Actum Florentie in populo Sancti Stefani Abbatie, presentibus ser Jacobo ser Mactei ser Dominici et ser Paulo Amerigi Bartoli Grassi, civibus et notariis florentinis, et Dominico Leonardi vocato Paleo populi Sancti Ambroxii de Florentia et aliis etc.

Johannes olim Filippi Bartolomei Baronci, filatotarius populi Sancti Laurentii de Florentia, constitutus in presentia et coram testibus suprascriptis et me notario infrascripto, dixit et exposuit et asseruit qualiter domina Lisa, uxor olim dicti Bartholomei, eius avia paterna, habuit et recepit in solutum et pagamentum de anno domini 1425 et die iii mensis Decembris ab egregio legum doctore domino Francisco de Salvestrinis de Nirsia, collaterali iudice quartierum Sancte Marie Novelle et Sancti Johannis curie potestatis civitatis Florentie, unum podere et bona pro extimatione florenorum auri ducentorum septuaginta pro creditis et expensis occaxione fl. auri x et libras xxviii et soldi xiii, prout constare dicitur et constare vidi per sententiam in publicam formam redactam. Quod podere et bona posita sunt etc. in populo Sancte Marie de Sancto Matero, olim comitatus Pistorii et tunc et nunc Florentie, et sic describitur et confinatur videlicet, unum podere cum domo pro domino et laboratore et cum terris laboratis, arboratis, et viniatis et cum omnibus petiis terre et bonis solitis laborari et seu teneri cum dicto podere, posito in dicto populo et loco, cui et quibus omnibus a primo via, a ii flumen vocatum la Pulicata, a iii domine Cilie... a iiii Angeli... calzolarii de Pistorio, a v Cambini alterius Cambini de Sancto Matho predicto. Et quod postea dicta domina Lisa, durante eius vita et semper dum vixit, dictum podere et bona ut supra idem adiudicata pro se et aliis tenentur pro ea habuit, tenuit, et possedit pro suis et tanquam sua bona propria, vigore dicte sententie iusta ratione, titulo, et causa, pacifice et quiete et bene in regula et in solidum, et in dictis bonis quamplurimas multas et varias expensas utiles et necessarias fecit. Et quod postea dicta domina Lisa, avia paterna dicti Johannis, et iam sunt plures et pluri anni mortuam est et decessit, relicto, remanente, et supervivente dicto Johanne, eius nepote ex filio predicto, videlicet nato ex dicto Filippo, filio legitimo et naturali dicte domine Lise, nato dicto Johanne ex dicto Filippo et domina Tita, eius uxore legitima et filia olim Michaellis Francisci tintoris, et nullis aliis relictis filiis masculis. Et quod postea dicta bona data et adiudicata fuerunt ipso domine Tite, matri dicti Johannis, pro dotibus suis confessatis per dictum Filippum et dominam Lisam et alios, et quod postea et post predicta omnia dictus Filippus et domina Tita et quilibet eorum mortui sunt et decesserunt, relicto dicto Johanne, eorum filio masculo legitimo et naturali, et nullis aliis relictis vel supervivientibus habentibus ipsum Johannem excludere ab hereditate dicte domine Lise, eius avie paterne, et domine Tite, eius matris. Qui Johannes dictas hereditates immo adhivit, et propterea dictus Johannes protestatus fuit et protestatur quod dicta bona tenuit et possedit et ea semper tenere et possidere vult et intendit ut et tanquam bona hereditaria dicte domine Lise, eius avie paterne, et ut bona postea data et adiudicata dicte domine Tite, eius matri, et propterea non discendo ab alia haditione alias quomodolibet, sed eis inherendo et insistendo ex nunc et ad cautelam ipsas hereditates dominarum Lise et Tite in solidum adhivit, et pro omni parte eidem delatas, protestando semper dicta bona tenuisse et tenere ut bona propria et non titulo aut aliquo iure paterno, cum ab hereditate paterna se abstinuerit et abstinere semper intendit et vult, et pro dicta repudiatione observante omnia requisita secundum formam statutorum communis Florentie, et cum dicta protestatione quod nullo iure intelligit aliquo modo adire vel se inmiscere aut aliquem actum prestare ut importetur quoquo modo aditio hereditatis paterne etc. sed solummodo ut heres avie paterne et matris, et sic semper protestatus fuit et protestatur et non titulo aut iure hereditario aliquo dicti sui patris etc. rogans etc.

Sources

Manuscript

Archivio di Stato, Florence (ASF)

Carte strozziane
Catasto
Consiglio del Cento
Consiglio dei Dugento
Mercanzia
Manoscritti
Notarile antecosimiano (NA)
Podestà
Provvisioni duplicati
Provvisioni registri
Ripudie d'eredità (RE)
Statuti del comune di Firenze

Biblioteca Nazionale Centrale, Florence (BNF)

Fondo principale, II, iv, 434 (Salvetti)
Fondo principale, II, iv, 435 (Bencivenni)
Landau Finaly 98
Magliabechiano xxix, 174
Magliabechiano xxix, 193

Web-based Source

Florentine Renaissance Resources: Online Catasto of 1427, ed. David Herlihy, Christiane Klapisch-Zuber, R. Burr Litchfield, and Anthony Molho (www.stg.brown.edu/projects/catasto).

Printed Sources

Sources for Ius Commune

Bartolo da Sassoferrato. *Opera omnia.* 10 vols. Venice, 1615.
Bottrigari, Jacopo. *Lectura super codice.* 1516; reprint ed., Bologna: Forni, 1973.
Cino da Pistoia. *In codicem et aliquot titulos primi pandectarum commentaria.* 2 vols. Frankfurt, 1575; facsimile ed., Turin: Bottega d'Erasmo, 1964.
Corpus iuris civilis. Edited by Th. Mommsen, P. Krueger, and R. Schoell. 3 vols. Berlin: Weidmann, 1928–29.
d'Ancarano, Pietro. *Consilia.* Pavia, 1496.
d'Arena, Jacopo. *Super iure civili.* 1541.
Formularium florentinum artis notariae (1220–1242). Edited by Gino Masi. Milan: Giuffrè, 1943.
Glossa ordinaria. 5 vols. Lyons 1568.
Paolo di Castro. *Consilia.* 3 vols. Venice, 1571.
———. *In primam infortiati partem.* Venice, 1593.
———. *In secundam codicis.* Lyon, 1548.
Passaggieri, Rolandino de'. *Apparatus super summa notariae.* Bologna, 1478.
Porcellini, Francesco. *Tractatus de confectione inventarii.* In *Tractatus universi iuris.* 29 vols. Vol. 8, part 2, fols. 156rb-65ra. Venice, 1584.
Romano, Andrea, ed. *Le sostituzioni ereditarie nell'inedita "Repetitio de substitutionibus" de Raniero Arsendi.* Catania: Giannotta, 1977.
Roselli, Antonio. *Tractatus de successionibus ab intestato.* In *Tractatus universi iuris.* Vol. 8, part 2, fols. 357vb-71va.
Salatiele. *Ars notariae.* Edited by Gianfranco Orlandelli. 2 vols. Milan: Giuffrè, 1961.
Tartagni, Alessandro. *Consilia.* 7 vols. in 4. Venice?, 1536.
———. *In primam et secundam codicis.* Venice, 1570.
———. *In primam et secundam infortiati.* Venice 1570.
Ubaldi, Angelo degli. *Consilia.* Frankfurt am Main, 1575.
———. *Super prima infortiati.* Lyon, 1522.
———. *Tractatus de inventario.* In *Tractatus universi iuris.* Vol. 8, part 2, fols. 155va-56rb.
Ubaldi, Baldo degli. *Consilia.* 6 vols. in 3. Venice, 1575; reprint ed., Turin: Bottega d'Erasmo, 1970.
———. *Opera omnia.* 9 vols. Venice, 1577.

Statutes

Statuta antiqua communis Collis Vallis Else (1307–1407). Edited by Renzo Ninci. 2 vols. Rome: Istituto Storico Italiano per il Medio Evo, 1999.
Statuta antiquissima Saone (1345). Edited by Laura Balletto. 2 vols. Genoa: Istituto Internazionale di Studi Liguri, 1971.
Statuta populi et communis Florentiae, anno salutis mccccxv. 3 vols. Freiburg [Florence], 1778–83. (Statuta)
Gli statuti del comune di Treviso (sec. xiii–xiv). Edited by Bianca Betto. 2 vols. Rome: Istituto Storico Italiano per il Medio Evo, 1986.
Statuti della repubblica fiorentina. Edited by Romolo Caggese. 2 vols. Vol. 1: *Statuto del capitano del popolo degli anni 1322–25.* Florence: Galileana, 1910. Vol. 2:

Statuto del podestà dell'anno 1325. Florence: Ariani, 1921. New edition, edited by Giuliano Pinto, Francesco Salvestrini, and Andrea Zorzi. Florence: Olschki, 1999. (Statuto)
Statuti di Verona del 1327. Edited by Silvana Anna Bianchi and Rosalba Granuzzo. 2 vols. Rome: Jouvence, 1992.
Statuti di Volterra (1210–1224). Edited by Enrico Fiumi. Florence: Deputazione di Storia Patria per la Toscana, 1951.
Statuto del comune di Montepulciano (1337). Edited by Ubaldo Morandi. Florence: Le Monnier, 1966.
Statuto del comune e del popolo di Perugia del 1342, in volgare. Edited by Mahmoud Salem Elsheikh. 3 vols. Perugia: Deputazione di Storia Patris per l'Umbria, 2000.
Statuto di Arezzo (1327). Edited by Giulia Marri Camerani. Florence: Deputazione per la Storia Patria per la Toscana, 1946.
Lo statuto di Bergamo di 1331. Edited by Claudia Storti Storchi. Milan: Giuffrè, 1986.
L'ultimo statuto della Repubblica di Siena (1545). Edited by Mario Ascheri. Siena: Accademia Senese degli Intronati, 1993.

Other Writings

Alberti, Leon Battista. *De Iciarchia*. In *Opere volgari*, edited by Cecil Grayson, 2: 185–286. Bari: Laterza, 1966.
———. *I libri della famiglia*. Edited by Ruggiero Romano and Alberti Tenenti. Turin: Einaudi, 1969. English *The Family in Renaissance Florence*. Translated by Renée Neu Watkins. Columbia: University of South Carolina Press, 1969.
Bec, Christian, ed. *Il libro degli affari proprii di casa de Lapo di Giovanni Niccolini de' Sirigatti*. Paris: SEVPEN, 1969.
Brucker, Gene, ed. *The Society of Renaissance Florence: A Documentary Study*. New York: Harper & Row, 1971.
Buonarroti, Michelangelo. *The Letters of Michelangelo*. Translated and edited by E. H. Ramsden. Vol. 1: *1496–1534*. Stanford: Stanford University Press, 1963.
Carozzini, Giuseppe Odoardo, ed. *Ricordanze di Bartolomeo Masi calderaio fiorentino dal 1478 al 1526*. Florence: Sansoni, 1906.
Castellani, Francesco di Matteo. *Ricordanze*. Vol. 1: *Ricordanze A (1436–1459)*. Edited by Giovanni Ciappelli. Florence: Olschki, 1992.
Corti, Gino, ed. "Le ricordanze trecentesche di Francesco e di Alessio Baldovinetti." *Archivio storico italiano* 112 (1954): 109–24.
Guicciardini, Francesco. *Ricordi diari memorie*. Edited by Mario Spinella. Rome: Riuniti, 1981. English *Maxims and Reflections of a Renaissance Statesman*. Translated by Mario Domandi. New York: Harper & Row, 1965.
Landucci, Luca. *A Florentine Diary from 1450 to 1516*. Translated by Alice de Rosen Jervis. Edited by Iodoco del Badia. London: J. M. Dent & Sons; New York: E. P. Dutton, 1927; reprint ed., 1969.
Machiavelli, Bernardo. *Libro di ricordi*. Edited by Cesare Olschki. Florence: Le Monnier, 1954.
Martelli, Ugolino di Niccolò. *Ricordanze dal 1433 al 1483*. Edited by Fulvio Pezzarossa. Rome: Edizioni di Storia e Letteratura, 1989.

Morelli, Giovanni di Pagolo. *Ricordi*. Abridged in *Mercanti scrittori: Ricordi nella Firenze tra Medioevo e Rinascimento*. Edited by Vittore Branca, 101–339. Milan: Rusconi, 1986.
Niccolini di Camugliano, Ginevra. *The Chronicles of a Florentine Family, 1200–1470*. London: Jonathan Cape, 1933.
Paolo da Certaldo. *Libro di buoni costumi*. In *Mercanti scrittori*, 1–99.
Petrucci, Armando, ed. *I ricordanze dei Corsini*. Rome: Isituto Storico Italiano per il Medio Evo, 1965.
Rucellai, Giovanni. *Zibaldone quaresimale*. Edited by Alessandro Perosa. London: Warburg Institute, 1960.
Sacchetti, Franco. *Il Trecento Novelle*. Edited by Antonio Lanza. Florence: Sansoni, 1984.
Strozzi, Alessandra. *Selected Letters of Alessandra Strozzi*. Translated by Heather Gregory. Berkeley: University of California Press, 1997.
Villani, Matteo. *Cronica con la continuazione di Filippo Villani*. 2 vols. Edited by Giusseppe Porta. Parma: Fondazione Pietro Bembo, 1995.

Index

Acciaiuoli, Dardano, 145, 147
Acciaiuoli, Francesco di Simone, 147
Acciaiuoli, Giovanni di Simone di Michele, 145, 147
Acciaiuoli, Lodovico (jurist), 206
Acciaiuoli, Zanobi di Simone, 147
Adimari, Domenico di Zanobi, 173
aditio, 7, 15, 16, 24, 26, 28–32, 34, 36–39, 43, 49, 51, 57, 59, 66, 70, 73, 93, 110, 153, 159, 160, 164–167, 175, 186, 194, 198, 200, 205, 207, 222
    tacit, 25, 55–57, 66, 72, 204, 207
adoption, 27
agnation. *See* lineage; family
Agnola (widow of Nozzo di Tuccio Manetti), 150
Albergotti, Lodovico di messer Francesco (jurist), 183, 187, 188
Alberico da Rosciate (jurist), 21
Alberti (family), 100, 130, 151, 153, 201
Alberti, Antonio di Francesco, 151
Alberti, Benedetto di Francesco di Giannozzo, 151
Alberti, Bernardo d'Antonio di Tommaso, 151
Alberti, Filippo di Tommaso, 151
Alberti, Francesco di Filippo, 151
Alberti, Giannozzo di Tommaso, 151
Alberti, Leon Battista, 87, 88, 100
Alberti, Matteo d'Antonio di Tommaso, 151
Alberti, Niccolò d'Antonio di Niccolò di Luigi, 147, 151
Alberti, Niccolò di Filippo, 151
Alberti, Riccardo d'Antonio di Riccardo, 151
Alberti, Simone, 147, 151
Albizzi, Alamanno d'Albizzo, 166
Albizzi, Baldassare di messer Francesco, 165
Albizzi, Giovanni di Piero di Vanni, 166
Albizzi, Luca di Salvestro, 78, 202
Albizzi, Piero d'Uberto, 166
Albizzi, Piero di Vanni, 165
Albizzi, Telda di Uberto, 165, 168
Albizzi, Tommaso d'Albizzo, 166
alienation
    prohibition of, 15, 87, 90, 108, 125, 134, 208, 210
    registration of, in Florence, 75
Altobianco di Giusto di Barone, 114
Altoviti, Giovangualberto d'Ubaldo, 125
Altoviti, Lionardo di Tommaso,
Ancarano, Pietro da (jurist), 48, 49, 183, 189–191
animus, 30, 44, 186. *See also* intent: to inherit
Antinori (family), 205
Antinori, Alessandro di Niccolò, 205, 206, 208
Antinori, Camillo di Niccolò, 205, 207
Antinori, Giovanbattista di Niccolò, 204, 206, 207
Antinori, Lorenzo di Alessandro, 205, 207
Antinori, Niccolò di Alessandro, 205, 206
Antinori, Niccolò di Thoma, 204
Antinori, Sebastiano di Alessandro, 205, 207
Antinori, Vincenzo di Alessandro, 205
Antonio da Butrio (jurist), 183
Antonio di Ghiere, 176
Antonio di Lodovico di Simone da Fighino, 127

Antonio di Michele di Giovanni, 162
Antonio di Paolo d'Antonio di Domenico, 156
arbitration, 88, 98, 106, 172–175, 184, 191, 196–198
Ardinghelli, Tommaso di Neri, 171
Arezzo, 130, 185
    statutes, 55
arms (right to bear), 175
Arnoldi, Francesca di Giovanni di Francesco, 114
Arsendi, Raniero (jurist), 41
Asini, Marco degli (jurist), 204–207
Astuzia, 102
Avignon, 158
Azo (jurist), 36

Badia Fiorentina, 96, 114
Badia of Settimo, 101
Baldesi, Antonio di Turino, 165
Baldesi, Vincenzo d'Antonio, 165
Baldovinetti, Alessio, 101
Baldovinetti, Francesco, 101
Baldovinetti, Francesco di Giovanni, 165
Baldovinetti, Giovanni di Guido di Francesco, 165
Baldovinetti, Paolo di Giovanni, 165
Balducci, Barone di Francesco, 144
Banchelli, Ginevra di Giovanni, 144
Banchi, Prierozzo, 148
Banchieri, Niccolò di Giovanni, 148
Banfield, Edward, 80
bankruptcy, 5, 52, 53, 64, 65, 71, 72, 76, 84, 97. See also *cessantes et fugitivi*
Barbadori, Antonio di Giovanni, 138
Barbadori, Giovanni, 138
Barbadori, Tommaso di Bartolomeo, 172
Bardi (family), 90, 173
Bardi da Vernia, Pietro, 91
Bardi, Andrea di Giovanni d'Andrea, 91
Bardi, Andrea di Lippaccio, 173
Bardi, Andrea, di Francesco, 172
Bardi, Benedetto, 173
Bardi, Bernardo di Gerozzo, 172
Bardi, Carlo di benedetto, 141
Bardi, Carlo di Benedetto, 173
Bardi, Filippo di Giovanni, 91
Bardi, Francesco di Benedetto, 141, 174
Bardi, Francesco di Gerozzo, 172
Bardi, Geronimo di Benedetto, 141
Bardi, Gerozzo di Francesco, 172
Bardi, Girolamo di Benedetto, 173

Bardi, Jacopo di Vannozzo, 90
Bardi, Larione di Lippaccio, 173
Bardi, Lippaccio di Benedetto, 141, 173
Bardi, Lutiano di Niccolò, 148
Bardi, Paolo di Giovanni, 91
Bardi, Piero di Luca di Maso
Bardi, Roberto di Rinaldo
Bardi, Simone di Vannozzo, 90
Bardi, Vannozzo di Jacopo, 90
Baronci, Giovanni di Filippo di Bartolomeo, 171
Barozzo di Bono
Bartolo da Sassoferrato (jurist), 20, 21, 28–31, 33, 35–37, 39, 43, 46, 47, 67, 181, 182, 194, 199
Bartolo di Luca of Settignano, 97
Basso della Penna (novella character), 94
Bastari, Filippozzo di Giovenco, 114
Bastiano di Chirico di Ghiotto da Seciano, 159
Bastiano di Francesco di Pasquino, 149
Bellomo, Manlio, 18, 54
Bellotto d'Andrrea (Artimino)
Benadusi, Giovanna, 11, 13
Benci, Dorato, 113
Benci, Giovanni di Niccolò, 113
Bencivenni, Alessandro (jurist), 67–71, 181, 183, 192
beneficium abstinendi, 24, 25
beneficium inventarii, 25, 56, 58. See also inventory
bequests. See *legatum*
Bergamo
    statutes, 56
Berlinghieri, Francesco di Berlinghiero, 170
Berlinghieri, Giovanni di Berlinghiero, 170
Berlinghieri, Girolamo di Berlinghiero, 170
Besta, Enrico, 15, 27, 52
Bettini, Francesco di Bettino, 160
Betto di Zanobi, 96
Biagio di Dino di Lottiere of Signa, 161
Bini, Bino di Niccolò, 175
Bischeri, Bernardo, 161
Bischeri, Piero di Jacopo, 114
Black Death. See plague
Bologna, 185
bona adventitia, 35
bona profectitia, 35
Bonaiuto di Ventura, 175
Bonfield, Lloyd, 8
bonorum possessio, 41
Bonsi, Bernardo d'Ugolino, 159

Index

Bonsi, Domenico (jurist), 206
Bonsi, Donato d'Ugolino, 159
Bonsi, Piero d'Ugolino, 159
Borromei, Antonio, 74
Borromei, Bartolomea, 75
Borromei, Beatrice (wife of Giovanni de' Pazzi), 74
Borromei, Carlo, 74
Borromei, Giovanni, 74
Borromei, Giuliano di Giuliano, 75
Boschetto, Luca, 100
Bostichi, Alessandro, 169
Bottrigari, Jacopo (jurist), 35, 46, 47, 181
Brucker, Gene, xi, xii, 53, 84
Brunelleschi, Simone di Niccolò, 163
Buonarroti, Michelangelo, 84
Burckhardt, Jakob, xiii, 2, 15
Busini, Maria di Nofri, 103
Busini, Nofri, 103

Canigiani, Piero di Carlo, 148
canon law, 26, 30, 49, 101
Capitano del Popolo, 53
capo di famiglia, 16. See also paterfamilias
Cappelli, Carlo di Filippo,
Capponi (family), 151, 153
Capponi, Agostino di Bernardo, 88, 152
Capponi, Bastiano di Piero, 152
Capponi, Donato di Giovanni, 152
Capponi, Filippo di Giovanni, 152
Capponi, Francesco di Giovanni, 152
Capponi, Francesco di Luca, 152
Capponi, Galeotto di Luca, 152
Capponi, Gherardo di Giovanni, 152
Capponi, Giovanni di Mico, 153
Capponi, Giovanni di Piero di Angelo, 152
Capponi, Luca d'Agostino, 152
Capponi, Luca d'Agostino, 66
Capponi, Neri di Gino, 88, 153
Capponi, Niccolò di Giovanni, 152
Capponi, Salvestro di Giovanni, 152
Capponi, Simone di Luca, 152
Capponi, Tommaso di Gino, 152
Carducci, Baldassare (jurist), 206
casa. See household
Casey, James, 2
Castellani, Francesco di Matteo, 85, 87, 88
Castellani, Michele d'Alberto, 88
Castro Franco, 172
catasto, 5, 17–19, 71, 84, 141, 148–150, 153, 173
    of 1427, 16, 136–40, 141–42, 151
    of 1457, 5, 139
    of 1469, 177
    of 1480, 137, 138, 142–143, 150, 176
Caterina di Tieri di Domenico di Tieri, 163
Cavalcanti, Bicie d'Archangelo, 148, 169
Cavalcanti, Francesco d'Archangelo di Bernardo, 148
Cavalcanti, Salvadore d'Archangelo, 148
Cavallo, Sandra, 11
Cavazza, Giovanni (novella character), 94
Cecchi, Domenico, 76
Ceffini (family), 162
Ceffini, Salvestro di Lodovico, 162
Ceffini, Serafino di Giovanni, 162
Cesare di Benedetto di Biagio da Certaldo, 126
cessantes et fugitivi, 65, 76
Champlin, Edward, 23
Checco di Checco, 127
Chiffoleau, Jacques, 10
Chojnacki, Stanley, 11
Ciallo di Dino da Certaldo, 126
Ciari, Bernardo di Filippo, 165
Cino da Pistoia (jurist), 28, 31, 36, 41, 46, 47, 188
Ciompi Revolt, 115
Ciurianni, Lapo di Valore, 101
Ciurianni, Valorino, 102
civil law, 30, 49, 70
Clavero, Bartolomé, 210
Cocchi, Antonio (jurist), 206
Code, 25, 27, 28, 45, 194, 206. See also *Corpus iuris civilis*
cognomen, 123, 144, 153
coheirs, 24, 34, 40–41, 156, 163–167, 194, 206
Cohen, Thomas, 95
coheredes. See coheirs
Cohn, Samuel K., 10, 12, 13, 15, 27, 91, 108
Cole, John, 7
Colle Val d'Elsa
    statutes, 57
Comi, Agostino di Giuliano, 145
Comi, Bastiano di Giuliano, 145
Comi, Domenico di Giuliano, 145
Comi, Giovanni di Giuliano, 145
Consiglio dei Dugento, 64
Consiglio del Cento, 77

consilium, 18, 19, 31, 45, 65, 69, 180–183, 187, 192, 206
  as persuasive precedent, 181
  iudiciale, 180
  pro parte, 180, 196, 198
Cooper, J. P., 93
Corbizi (family), 107, 110
Corbizi, Antonio di Filippo, 106
Corbizi, Bernardo di Filippo, 106
Corbizi, Filippo di Giovanni, 106
Corbizi, Giovanni di Filippo, 106
Corbizi, Giovanni di Filippo di Giovanni, 106, 107
Corbizi, Roberto di Filippo, 106
Corpus iuris canonici, 21
Corpus iuris civilis, 20, 21, 49
Corsellini, Stefano, 149
Corsini, Filippo (jurist), 68, 183, 187, 188
Corsini, Giovanni di Matteo, 92, 93
Corsini, Matteo di Niccolò, 85
Costa San Giorgio, 149
cousin, 38, 93, 96, 103, 104, 166, 168, 178, 193, 195, 207
credit, 81, 104, 136. *See also* trust
  circumstantial, 5, 84
creditors, 36, 45, 62, 64, 66, 68, 71, 72, 75, 76, 84, 125, 166, 177, 189, 192, 211
  of deceased, 15, 24, 35, 42, 45, 47, 52, 55, 56, 59, 60, 63, 70, 72, 73, 79, 102, 104, 175–177, 179, 185–187, 199, 206, 208, 209
Cresci, Francesco di Piero di Lorenzo, 174
Cresci, Raffaele di Piero, 174
Cristofano di Piero d'Arrigo di ser Orsino, 149
Cristoforo di Lorenzo,
cura (minorum), 35

da Ghiacceto, Paolo di Zanobi di Paolo, 123
da Laterino, Piero di ser Cristofano, 96
da Laterino, Sandra (widow), 96
da Panzano, Angelo di Totto, 196, 197
da Panzano, Antonio di messer Luca, 103, 104, 110
da Panzano, Guerriante, 196, 197
da Panzano, Luca, 100, 103, 104
da Panzano, Luca di Matteo, 93
da Panzano, Totto d'Antonio di messer Luca, 103
da Saliceto, Bartolomeo (jurist), 189, 191
da Terranuova, Nardo di Francesco di Giovanni di ser Niccolò, 150
da Terranuova, Niccolò di Guasparre di Giovanni, 150
da Terranuova, Vangelista di Francesco, 150
da Uzzano, Giovanni di Bernardo, 97
da Uzzano, Niccolò, 97
Dalma di Falchino, 127
Dameron, George, 13
damnosa, 154
  hereditas as, xi, 24, 27, 31, 32, 79, 84, 136, 161, 188, 189
Davis, Natalie Zemon, 92
debt, 5, 14, 58, 67, 69, 92, 102, 106, 137, 141, 189
  as feature of social life, xii, 4, 19, 52, 53, 84, 104
  of deceased, 14, 25, 81, 101, 107, 110, 125, 136, 150, 168
  of heir, 78, 105
deceit, 5, 79, 81, 88, 93, 101–103, 111, 199, 212
deceptive practices. *See* fraud
del Bene, Ricciardo di Francesco (jurist), 69, 175
del Chiaro, Bartolomeo di Giovanni, 202
del Chiaro, Chiaro di Giovanni di Niccolò, 202
del Guanto, Francesco di Girolamo, 170
del Guanto, Simone di Girolamo di Piero, 170
del Nero, Carlo di Piero, 147
del Nero, Nerozzo di Piero di Filippo, 147
del Pecha, Ginevra d'Antonio,
del Sena, Caterina di Francesco di Luca (wife of Uguccione Pazzi), 160
delata hereditas, 32, 34
Deti, Ormannozzo (jurist), 198, 200, 206, 207
Diana (wife of Buonaccorso Torelli), 126
Digest, 25, 27, 29, 35, 67. *See also Corpus iuris civilis*
dignitas, 21
Dimitilla di Giuliano di Nerlo, 177
Dino di Biagio di Dino of Signa, 161
disinheritance, 86, 92, 94
division of inheritance, 77, 88, 173, 210
doctrine, legal. *See ius commune*
Dodici Buonuomini, 201
Domenico di Giovanni di Feo, 164
donatio propter nuptias, 55

Index

dowry, 3, 19, 26, 48, 51, 68, 75, 76, 82, 84, 90, 91, 93, 96, 97, 101, 102, 105, 106, 109, 110, 140–142, 144, 148, 160, 162, 163, 165, 167–170, 173, 174, 177, 179, 184, 185, 187, 188, 192–194, 197, 198, 210, 212
  daughter's right to, 66
  hypothecated on husband's property, 45, 59
  maternal, 46, 54, 55, 68, 69, 72, 76, 97, 100, 105, 119, 149, 158, 174, 183, 185, 192, 195, 198
  maternal, and repudiation in Florentine law, 59–61
  return of, 5, 12, 64, 66, 76, 84, 97, 105, 106, 150, 171, 174
  right retained by repudiating woman, 38
Durante, Guglielmo (jurist), 180
Durkheim, Émile, xi, 2

emancipation, xv, 46, 48, 62–65, 68, 69, 71, 101–103, 110, 159, 160, 165, 172–174, 184, 190, 191, 212
Epstein, Steven, 10, 12, 91
executor, 99
extranei, 23–25, 41, 55

Fabbrica, 147
Falconieri, Nadda di Paolo, 162
Faldino di Tino di Faldino, 165
fama, 102. *See also* honor
familism, amoral, 80, 111, 213
family, 3, 4, 6, 15, 19, 80, 130
  discord within, 89
family name. *See* cognomen
family property. *See* patrimony
favor agnationis, 51
Federighi, Filippo di Federigo, 148
Feo di Giovanni di Feo, 164
fideicommissum, 7, 25, 54, 75, 110, 111, 113, 125, 134, 170, 204–207, 210
fideiussor, 98, 162
Filippo d'Antonio di Guccio, 142
Filippo di Bartolomeo di Girello (Gangalandi), 127
Filippo di Buono di Michele, 159
Findlen, Paula, xiii
Fini, Tommaso di Giovanni, 138
finis, 98, 167
Fitzpatrick, Peter, 18
Florence, xii–xv, 2, 4, 5, 10, 13, 14, 16, 21, 36–38, 42, 43, 52, 54–62, 64, 67, 76, 79, 82, 102, 104–106, 108, 112, 130, 136, 137, 141, 181, 195, 200, 211
  age of majority in, 54
  population, 117
  statute on husband's rights on predeceased wife's dowry, 168
  statute on inheritance by women, 51, 101, 164
  statute on obligations of heirs, 54–55, 57, 58, 62, 67–72, 101, 149, 157, 158, 179, 205, 207
  statutes, 28, 53–54
Floriano di San Pietro, 191
Floriano di San Pietro (jurist), 189
fragilitas sexus, 37
Francesca di Zanobi di Maso di Valore, 174
Francesco di Bonaiuto di Ventura, 175
Francesco di Giovanni di Lippo, 114
Francesco di Giuliano di Nerlo, 177
Franzesi, Caterina di Napoleone, 167
fraud, 17, 29, 45–48, 56, 60, 62, 63, 70, 73, 76, 79, 186, 188, 192, 195, 196, 199, 206, 210
  legislation concerning, 52, 71
  presumptions of, in repudiation, 46–48
furberia, 102

Gavitt, Philip, 11
gestio pro herede, 30, 46, 49, 183
gestio pro non herede, 30
Gherardini, Antonio di Giovanni, 167
Gherardini, Catalano di Giovanni, 167
Gherardini, Caterina di Giovanni, 167
Gherardini, Giovanni d'Antonio, 167
Gherardini, Piero di Gherardo, 144
Ghiere d'Antonio di Ghiere, 164, 176
Ghirlandaio, Domenico (artist), 167
Gianfigliazzi, Antonio di Adovardo, 142
Gianfigliazzi, Lorenzo, 142
Gigoli, Gapa (wife of Marco), 127
Gigoli, Marco, 127
Gini, Giuliano di Bartolo, 92
Giovanna di Francesco di Michele of Giogoli, 169
Giovanni d'Agnolo di Guido, 175
Giovanni d'Andrea (jurist), 183
Giovanni d'Andrea d'Antonio, 156
Giovanni di Buono, 175
Giovanni di Domenico di Zanobi, 171
Giovanni di Giusto di Barone, 114
Giovanni di Lorenzo (Castel San Giovanni), 127

Giovanni di Luca di Duccio, 175
Giovanni di Michele di Giovanni, 162
Giovanni di Michele di Torello, 115
Giovanni di Sodo di Lorenzo, 169
Giovanni di Stefano di Vanni, 159
Giugni, Bernardo di Domenico, 165
Giugni, Niccolò di Domenico, 165
Giuliano di Bettino di Sante,
Giuliano di Nerlo, 176
Giuntini, Lorenzo di Cristoforo (Montevarchi), 169
Glossa ordinaria, 43, 194
good faith (in repudiation), 45
Goody, Jack, 3
Gostanza di Lorenzo di Giovanni, 127
Gottlieb, Beatrice, xii, 7
grandfather, 42, 113, 123, 139, 144, 147, 157, 170, 173, 190, 202, 205
grandpaternal estate, 34, 41, 42, 96, 102
Graziano di Bernaba, 115
Gualterotti, Lorenzo di Totto, 90
guardianship, xii, 6, 26, 35, 36, 59, 83, 92, 149, 157, 166, 169, 170, 173
  and repudiation, 161–162
  of *hereditas iacens*, 176
  of women, 169. See also *mundualdus*
Guasconi, Jacopo di Niccolò, 114, 142
Guasconi, Lattanzio di Bindo, 114, 142
Guasconi, Tinoro di messer Niccolò, 164
Guasconi, Ubaldino di Bindo, 141, 142, 173, 174
Guicciardini, Francesco, 87, 102
Guidalotti, Angela di Giovanni, 163
Guidalotti, Antonia di Giovanni, 163
Guidalotti, Bernardo di Giovanni, 163–164, 167
Guidalotti, Caterina di Giovanni, 163
Guidalotti, Gostanza di Bernardo, 163
Guidalotti, Piera di Giovanni, 163
Guidetti, Lorenzo di Francesco, 125
Guidi, Paolo d'Antonio, 163
Guiducci, Andrea di Nastagio, 145
guild, 84, 176, 184

head of household, 5, 137. See also *paterfamilias*
heirship, 7, 19
  strategies of, 8, 10, 19, 177
hereditas, 29
hereditas iacens, 24, 61, 79, 81, 98, 150, 175–177
  in Florentine legislation, 72–74

Herlihy, David, 16, 136, 140, 141
honor, 82, 86, 94, 169
household, xii, 2–4, 14, 141, 167, 178
household wealth
  from catasto, 138, 141

illegitimate children, xii, 90, 106
imbecillitas, 38. See also *fragilitas sexus*,
immobilia, 54, 62, 75, 149, 204, 207
impubes, 36
in integrum restitutio, 37
individual, 2, 9, 15, 24, 45, 110
individual, and family, xii, xiii, 2, 6, 7, 19, 27, 48, 77, 88, 89, 108, 109, 177, 211, 212
infans, 36
inheritance
  as process, 5–6, 8–9, 11, 16–17, 167
  as social reproduction, xi, xv, 1–5, 7, 14, 17, 21, 22, 27, 49, 79, 82, 83, 86, 200
  impartible, 3, 7
  partible, 3, 7, 123
inmiscere, 24, 30, 40, 45, 193, 194, 222
inmixtio, 25, 30, 44, 46, 47, 55
Innocenti (hospital), 11
inofficiosum (testament), 91, 189
intent
  fraudulent, 47, 195
  of legislator, 70, 73, 77, 134, 206, 207
  of repudiator, 34
  of testator, 1, 12, 92, 93, 95, 207
  to inherit, 30, 39, 44, 46, 59, 186. See also *animus*
intermingle. See *inmiscere*
intermingling, 45, 46
interval (between death and repudiation), 24, 31, 157–158, 168. See also *ius deliberandi*
intestacy, xv, 9, 12–13, 23, 34, 40, 51, 57, 74, 91–92, 106, 113, 132–134, 145, 154, 156, 159, 162–164, 167, 169, 177, 186, 210
  horror of, among Romans, 1, 12, 23, 89
inventory, 54–57, 59, 60, 68, 69, 102, 106, 159, 161, 162, 165–167, 176, 184, 194, 198, 205. See also *beneficium inventarii*
  as limiting liability, 32
  in Florentine statute, 69
ius accrescendi, 40, 163
ius commune, xiv, 18, 21, 31, 32, 37, 39, 48, 51, 52, 54, 55, 57, 67, 69, 70, 72, 77, 89, 114, 158, 181, 182, 184–186, 188, 189, 192, 195, 199, 200, 203, 205, 208

Index

ius deliberandi, 24, 41, 42
ius familiaritatis, 68, 69, 165, 172
ius gentium, 30
ius proprium, xiv, 26, 39, 49, 51

Jacopo d'Antonio di Domenico, 156
Jacopo d'Arena (jurist), 28, 37, 181
Jacopo di Giovanni di Lippo, 114
Jacopo di Guido, 179, 183, 184
Jacopo di Simone dal Orna, 139

Kent, Francis William, 110
kinship, 111, 210, 212. *See also* lineage; family
Kirshner, Julius, xii
Klapisch-Zuber, Christiane, 16, 136, 140, 141

La Roncière, Charles de, 85, 107
Lamberteschi, Piero di Domenico, 75, 146
Landucci, Luca, 86
law, 17–18
Le Play, Frédéric, xi, 3
legal history, 18
legatarius (beneficiary), 29, 35
  contrasted to *heres*, 23, 40, 199
legatum, 12, 25, 28–30, 49, 54, 90–92, 94, 96, 99, 110, 114, 149, 174, 189, 198, 199, 207, 208
  as burdens on estate, 29, 95–97, 142, 190
  repudiation of, 32, 40
legislation, 125. *See* statutes
legitima, 189–191, 198, 205, 208
  and repudiation, 43, 70
liability (of fathers and sons in Florence), 61, 62, 65, 76
Ligi, Bartolo di Piero di Bartolo, 113
lineage, xiv, 9, 26, 27, 48, 82, 88, 90, 108, 109, 111, 134, 151, 168, 172, 211
Lombardo, Maria Luisa, 11
Longo, Alfonso, 211
Luca di Bartolo di Luca of Settignano, 97
lucrosa, inheritance as, 31, 40, 49
Lynch, Katherine, 79

Machiavelli, Battista di Boninsegna, 105
Machiavelli, Bernardo, 104
Machiavelli, Boninsegna di Guido, 105, 110
Machiavelli, Guido di Pietro Pagolo, 105
Machiavelli, Niccolò di Bernardo, 103, 104
Machiavelli, Piero Amadio, 105
Machiavelli, Pietro Pagolo, 105

Magistrato dei Pupilli, 105
magnate, 65
Magnesi, Francesco di Rinaldo di Bardo, 126
Maine, Henry Sumner, xi, 1, 2, 6, 14, 22, 23, 211
mala fides, 47, 195
Malegonelli, Antonio (jurist), 206
Malegonelli, Bartolomea di Piero, 165
Malegonelli, Piero di Nello, 165
Malegonelli, Simona di Piero, 165
Manetti, Nozo di Tuccio di Marabottino, 150
Mangioni, Lippozzo di Cipriano, 92
Mannelli (family), 107, 110
Mannelli, Raimondo, 106
Marco di Giovanni (Gangalandi), 127
Maria di Niccolò di Battista di Jacopo, 128
Martelli, Bino di Niccolò, 98
Martelli, Carlo, 88
Martelli, Ugolino di Niccolò, 87, 98, 175
Martines, Lauro, 74
Masi, Bartolomeo, 100, 102
Masi, Matteo, 101
Masi, Romolo, 101
massaio, 86
maternal estate, 67, 86, 93, 104, 107, 110, 127, 128, 141, 143, 147, 150–152, 156, 158, 160, 162–170, 172, 176, 177, 179, 193. *See also* dowry, maternal
Matteo di Duccio, 175
Mazzei, Giovanni di Lapo, 141
Mazzei, Piero, 141
Mazzi, Maria Serena, 100, 136
Medici (family), xv, 63, 79, 92, 99, 108, 118, 119, 130, 134, 169, 201, 212
Medici, Alessio di Gerozzo, 166
Medici, Bernardo di Giovenco, 165
Medici, Cambio di Gerozzo, 166
Medici, Cosimo, 91, 92, 137
Medici, Gabriele di Cambio, 166
Medici, Gerozzo di Cambio di Vieri, 166
Medici, Giuliano, 160
Medici, Lorenzo, 74, 88, 146, 160, 169
Medici, Lorenzo di Cosimo, 5
Medici, Lorenzo di Giovanni di Bici, 115
Medici, messer Matteo, 166
Medici, Niccolò di Francesco, 163
Medici, Niccolò di Tollosino di Francesco, 162
Medici, Piero, 63, 99, 108
Medici, Tollosino di Francesco, 162
Medici, Tommaso di Francesco, 163
memoria (familial), 21
Mercanzia, 62, 71, 84, 85, 104–106

Mercato Vecchio, 148
mezzadria, 131, 210
Michele di Bernaba, 115
Michele di Buono di Michele, 159
Michele di Giovanni, 162
minor, 40, 72, 165, 166, 195
  benefit of inventory in Florence, 58–59, 69, 102, 166
  repudiation by, 35–37, 44, 49
modernity and inheritance, 2
Molho, Anthony, 27, 138, 142, 144, 146, 151
Monachi, Monaco d'Antonio, 158
Monachi, Piero d'Antonio, 158
Monte comune, 73, 78, 169, 170, 202
Monte delle doti, 71, 118, 142, 148
Montepulciano
  statutes, 55
Montevarchi, 172
Morelli, Calandro, 83
Morelli, Giovanni di Pagolo, 83, 161
Morelli, Mirella, 11
Morelli, Morello di Giraldo, 83
Morelli, Pagolo di Bartolomeo, 83
Mori, Bartolo, 145
Mori, Filippo di Niccolò, 145
Mori, Francesco di Niccolo, 145
mother
  inheritance from, in Florence, 59
  repudians as heir to, 45–46
mundualdus, 37, 162, 163
Muratori, Lodovico Antonio, 211

Nacchianti, Andrea di Cristoforo, 170
Nanna (widow of Cristofano di Piero d'Arrigo di ser Orsino), 149
necessary heir, 22–25, 41, 44
Nerli, Lisa di Pera, 126
Nerlo di Giuliano di Nerlo, 177
Nero di Filippo di Nero, 164
Niccolai, Franco, 15, 52, 58
Niccolini, Biagio di Lapo, 110
Niccolini, Giovanni di Lapo, 110
Niccolini, Giovanni di Niccolaio, 93
Niccolini, Lapo di Giovanni, 85, 87, 93, 104, 105, 110
Niccolini, Lodovico di Paolo, 102
Niccolini, Niccolaio di Lapo, 106
Niccolini, Paolo di Lapo, 94, 102
Niccolò di Giovanni di Feo, 164
Niccolò di Guido, 179, 183
Nobili, Filippo d'Antonio, 142
Nobili, Lionardo d'Antonio, 142

Norducci, Francesco di Benedetto, 160

obligations
  contractual, extended to heirs, 98–99
  of heirs, 5, 6, 16, 29–31, 41, 49, 52, 54–56, 87, 118, 132, 134, 139, 144, 150, 159, 165, 190
  of heirs, in *ius commune*, 30
occupations of repudiating persons, 115
Odofredus (jurist), 46
officeholding, 78, 79, 109, 146, 147, 150, 182
  and fiscal obligations, 200–204
  and repudiation, 79
Or San Michele, 167
Orlandi, Rosso d'Andreozzo, 103
Ostinelli, Gianna Lumia, 11

Paganelli, Antonio di Bernardo, 169
Paganelli, Jacopo di Niccolò, 149
Palmieri, Matteo, 102
Pandolfini, Pierfilippo di messer Giannozzo, 96
Paolo da Certaldo (writer), 86, 89, 94
Paolo di Castro (jurist), 28, 33, 36, 38, 39, 43, 46, 60, 61, 183, 194, 199
parentado, 109
paterfamilias, 104, 111
paternal estate, 120, 127, 134, 138, 144, 147–151, 153, 156, 158, 161, 168–170, 172, 177, 179, 193, 196
patria potestas, 14, 22, 26, 35, 165, 184, 190
patrimony, 2, 3, 9, 27, 77, 85, 86, 89, 108, 110, 150, 207
Pavia
  statutes, 57
Pazzi (family), 75, 169, 201
Pazzi Conspiracy, 119, 177
Pazzi, Filippo di Leonardo d'Uguccione, 169
Pazzi, Francesco di Francesco, 113
Pazzi, Ghinozzo d'Uguccione, 160
Pazzi, Gianna di Francesco di Ghinozzo, 113
Pazzi, Giovanna d'Uguccione, 160
Pazzi, Giovanni, 74
Pazzi, Jacopo d'Andrea, 146
Pazzi, Uguccione di Ghinozzo, 160
Pepi, Francesco (jurist), 206
period for deliberation (to inherit), 25, 38–42, 54, 55, 72, 77, 156, 167, 181. *See also ius deliberandi*
  in Florence, 54, 73, 183, 187, 205
  in Siena, 56

period for reconsideration, 194
persona, 45, 67, 208, 211
personality of the decedent. *See universum ius*
Pertile, Antonio, 3
Perugia
  statutes, 57
Peruzzi, Lisa (wife of Ridolfo), 127
Peruzzi, Ridolfo, 127
Piero d'Andrea di Sante, 165
Piero di Bernardo, 96
Piero di Graziano, 115
Piero di Vanni di Rinaldo, 96
Pirandello, Luigi, xiii, 177
Pisa, 130, 137
Pistoia, 193, 204
plague, 10, 93, 104, 114, 119, 136, 149, 167, 172, 211
Podestà, 53, 60, 66, 85, 105, 107, 150, 161, 172, 193
Politto di Jacopo di Simone dal Orna, 139
Pomata, Gianna, 109
Pontano, Lodovico, 195
Popoleschi, Bartolomeo, 176
possessio, 68, 187
Pottage, Alain, 2
Prato, 130, 164
prelegata, 199
prestanza, 78
primogeniture, 9, 211
procurator, 159, 163, 169, 172, 195
proprietas, 35
protestationes regarding inheritance, 170–172
Pullan, Brian, 11
pupillus maior infante, 36
Putnam, Robert, 79, 80

Quercitani, Fruosino di Bernardo, 100
Quercitani, Simone, 102

Raveggi, Sergio, 100, 136
renunciation of inheritance (by religious), 32–33, 100–101, 162–164
repudiation, xi, xv, 4, 6, 13–19, 22, 26–28, 30, 35, 40, 43, 49, 52, 82, 100, 103, 110, 175, 177, 186, 189, 211, 212
  and ages, 141
  and household wealth, 138–147, 153, 164, 173
  and residence, 130–131
  as "favorable", 28
  as inheritance strategy, xii, 32, 93, 109, 111, 126, 136, 142, 144, 148, 150–152, 159, 168, 177, 213
  as odious, 28, 52, 107
  by a religious institution, 70, 114, 162, 167
  by daughters, 128
  certain knowledge required, 32–34, 45
  chronological analysis, 115–118, 134–135
  economic effects of, 212
  in Florentine *ricordi*, 101–102
  in Roman law, 23–25
  notarial instruments, 58, 154, 156–161
  notarial text, 44
  of brothers, 120, 123, 125, 128, 132, 134, 143–145, 147, 148, 150–152, 156, 159, 164, 165, 170, 204, 208
  of cousins, 120, 123, 125, 128, 134, 147, 152, 158, 208
  of guild membership, 112
  of uncles, 120, 123, 125, 128, 134, 143, 145, 147, 151, 152, 156, 158, 208
  partial, 45, 131–132, 140, 144, 156
  proof not required, 32
  registration of, 60–64, 70, 71, 75, 111, 113, 182, 186–187, 189
  registry of, 16, 18, 112–113, 134, 137, 154, 182, 208
  reversal of, 36
  some rights not terminated by it, 71
  tacit, 39, 72, 73
Ricasoli, India d'Ugo d'Arrigo, 127
Ricasoli, Roba di Bindo, 165
Ricci, Ardingo di Corso, 165
Ricci, Corso di Zanobi, 160
Ricci, Giovanni di Zanobi, 160
Ricci, Guido di Zanobi, 160
Ricci, Matteo, 165
Ricci, Sandro di Zanobi, 160
Ricci, Simona, 10, 13
ricordanze, 16
ricordi, 85, 101
Rinaldeschi, Antonio di Giovanni, 105
Rinaldeschi, Giovanni, 105
Rinieri, Guglielmo di Luca, 138
Rinieri, Luca di Piero, 138
rinuncia all'eredità (in Italian national law), 209
Ripoli, 164
Risaliti, Antonio di Tommaso, 125
Risaliti, Geri d'Ubertino di Gherardo, 123
Risaliti, Jacopo di Mariotto, 125

Risaliti, Rosso d'Ubertino, 125
Risaliti, Stefano di Girolamo, 125
Risaliti, Ubertino di Simone, 125
Roberto d'Antonio di Guccio, 142
Romano, Andrea, 3, 9, 27
Rome, 130, 158
Rondinelli, Piera di Ghino, 114
Roselli, Antonio (jurist), 42
Roselli, Rosello (jurist), 185, 186
Rossi, Piero, 148
Rucellai (family), 151, 152
Rucellai, Alessandra di Piero, 171
Rucellai, Arrigo di Filippo, 127
Rucellai, Brancazio di Niccolò, 113, 151, 171
Rucellai, Cardinale di Guglielmo, 152
Rucellai, Francesco di Filippo di Vanni, 171
Rucellai, Giovanni di Paolo, 5, 114, 151, 153, 171
Rucellai, Guglielmo di Cardinale, 152
Rucellai, Piero di Niccolò, 113, 114, 151, 171
Ruggieri, Bonifazio di Niccolò, 145
Ruggieri, Zanobi di Niccolo, 145

Sacchetti, Franco (writer), 94
Salvetti, Tommaso (jurist), 67–70, 181, 183, 192
Salviati (family), 151
Salviati, Bernardo di Marco di Forese, 152
Salviati, Filippo di Forese, 152
Salviati, Francesco d'Alamanno, 153
Salviati, Francesco di Forese, 152
Salviati, Lotto di Giovanni di Forese, 152
San Benedetto, 162
San Casciano (Mugello), 165
San Giorgio, 148
San Jacopo (Ripoli), 163
San Marco, 163
San Martino a Pagliariccio, 159
San Martino di Buonuomini, 167
San Niccolò (Prato), 163
San Salvatore (Settimo), 75
Sandro di Goro d'Antonio (Castro Franco), 172
Santa Maria da Spagnola, 165
Santa Maria de Avena, 170
Santa Maria degli Angeli, 163
Santa Maria del Campo, 156
Santa Maria Novella, 159
Santa Maria Nuova, 70, 96, 114
Santa Trinita, 175

Santissima Annunziata, 114
satisdations of new citizens, 112
Savona
  statutes, 57
scaltrezza, 102
Scarlatti, Carlo d'Antonio, 125
Sedici Gonfalonieri di Compagnia, 201
separatio bonorum, 25. *See also inmixtio*
ser Paolo di ser Andrea, 176
Serristori, Francesco di Leonardo di Tommaso, 161
Sesto, 130
Siena, 10, 11
  statutes, 56
Signoria, 63, 64, 71, 72, 76, 78, 84, 103, 134, 147, 154, 201
Simone di Giovanni d'Orna, 139
slave, inheritance of, 138
Smail, Daniel, 5, 18, 84
Soderini (family), 130
Soderini, Raynerio di Lorenzo, 166
Soderini, Tommaso di Lorenzo, 166
Sozzini, Bartolomeo (jurist), 193–196, 206, 207
speculum, 78
Spinelli (family), 151, 152
Spinelli, Bartolomeo, 167
Spinelli, Carlo di Jacopo, 114, 152, 153
Spinelli, Francesco di Domenico, 152
Spinelli, Girolamo d'Antonio, 152
Spinelli, Jacopo di Lorenzo, 152
Spinelli, Lionardo di Francesco, 152
Spinelli, Lorenzo d'Antonio, 152, 153
Spinelli, Lorenzo di Francesco, 114, 152
Spinelli, Nanna di Lorenzo, 152
Spinelli, Riccardo, 138
Spinelli, Tommaso di Lionardo, 153
Spini, Dego di Piero degli, 172
statutes. *See ius proprium*
Stinche, 176
Strozzi (family), 201
Strozzi, Alessandra, 96, 99, 100, 102
Strozzi, Antonio di Vanni (jurist), 65, 193, 196, 198, 201–204
Strozzi, Benedetto di Marco, 98
Strozzi, Carlo di Marco, 98
Strozzi, Filippo, 96, 100, 102
Strozzi, Jacopo di Leonardo, 99
Strozzi, Lorenzo, 99, 100
Strozzi, Marco di Giovanni, 101
Strozzi, Matteo, 100
Strozzi, Palla, 5

substantia, 213
  family as, 20–21
substitution, 40, 41, 48, 70, 90, 91, 125, 165, 167, 168, 170, 171, 190, 208, 210. *See also* fideicommissum
succession, 1, 14, 16, 22, 23, 28, 30, 42, 52, 63, 97, 112, 182. *See also universum ius*

Tartagni, Alessandro (jurist), 31, 32, 39, 43, 44, 46, 61, 194, 199
tenuta, 68, 95, 191
testament, 9, 15, 23, 26, 57, 74, 89–95, 158, 190, 199
  as historical source, 9–13
Tino di Faldino, 165
Tocqueville, Alexis de, 2
Torelli, Buonaccorso di Niccolò, 126
Tornabuoni, Giovanni, 99
Tornabuoni, Lorenzo, 99
Tosinghi, Baschiere di Franceschino, 174
Tosinghi, Beltramone, 144
Tosinghi, Madalena, 144
Treviso
  statutes, 56
trust, 52, 53, 88, 102, 111. *See also* credit
tutela. *See* guardianship

Ubaldi, Angelo degli (jurist), 20, 21, 28, 29, 31, 33, 35, 37, 42, 46, 47, 66, 115, 182–187, 194, 196, 207
Ubaldi, Baldo degli (jurist), 28, 30, 31, 34–37, 40, 41, 43, 46, 47, 64, 65, 115, 181, 182, 195
Uguccioni, Benedetto, 202, 203
Uguccioni, Bernardo di Benedetto, 201
Uguccioni, Giovanbattista di Benedetto, 201

universum ius, 22, 30, 42, 199. *See* Roman heirship

Venice, xv, 11, 82, 130, 212
Verona, 212
  statutes, 57
Vettori, Giannozzo di Neri, 127
Villani, Matteo (writer), 62
Vincenzo di Domenico, 193, 195, 207
Volterra
  statutes, 57
voluntas (to inherit), 30–31, 35. *See also animus*
Vovelle, Michel, 10
Vulpi da Soncino, Bartolomeo (jurist), 183

warranty (on sale), 99
Weber, Max, xi, 2, 4
Welch, Evelyn, 52
widow, 11, 76, 96, 97, 105, 106, 126, 128, 144, 148–150, 161, 163, 165, 167, 174, 177, 205
Wilson, Stephen, 135
Wolf, Eric, 7
women, xii, 11, 145, 167, 177, 185. *See also fragillitas sexus*; widow
  and lineage, 82, 108
  estates of, 76
  inheritance by, 74, 210
  inheritance rights of, 38, 43, 51
  liabilities of, in Florentine law, 59, 69
  married, 128
  repudiation by, 37–38, 64
  repudiations of and by, 123, 126–130, 134
  rights of in Florentine law, xiv

Yanagisako, Sylvia Junko, xiii